# BLUE PERIOD

TSUBASA YAMAGUCHI

5

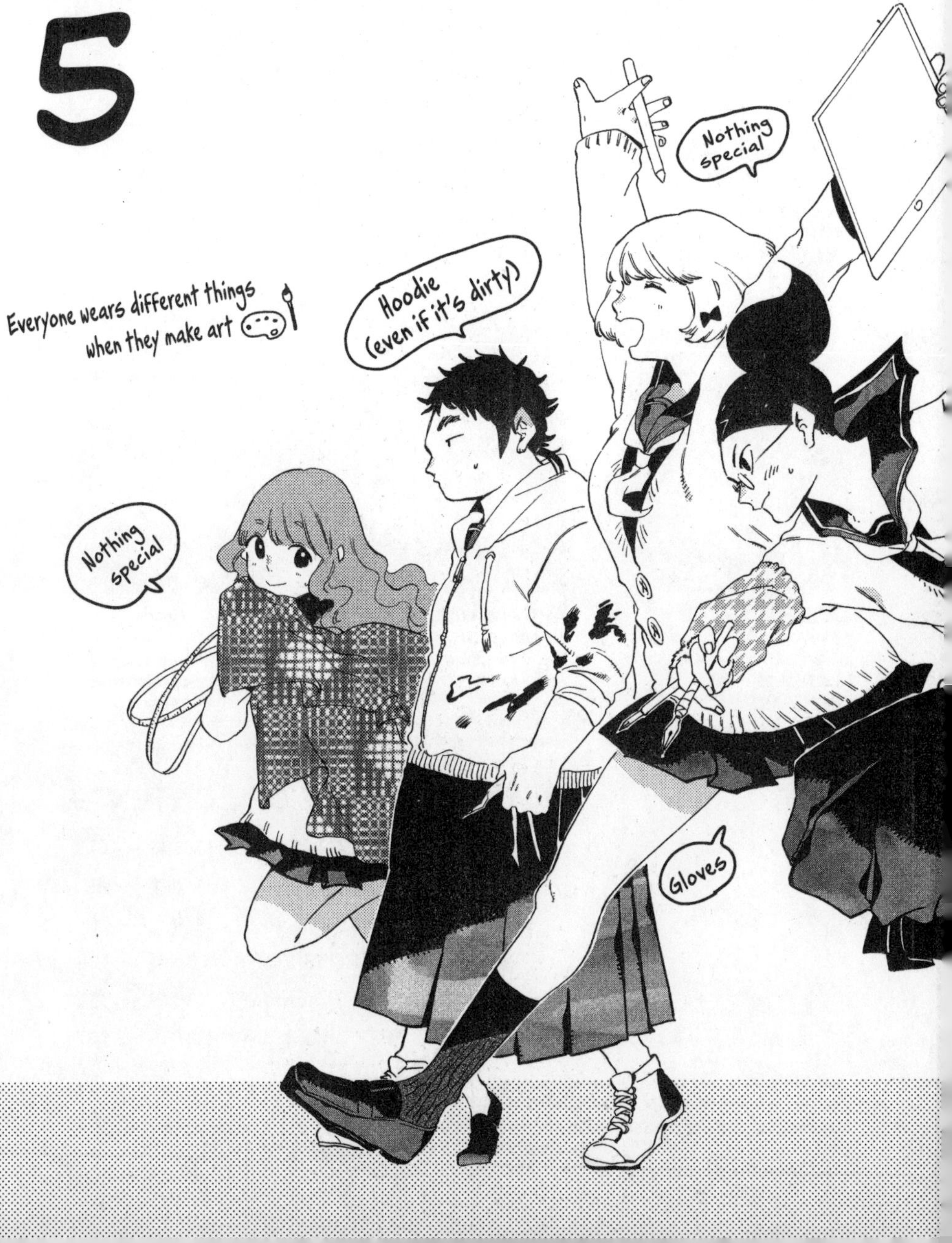
Everyone wears different things when they make art
Nothing special
Hoodie (even if it's dirty)
Gloves
Nothing special

# CHARACTERS

## Yotasuke Takahashi
A third-year high school student who used to attend the same prep school as Yatora. His talent, skill, and unsociable character inspire Yatora to be a better artist.

## Ryuji Ayukawa
Goes by the name Yuka. A boy who dresses in women's clothing. A member of the Art Club who's in the same class as Yatora. Yuka invited Yatora to the Art Club.

## Yatora Yaguchi
A third-year in high school. After seeing Mori-senpai's painting, he discovered the joy of making art and was hooked. He sets his sights on Tokyo University of the Arts, the most competitive of all Japanese art colleges.

## Ooba-sensei
An instructor at the art prep school that Yatora attends. Her height matches the volume of her voice.

## Maki Kuwana
A third-year in high school. She attends the same prep school as Yatora. Her parents are TUA alumni, and her older sister, who is a bit of a "campus celebrity," currently attends TUA.

## Haruka Hashida
A student who's in the same year and school as Yotasuke. He attends the same prep school as Yatora. As an art connoisseur of sorts, he enjoys museum outings and the like.

# TABLE OF CONTENTS

**WARNING:** This volume contains mentions of suicide. If you are experiencing suicidal thoughts or feelings, you are not alone, and there is free, 24/7 help.

**National Suicide Prevention Lifeline** offers specific resources for kids, LGBTQ+ people, survivors, and more. You can call 1-800-273-TALK (8255) or go to SuicidePreventionLifeline.org

**The Trevor Project** offers call, text, and online chat for LGBTQ+ youth. You can call 1-866-488-7386, or go to TheTrevorProject.org

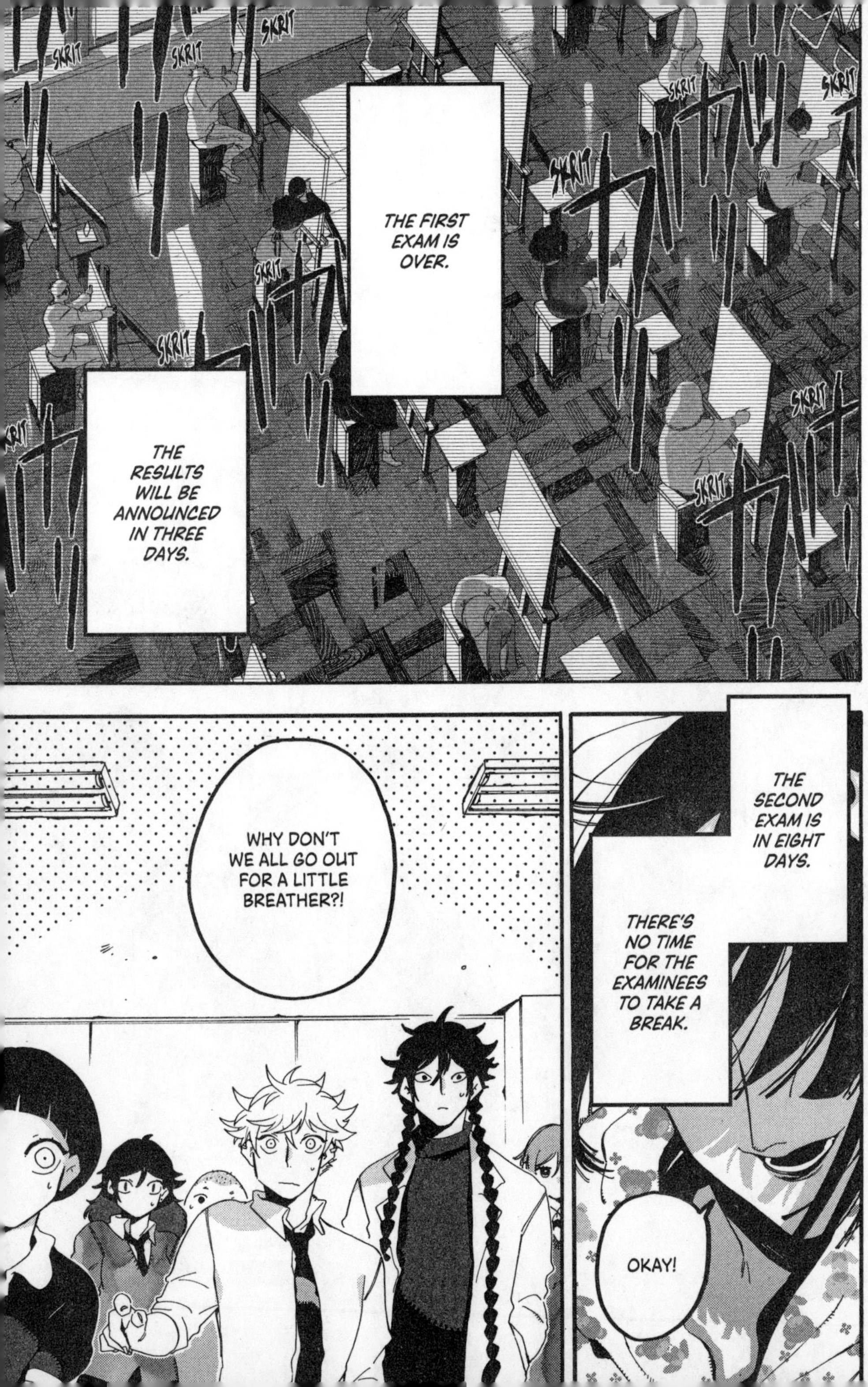
SKRIT
SKRIT
SKRIT
SKRIT
SKRIT
SKRIT
SKRIT
SKRIT
SKRIT
SKRIT
THE FIRST EXAM IS OVER.
THE RESULTS WILL BE ANNOUNCED IN THREE DAYS.
THE SECOND EXAM IS IN EIGHT DAYS.
THERE'S NO TIME FOR THE EXAMINEES TO TAKE A BREAK.
OKAY!
WHY DON'T WE ALL GO OUT FOR A LITTLE BREATHER?!

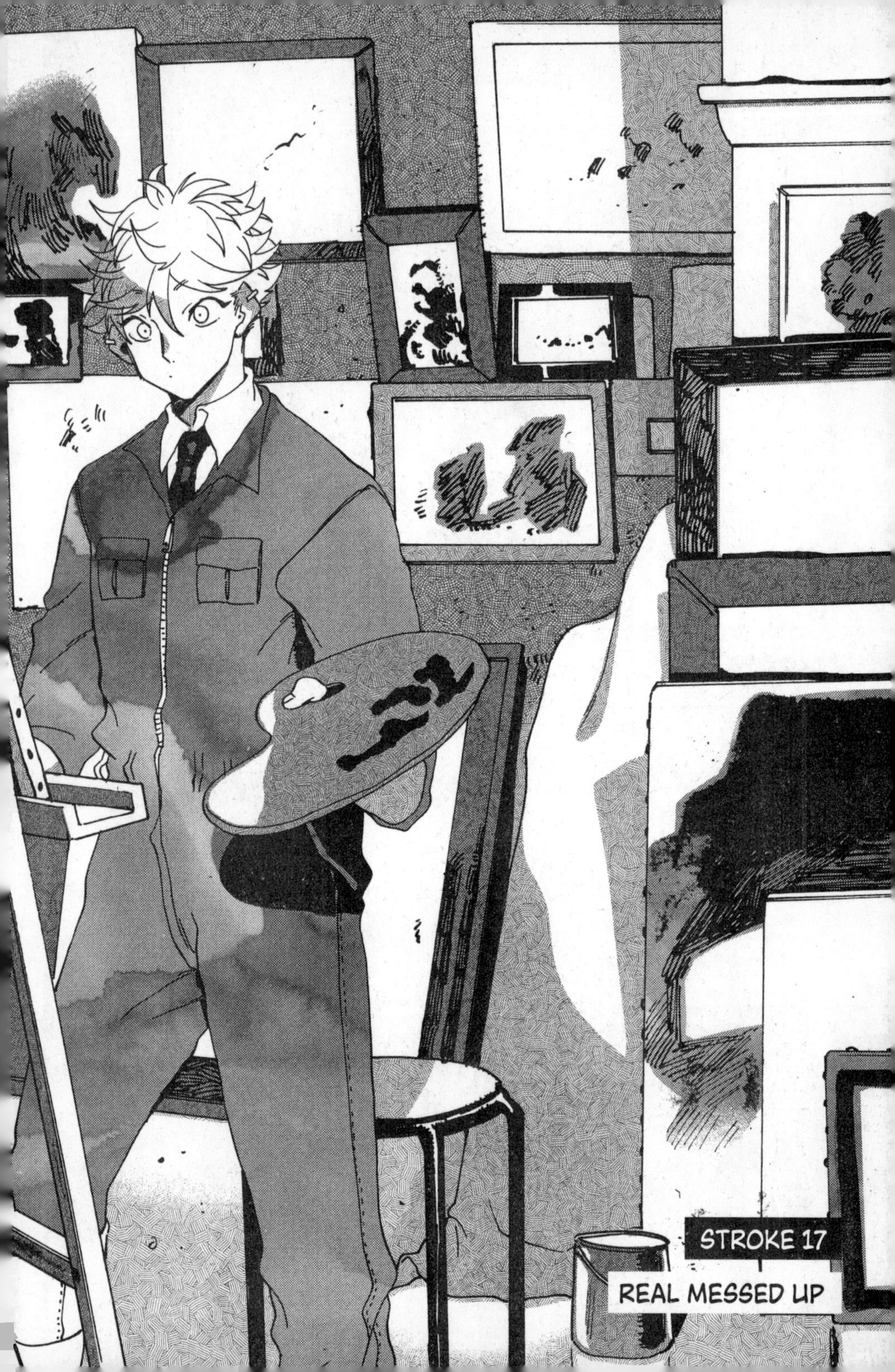
STROKE 17
REAL MESSED UP

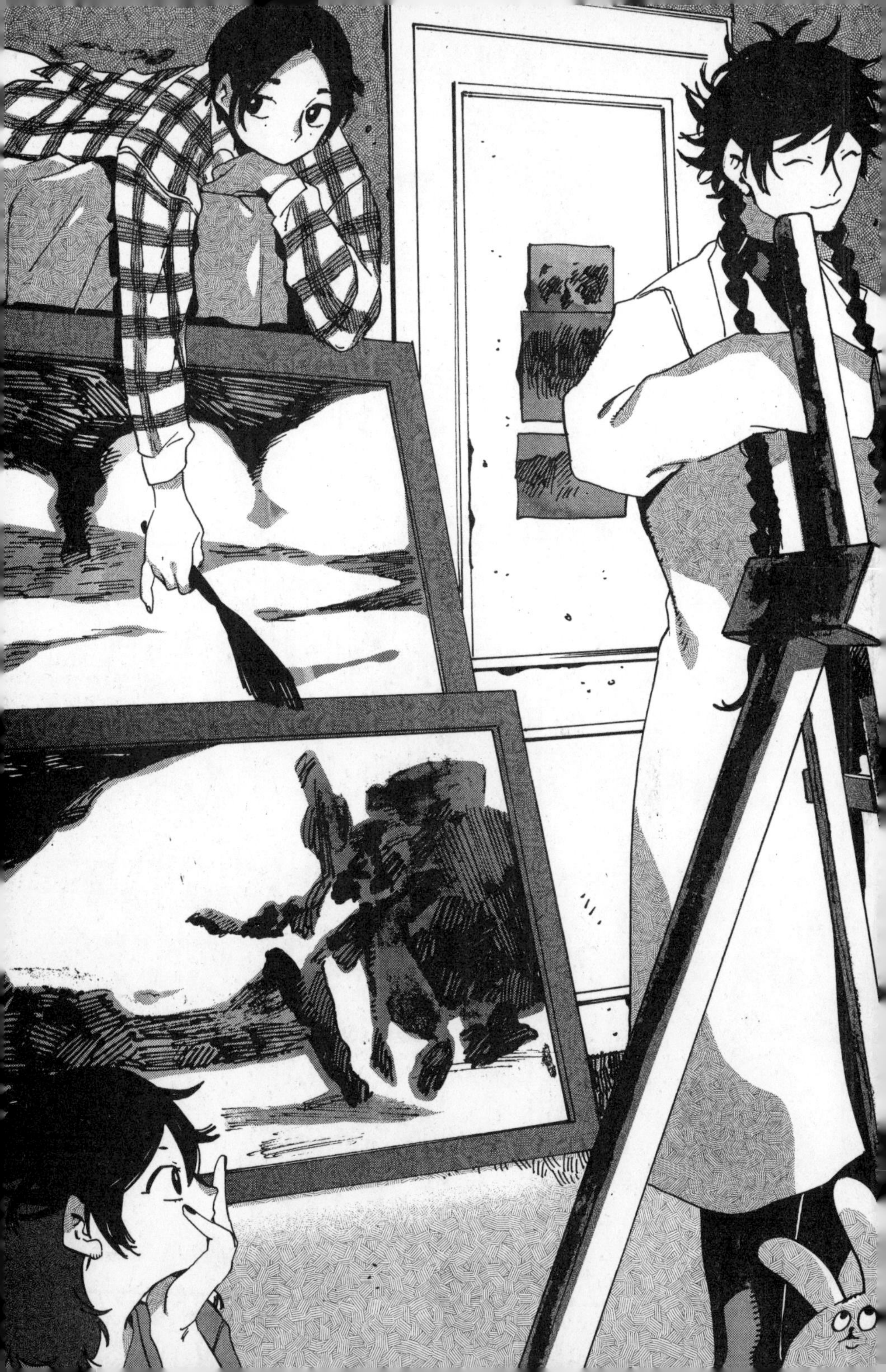

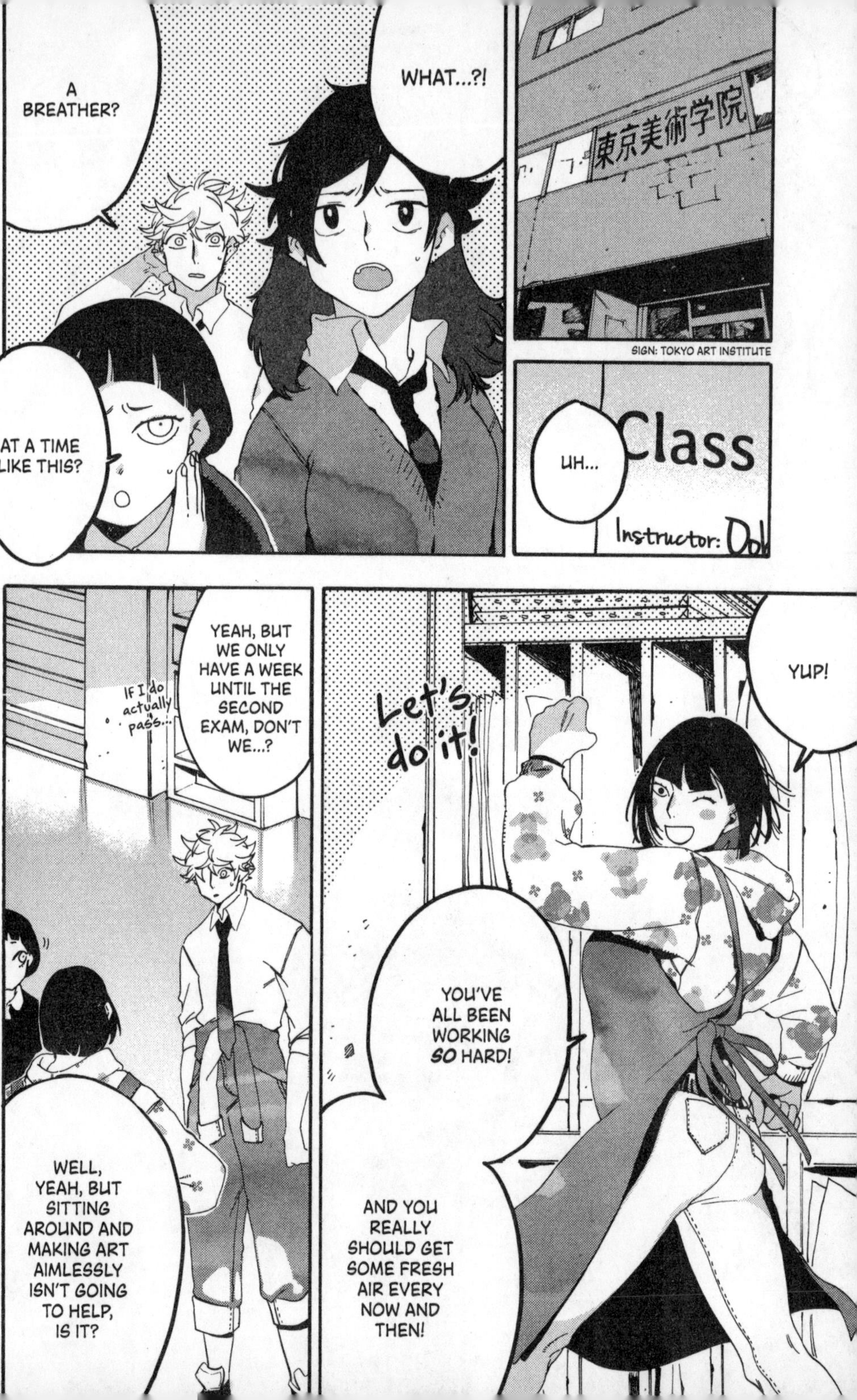
東京美術学院
SIGN: TOKYO ART INSTITUTE
Class
Instructor:
UH...
WHAT...?!
A BREATHER?
AT A TIME LIKE THIS?
YUP!
Let's do it!
YOU'VE ALL BEEN WORKING *SO* HARD!
AND YOU REALLY SHOULD GET SOME FRESH AIR EVERY NOW AND THEN!
YEAH, BUT WE ONLY HAVE A WEEK UNTIL THE SECOND EXAM, DON'T WE...?
If I do actually pass...
WELL, YEAH, BUT SITTING AROUND AND MAKING ART AIMLESSLY ISN'T GOING TO HELP, IS IT?

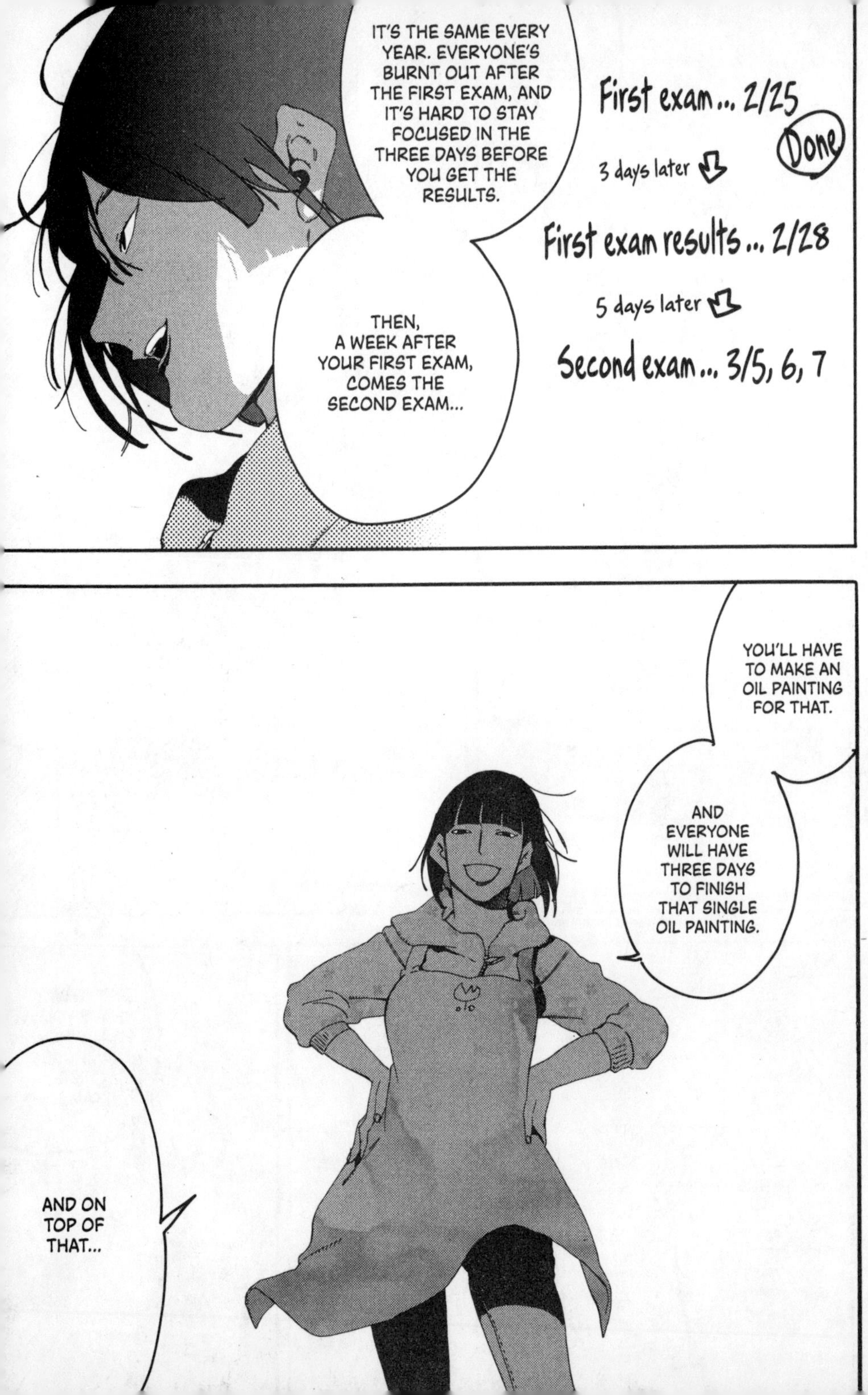
IT'S THE SAME EVERY YEAR. EVERYONE'S BURNT OUT AFTER THE FIRST EXAM, AND IT'S HARD TO STAY FOCUSED IN THE THREE DAYS BEFORE YOU GET THE RESULTS.
First exam... 2/25
Done
3 days later
First exam results... 2/28
5 days later
Second exam... 3/5, 6, 7
THEN, A WEEK AFTER YOUR FIRST EXAM, COMES THE SECOND EXAM...
YOU'LL HAVE TO MAKE AN OIL PAINTING FOR THAT.
AND EVERYONE WILL HAVE THREE DAYS TO FINISH THAT SINGLE OIL PAINTING.
AND ON TOP OF THAT...

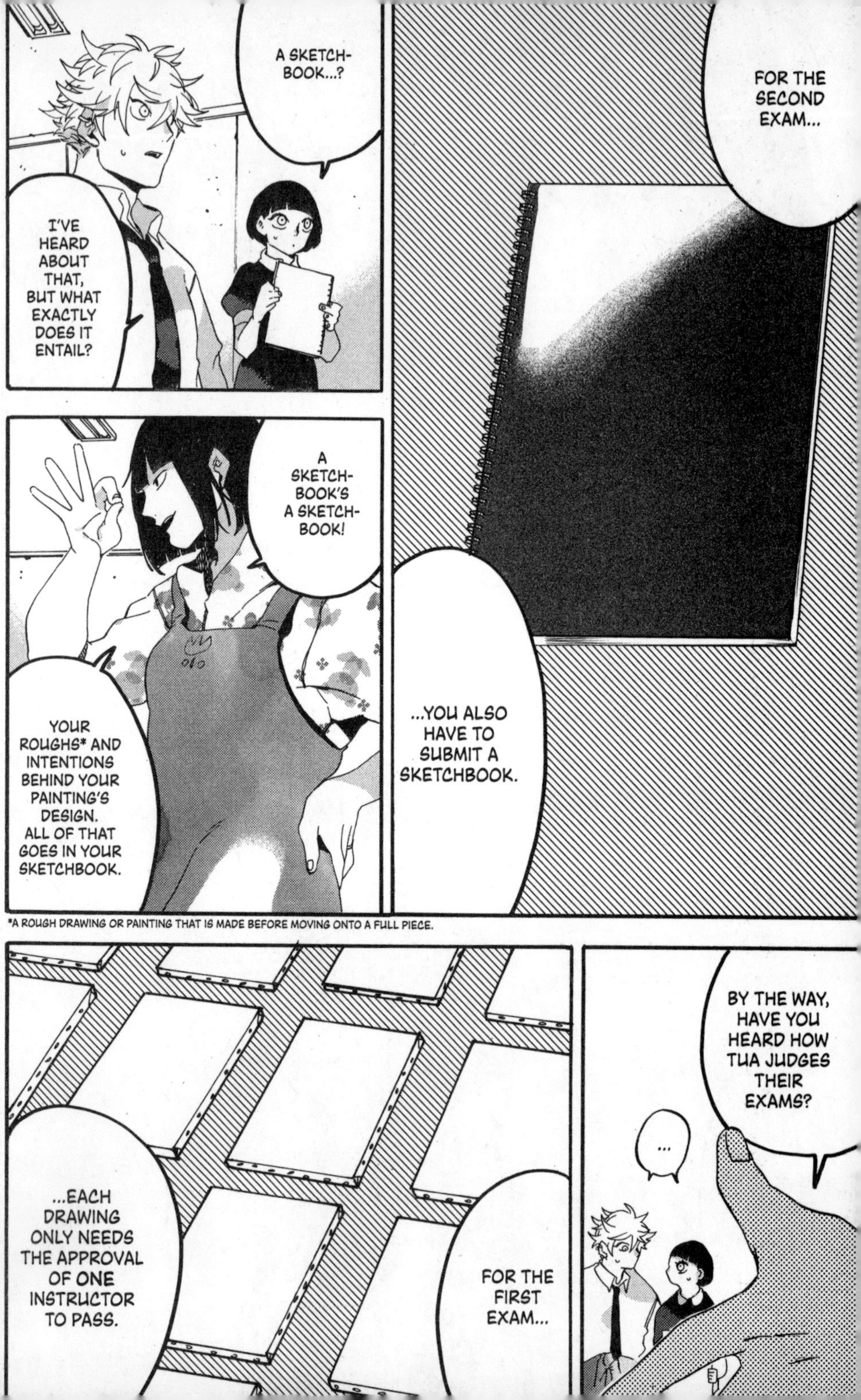
FOR THE SECOND EXAM...
...YOU ALSO HAVE TO SUBMIT A SKETCHBOOK.
A SKETCH-BOOK...?
I'VE HEARD ABOUT THAT, BUT WHAT EXACTLY DOES IT ENTAIL?
A SKETCH-BOOK'S A SKETCH-BOOK!
YOUR ROUGHS* AND INTENTIONS BEHIND YOUR PAINTING'S DESIGN. ALL OF THAT GOES IN YOUR SKETCHBOOK.
*A ROUGH DRAWING OR PAINTING THAT IS MADE BEFORE MOVING ONTO A FULL PIECE.
BY THE WAY, HAVE YOU HEARD HOW TUA JUDGES THEIR EXAMS?
...
FOR THE FIRST EXAM...
...EACH DRAWING ONLY NEEDS THE APPROVAL OF ONE INSTRUCTOR TO PASS.

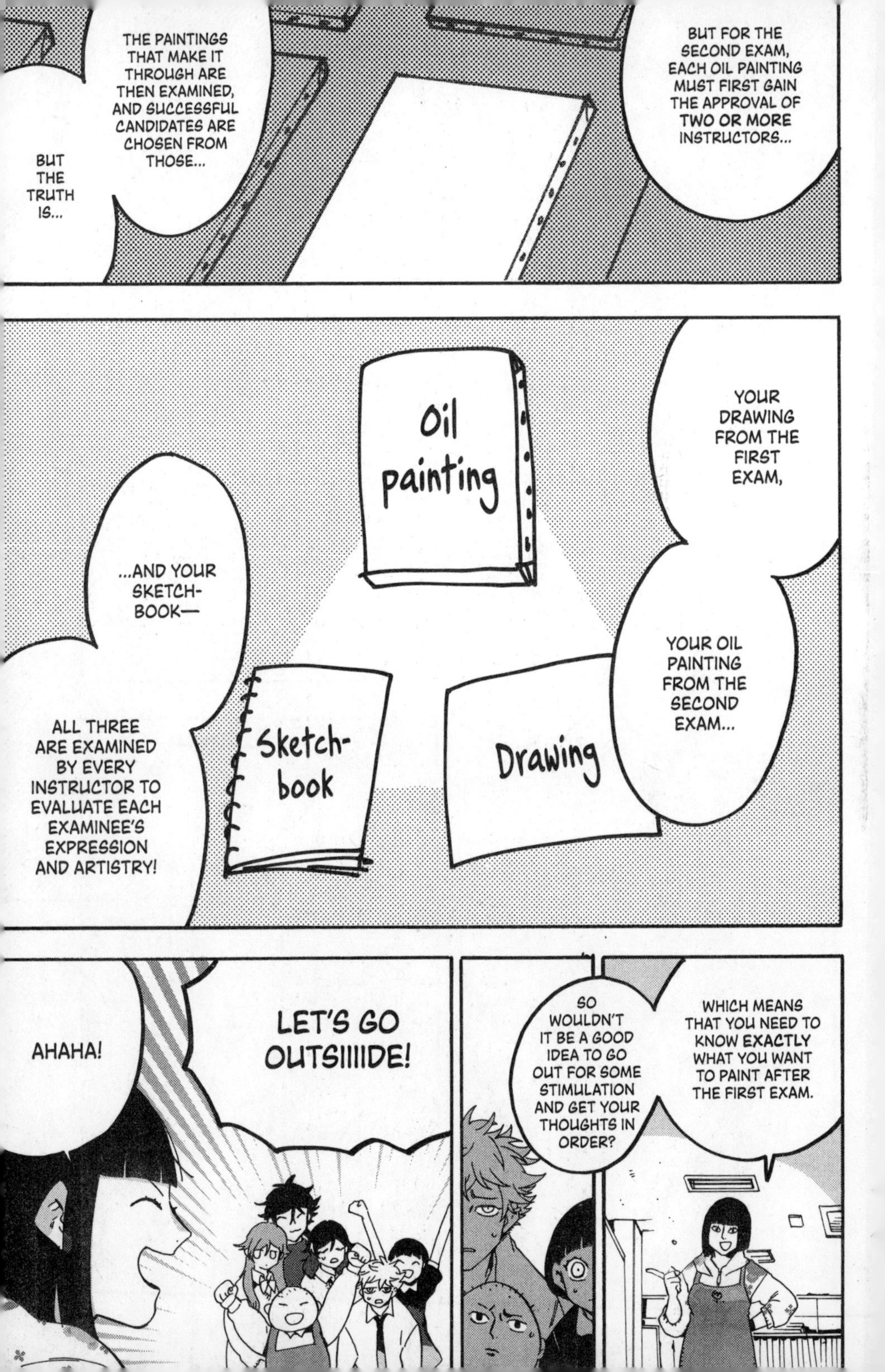
BUT FOR THE SECOND EXAM, EACH OIL PAINTING MUST FIRST GAIN THE APPROVAL OF TWO OR MORE INSTRUCTORS...
THE PAINTINGS THAT MAKE IT THROUGH ARE THEN EXAMINED, AND SUCCESSFUL CANDIDATES ARE CHOSEN FROM THOSE...
BUT THE TRUTH IS...
YOUR DRAWING FROM THE FIRST EXAM,
YOUR OIL PAINTING FROM THE SECOND EXAM...
Oil painting
...AND YOUR SKETCHBOOK—
Drawing
Sketch-book
ALL THREE ARE EXAMINED BY EVERY INSTRUCTOR TO EVALUATE EACH EXAMINEE'S EXPRESSION AND ARTISTRY!
WHICH MEANS THAT YOU NEED TO KNOW EXACTLY WHAT YOU WANT TO PAINT AFTER THE FIRST EXAM.
SO WOULDN'T IT BE A GOOD IDEA TO GO OUT FOR SOME STIMULATION AND GET YOUR THOUGHTS IN ORDER?
LET'S GO OUTSIIIIDE!
AHAHA!

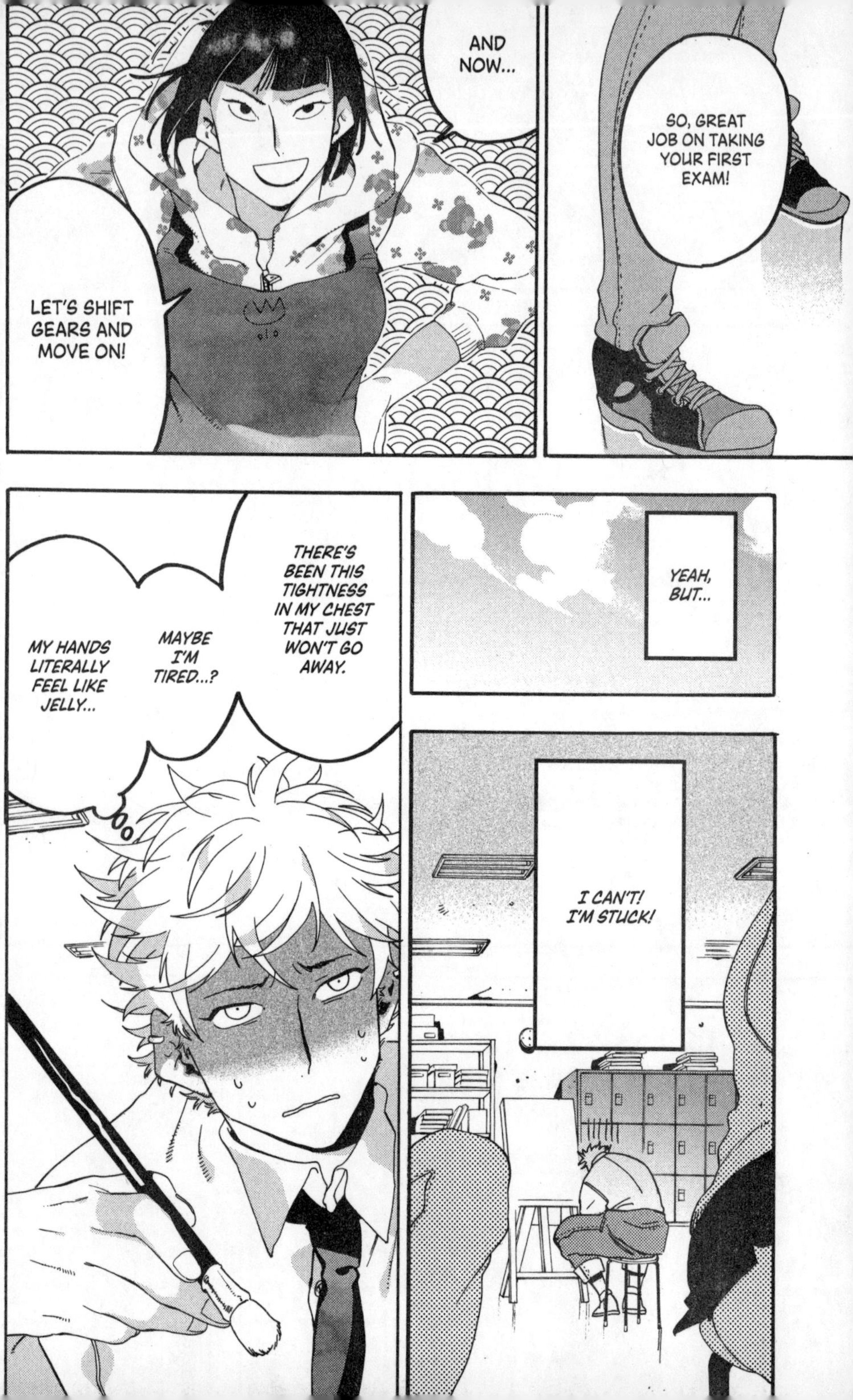
SO, GREAT JOB ON TAKING YOUR FIRST EXAM!
AND NOW...
LET'S SHIFT GEARS AND MOVE ON!
YEAH, BUT...
I CAN'T! I'M STUCK!
THERE'S BEEN THIS TIGHTNESS IN MY CHEST THAT JUST WON'T GO AWAY.
MAYBE I'M TIRED...?
MY HANDS LITERALLY FEEL LIKE JELLY...

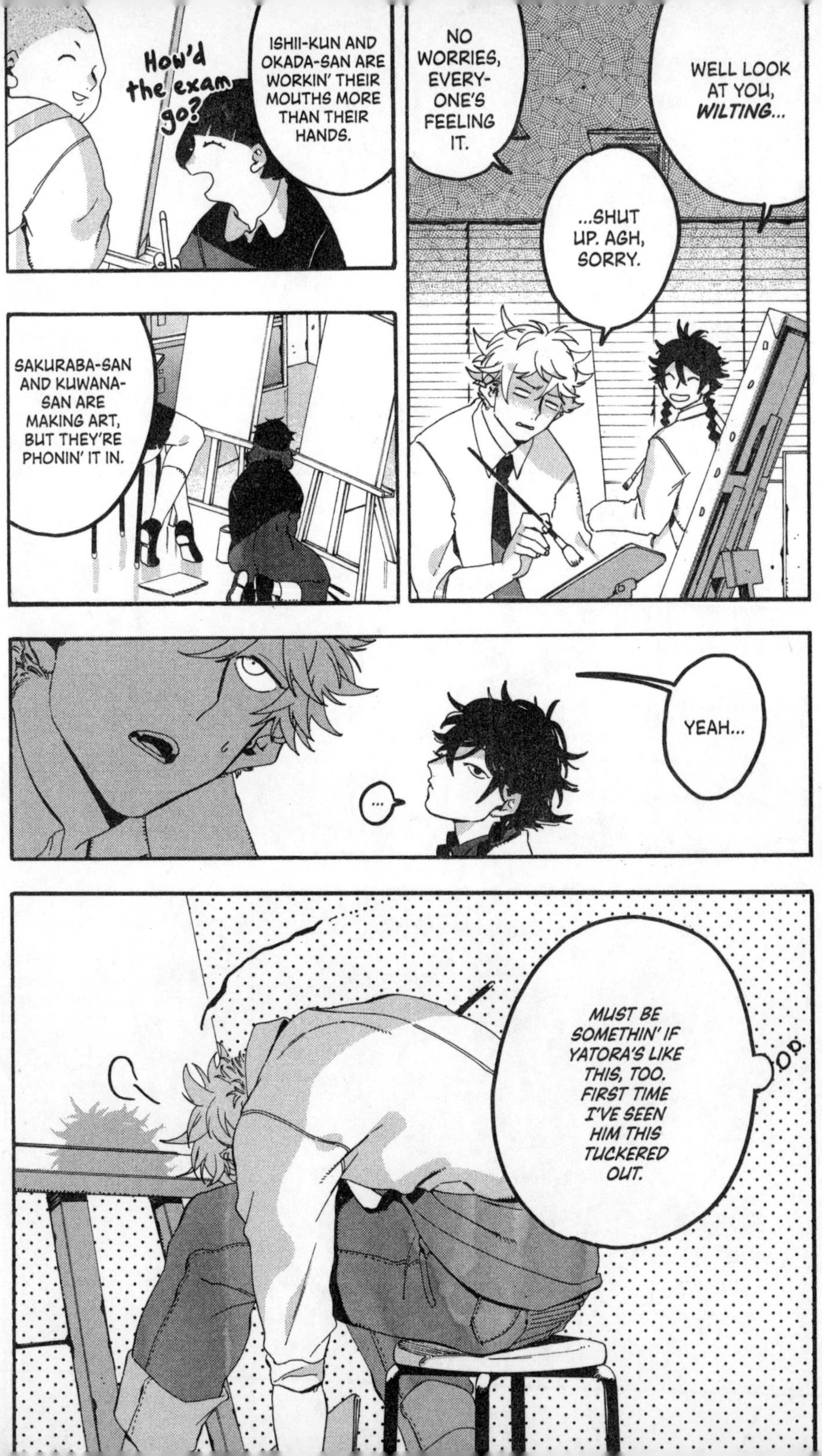
WELL LOOK AT YOU, *WILTING*...
NO WORRIES, EVERY-ONE'S FEELING IT.
...SHUT UP. AGH, SORRY.
ISHII-KUN AND OKADA-SAN ARE WORKIN' THEIR MOUTHS MORE THAN THEIR HANDS.
How'd the exam go?
SAKURABA-SAN AND KUWANA-SAN ARE MAKING ART, BUT THEY'RE PHONIN' IT IN.
YEAH...
...
*MUST BE SOMETHIN' IF YATORA'S LIKE THIS, TOO. FIRST TIME I'VE SEEN HIM THIS TUCKERED OUT.*

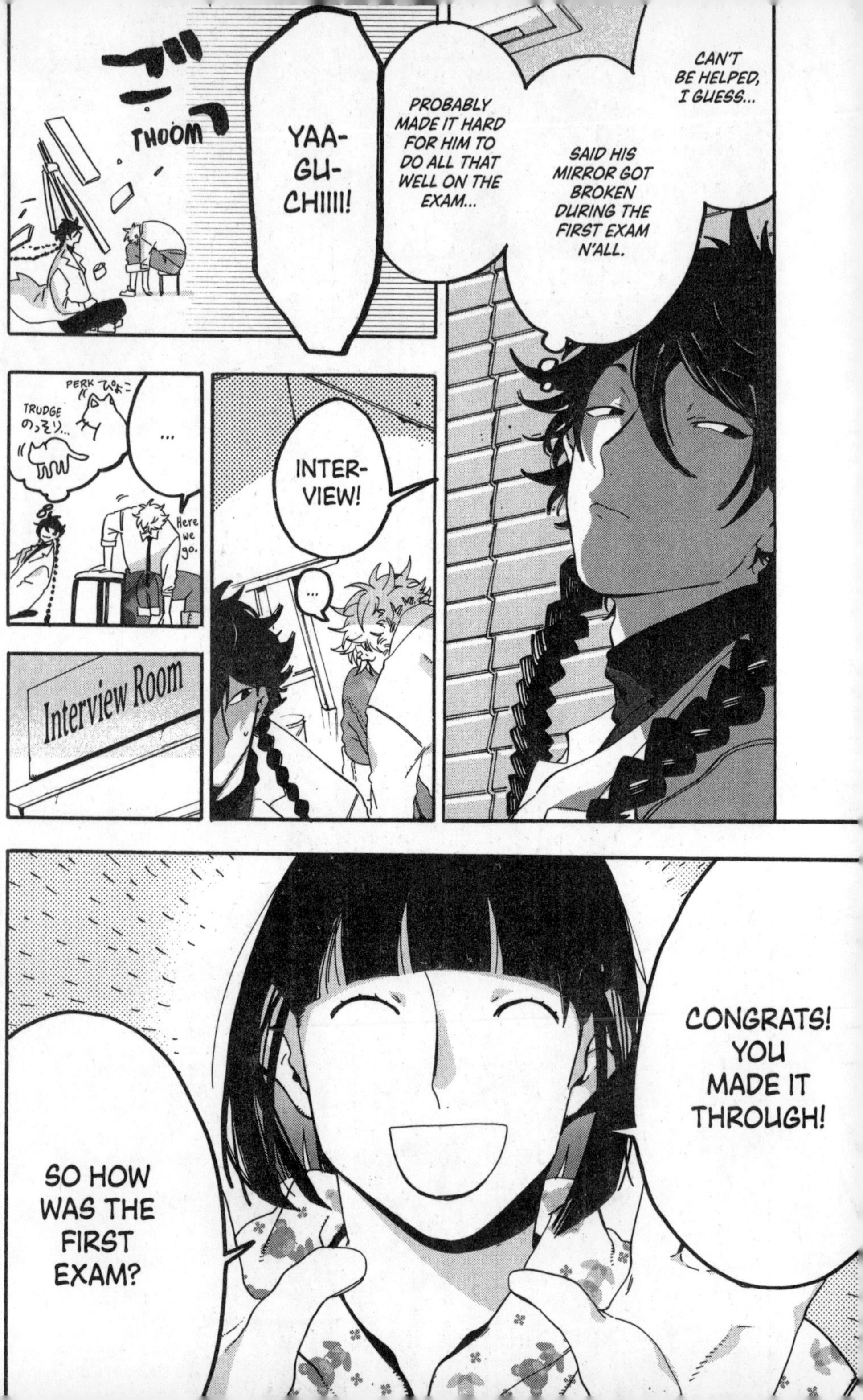
CAN'T BE HELPED, I GUESS...
SAID HIS MIRROR GOT BROKEN DURING THE FIRST EXAM N'ALL.
PROBABLY MADE IT HARD FOR HIM TO DO ALL THAT WELL ON THE EXAM...
YAA-GU-CHIIIII!
THOOM
INTER-VIEW!
...
...
PERK
TRUDGE
のっそり...
Here we go.
Interview Room
CONGRATS! YOU MADE IT THROUGH!
SO HOW WAS THE FIRST EXAM?

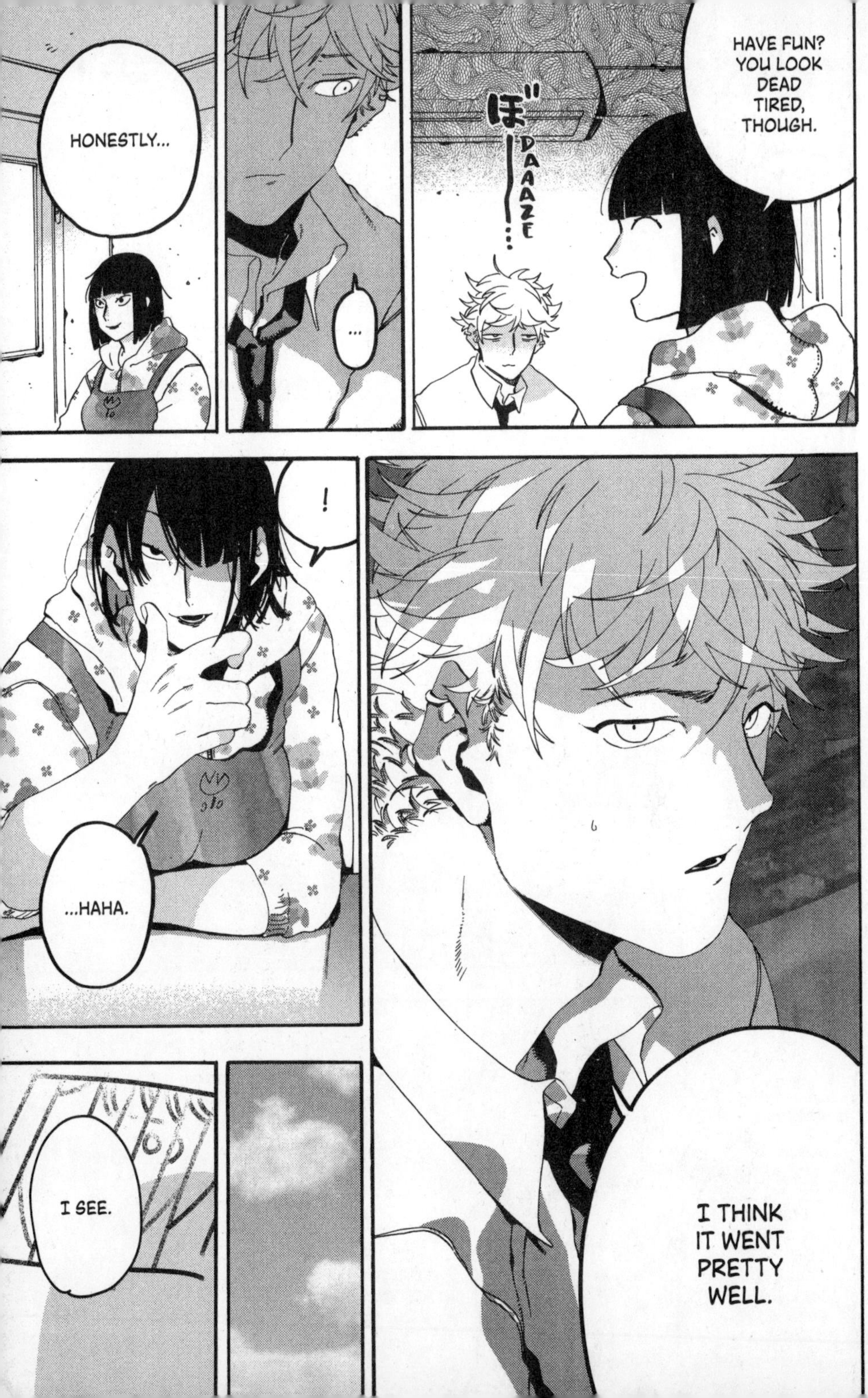
HAVE FUN? YOU LOOK DEAD TIRED, THOUGH.
ぼーー…
DAAAZE
...
HONESTLY...
I THINK IT WENT PRETTY WELL.
!
...HAHA.
I SEE.

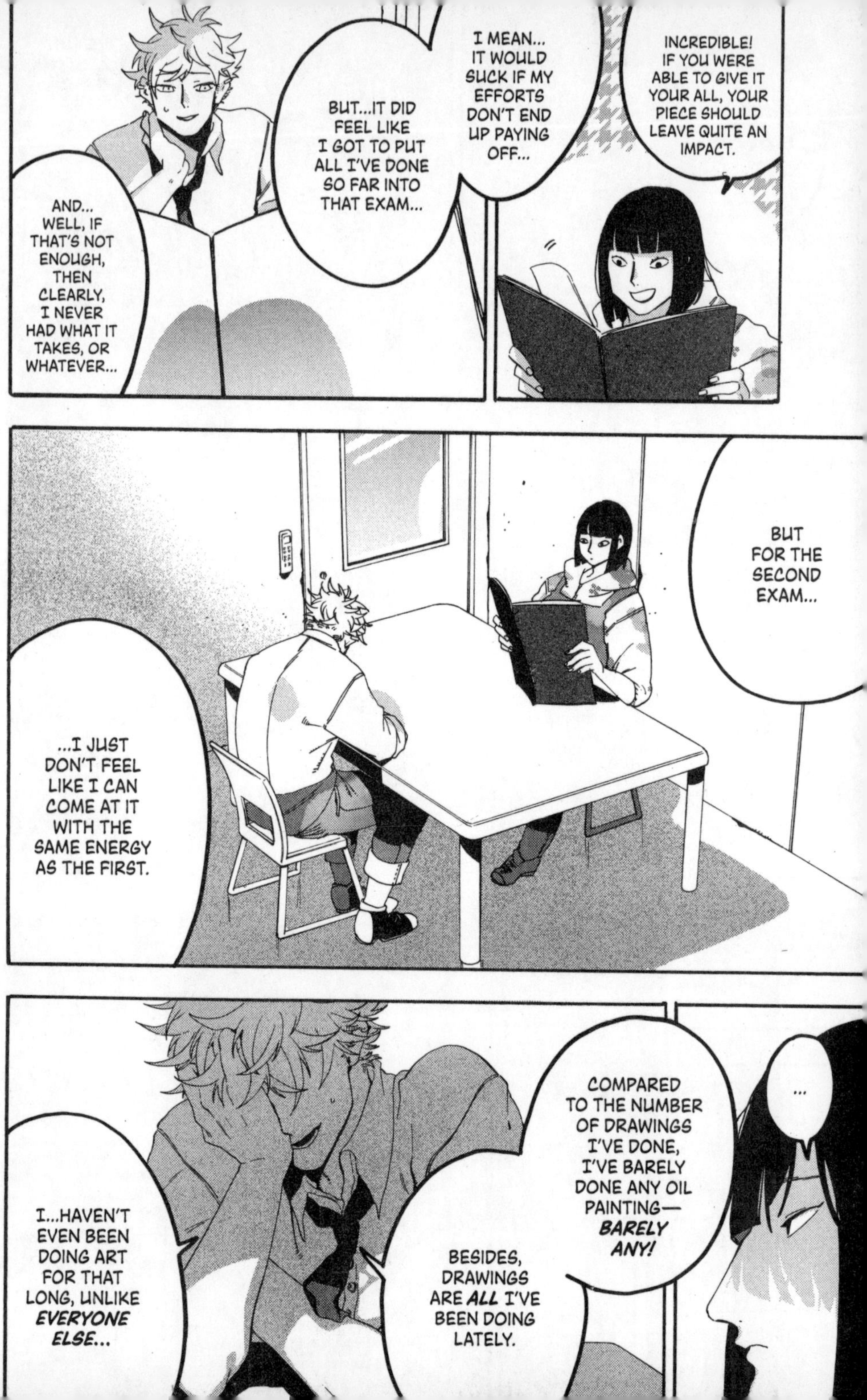
INCREDIBLE! IF YOU WERE ABLE TO GIVE IT YOUR ALL, YOUR PIECE SHOULD LEAVE QUITE AN IMPACT.
I MEAN... IT WOULD SUCK IF MY EFFORTS DON'T END UP PAYING OFF...
BUT...IT DID FEEL LIKE I GOT TO PUT ALL I'VE DONE SO FAR INTO THAT EXAM...
AND... WELL, IF THAT'S NOT ENOUGH, THEN CLEARLY, I NEVER HAD WHAT IT TAKES, OR WHATEVER...
BUT FOR THE SECOND EXAM...
...I JUST DON'T FEEL LIKE I CAN COME AT IT WITH THE SAME ENERGY AS THE FIRST.
...
COMPARED TO THE NUMBER OF DRAWINGS I'VE DONE, I'VE BARELY DONE ANY OIL PAINTING—*BARELY ANY!*
BESIDES, DRAWINGS ARE *ALL* I'VE BEEN DOING LATELY.
I...HAVEN'T EVEN BEEN DOING ART FOR THAT LONG, UNLIKE *EVERYONE ELSE*...

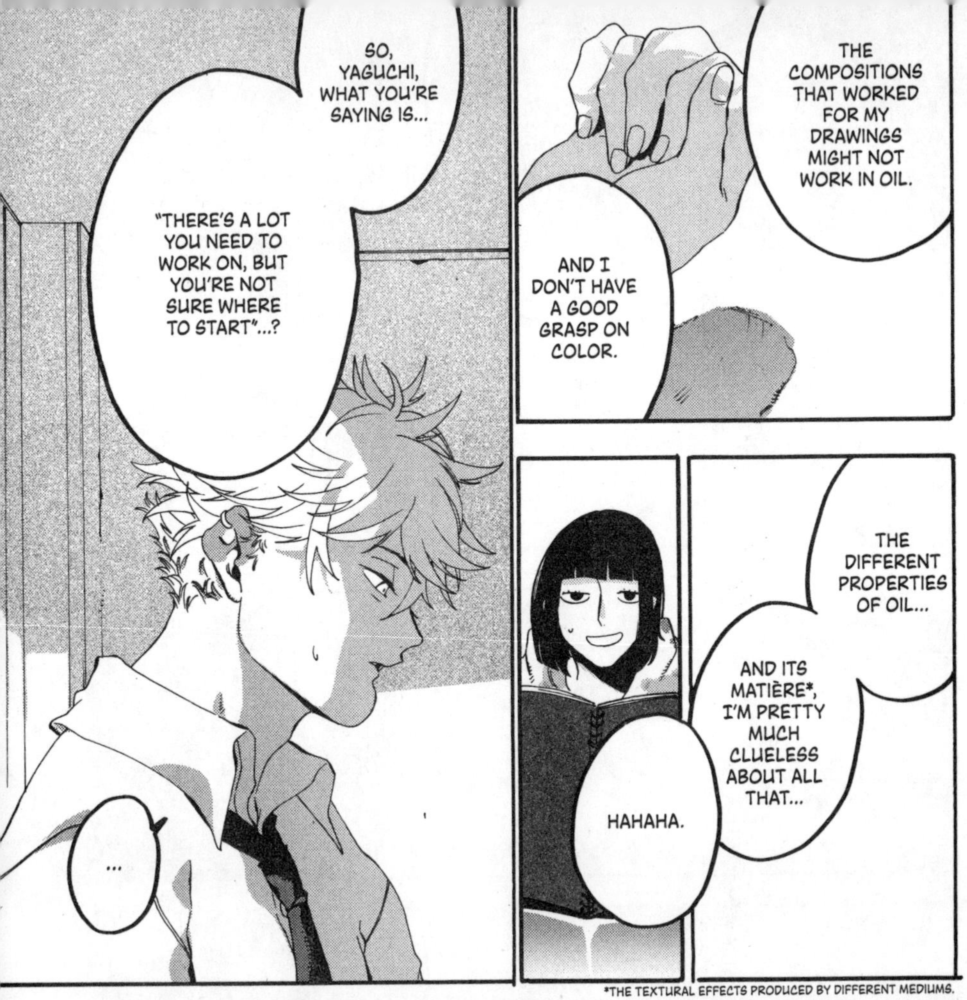
THE COMPOSITIONS THAT WORKED FOR MY DRAWINGS MIGHT NOT WORK IN OIL.
AND I DON'T HAVE A GOOD GRASP ON COLOR.
THE DIFFERENT PROPERTIES OF OIL...
AND ITS MATIÈRE*, I'M PRETTY MUCH CLUELESS ABOUT ALL THAT...
HAHAHA.
SO, YAGUCHI, WHAT YOU'RE SAYING IS...
"THERE'S A LOT YOU NEED TO WORK ON, BUT YOU'RE NOT SURE WHERE TO START"...?
...

*THE TEXTURAL EFFECTS PRODUCED BY DIFFERENT MEDIUMS.

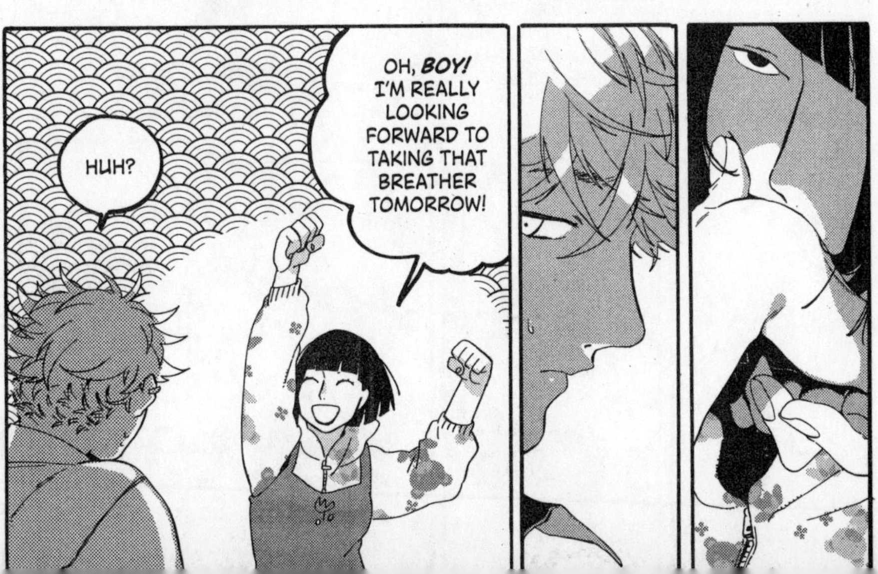
OH, ***BOY!*** I'M REALLY LOOKING FORWARD TO TAKING THAT BREATHER TOMORROW!
HUH?

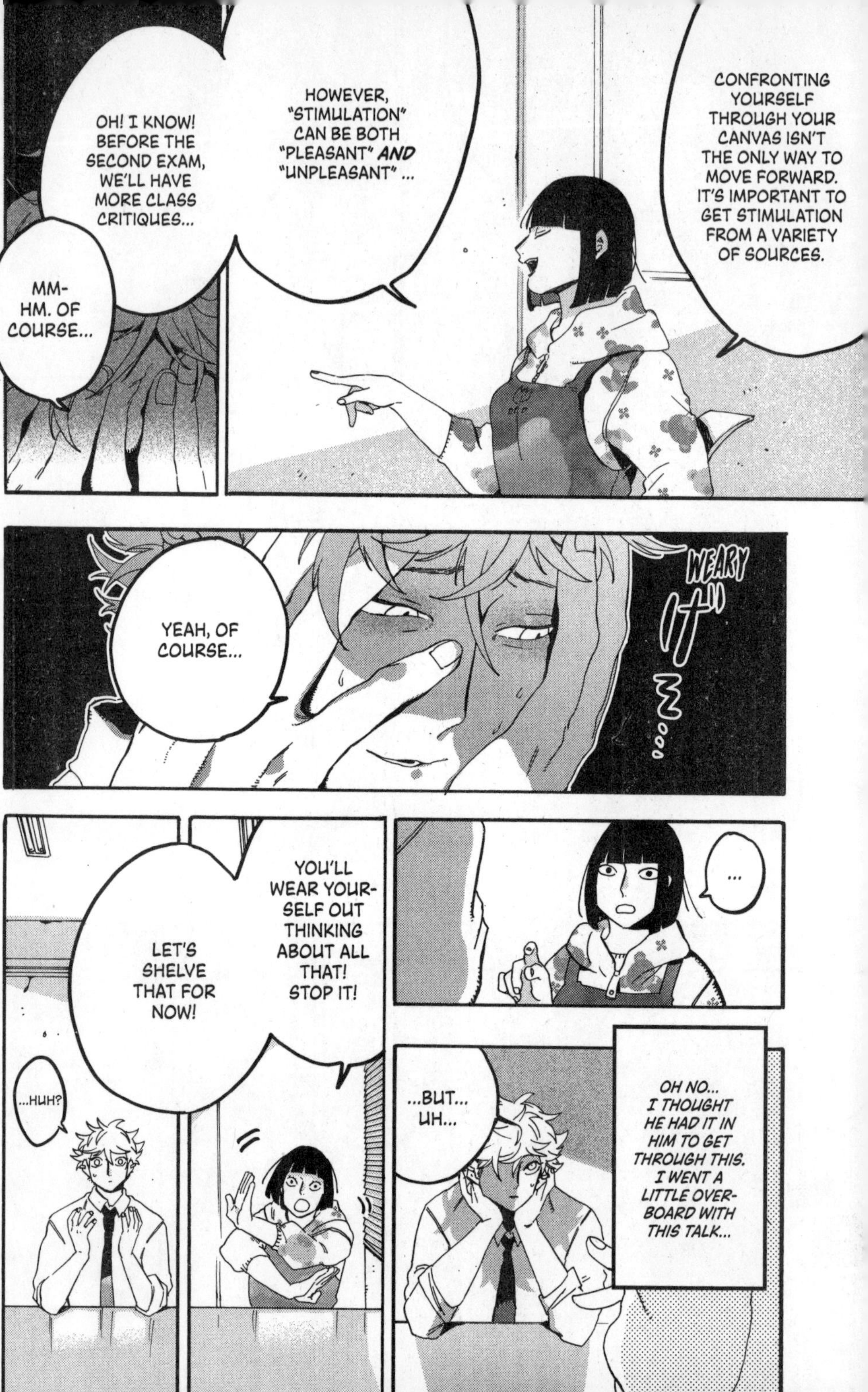
CONFRONTING YOURSELF THROUGH YOUR CANVAS ISN'T THE ONLY WAY TO MOVE FORWARD. IT'S IMPORTANT TO GET STIMULATION FROM A VARIETY OF SOURCES.
HOWEVER, "STIMULATION" CAN BE BOTH "PLEASANT" *AND* "UNPLEASANT"...
OH! I KNOW! BEFORE THE SECOND EXAM, WE'LL HAVE MORE CLASS CRITIQUES...
MM-HM. OF COURSE...
WEARY
YEAH, OF COURSE...
...
*OH NO... I THOUGHT HE HAD IT IN HIM TO GET THROUGH THIS. I WENT A LITTLE OVER-BOARD WITH THIS TALK...*
...BUT... UH...
YOU'LL WEAR YOURSELF OUT THINKING ABOUT ALL THAT! STOP IT!
LET'S SHELVE THAT FOR NOW!
...HUH?

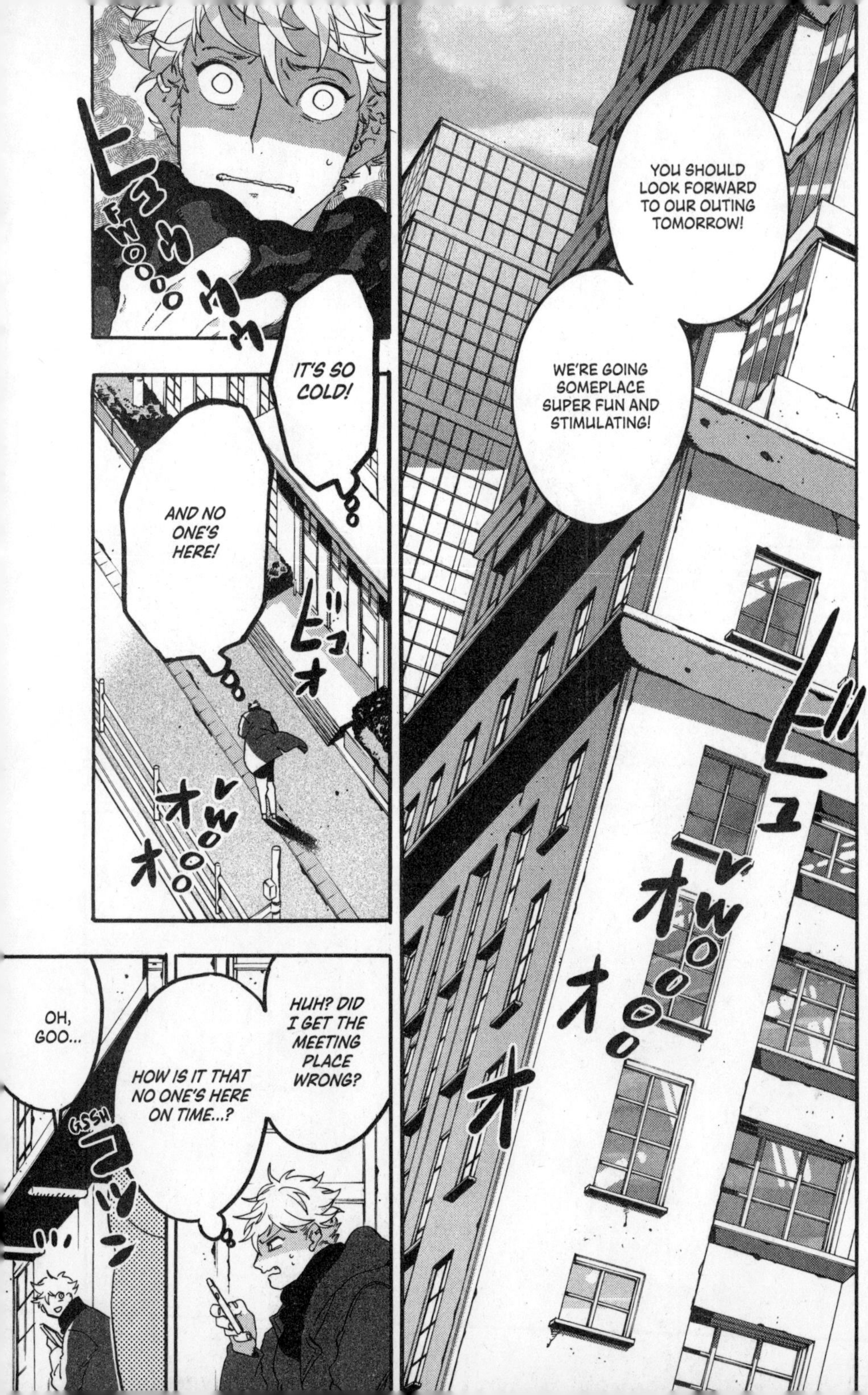
YOU SHOULD LOOK FORWARD TO OUR OUTING TOMORROW!
WE'RE GOING SOMEPLACE SUPER FUN AND STIMULATING!
FWOOOO
FWOOOO
IT'S SO COLD!
AND NO ONE'S HERE!
FWOOOO
HUH? DID I GET THE MEETING PLACE WRONG?
HOW IS IT THAT NO ONE'S HERE ON TIME...?
OH, GOO...
GSSH

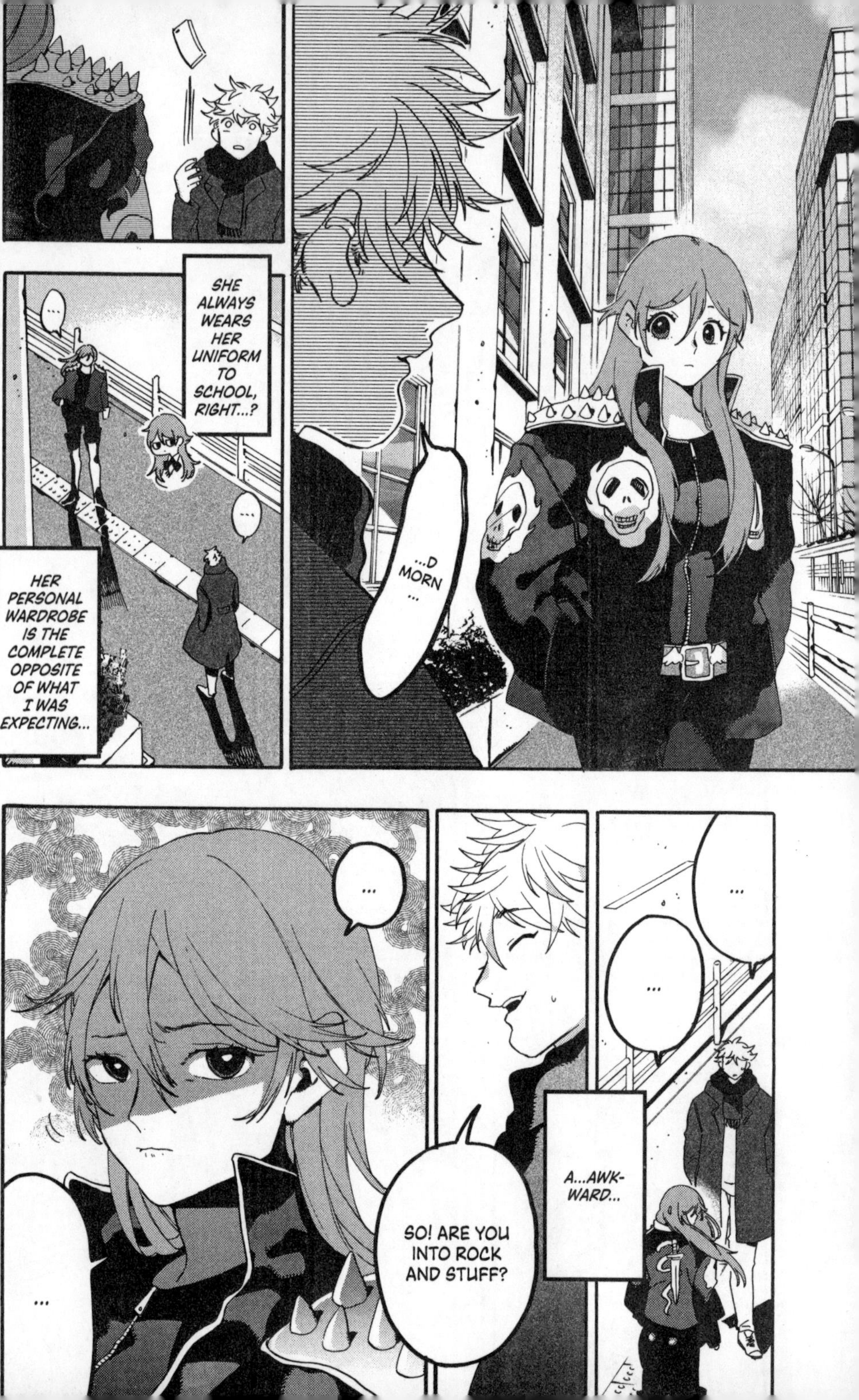
...D MORN ...
SHE ALWAYS WEARS HER UNIFORM TO SCHOOL, RIGHT...?
...
...
HER PERSONAL WARDROBE IS THE COMPLETE OPPOSITE OF WHAT I WAS EXPECTING...
...
...
A...AWK-WARD...
SO! ARE YOU INTO ROCK AND STUFF?
...
...

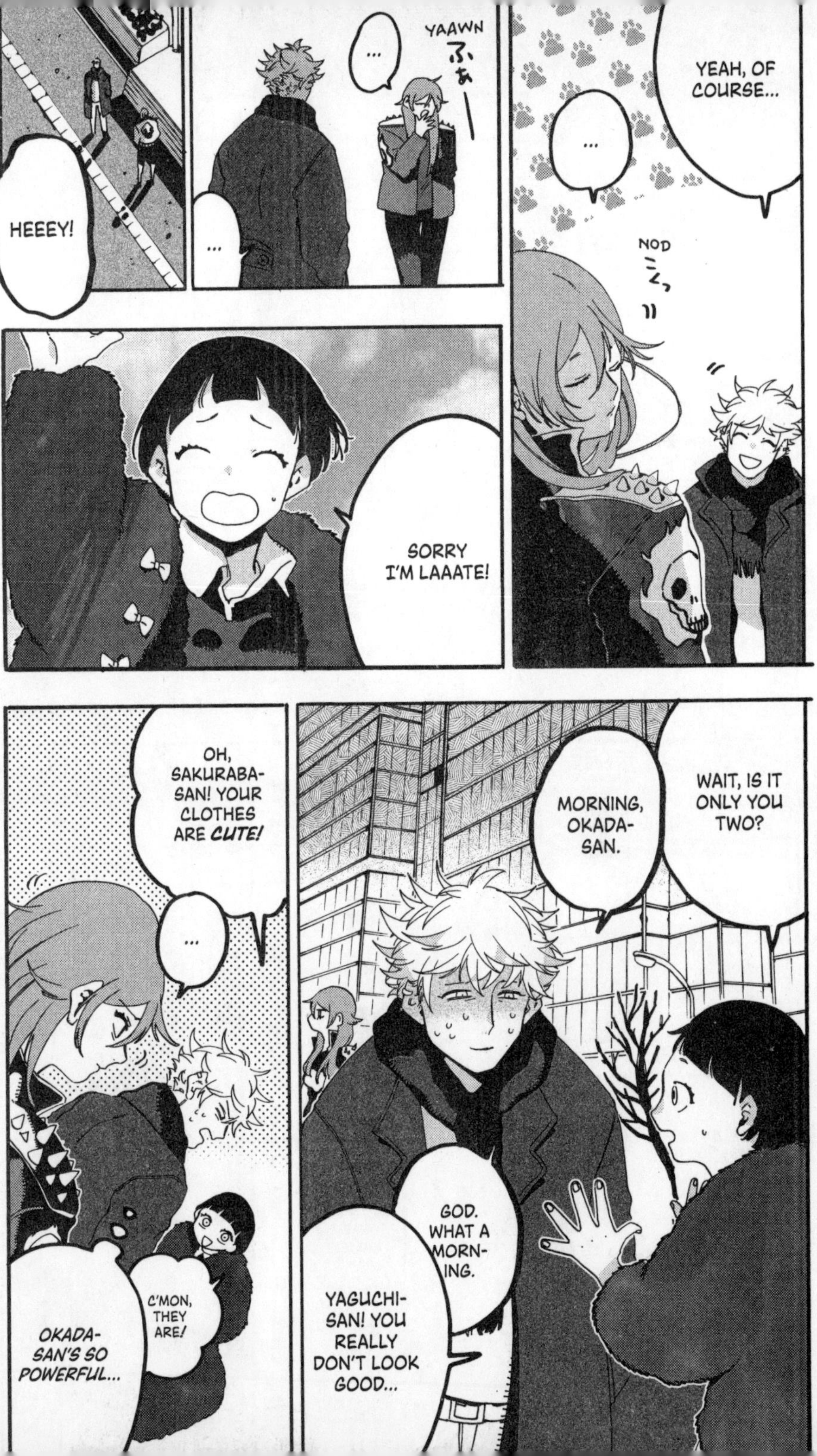
YEAH, OF COURSE...
...
NOD
こくっ
YAAWN
ふぁー
...
...
HEEEY!
SORRY I'M LAAATE!
WAIT, IS IT ONLY YOU TWO?
MORNING, OKADA-SAN.
GOD. WHAT A MORNING.
YAGUCHI-SAN! YOU REALLY DON'T LOOK GOOD...
OH, SAKURABA-SAN! YOUR CLOTHES ARE *CUTE!*
...
C'MON, THEY ARE!
*OKADA-SAN'S SO POWERFUL...*

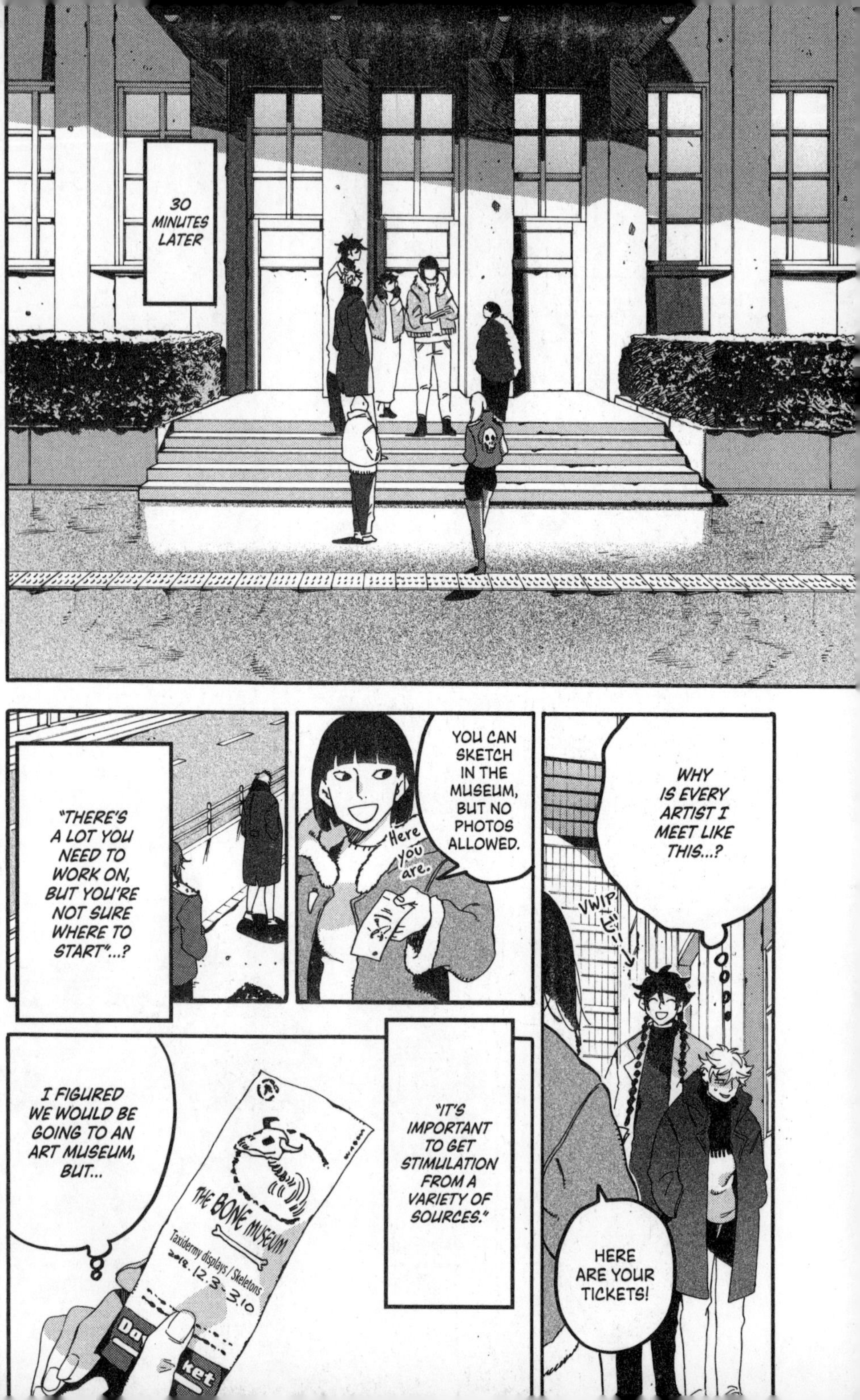
30 MINUTES LATER
WHY IS EVERY ARTIST I MEET LIKE THIS...?
VWIP
HERE ARE YOUR TICKETS!
YOU CAN SKETCH IN THE MUSEUM, BUT NO PHOTOS ALLOWED.
Here you are.
"THERE'S A LOT YOU NEED TO WORK ON, BUT YOU'RE NOT SURE WHERE TO START"...?
"IT'S IMPORTANT TO GET STIMULATION FROM A VARIETY OF SOURCES."
I FIGURED WE WOULD BE GOING TO AN ART MUSEUM, BUT...
THE BONE MUSEUM
Taxidermy displays / Skeletons

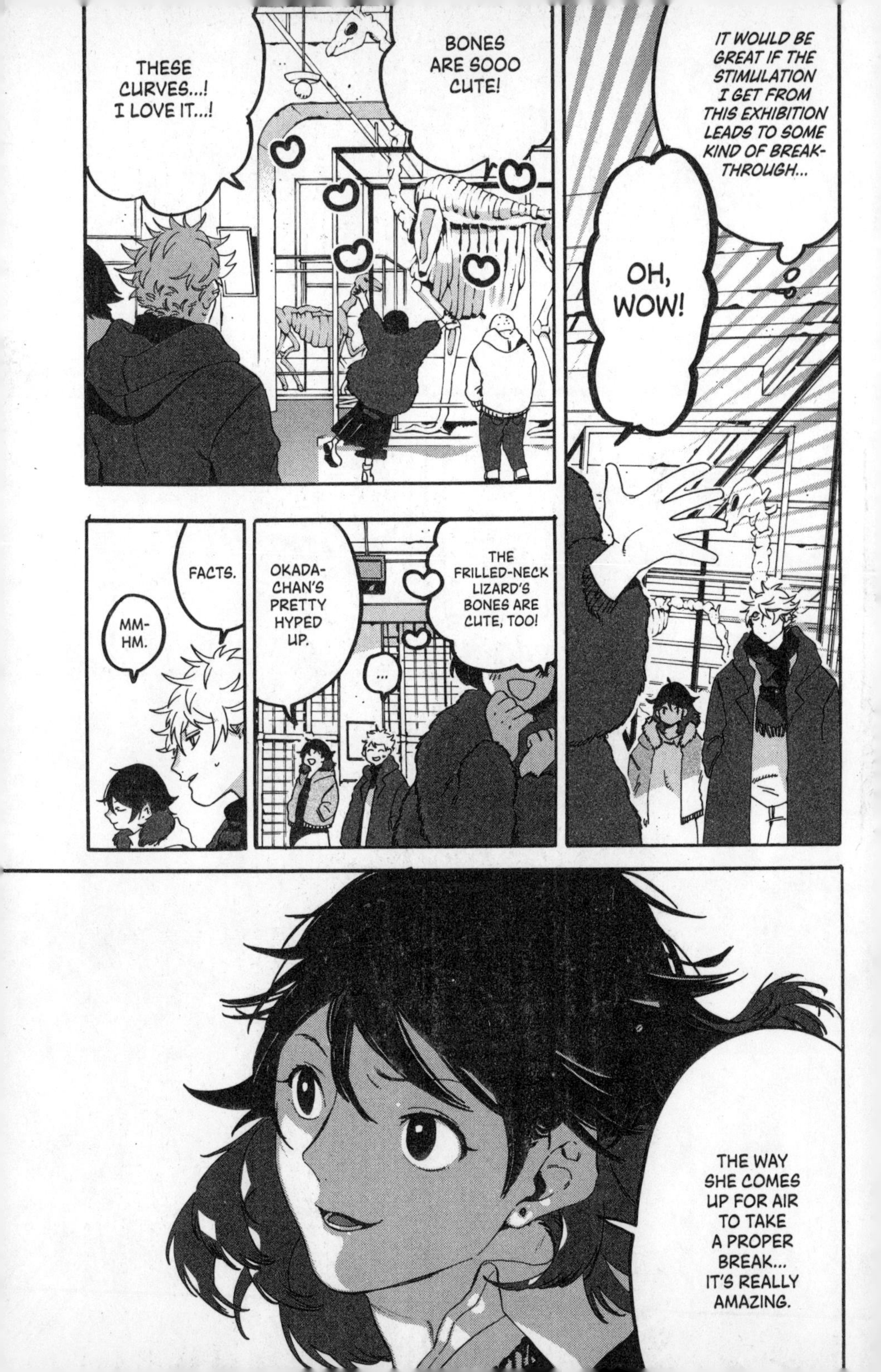
IT WOULD BE GREAT IF THE STIMULATION I GET FROM THIS EXHIBITION LEADS TO SOME KIND OF BREAK-THROUGH...
OH, WOW!
BONES ARE SOOO CUTE!
THESE CURVES...! I LOVE IT...!
THE FRILLED-NECK LIZARD'S BONES ARE CUTE, TOO!
OKADA-CHAN'S PRETTY HYPED UP.
...
FACTS.
MM-HM.
THE WAY SHE COMES UP FOR AIR TO TAKE A PROPER BREAK... IT'S REALLY AMAZING.

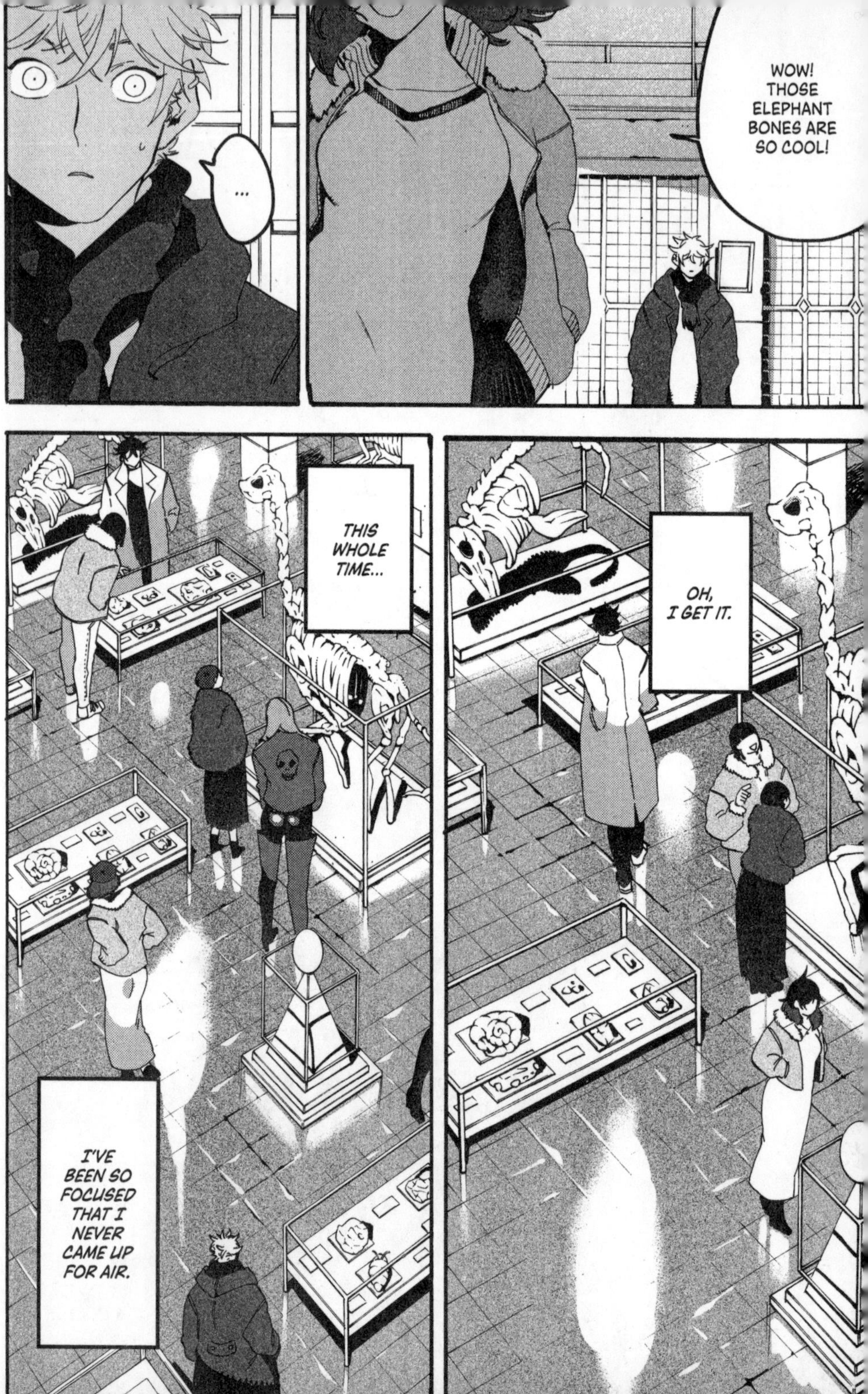
WOW! THOSE ELEPHANT BONES ARE SO COOL!
...
OH, I GET IT.
THIS WHOLE TIME...
I'VE BEEN SO FOCUSED THAT I NEVER CAME UP FOR AIR.

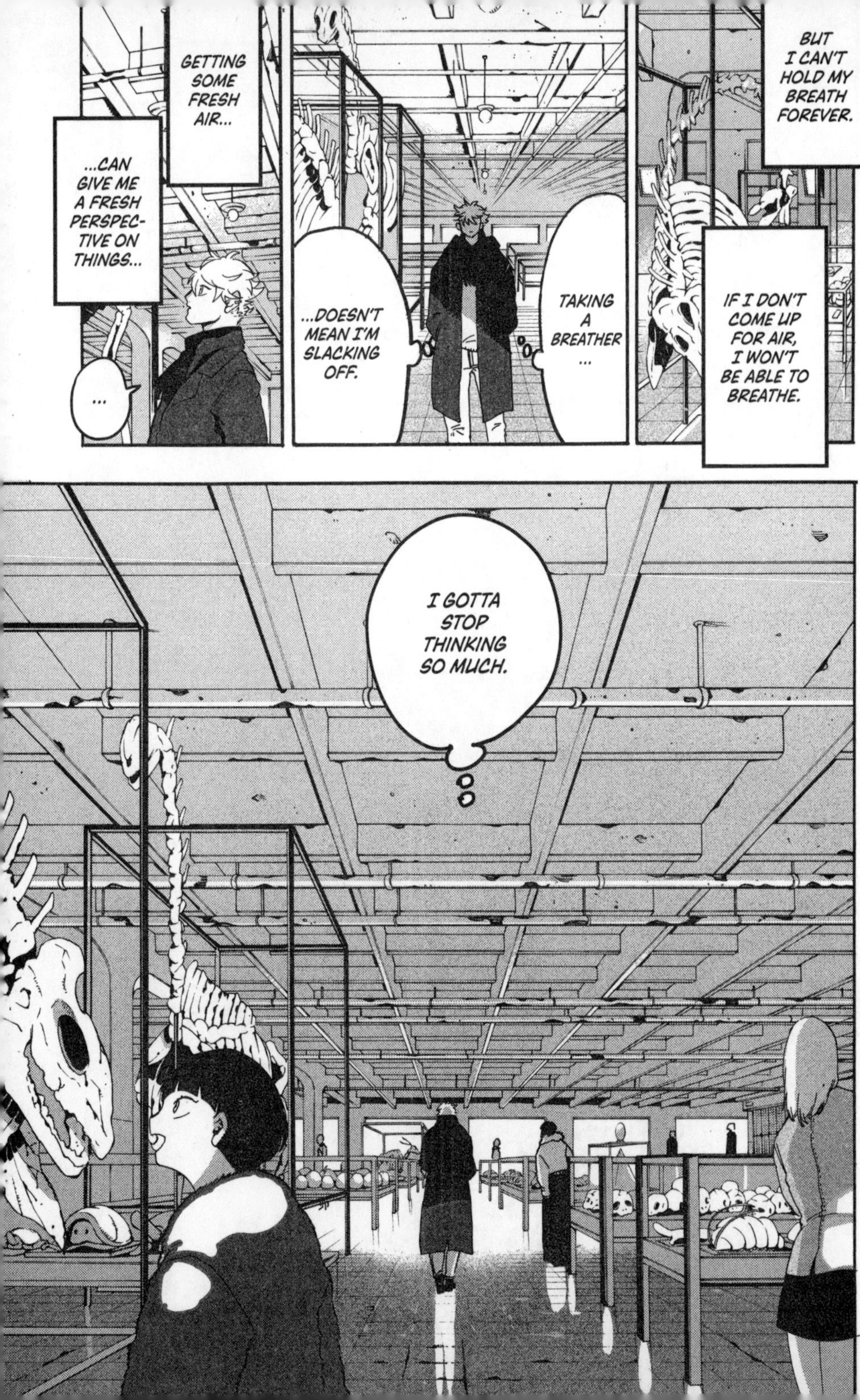
BUT I CAN'T HOLD MY BREATH FOREVER.
IF I DON'T COME UP FOR AIR, I WON'T BE ABLE TO BREATHE.
TAKING A BREATHER...
...DOESN'T MEAN I'M SLACKING OFF.
GETTING SOME FRESH AIR...
...CAN GIVE ME A FRESH PERSPEC-TIVE ON THINGS...
...
I GOTTA STOP THINKING SO MUCH.

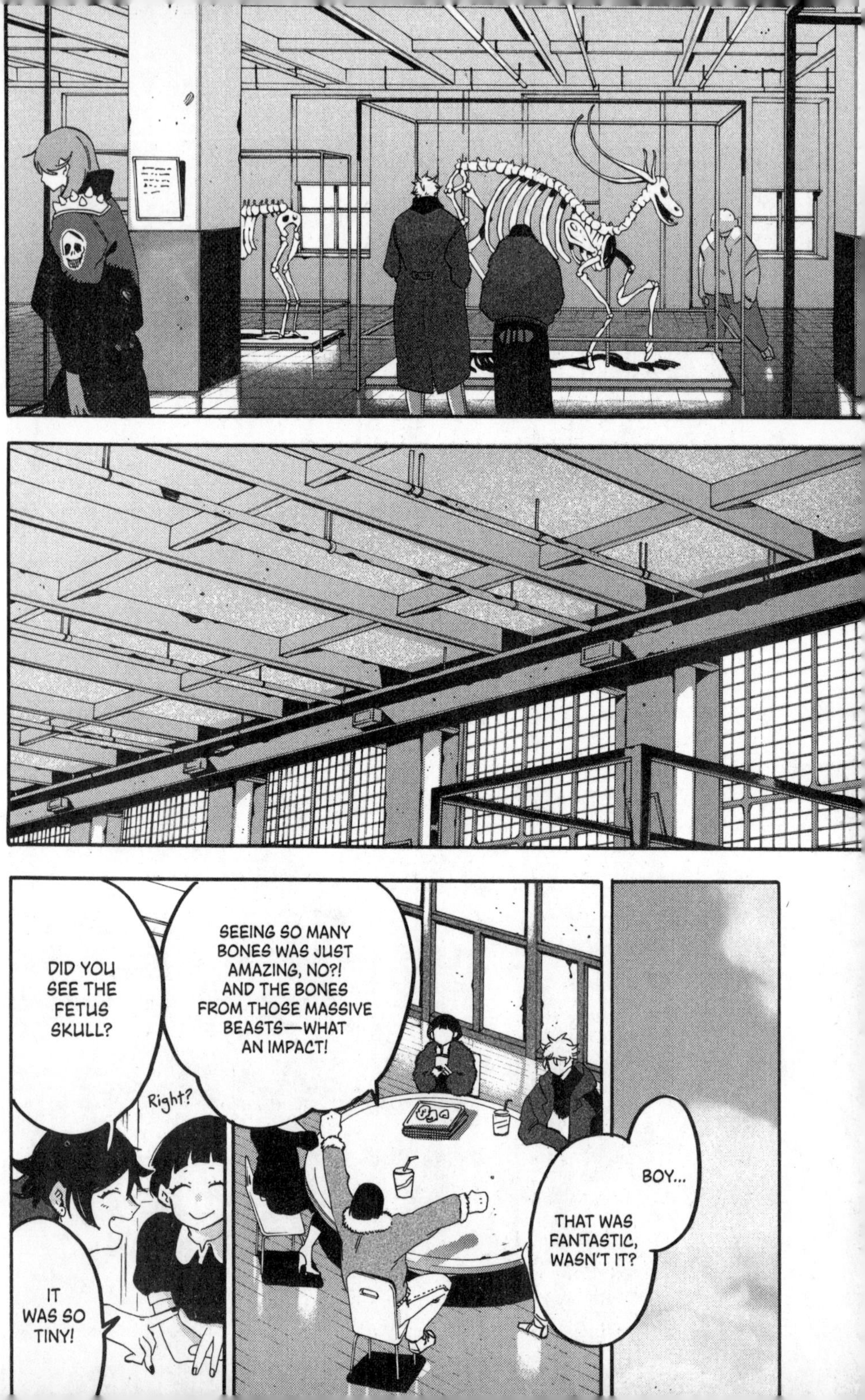
BOY...
THAT WAS FANTASTIC, WASN'T IT?
SEEING SO MANY BONES WAS JUST AMAZING, NO?! AND THE BONES FROM THOSE MASSIVE BEASTS—WHAT AN IMPACT!
DID YOU SEE THE FETUS SKULL?
Right?
IT WAS SO TINY!

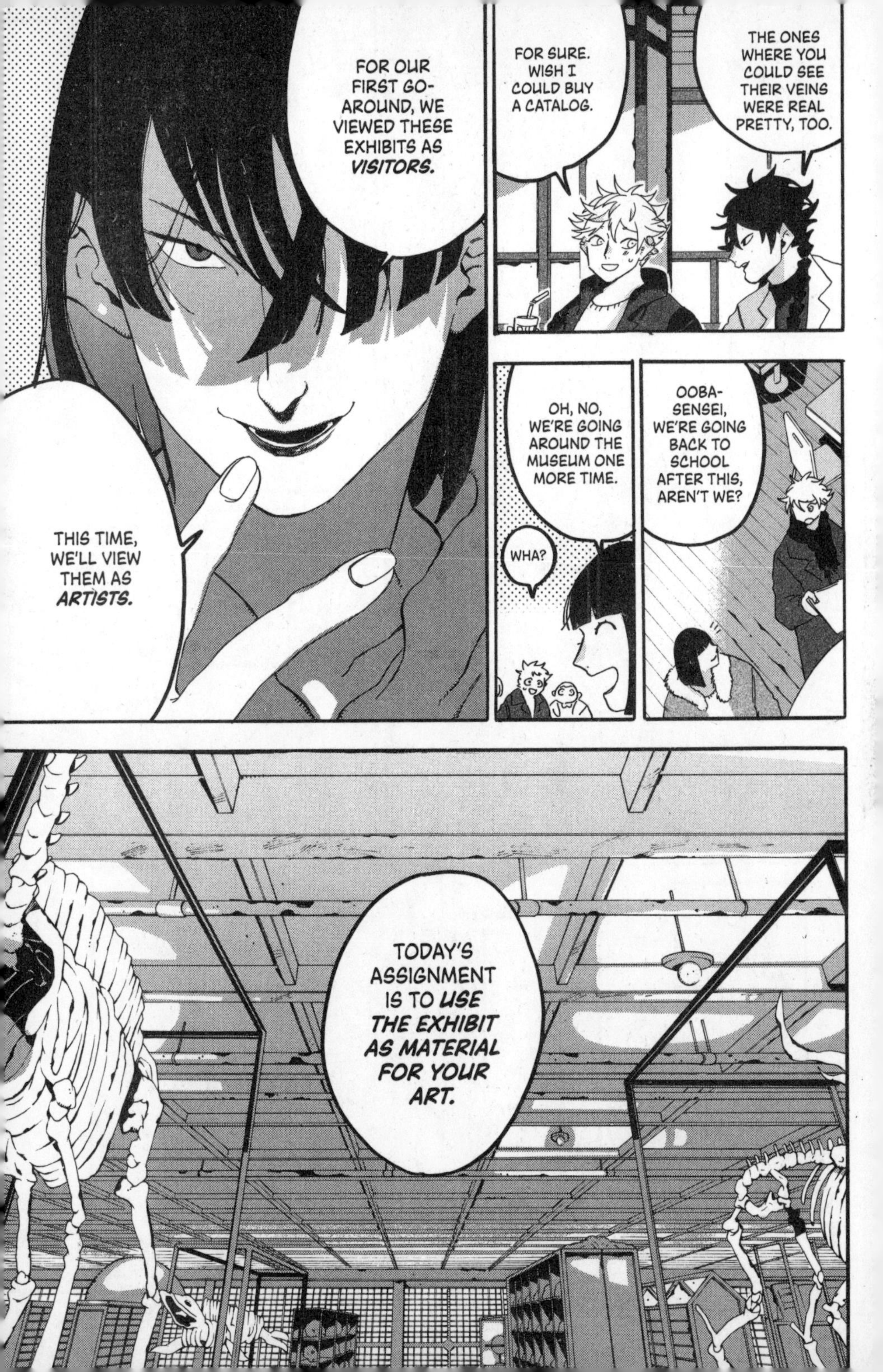
THE ONES WHERE YOU COULD SEE THEIR VEINS WERE REAL PRETTY, TOO.
FOR SURE. WISH I COULD BUY A CATALOG.
OOBA-SENSEI, WE'RE GOING BACK TO SCHOOL AFTER THIS, AREN'T WE?
OH, NO, WE'RE GOING AROUND THE MUSEUM ONE MORE TIME.
WHA?
FOR OUR FIRST GO-AROUND, WE VIEWED THESE EXHIBITS AS *VISITORS.*
THIS TIME, WE'LL VIEW THEM AS *ARTISTS.*
TODAY'S ASSIGNMENT IS TO *USE THE EXHIBIT AS MATERIAL FOR YOUR ART.*

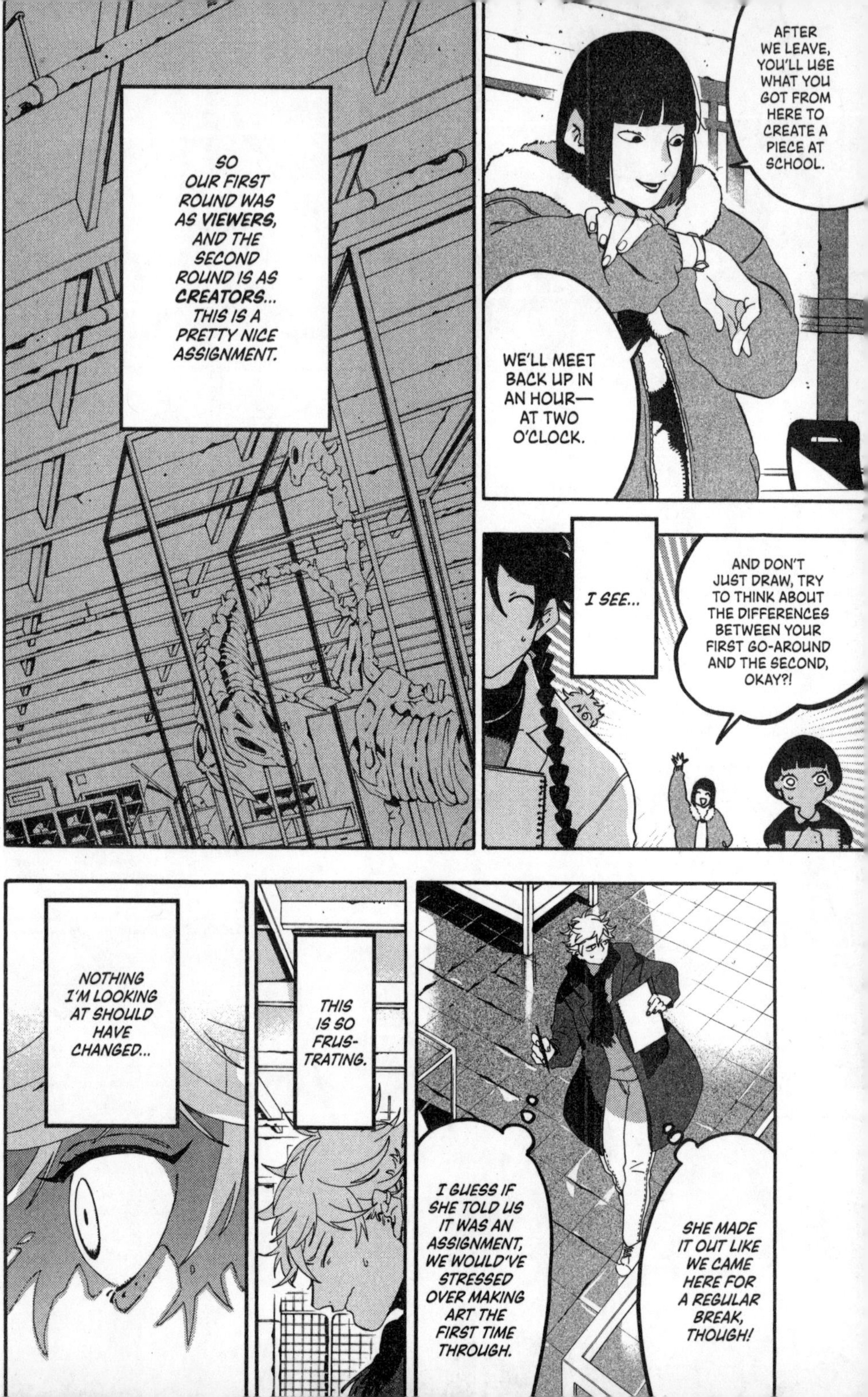
AFTER WE LEAVE, YOU'LL USE WHAT YOU GOT FROM HERE TO CREATE A PIECE AT SCHOOL.
WE'LL MEET BACK UP IN AN HOUR—AT TWO O'CLOCK.
AND DON'T JUST DRAW, TRY TO THINK ABOUT THE DIFFERENCES BETWEEN YOUR FIRST GO-AROUND AND THE SECOND, OKAY?!
I SEE...
SO OUR FIRST ROUND WAS AS VIEWERS, AND THE SECOND ROUND IS AS CREATORS... THIS IS A PRETTY NICE ASSIGNMENT.
SHE MADE IT OUT LIKE WE CAME HERE FOR A REGULAR BREAK, THOUGH!
I GUESS IF SHE TOLD US IT WAS AN ASSIGNMENT, WE WOULD'VE STRESSED OVER MAKING ART THE FIRST TIME THROUGH.
THIS IS SO FRUS-TRATING.
NOTHING I'M LOOKING AT SHOULD HAVE CHANGED...

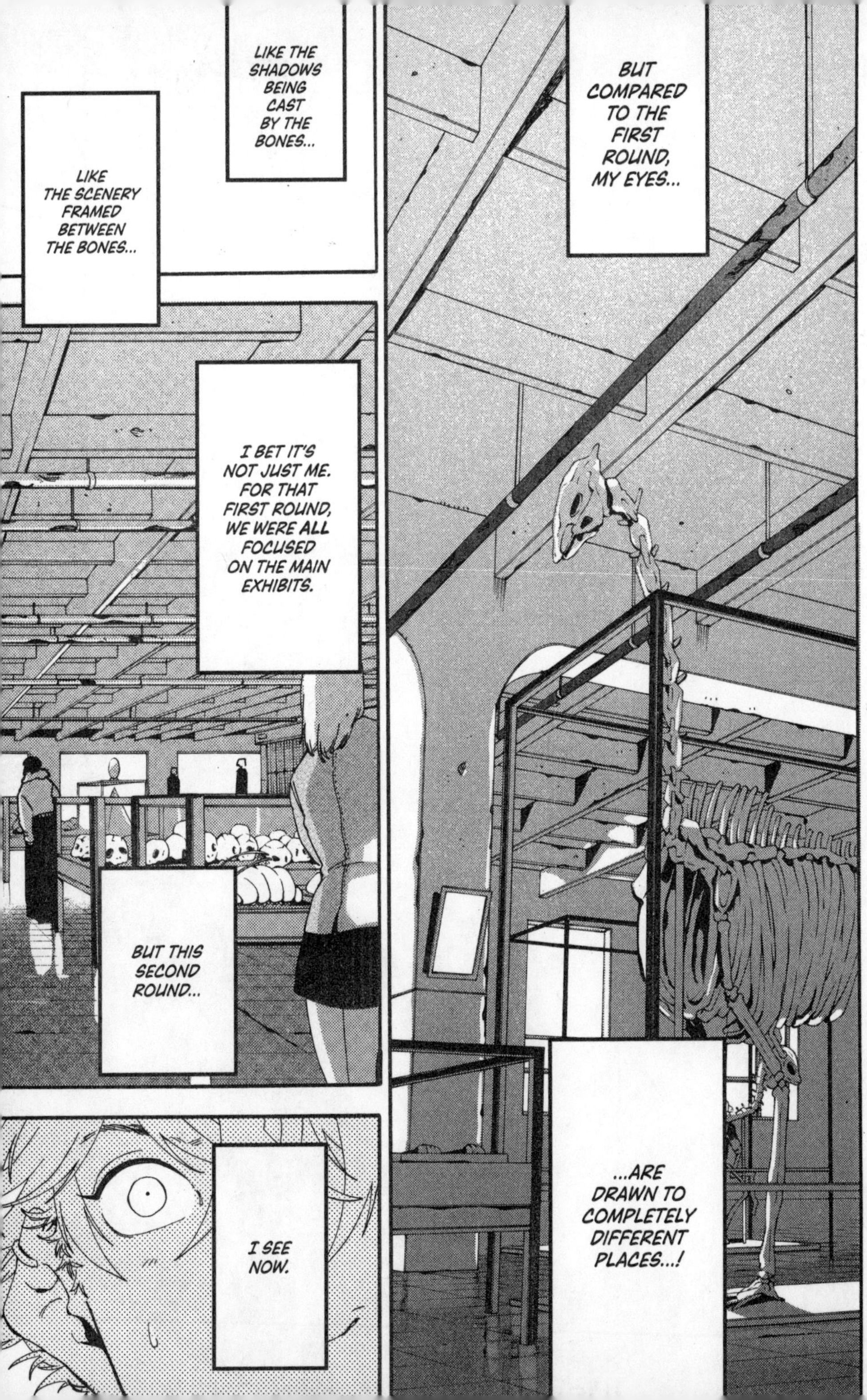
BUT COMPARED TO THE FIRST ROUND, MY EYES...
...ARE DRAWN TO COMPLETELY DIFFERENT PLACES...!
LIKE THE SHADOWS BEING CAST BY THE BONES...
LIKE THE SCENERY FRAMED BETWEEN THE BONES...
I BET IT'S NOT JUST ME. FOR THAT FIRST ROUND, WE WERE ALL FOCUSED ON THE MAIN EXHIBITS.
BUT THIS SECOND ROUND...
I SEE NOW.

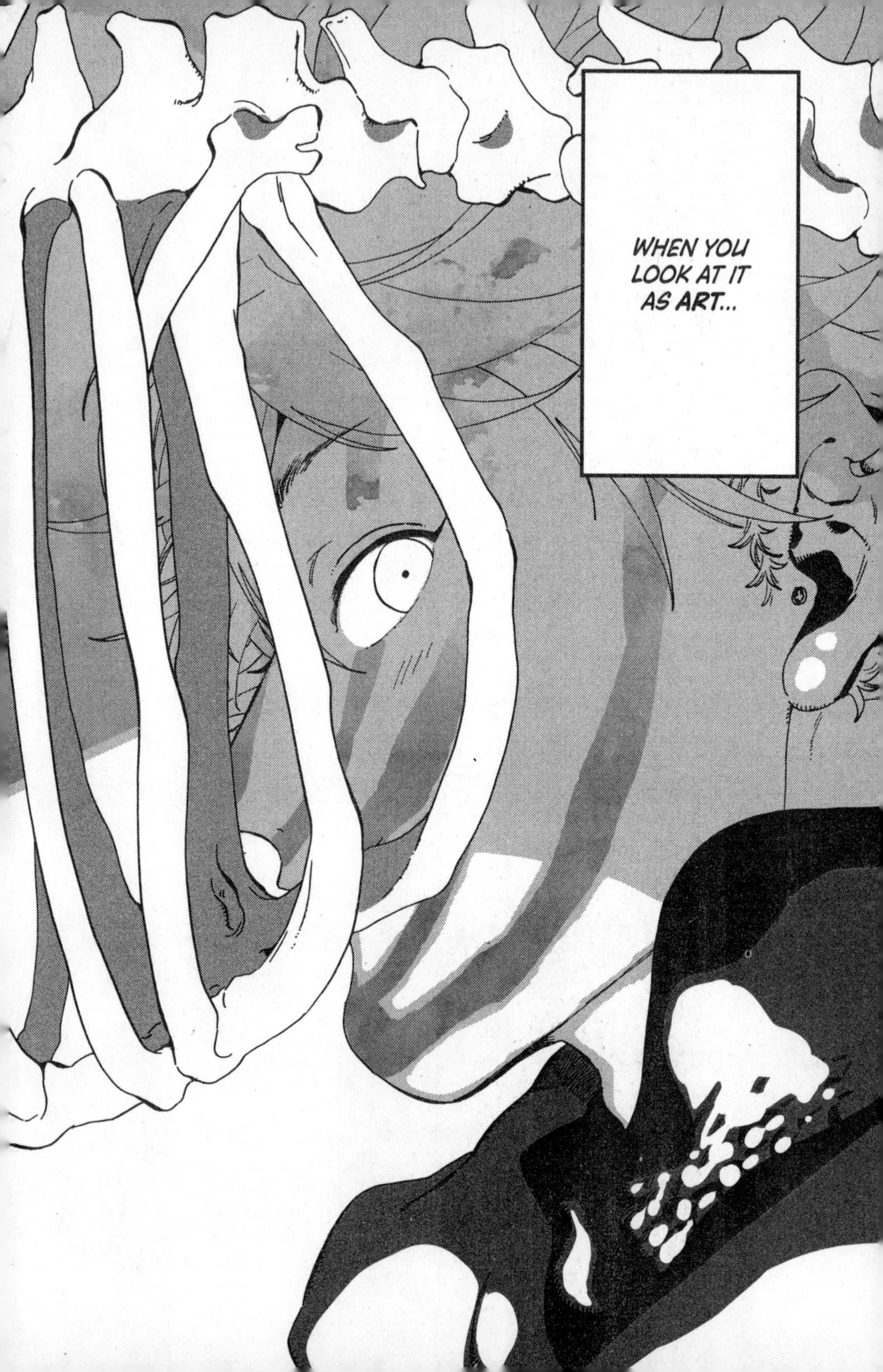
WHEN YOU LOOK AT IT AS ART...

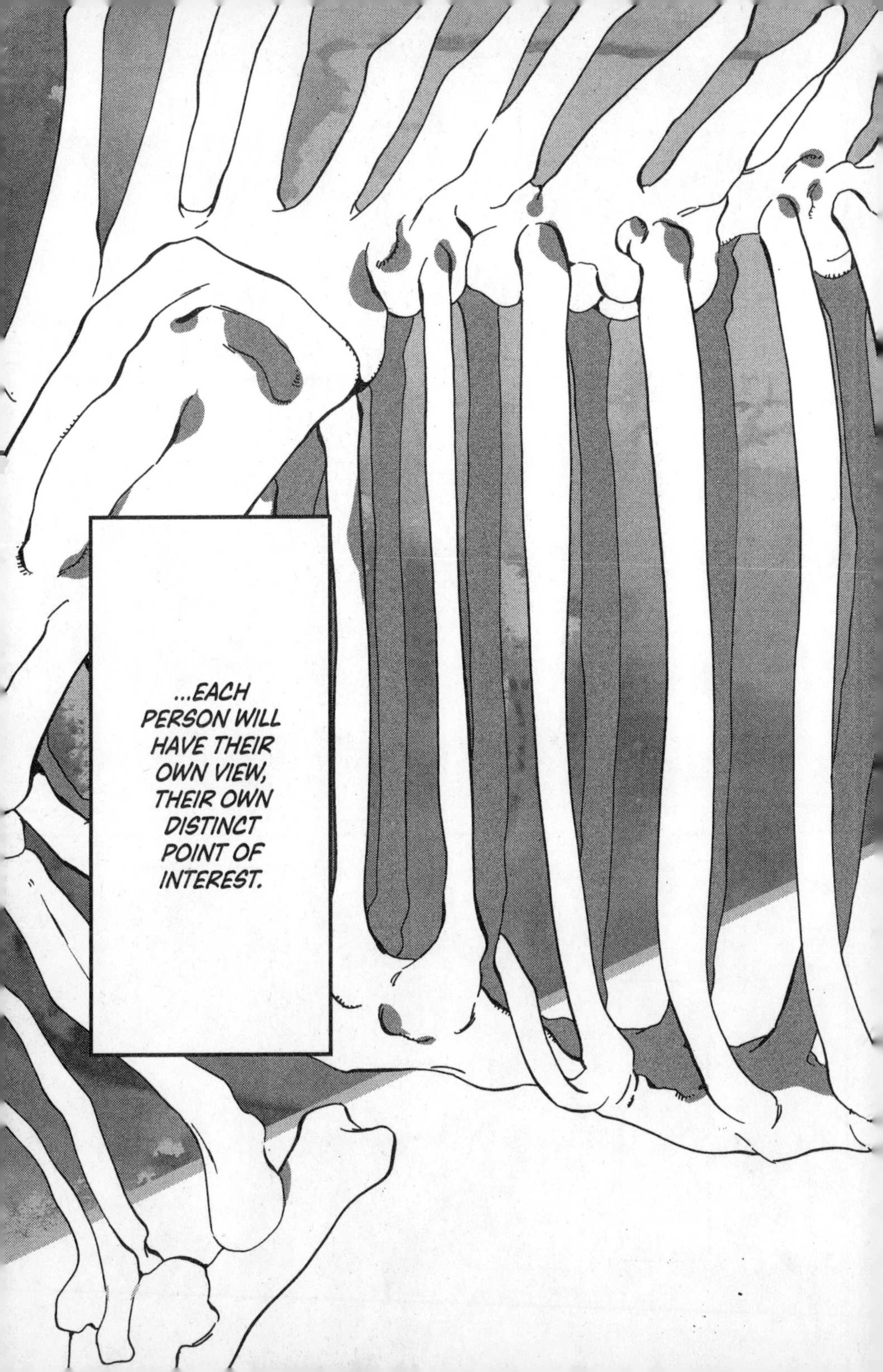
...EACH PERSON WILL HAVE THEIR OWN VIEW, THEIR OWN DISTINCT POINT OF INTEREST.

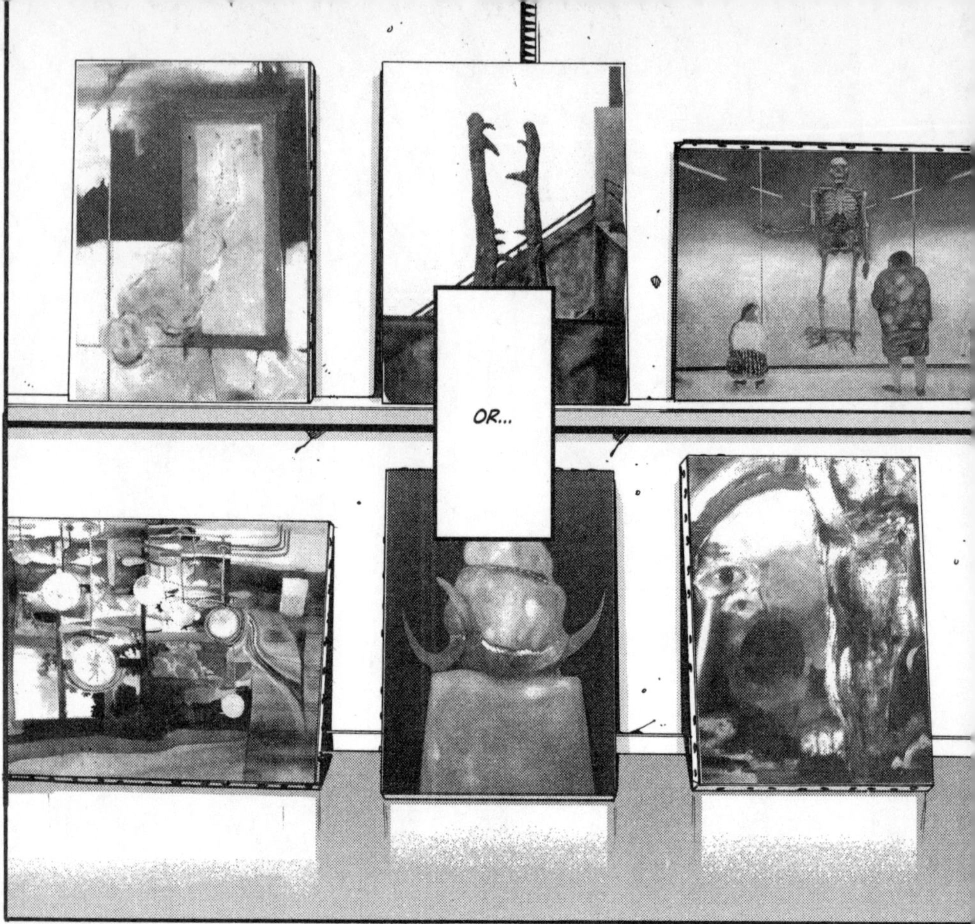
OR...

ART: (TOP, L TO R) MOEKO NATSUI, SHOTA YAMAMICHI, TAKERU NAKAJIMA. (BOTTOM, L TO R) SAKI UCHIDA, MATSUBA YACHIGUSA, HARU OOKAWA.

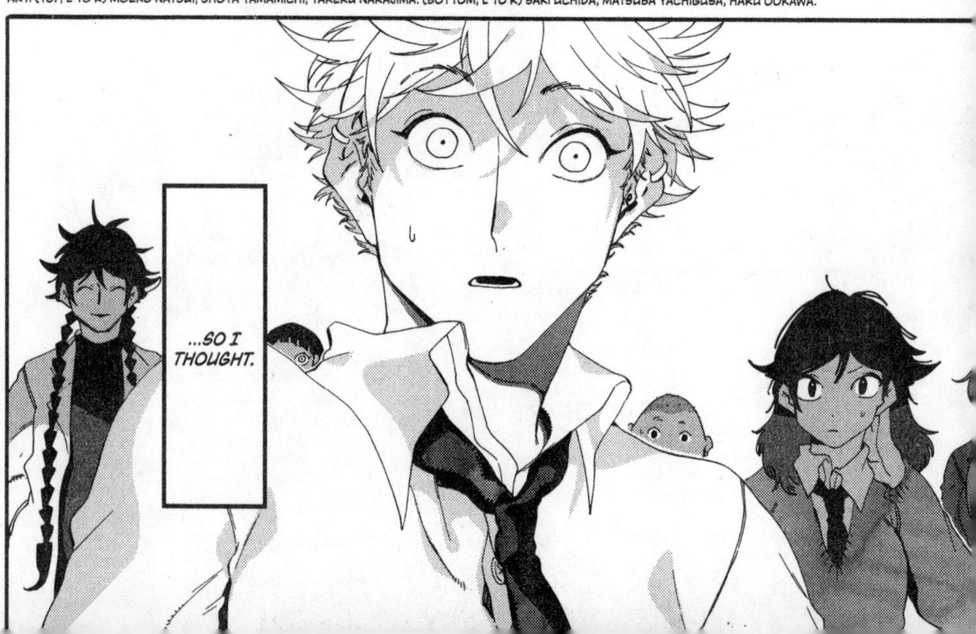
...SO I THOUGHT.

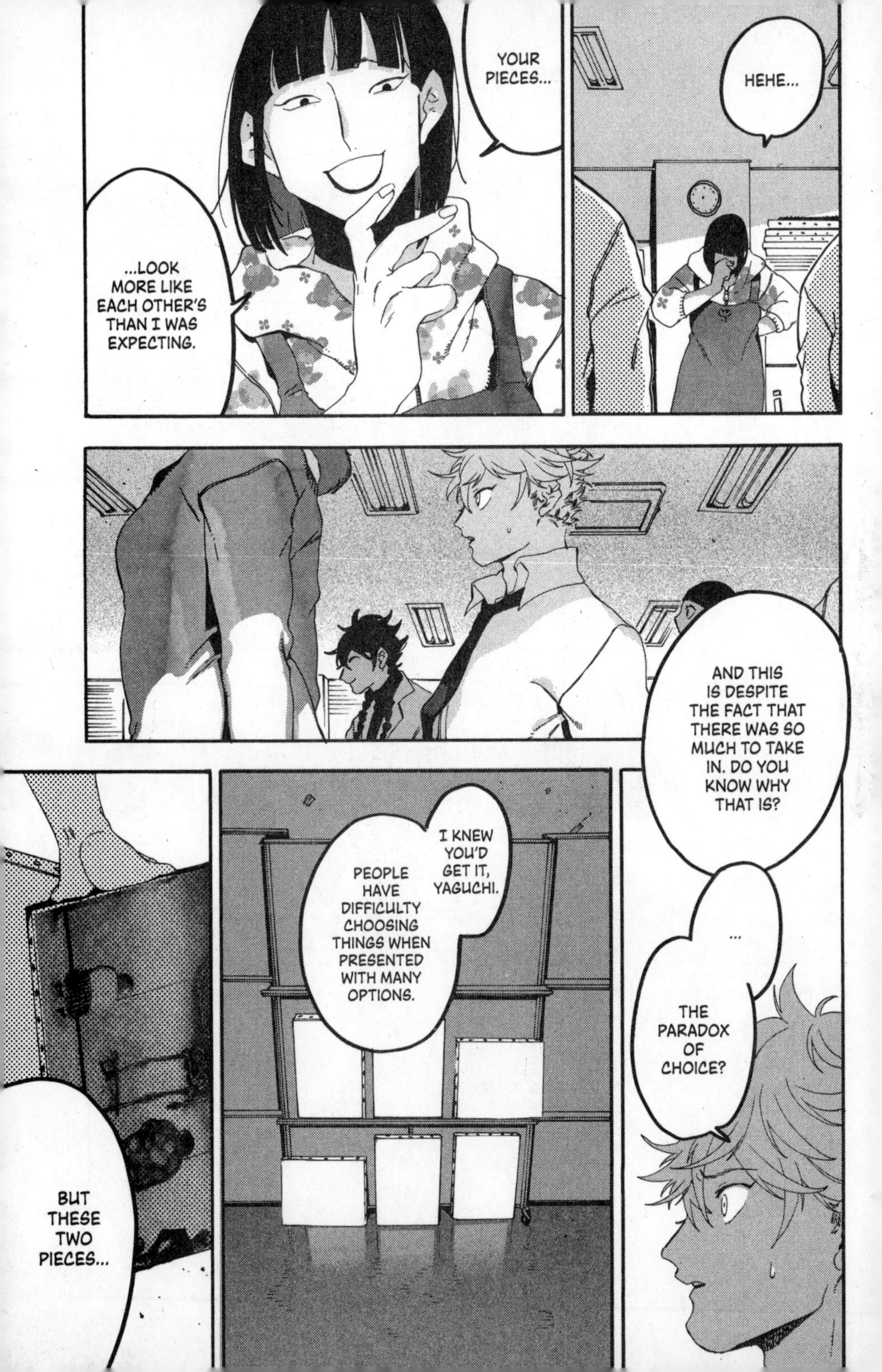
HEHE...
YOUR PIECES...
...LOOK MORE LIKE EACH OTHER'S THAN I WAS EXPECTING.
AND THIS IS DESPITE THE FACT THAT THERE WAS SO MUCH TO TAKE IN. DO YOU KNOW WHY THAT IS?
...
THE PARADOX OF CHOICE?
I KNEW YOU'D GET IT, YAGUCHI.
PEOPLE HAVE DIFFICULTY CHOOSING THINGS WHEN PRESENTED WITH MANY OPTIONS.
BUT THESE TWO PIECES...

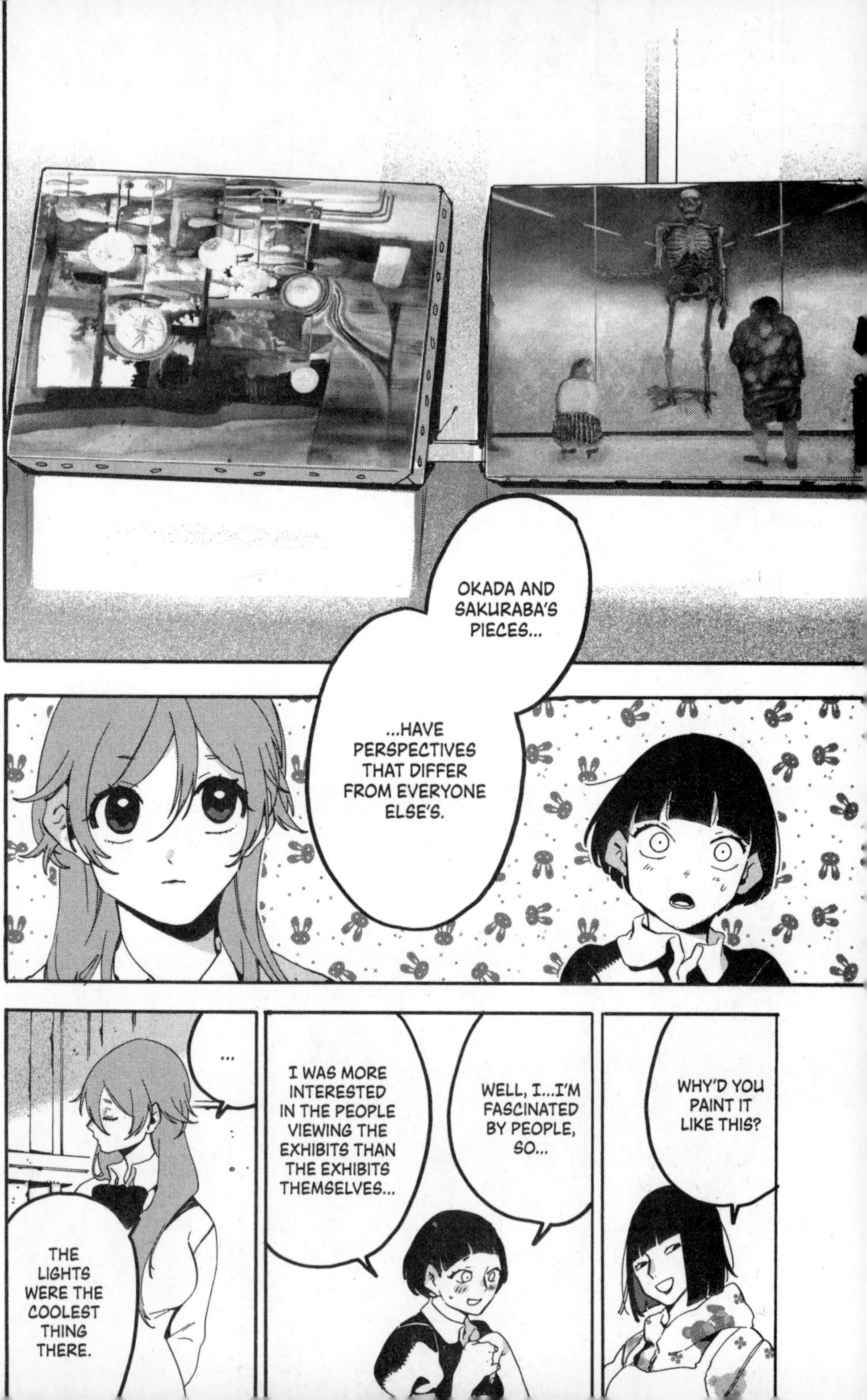
OKADA AND SAKURABA'S PIECES...
...HAVE PERSPECTIVES THAT DIFFER FROM EVERYONE ELSE'S.
WHY'D YOU PAINT IT LIKE THIS?
WELL, I...I'M FASCINATED BY PEOPLE, SO...
I WAS MORE INTERESTED IN THE PEOPLE VIEWING THE EXHIBITS THAN THE EXHIBITS THEMSELVES...
...
THE LIGHTS WERE THE COOLEST THING THERE.

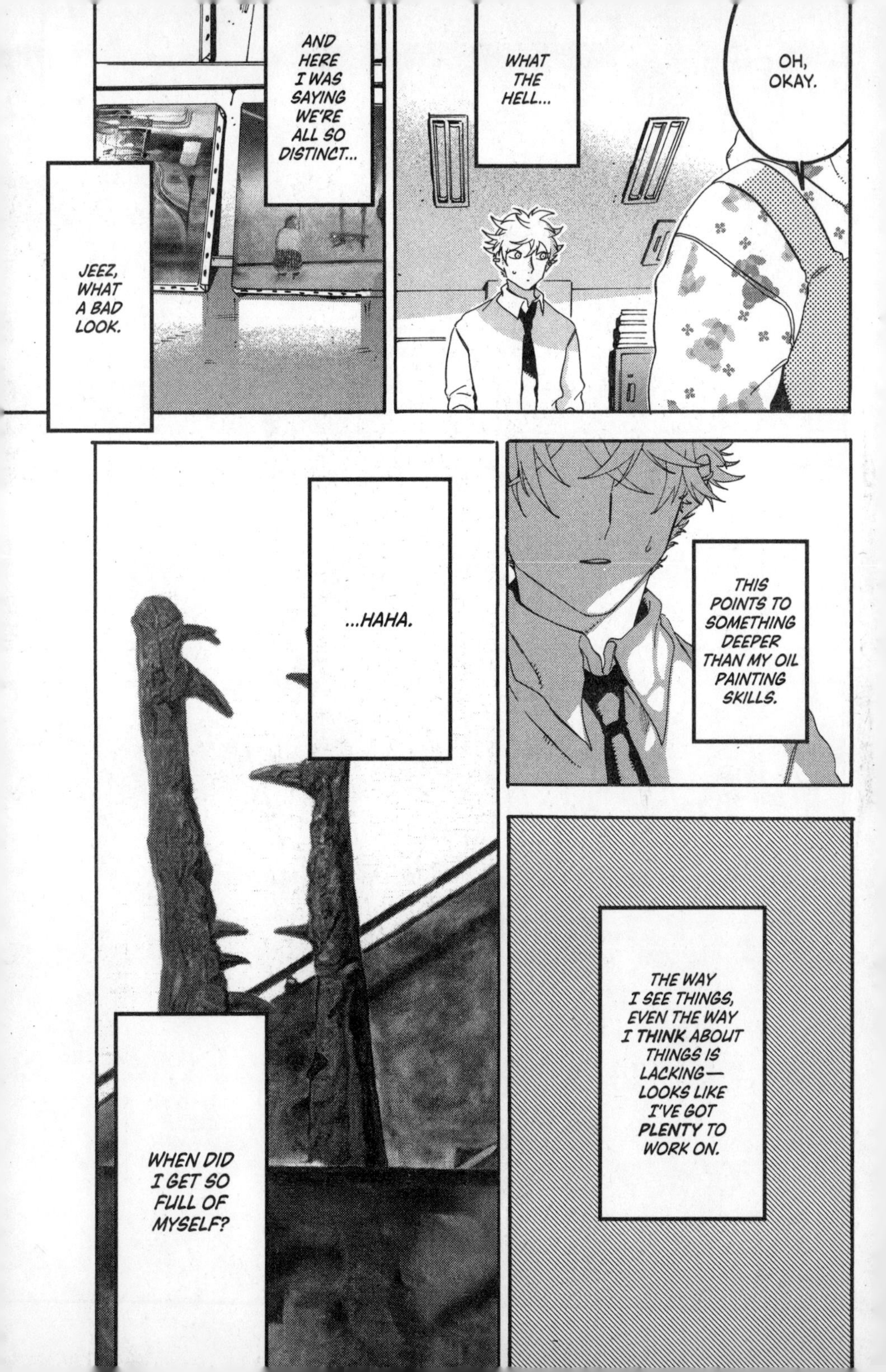
OH, OKAY.
WHAT THE HELL...
AND HERE I WAS SAYING WE'RE ALL SO DISTINCT...
JEEZ, WHAT A BAD LOOK.
THIS POINTS TO SOMETHING DEEPER THAN MY OIL PAINTING SKILLS.
THE WAY I SEE THINGS, EVEN THE WAY I THINK ABOUT THINGS IS LACKING—LOOKS LIKE I'VE GOT PLENTY TO WORK ON.
...HAHA.
WHEN DID I GET SO FULL OF MYSELF?

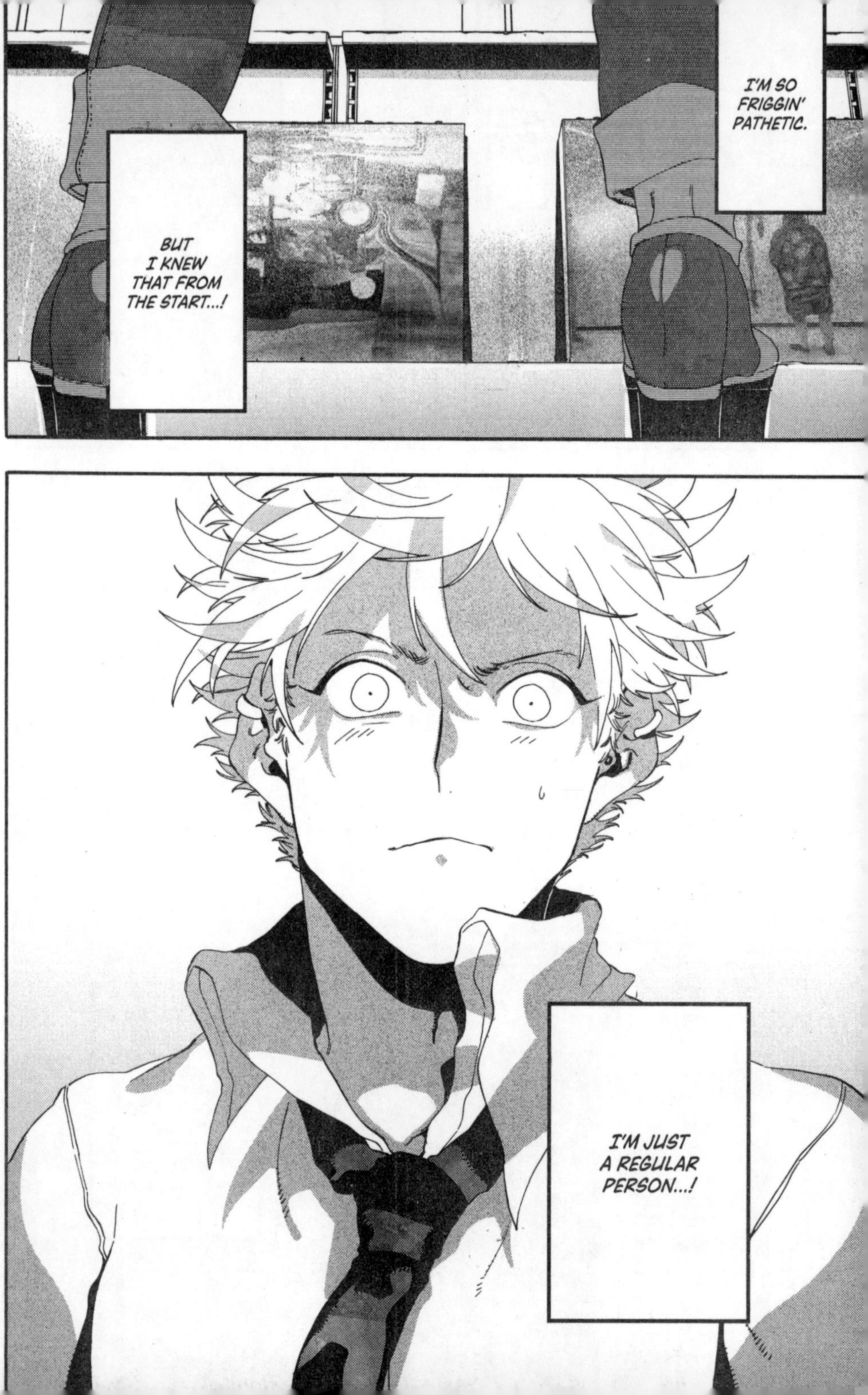
I'M SO FRIGGIN' PATHETIC.
BUT I KNEW THAT FROM THE START...!
I'M JUST A REGULAR PERSON...!

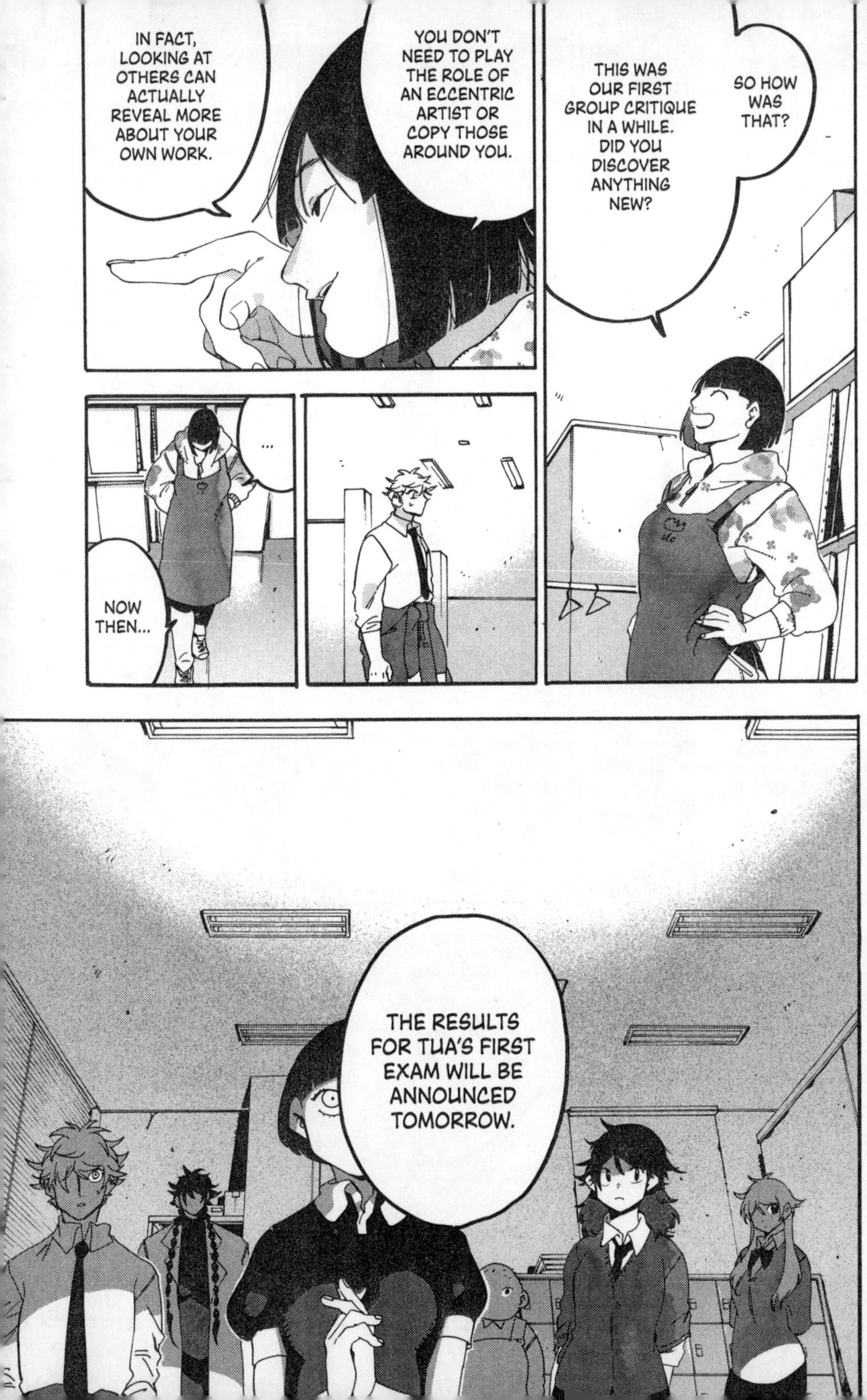
SO HOW WAS THAT?
THIS WAS OUR FIRST GROUP CRITIQUE IN A WHILE. DID YOU DISCOVER ANYTHING NEW?
YOU DON'T NEED TO PLAY THE ROLE OF AN ECCENTRIC ARTIST OR COPY THOSE AROUND YOU.
IN FACT, LOOKING AT OTHERS CAN ACTUALLY REVEAL MORE ABOUT YOUR OWN WORK.
...
NOW THEN...
THE RESULTS FOR TUA'S FIRST EXAM WILL BE ANNOUNCED TOMORROW.

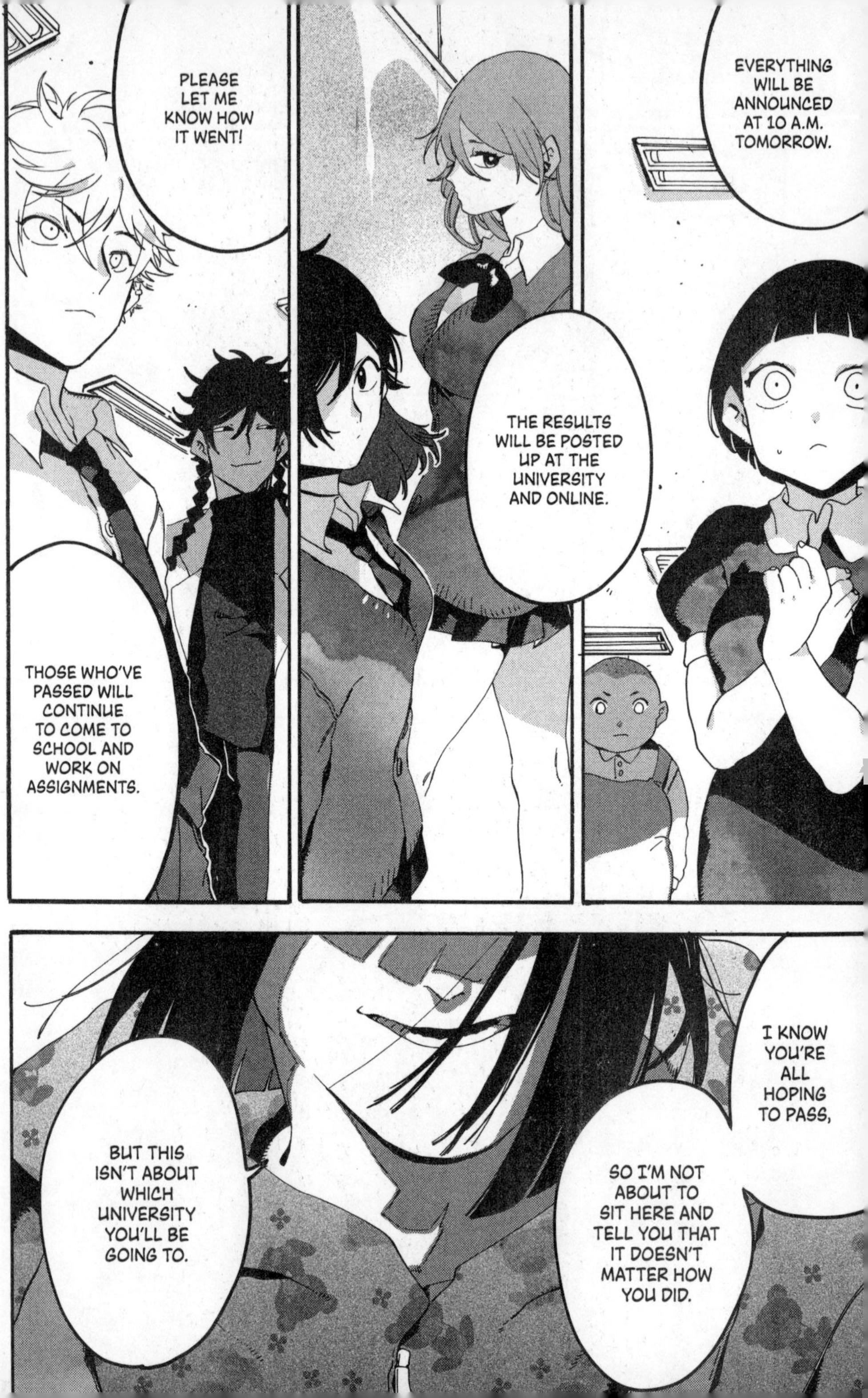
EVERYTHING WILL BE ANNOUNCED AT 10 A.M. TOMORROW.
THE RESULTS WILL BE POSTED UP AT THE UNIVERSITY AND ONLINE.
PLEASE LET ME KNOW HOW IT WENT!
THOSE WHO'VE PASSED WILL CONTINUE TO COME TO SCHOOL AND WORK ON ASSIGNMENTS.
I KNOW YOU'RE ALL HOPING TO PASS,
SO I'M NOT ABOUT TO SIT HERE AND TELL YOU THAT IT DOESN'T MATTER HOW YOU DID.
BUT THIS ISN'T ABOUT WHICH UNIVERSITY YOU'LL BE GOING TO.

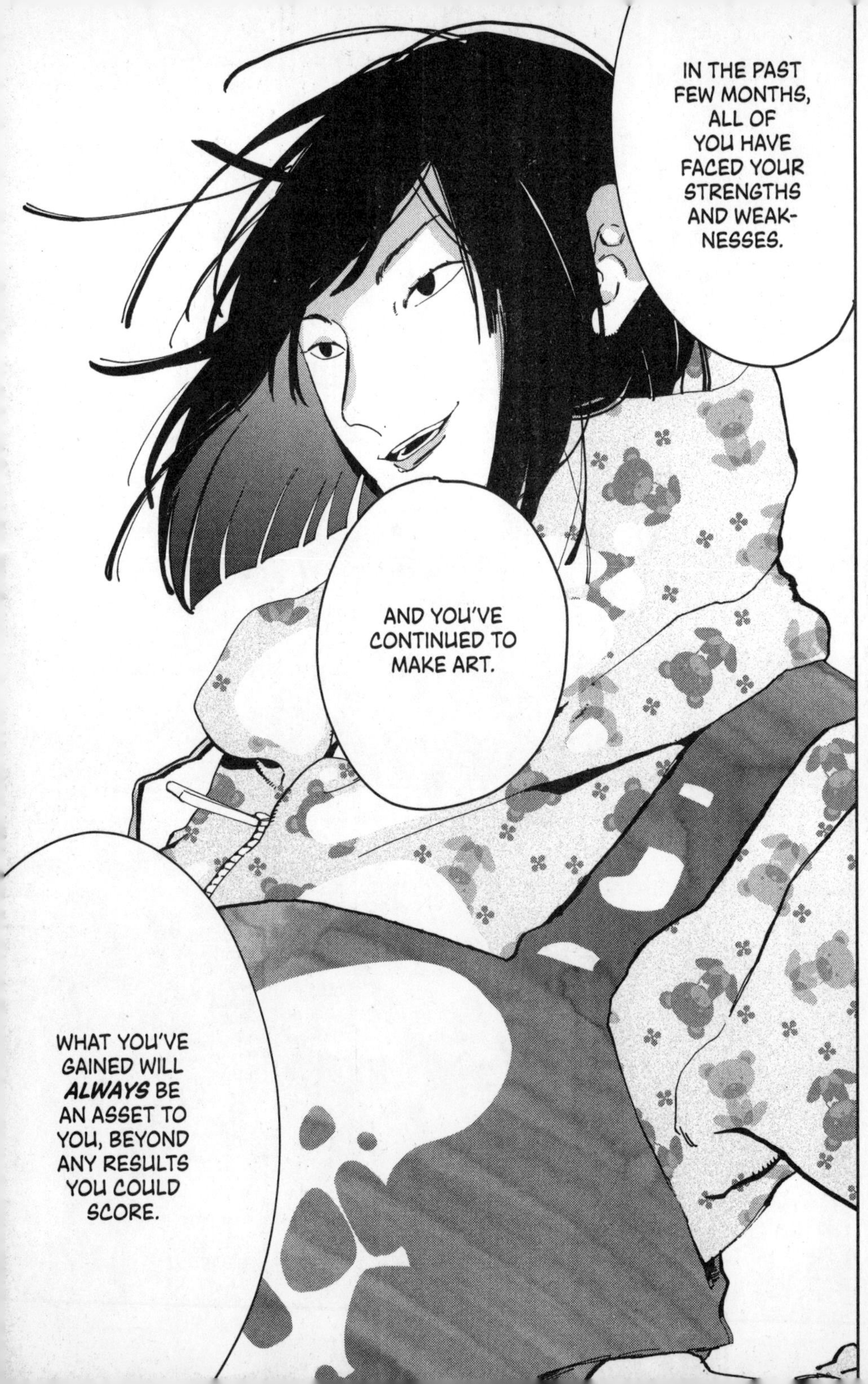
IN THE PAST FEW MONTHS, ALL OF YOU HAVE FACED YOUR STRENGTHS AND WEAK-NESSES.
AND YOU'VE CONTINUED TO MAKE ART.
WHAT YOU'VE GAINED WILL *ALWAYS* BE AN ASSET TO YOU, BEYOND ANY RESULTS YOU COULD SCORE.

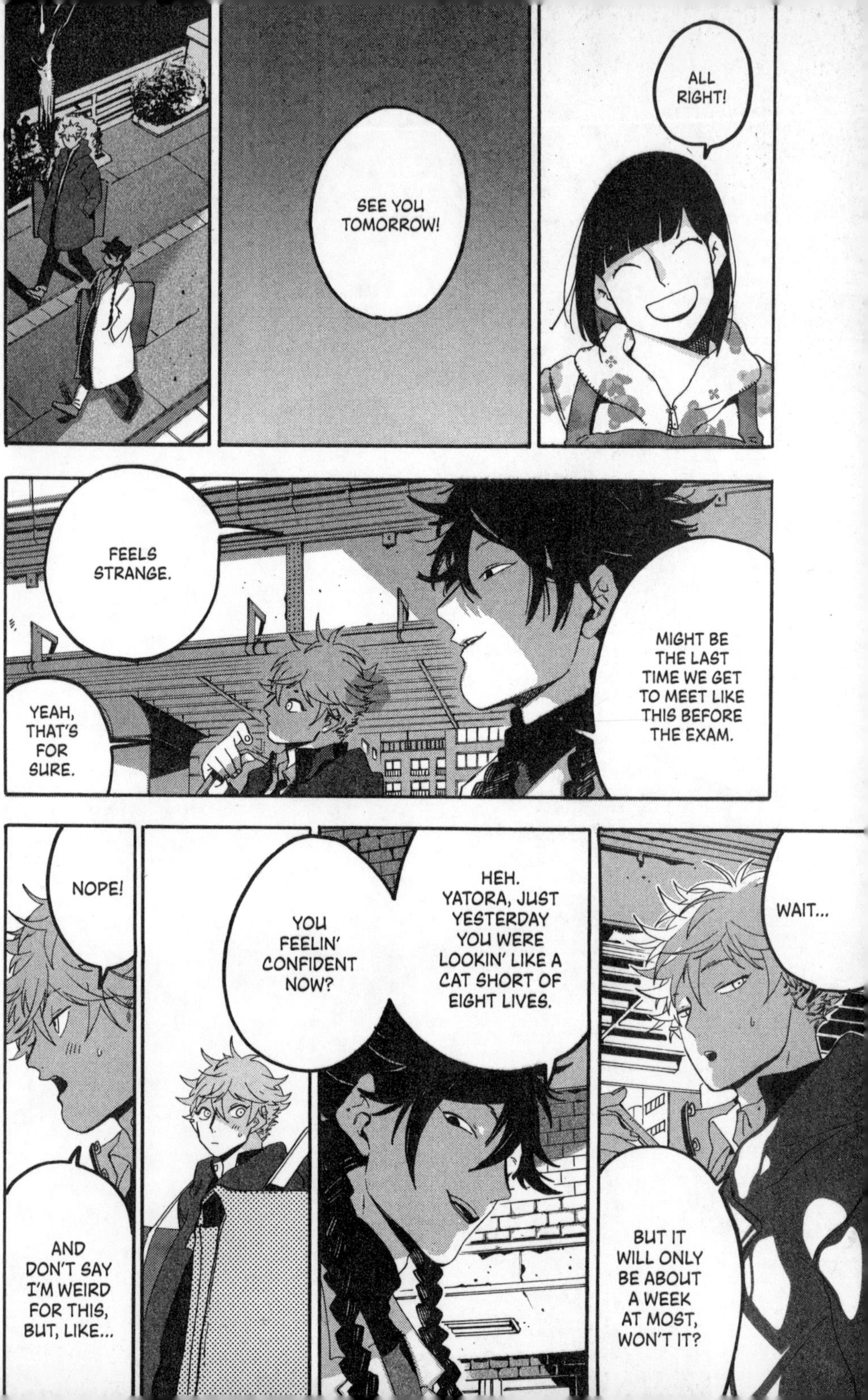
ALL RIGHT!
SEE YOU TOMORROW!
MIGHT BE THE LAST TIME WE GET TO MEET LIKE THIS BEFORE THE EXAM.
FEELS STRANGE.
YEAH, THAT'S FOR SURE.
WAIT...
BUT IT WILL ONLY BE ABOUT A WEEK AT MOST, WON'T IT?
HEH. YATORA, JUST YESTERDAY YOU WERE LOOKIN' LIKE A CAT SHORT OF EIGHT LIVES.
YOU FEELIN' CONFIDENT NOW?
NOPE!
AND DON'T SAY I'M WEIRD FOR THIS, BUT, LIKE...

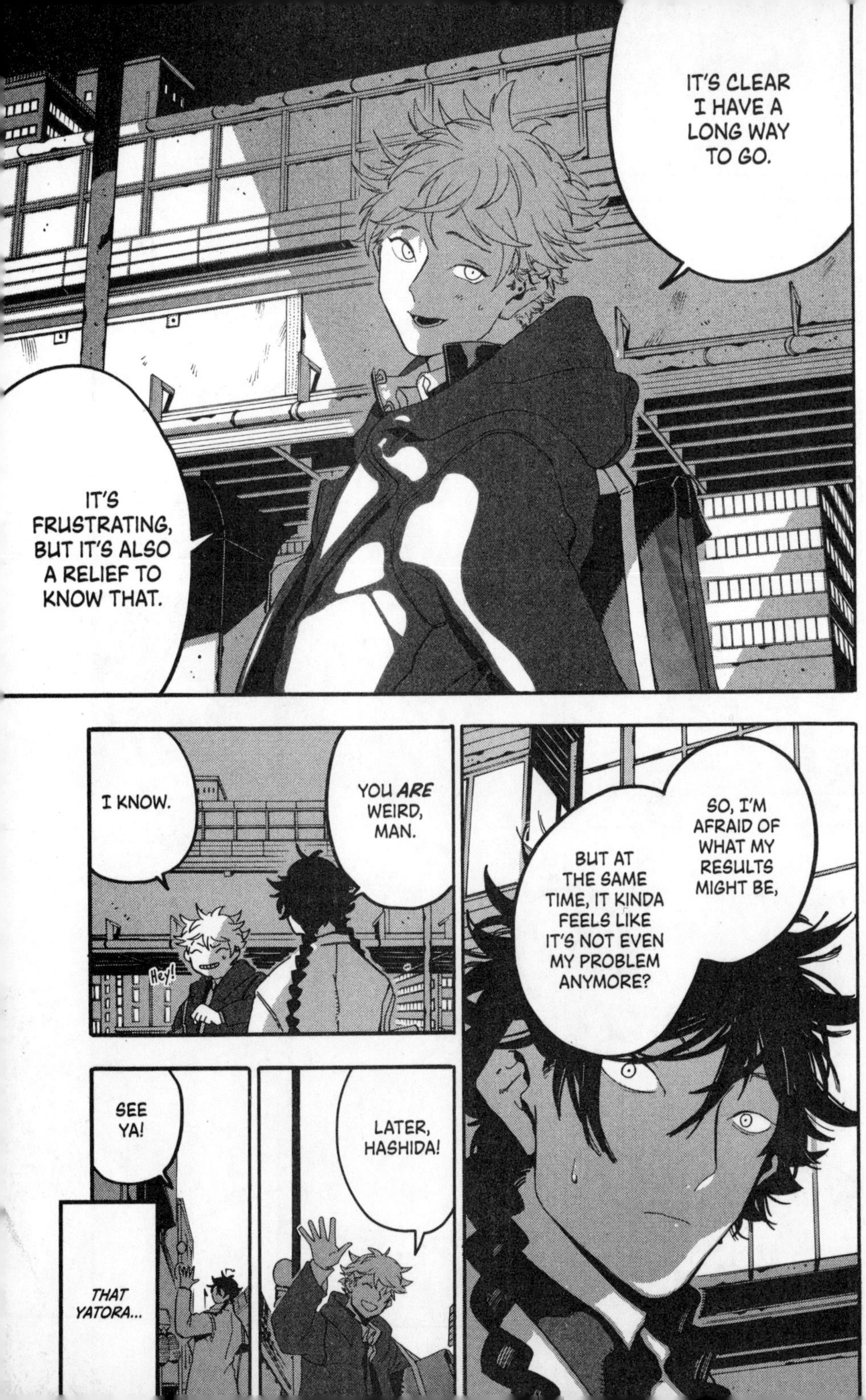
IT'S CLEAR I HAVE A LONG WAY TO GO.
IT'S FRUSTRATING, BUT IT'S ALSO A RELIEF TO KNOW THAT.
SO, I'M AFRAID OF WHAT MY RESULTS MIGHT BE,
BUT AT THE SAME TIME, IT KINDA FEELS LIKE IT'S NOT EVEN MY PROBLEM ANYMORE?
YOU *ARE* WEIRD, MAN.
I KNOW.
Hey!
LATER, HASHIDA!
SEE YA!
THAT YATORA...

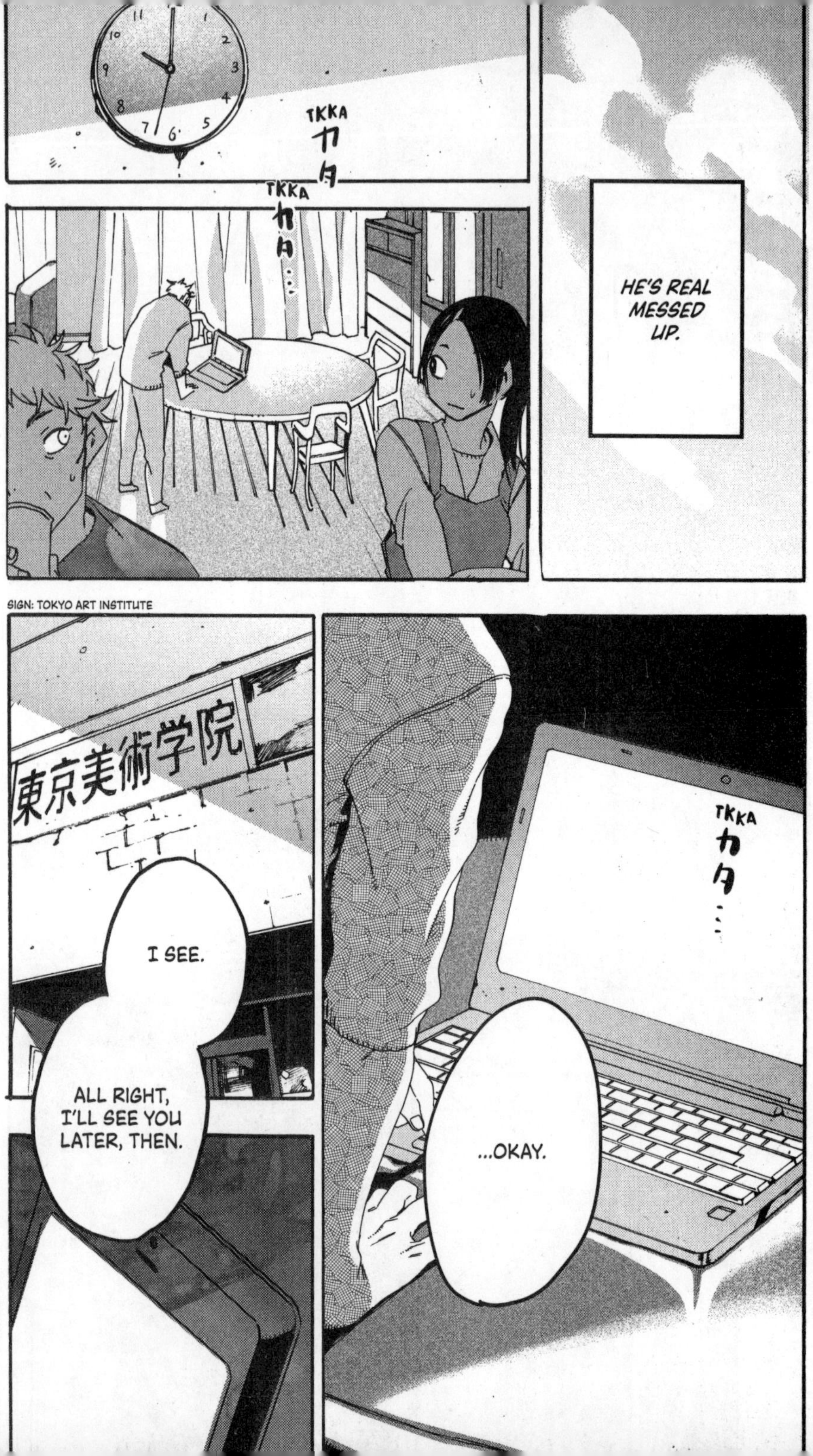
HE'S REAL MESSED UP.
TKKA
カタ
TKKA
カタ…
TKKA
カタ…
...OKAY.
SIGN: TOKYO ART INSTITUTE
東京美術学院
I SEE.
ALL RIGHT, I'LL SEE YOU LATER, THEN.

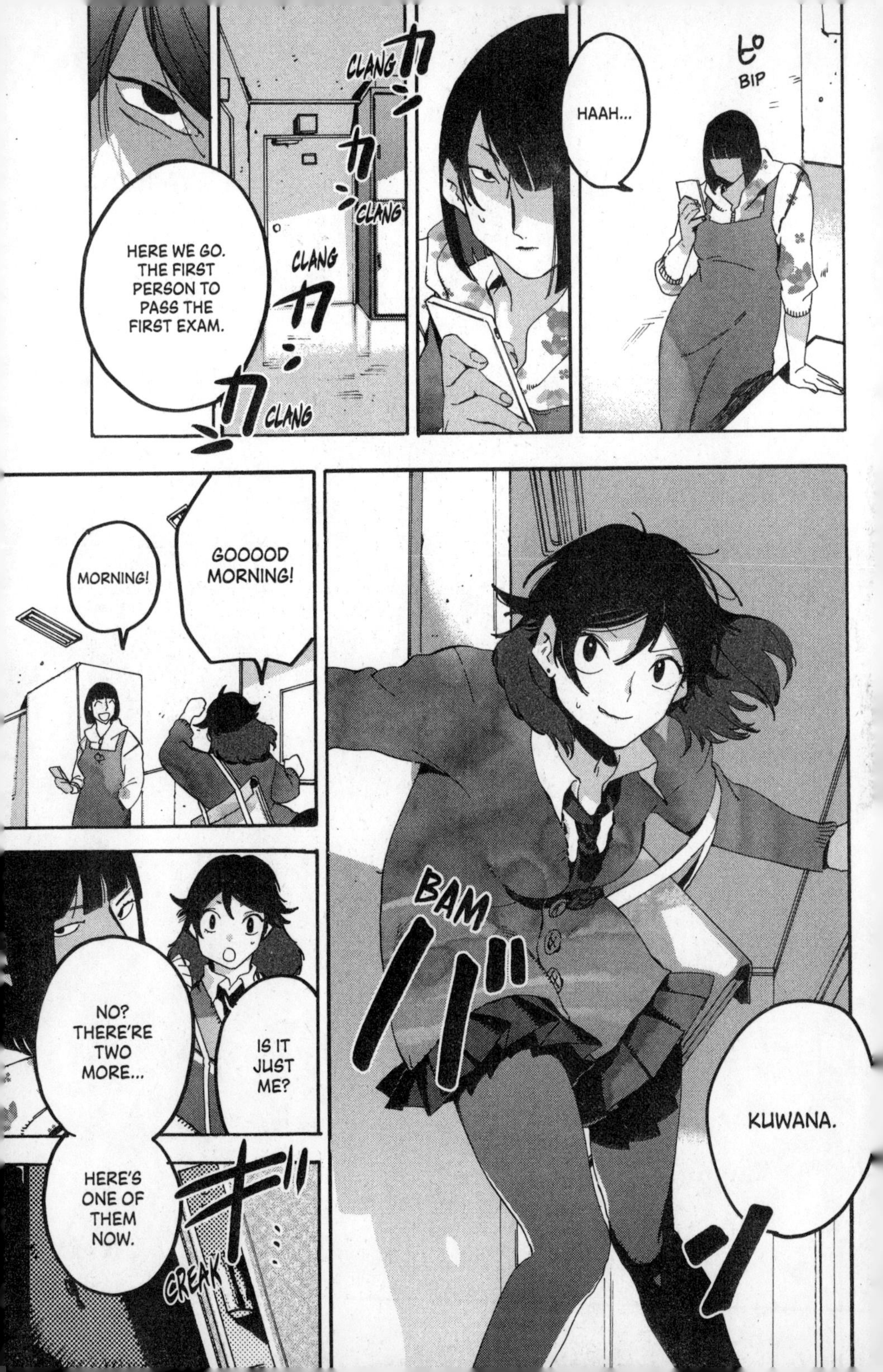
BIP
HAAH...
CLANG
CLANG
CLANG
HERE WE GO. THE FIRST PERSON TO PASS THE FIRST EXAM.
CLANG
BAM
KUWANA.
GOOOOD MORNING!
MORNING!
IS IT JUST ME?
NO? THERE'RE TWO MORE...
HERE'S ONE OF THEM NOW.
CREAK

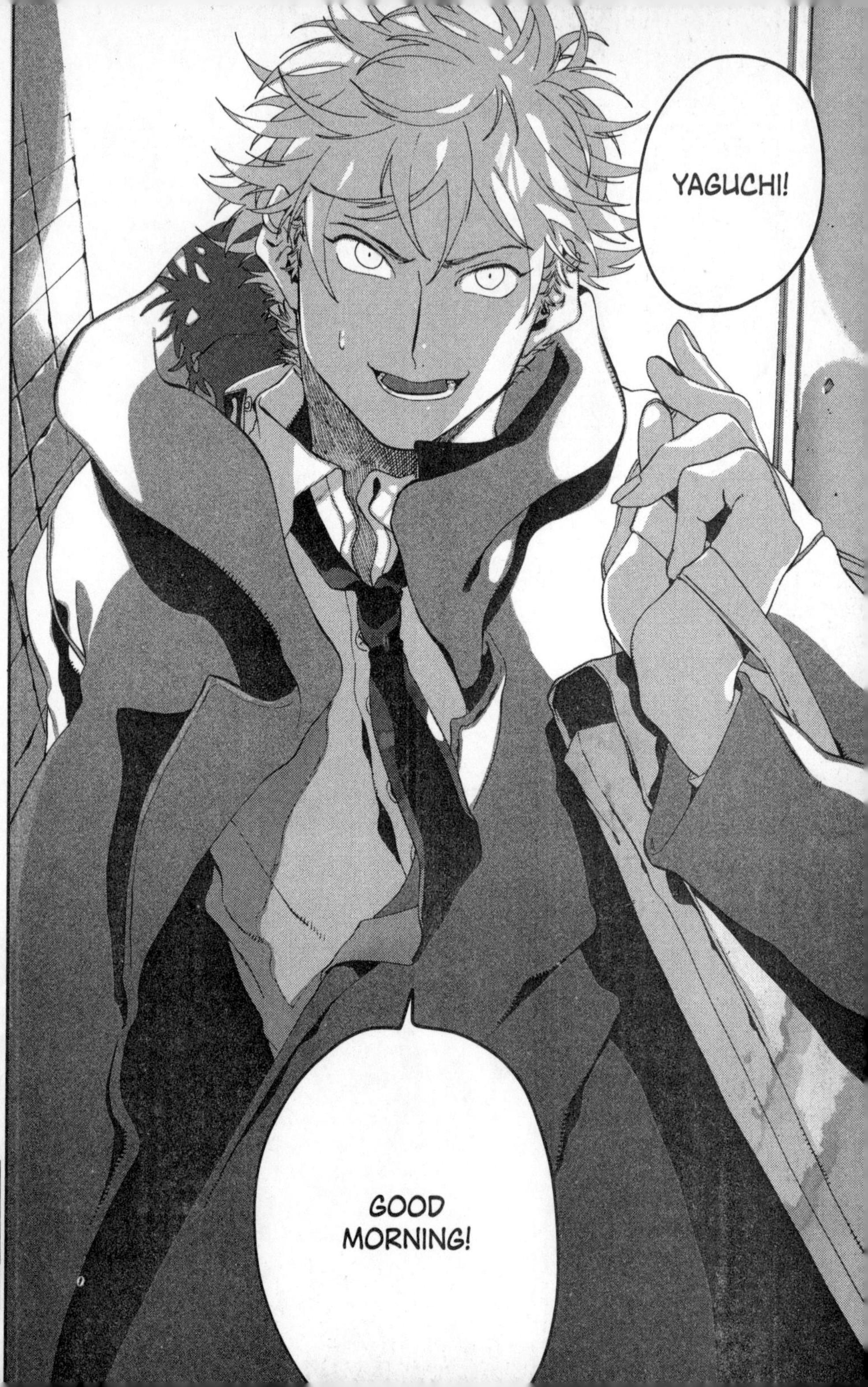
YAGUCHI!
GOOD MORNING!

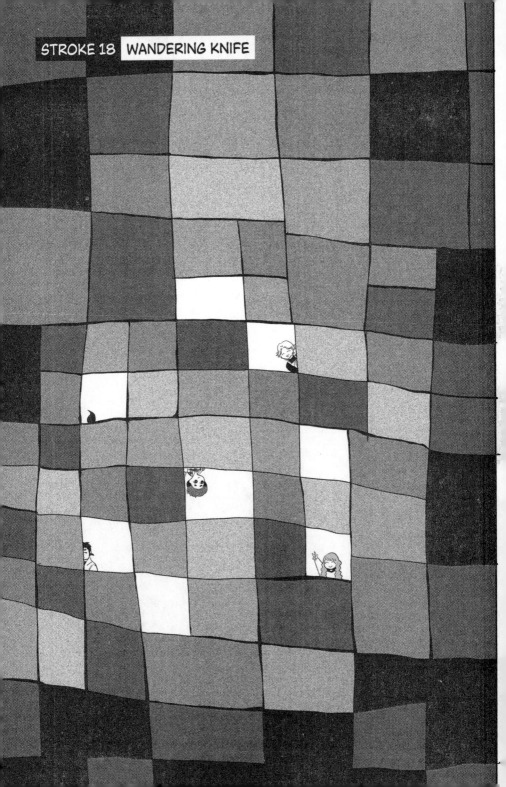

STROKE 18 WANDERING KNIFE

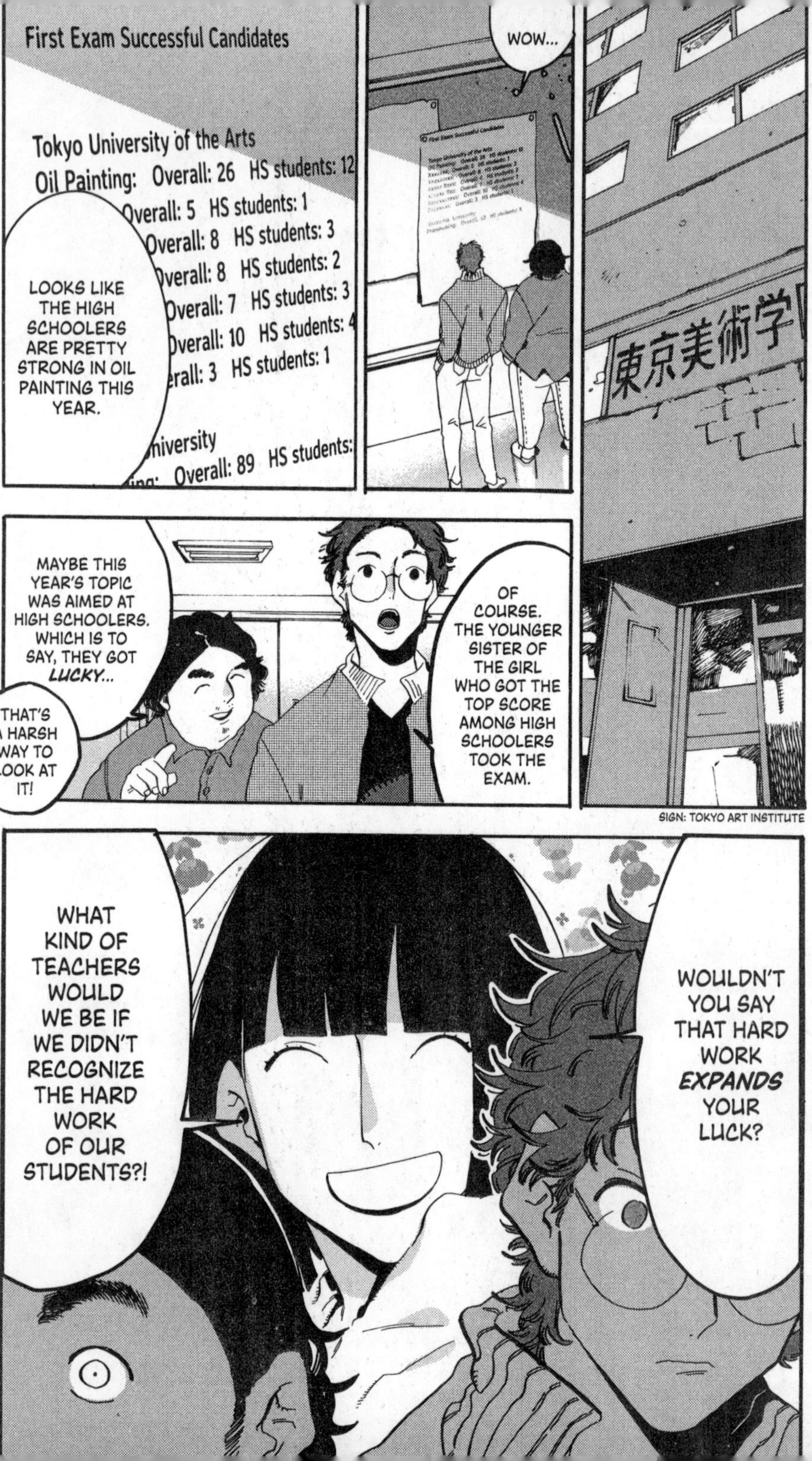
東京美術学
SIGN: TOKYO ART INSTITUTE
WOW...
First Exam Successful Candidates
Tokyo University of the Arts
Oil Painting: Overall: 26 HS students: 12
Overall: 5 HS students: 1
Overall: 8 HS students: 3
Overall: 8 HS students: 2
Overall: 7 HS students: 3
Overall: 10 HS students: 4
Overall: 3 HS students: 1
Overall: 89 HS students:
LOOKS LIKE THE HIGH SCHOOLERS ARE PRETTY STRONG IN OIL PAINTING THIS YEAR.
OF COURSE. THE YOUNGER SISTER OF THE GIRL WHO GOT THE TOP SCORE AMONG HIGH SCHOOLERS TOOK THE EXAM.
MAYBE THIS YEAR'S TOPIC WAS AIMED AT HIGH SCHOOLERS. WHICH IS TO SAY, THEY GOT *LUCKY*...
THAT'S A HARSH WAY TO LOOK AT IT!
WOULDN'T YOU SAY THAT HARD WORK ***EXPANDS*** YOUR LUCK?
WHAT KIND OF TEACHERS WOULD WE BE IF WE DIDN'T RECOGNIZE THE HARD WORK OF OUR STUDENTS?!

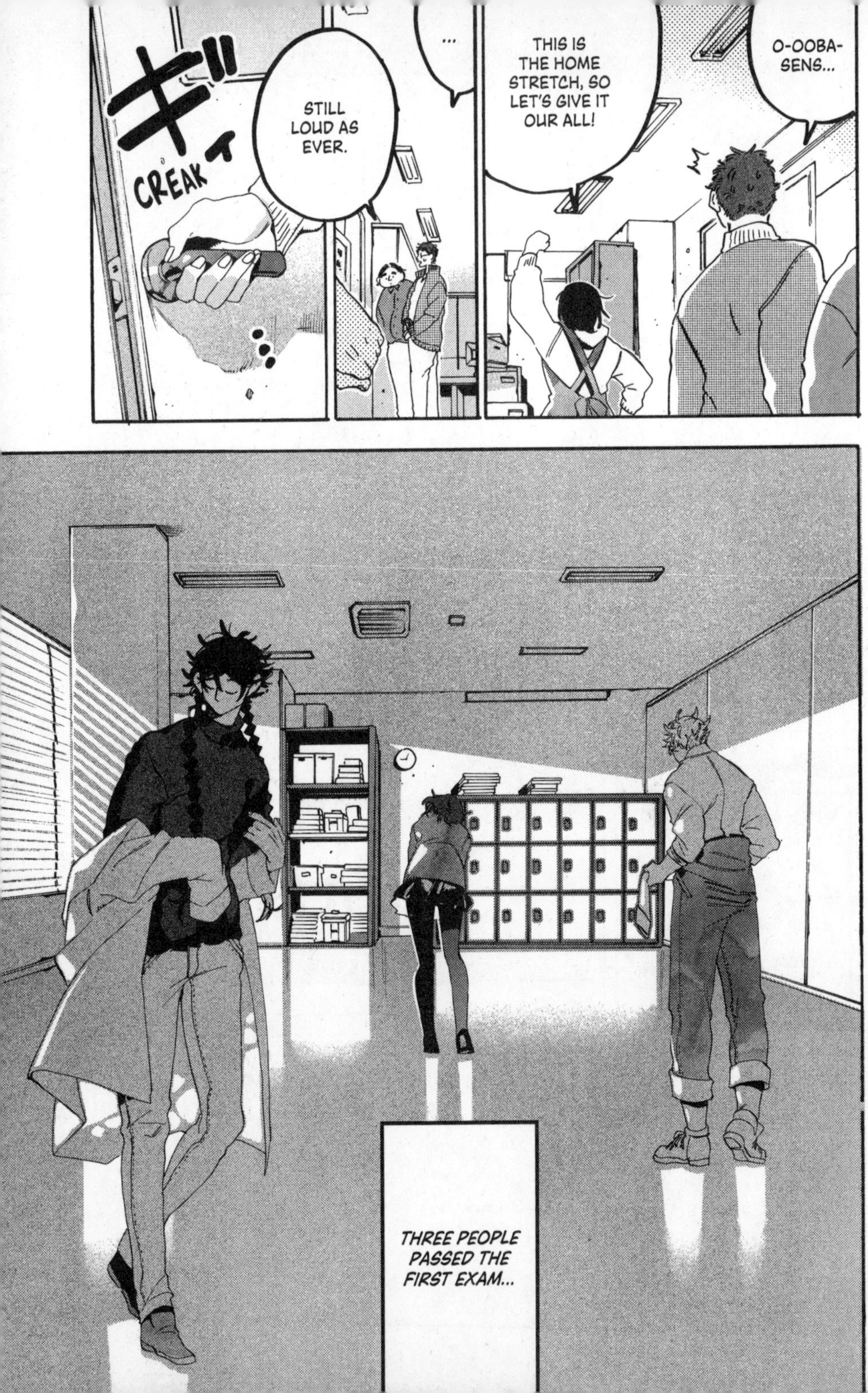
O-OOBA-SENS...
THIS IS THE HOME STRETCH, SO LET'S GIVE IT OUR ALL!
...
STILL LOUD AS EVER.
ギィ
CREAK
THREE PEOPLE PASSED THE FIRST EXAM...

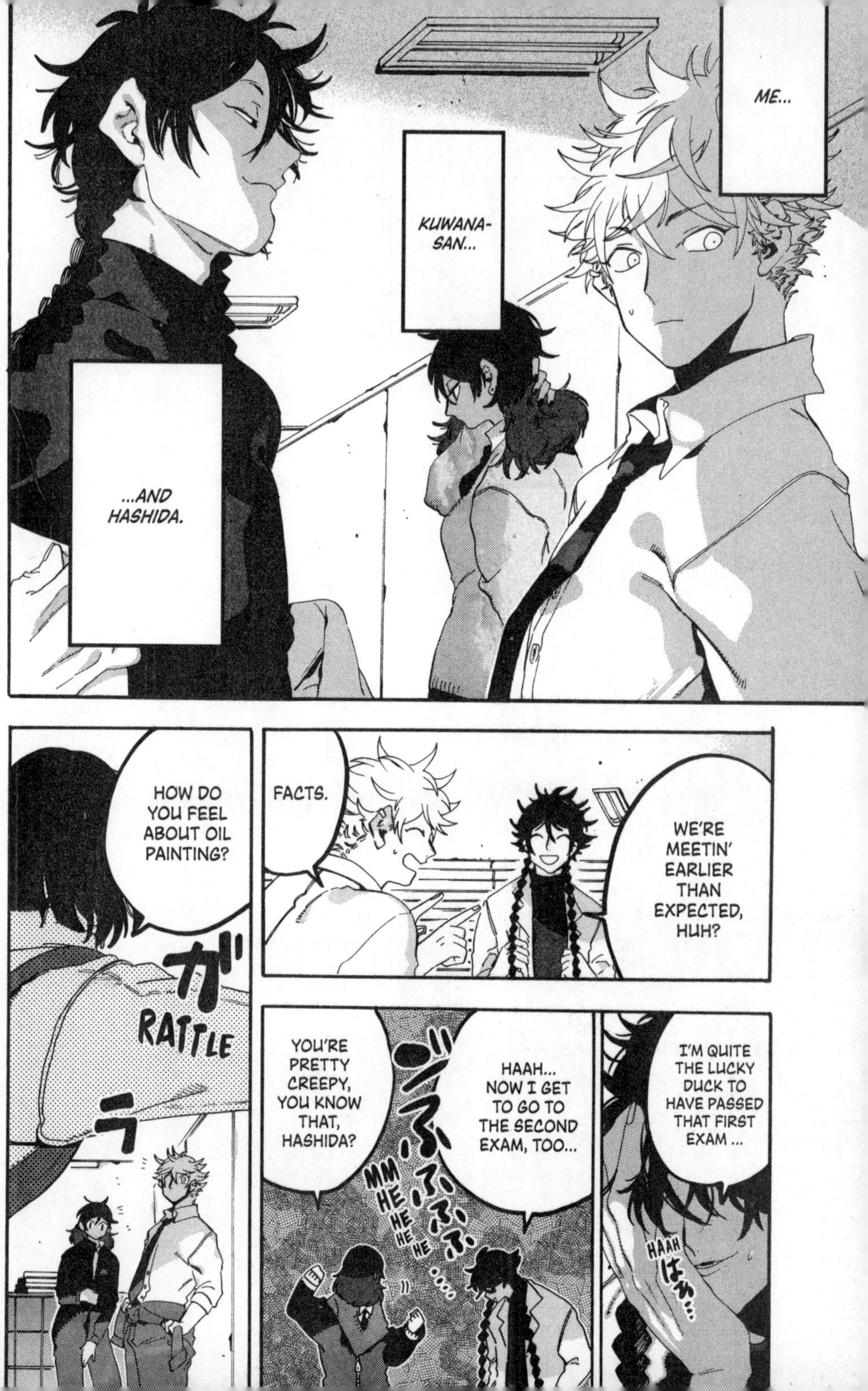
ME...
KUWANA-SAN...
...AND HASHIDA.
WE'RE MEETIN' EARLIER THAN EXPECTED, HUH?
FACTS.
I'M QUITE THE LUCKY DUCK TO HAVE PASSED THAT FIRST EXAM ...
HAAH
はぁ…
HAAH... NOW I GET TO GO TO THE SECOND EXAM, TOO...
MM HE HE HE HE ....
YOU'RE PRETTY CREEPY, YOU KNOW THAT, HASHIDA?
HOW DO YOU FEEL ABOUT OIL PAINTING?
ガ
RATTLE
ラ

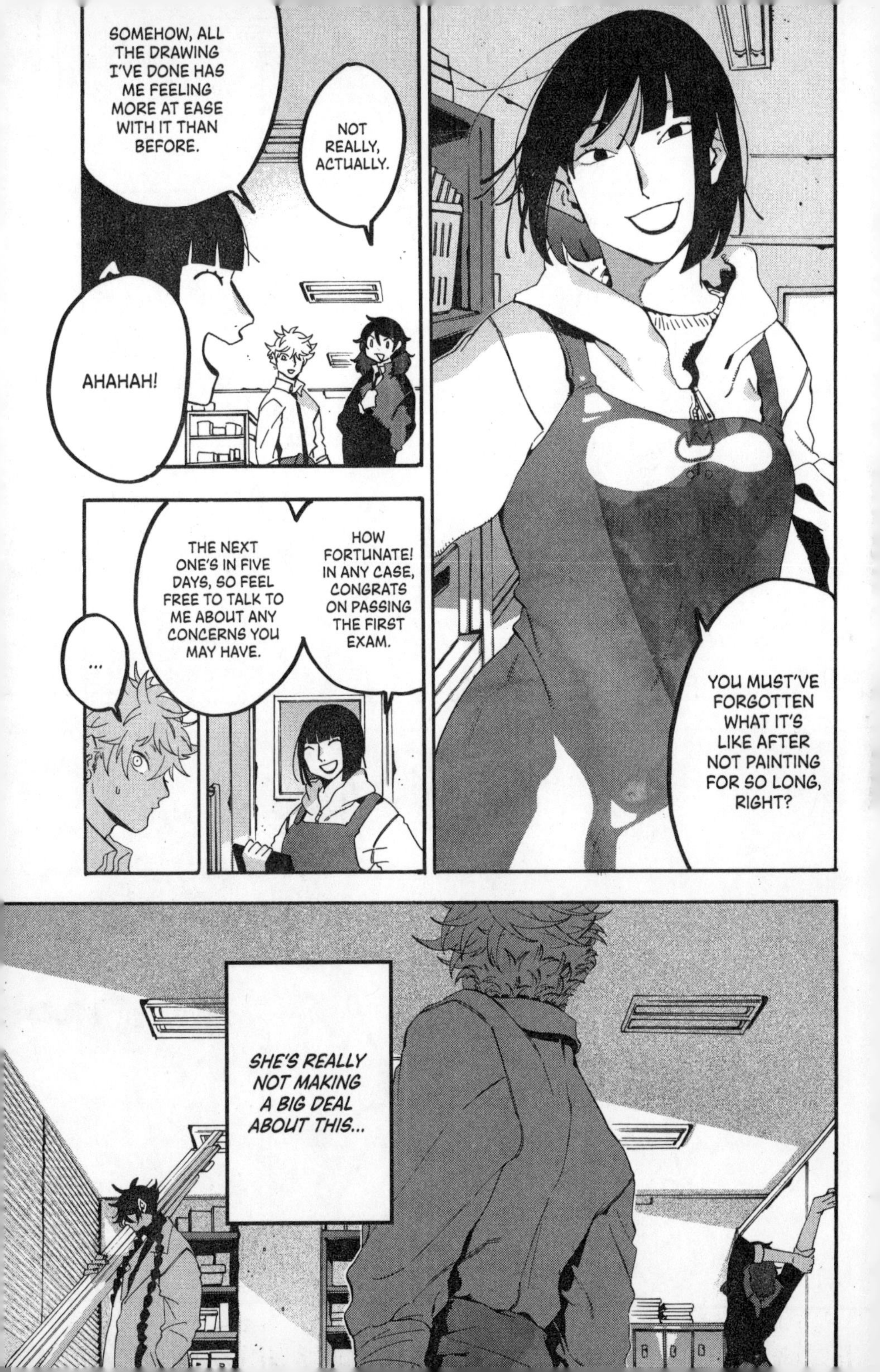
YOU MUST'VE FORGOTTEN WHAT IT'S LIKE AFTER NOT PAINTING FOR SO LONG, RIGHT?
NOT REALLY, ACTUALLY.
SOMEHOW, ALL THE DRAWING I'VE DONE HAS ME FEELING MORE AT EASE WITH IT THAN BEFORE.
AHAHAH!
HOW FORTUNATE! IN ANY CASE, CONGRATS ON PASSING THE FIRST EXAM.
THE NEXT ONE'S IN FIVE DAYS, SO FEEL FREE TO TALK TO ME ABOUT ANY CONCERNS YOU MAY HAVE.
...
SHE'S REALLY NOT MAKING A BIG DEAL ABOUT THIS...

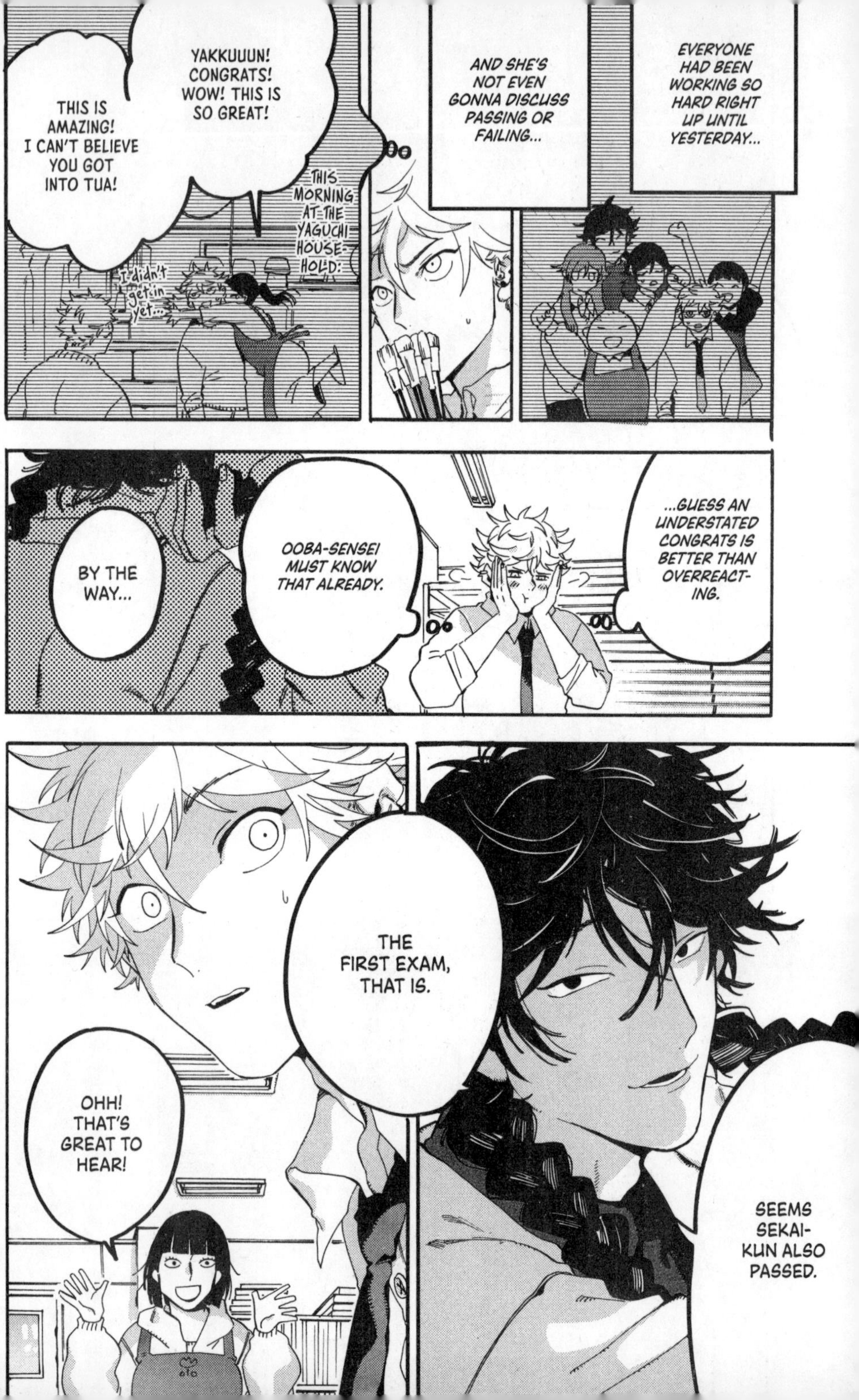
EVERYONE HAD BEEN WORKING SO HARD RIGHT UP UNTIL YESTERDAY...
AND SHE'S NOT EVEN GONNA DISCUSS PASSING OR FAILING...
THIS MORNING AT THE YAGUCHI HOUSEHOLD:
YAKKUUUN! CONGRATS! WOW! THIS IS SO GREAT!
THIS IS AMAZING! I CAN'T BELIEVE YOU GOT INTO TUA!
I didn't get in yet...
...GUESS AN UNDERSTATED CONGRATS IS BETTER THAN OVERREACTING.
OOBA-SENSEI MUST KNOW THAT ALREADY.
BY THE WAY...
SEEMS SEKAI-KUN ALSO PASSED.
THE FIRST EXAM, THAT IS.
OHH! THAT'S GREAT TO HEAR!

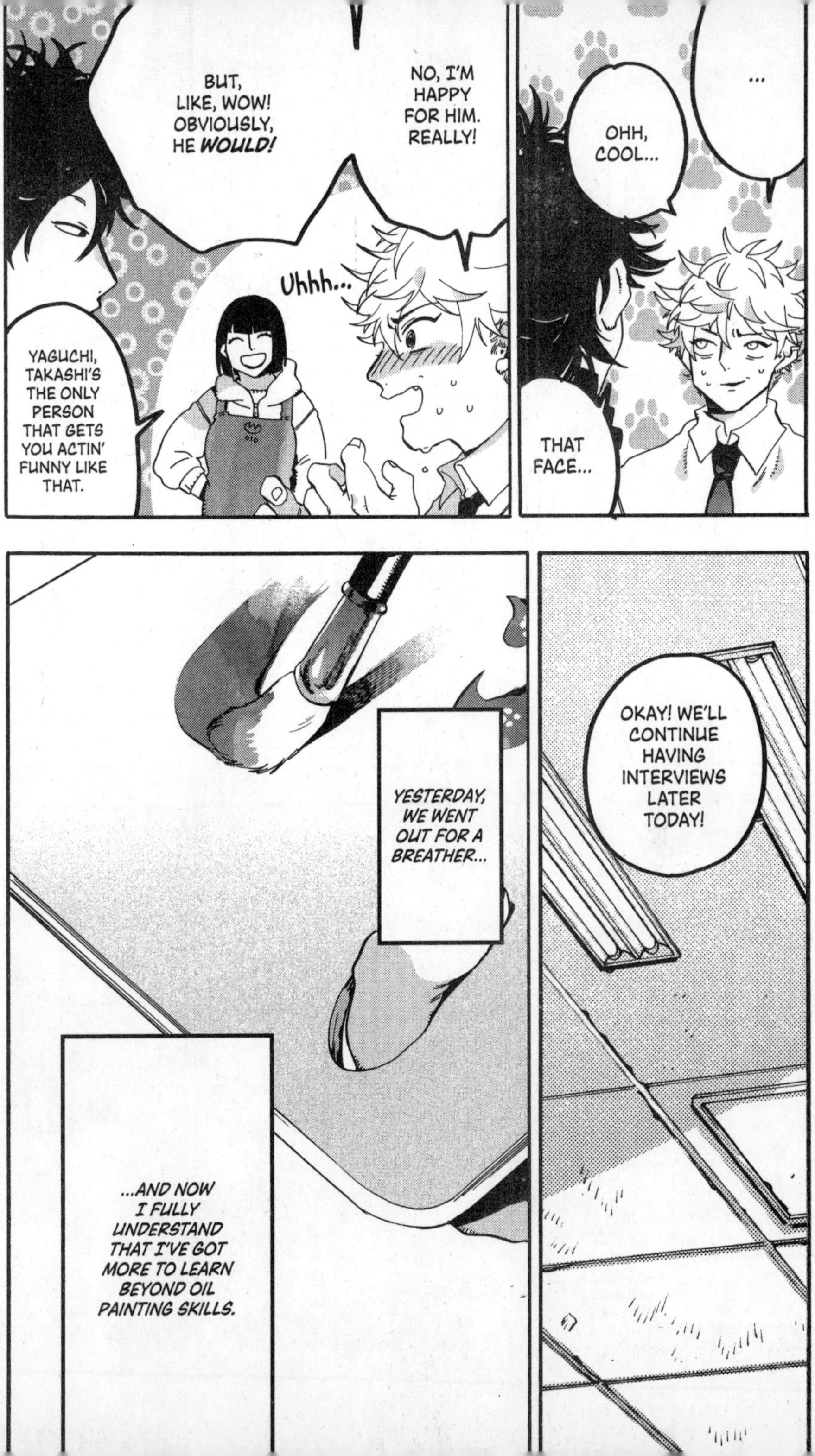
...
OHH, COOL...
THAT FACE...
NO, I'M HAPPY FOR HIM. REALLY!
BUT, LIKE, WOW! OBVIOUSLY, HE ***WOULD!***
Uhhh...
YAGUCHI, TAKASHI'S THE ONLY PERSON THAT GETS YOU ACTIN' FUNNY LIKE THAT.
OKAY! WE'LL CONTINUE HAVING INTERVIEWS LATER TODAY!
*YESTERDAY, WE WENT OUT FOR A BREATHER...*
*...AND NOW I FULLY UNDERSTAND THAT I'VE GOT MORE TO LEARN BEYOND OIL PAINTING SKILLS.*

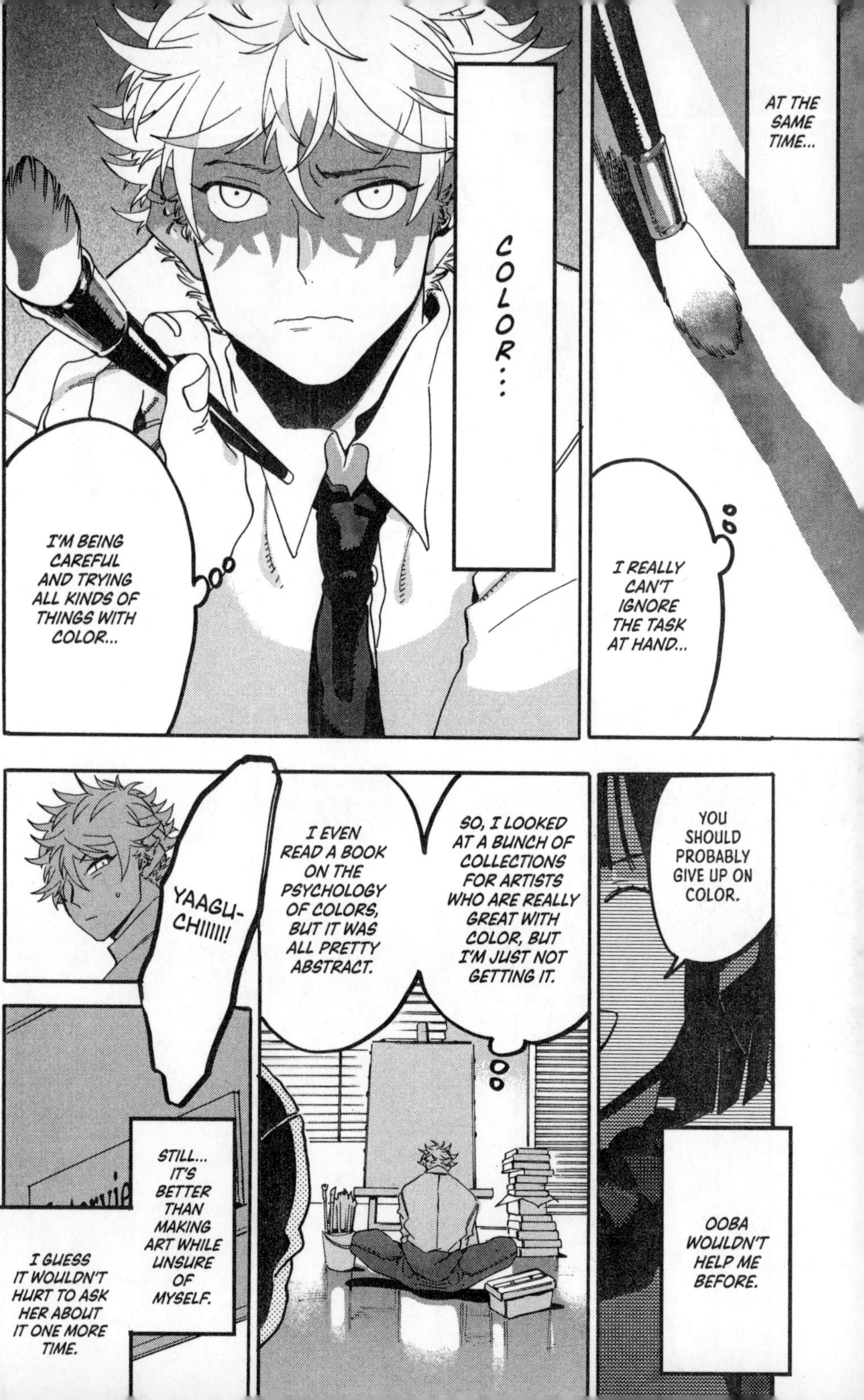
AT THE SAME TIME...
I REALLY CAN'T IGNORE THE TASK AT HAND...
COLOR...
I'M BEING CAREFUL AND TRYING ALL KINDS OF THINGS WITH COLOR...
YOU SHOULD PROBABLY GIVE UP ON COLOR.
OOBA WOULDN'T HELP ME BEFORE.
SO, I LOOKED AT A BUNCH OF COLLECTIONS FOR ARTISTS WHO ARE REALLY GREAT WITH COLOR, BUT I'M JUST NOT GETTING IT.
I EVEN READ A BOOK ON THE PSYCHOLOGY OF COLORS, BUT IT WAS ALL PRETTY ABSTRACT.
YAAGU-CHIIIIII!
STILL... IT'S BETTER THAN MAKING ART WHILE UNSURE OF MYSELF.
I GUESS IT WOULDN'T HURT TO ASK HER ABOUT IT ONE MORE TIME.

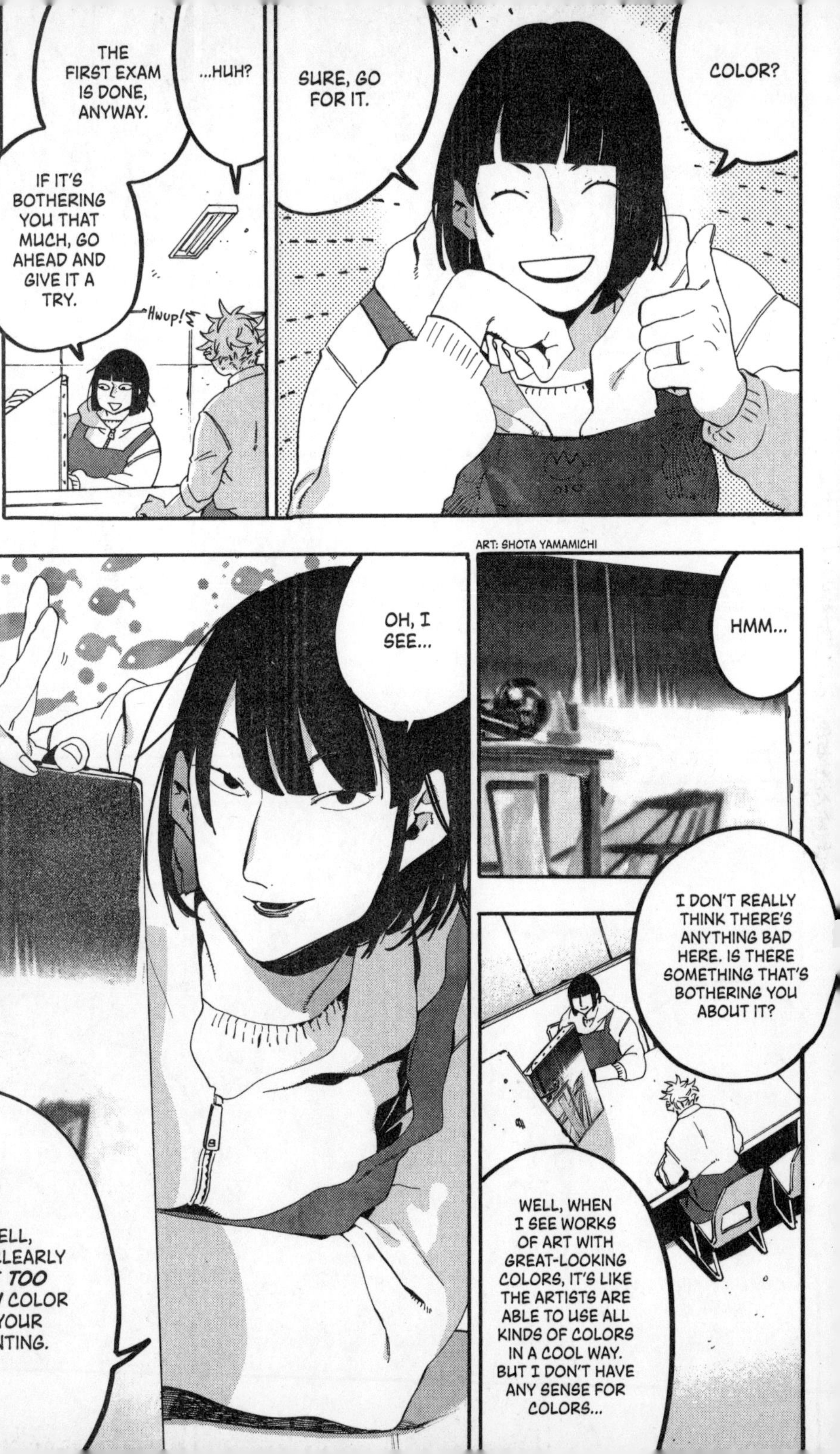
COLOR?
SURE, GO FOR IT.
...HUH?
THE FIRST EXAM IS DONE, ANYWAY.
IF IT'S BOTHERING YOU THAT MUCH, GO AHEAD AND GIVE IT A TRY.
Hwup!
ART: SHOTA YAMAMICHI
HMM...
I DON'T REALLY THINK THERE'S ANYTHING BAD HERE. IS THERE SOMETHING THAT'S BOTHERING YOU ABOUT IT?
WELL, WHEN I SEE WORKS OF ART WITH GREAT-LOOKING COLORS, IT'S LIKE THE ARTISTS ARE ABLE TO USE ALL KINDS OF COLORS IN A COOL WAY. BUT I DON'T HAVE ANY SENSE FOR COLORS...
OH, I SEE...
WELL, YOU CLEARLY PUT *TOO MUCH* COLOR IN YOUR PAINTING.

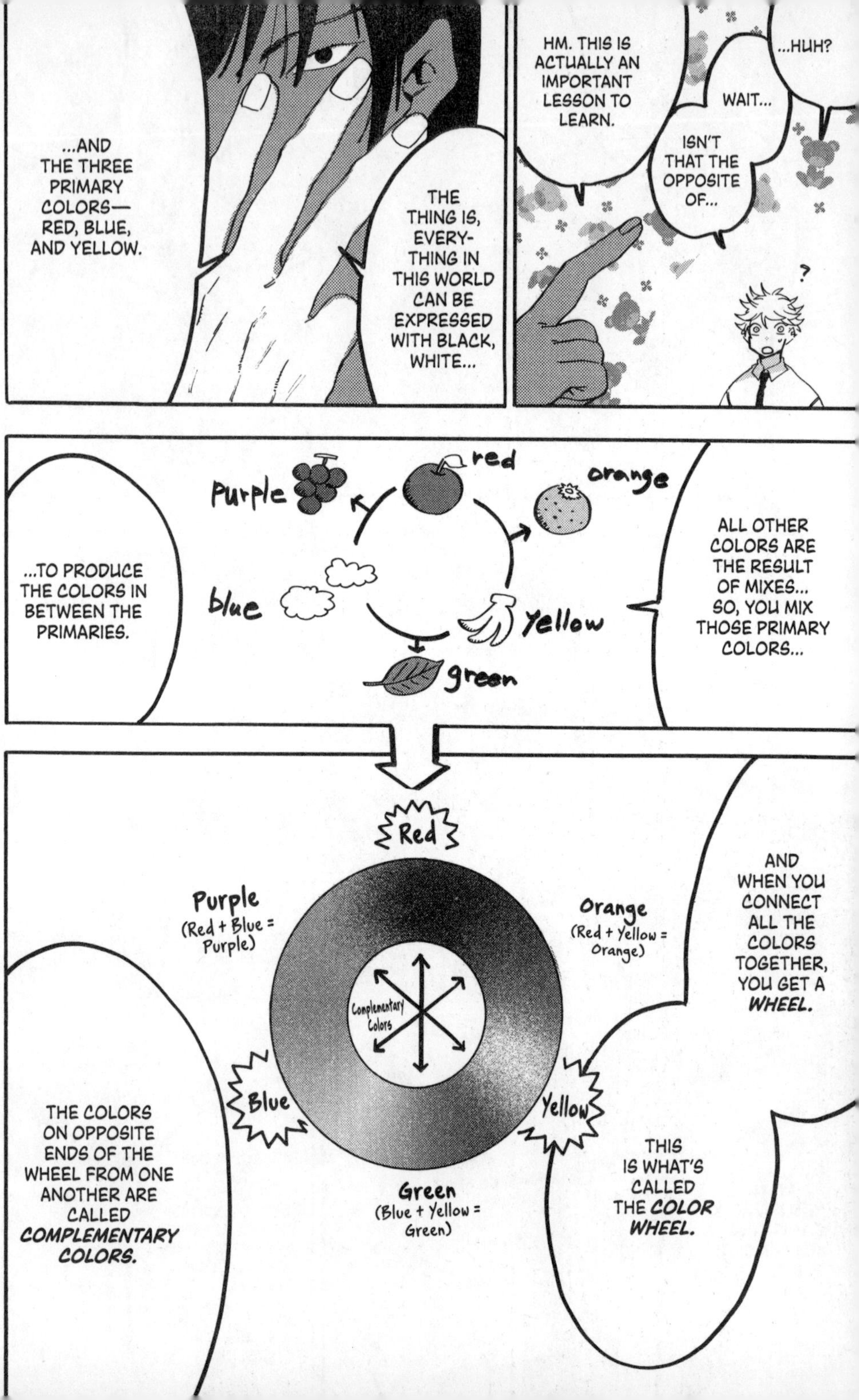

...HUH?
WAIT...
ISN'T THAT THE OPPOSITE OF...
HM. THIS IS ACTUALLY AN IMPORTANT LESSON TO LEARN.
THE THING IS, EVERY-THING IN THIS WORLD CAN BE EXPRESSED WITH BLACK, WHITE...
...AND THE THREE PRIMARY COLORS—RED, BLUE, AND YELLOW.
ALL OTHER COLORS ARE THE RESULT OF MIXES... SO, YOU MIX THOSE PRIMARY COLORS...
red
orange
Yellow
green
blue
purple
...TO PRODUCE THE COLORS IN BETWEEN THE PRIMARIES.
AND WHEN YOU CONNECT ALL THE COLORS TOGETHER, YOU GET A ***WHEEL.***
THIS IS WHAT'S CALLED THE ***COLOR WHEEL.***
Red
Orange (Red + Yellow = Orange)
Yellow
Green (Blue + Yellow = Green)
Blue
Purple (Red + Blue = Purple)
Complementary Colors
THE COLORS ON OPPOSITE ENDS OF THE WHEEL FROM ONE ANOTHER ARE CALLED ***COMPLEMENTARY COLORS.***

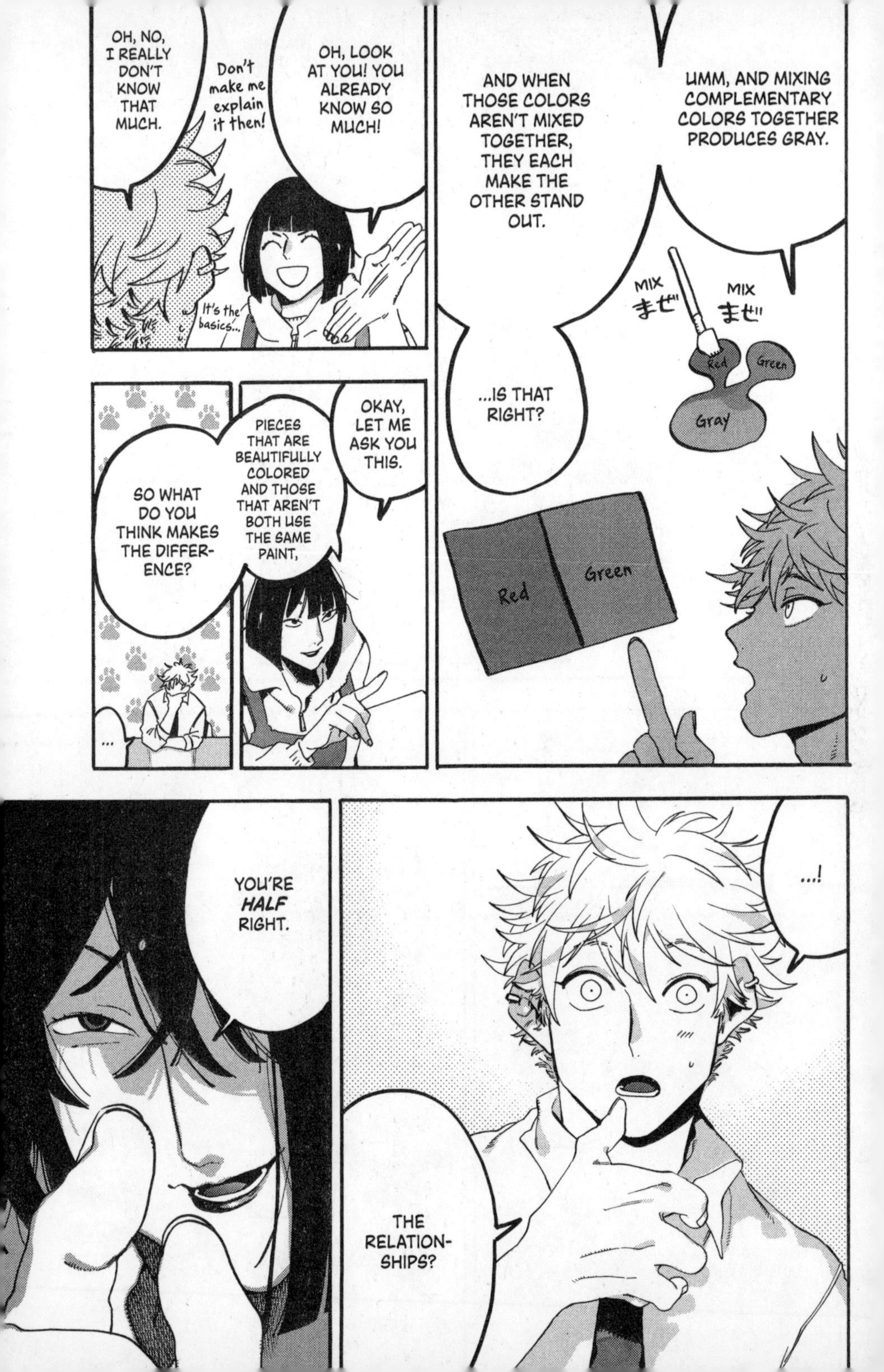
UMM, AND MIXING COMPLEMENTARY COLORS TOGETHER PRODUCES GRAY.
AND WHEN THOSE COLORS AREN'T MIXED TOGETHER, THEY EACH MAKE THE OTHER STAND OUT.
MIX まぜ
MIX まぜ
Red
Green
Gray
...IS THAT RIGHT?
Green
Red
OH, LOOK AT YOU! YOU ALREADY KNOW SO MUCH!
Don't make me explain it then!
OH, NO, I REALLY DON'T KNOW THAT MUCH.
It's the basics...
OKAY, LET ME ASK YOU THIS.
PIECES THAT ARE BEAUTIFULLY COLORED AND THOSE THAT AREN'T BOTH USE THE SAME PAINT,
SO WHAT DO YOU THINK MAKES THE DIFFERENCE?
...
...!
THE RELATION-SHIPS?
YOU'RE *HALF* RIGHT.

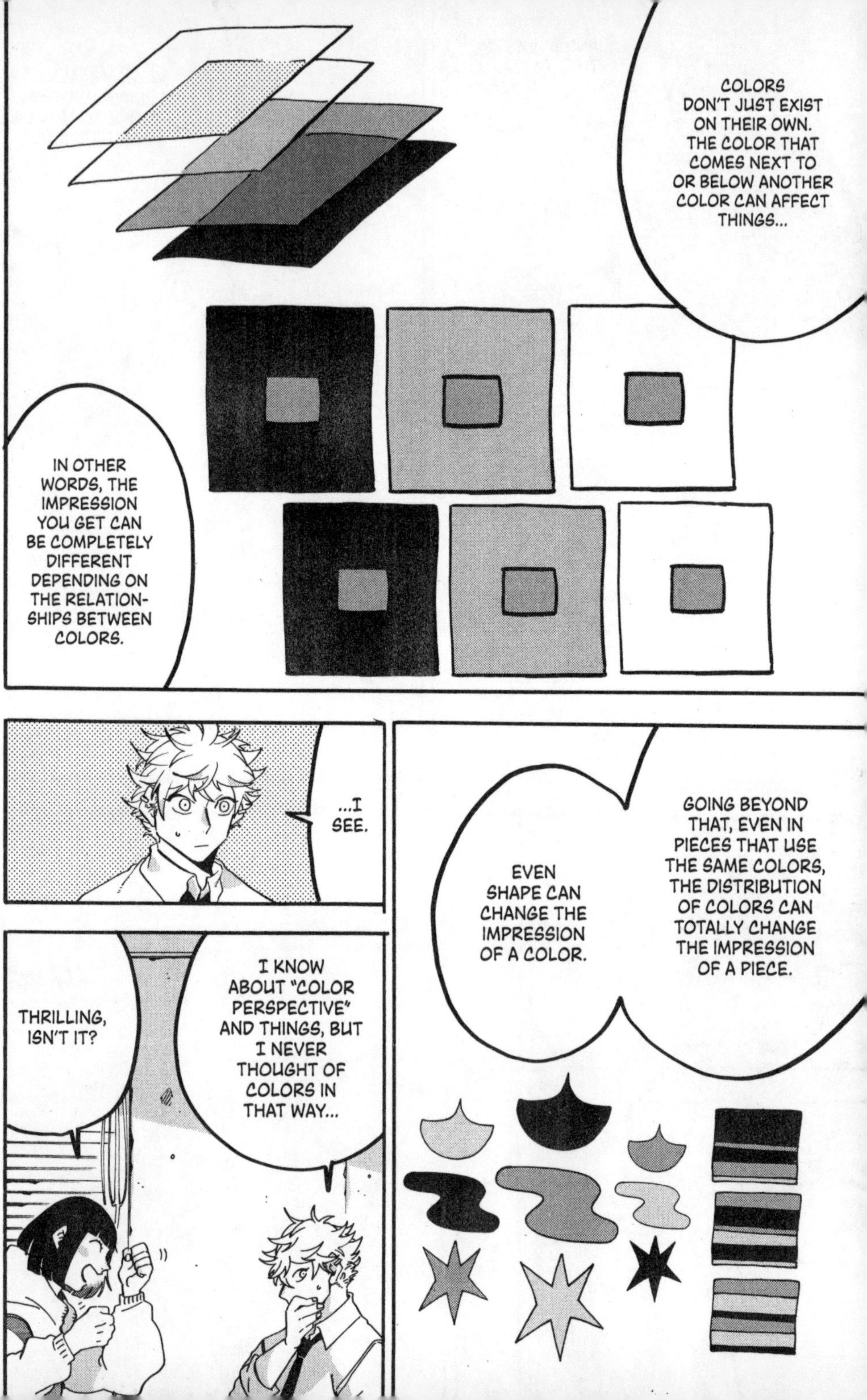
COLORS DON'T JUST EXIST ON THEIR OWN. THE COLOR THAT COMES NEXT TO OR BELOW ANOTHER COLOR CAN AFFECT THINGS...
IN OTHER WORDS, THE IMPRESSION YOU GET CAN BE COMPLETELY DIFFERENT DEPENDING ON THE RELATIONSHIPS BETWEEN COLORS.
GOING BEYOND THAT, EVEN IN PIECES THAT USE THE SAME COLORS, THE DISTRIBUTION OF COLORS CAN TOTALLY CHANGE THE IMPRESSION OF A PIECE.
EVEN SHAPE CAN CHANGE THE IMPRESSION OF A COLOR.
...I SEE.
I KNOW ABOUT "COLOR PERSPECTIVE" AND THINGS, BUT I NEVER THOUGHT OF COLORS IN THAT WAY...
THRILLING, ISN'T IT?

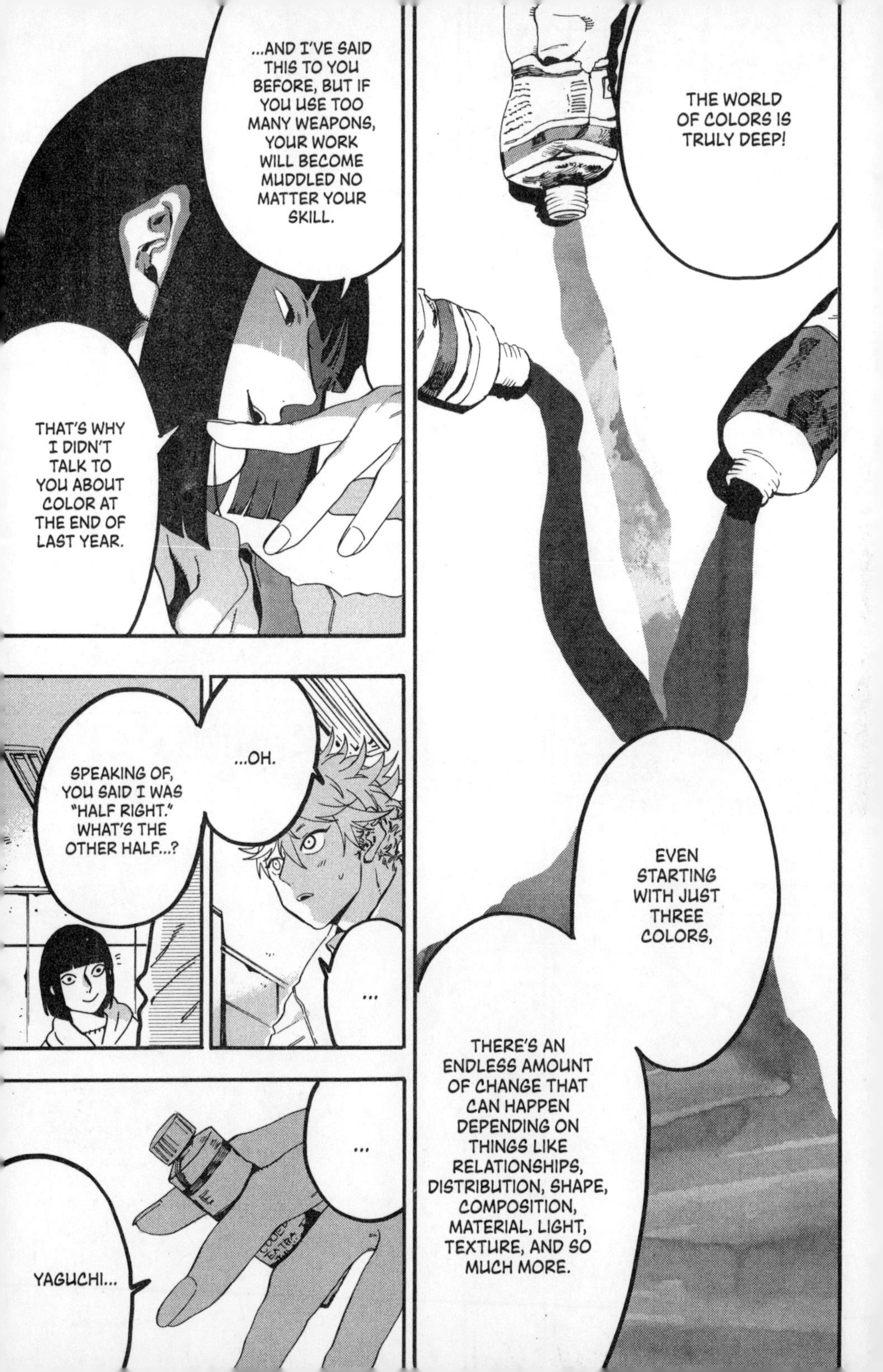
THE WORLD OF COLORS IS TRULY DEEP!
EVEN STARTING WITH JUST THREE COLORS,
THERE'S AN ENDLESS AMOUNT OF CHANGE THAT CAN HAPPEN DEPENDING ON THINGS LIKE RELATIONSHIPS, DISTRIBUTION, SHAPE, COMPOSITION, MATERIAL, LIGHT, TEXTURE, AND SO MUCH MORE.
...AND I'VE SAID THIS TO YOU BEFORE, BUT IF YOU USE TOO MANY WEAPONS, YOUR WORK WILL BECOME MUDDLED NO MATTER YOUR SKILL.
THAT'S WHY I DIDN'T TALK TO YOU ABOUT COLOR AT THE END OF LAST YEAR.
...OH.
...
SPEAKING OF, YOU SAID I WAS "HALF RIGHT." WHAT'S THE OTHER HALF...?
...
YAGUCHI...

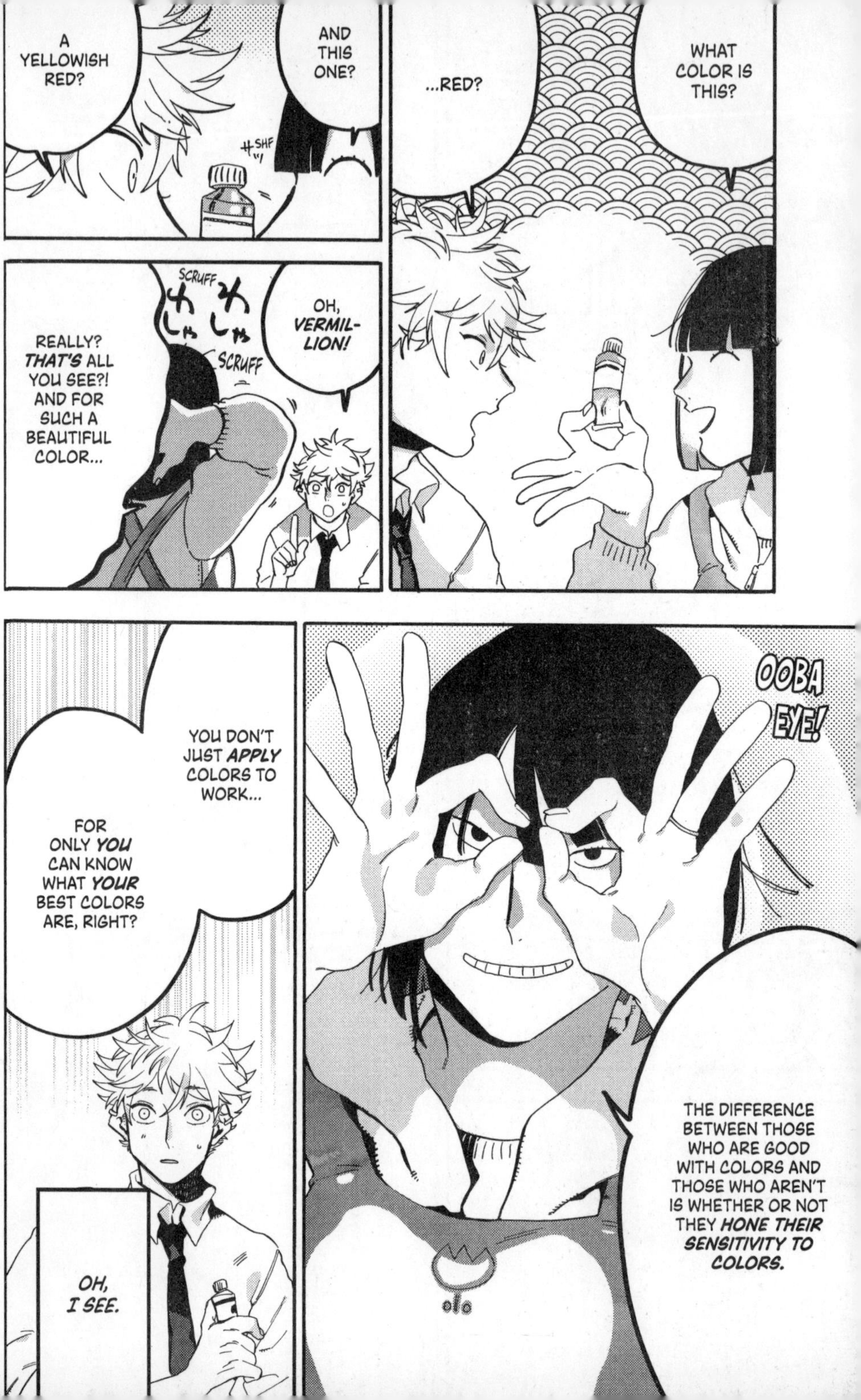
WHAT COLOR IS THIS?
...RED?
AND THIS ONE?
A YELLOWISH RED?
SHF
OH, VERMIL-LION!
SCRUFF
SCRUFF
REALLY? THAT'S ALL YOU SEE?! AND FOR SUCH A BEAUTIFUL COLOR...
OOBA EYE!
THE DIFFERENCE BETWEEN THOSE WHO ARE GOOD WITH COLORS AND THOSE WHO AREN'T IS WHETHER OR NOT THEY HONE THEIR SENSITIVITY TO COLORS.
YOU DON'T JUST APPLY COLORS TO WORK...
FOR ONLY YOU CAN KNOW WHAT YOUR BEST COLORS ARE, RIGHT?
OH, I SEE.

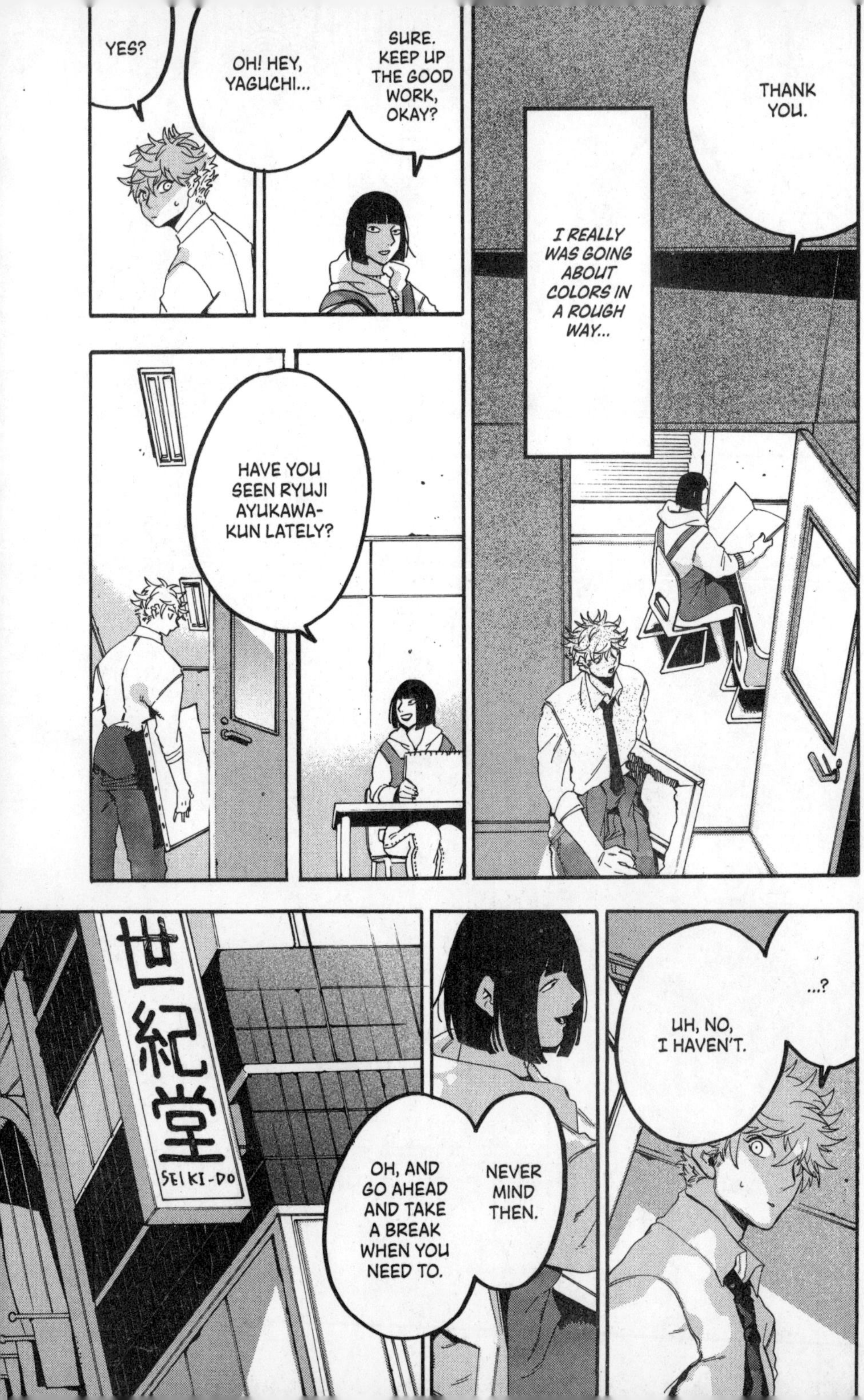
THANK YOU.
I REALLY WAS GOING ABOUT COLORS IN A ROUGH WAY...
OH! HEY, YAGUCHI...
SURE. KEEP UP THE GOOD WORK, OKAY?
YES?
HAVE YOU SEEN RYUJI AYUKAWA-KUN LATELY?
...?
UH, NO, I HAVEN'T.
NEVER MIND THEN.
OH, AND GO AHEAD AND TAKE A BREAK WHEN YOU NEED TO.
世紀堂
SEIKI-DO

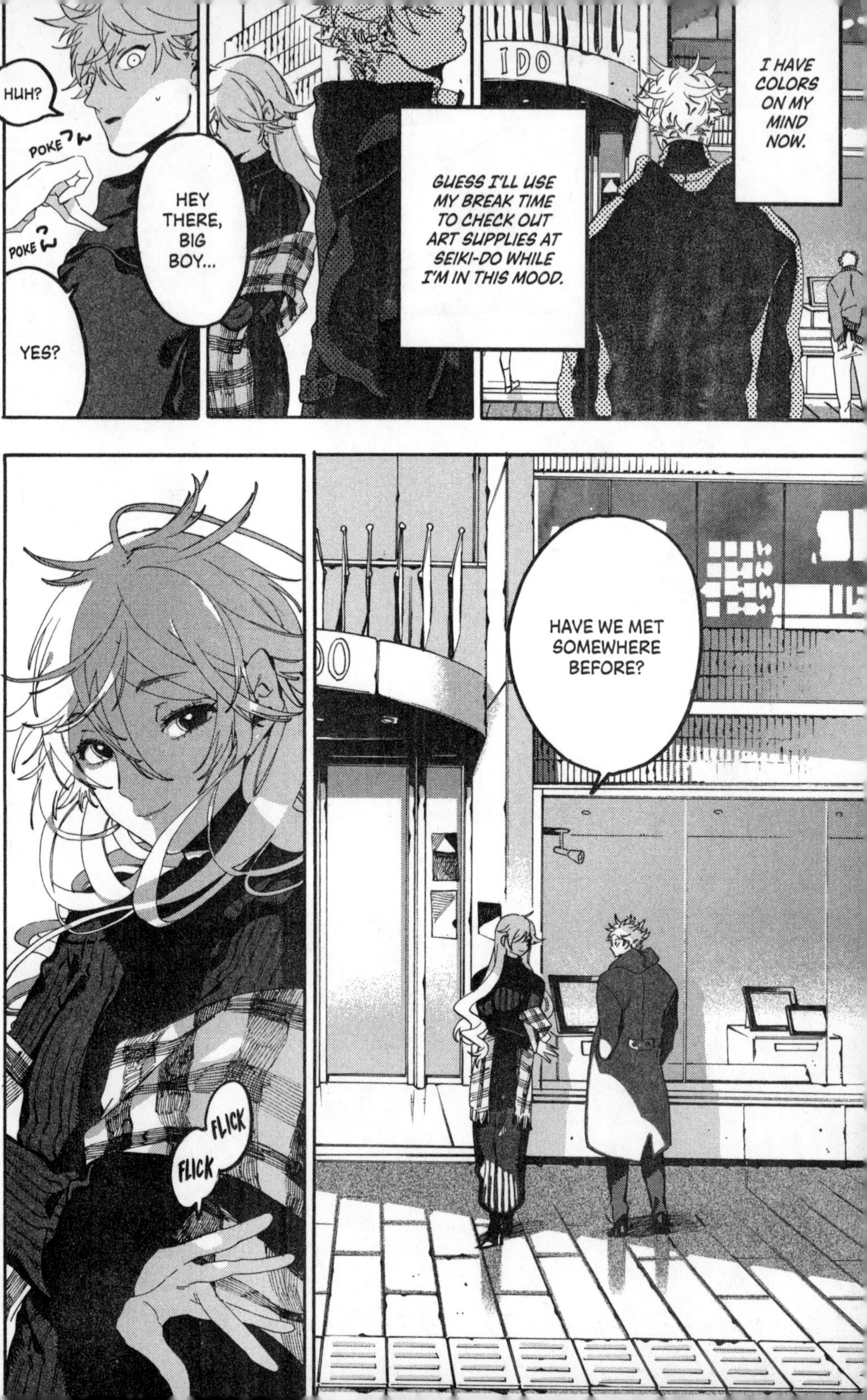
I HAVE COLORS ON MY MIND NOW.
GUESS I'LL USE MY BREAK TIME TO CHECK OUT ART SUPPLIES AT SEIKI-DO WHILE I'M IN THIS MOOD.
HUH?
POKE
HEY THERE, BIG BOY...
POKE
YES?
IDO
HAVE WE MET SOMEWHERE BEFORE?
FLICK
FLICK

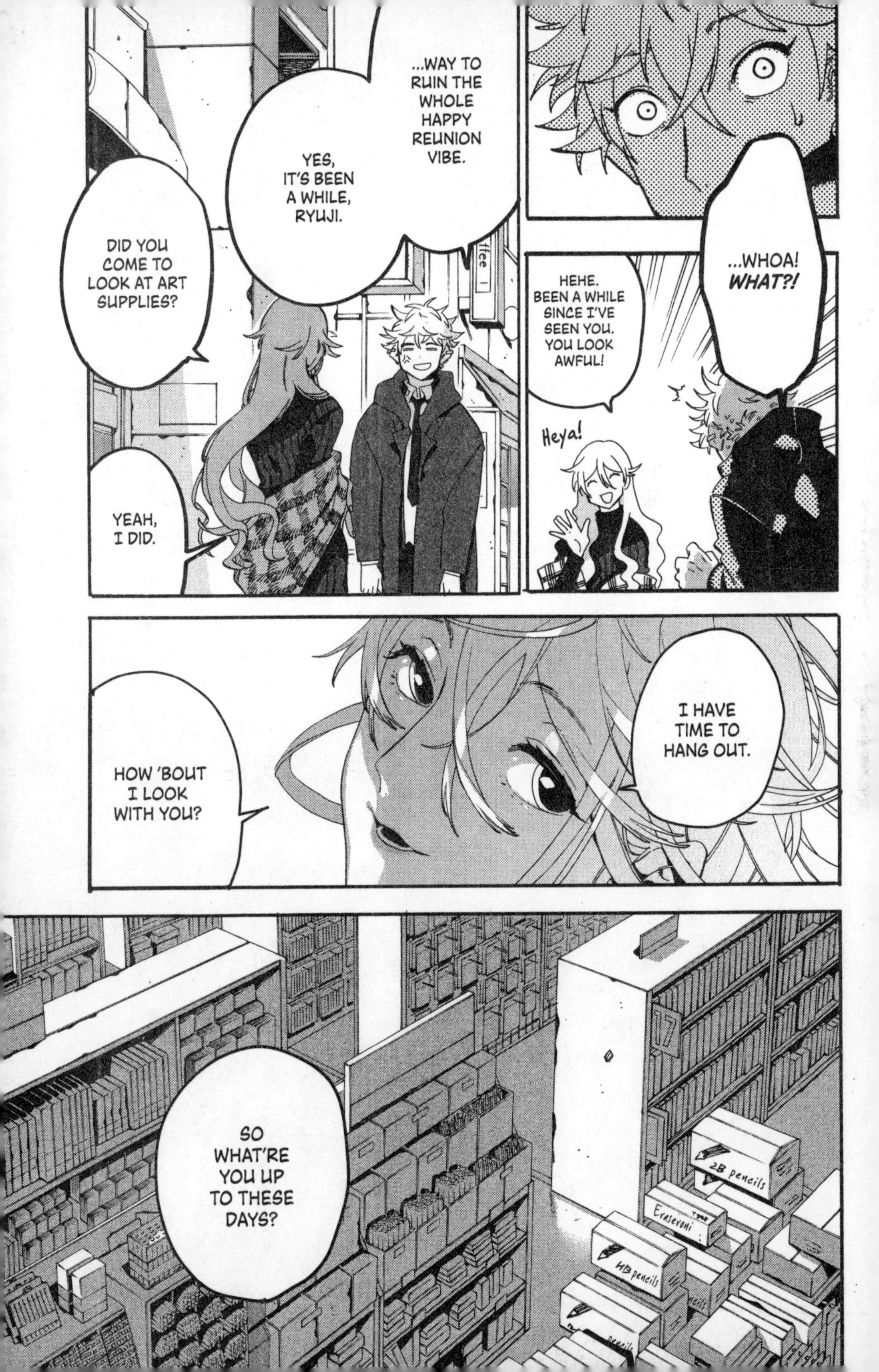
...WHOA! *WHAT?!*
HEHE. BEEN A WHILE SINCE I'VE SEEN YOU. YOU LOOK AWFUL!
Heya!
...WAY TO RUIN THE WHOLE HAPPY REUNION VIBE.
YES, IT'S BEEN A WHILE, RYUJI.
DID YOU COME TO LOOK AT ART SUPPLIES?
YEAH, I DID.
I HAVE TIME TO HANG OUT.
HOW 'BOUT I LOOK WITH YOU?
SO WHAT'RE YOU UP TO THESE DAYS?
2B pencils
Eraseroni
HB pencils

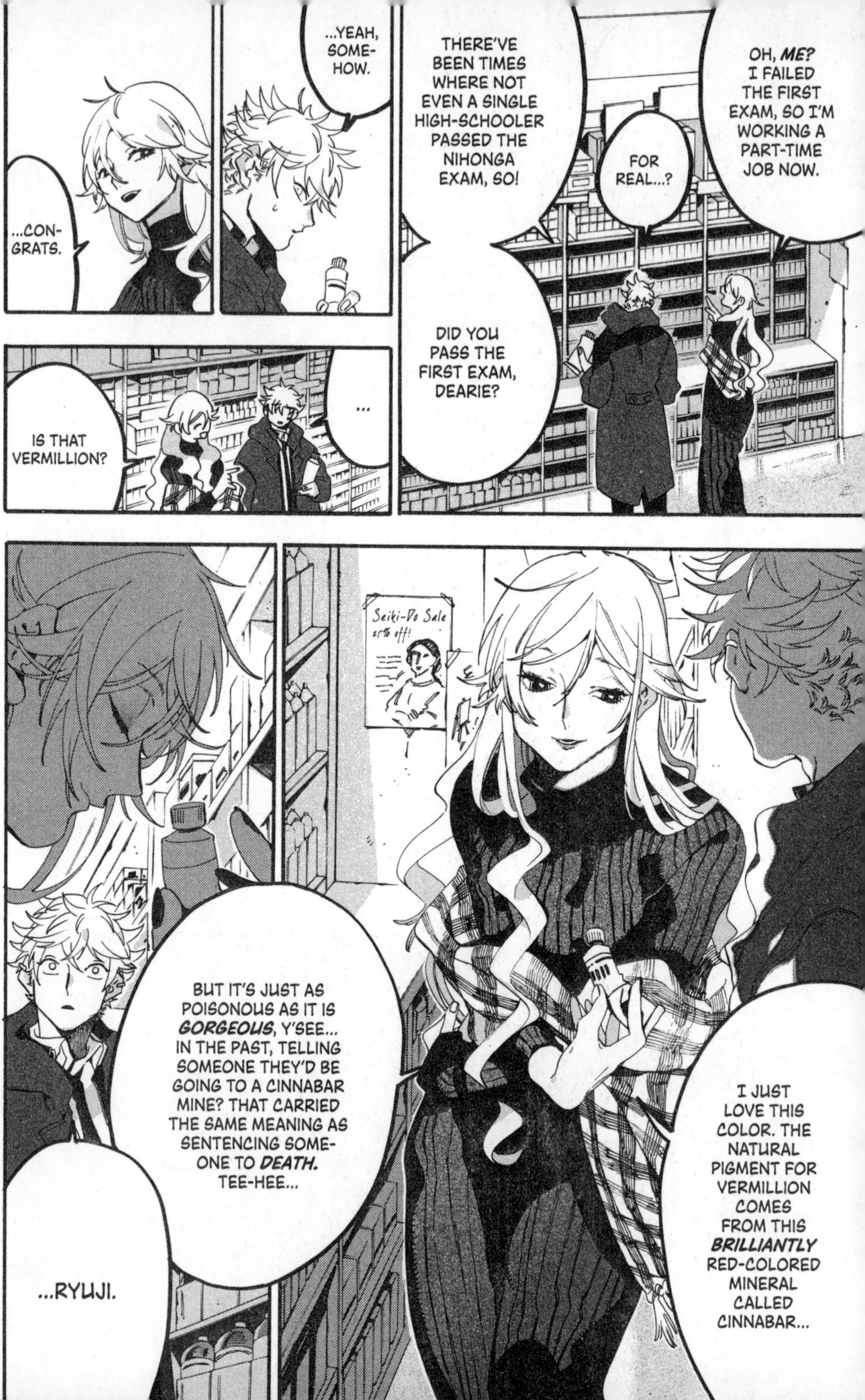
OH, *ME?* I FAILED THE FIRST EXAM, SO I'M WORKING A PART-TIME JOB NOW.
FOR REAL...?
THERE'VE BEEN TIMES WHERE NOT EVEN A SINGLE HIGH-SCHOOLER PASSED THE NIHONGA EXAM, SO!
DID YOU PASS THE FIRST EXAM, DEARIE?
...YEAH, SOME-HOW.
...CON-GRATS.
...
IS THAT VERMILLION?
Seiki-Do Sale
25% off!
I JUST LOVE THIS COLOR. THE NATURAL PIGMENT FOR VERMILLION COMES FROM THIS *BRILLIANTLY* RED-COLORED MINERAL CALLED CINNABAR...
BUT IT'S JUST AS POISONOUS AS IT IS *GORGEOUS*, Y'SEE... IN THE PAST, TELLING SOMEONE THEY'D BE GOING TO A CINNABAR MINE? THAT CARRIED THE SAME MEANING AS SENTENCING SOME-ONE TO *DEATH.* TEE-HEE...
...RYUJI.

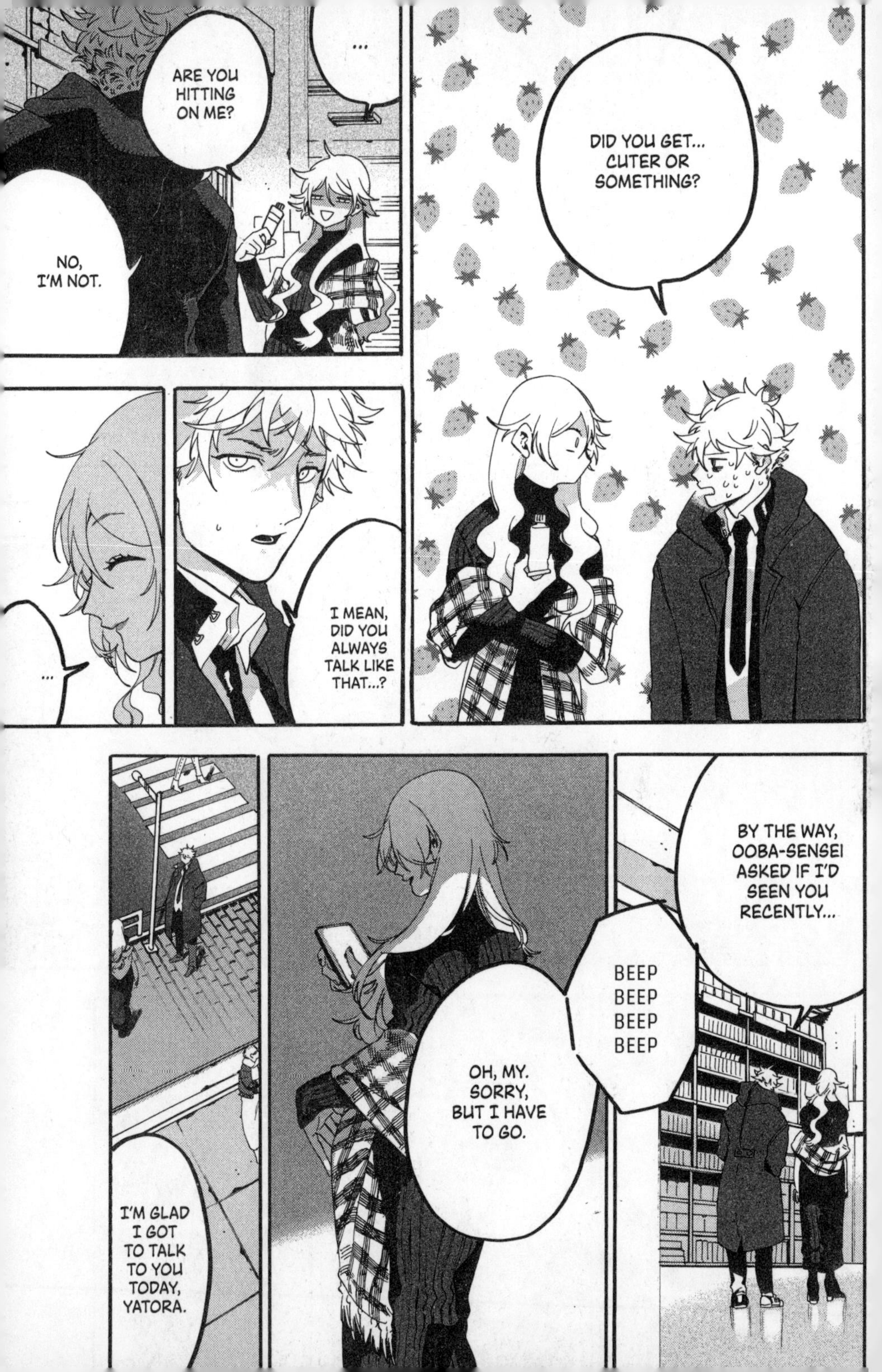
DID YOU GET... CUTER OR SOMETHING?
...
ARE YOU HITTING ON ME?
NO, I'M NOT.
I MEAN, DID YOU ALWAYS TALK LIKE THAT...?
...
BY THE WAY, OOBA-SENSEI ASKED IF I'D SEEN YOU RECENTLY...
BEEP BEEP BEEP BEEP
OH, MY. SORRY, BUT I HAVE TO GO.
I'M GLAD I GOT TO TALK TO YOU TODAY, YATORA.

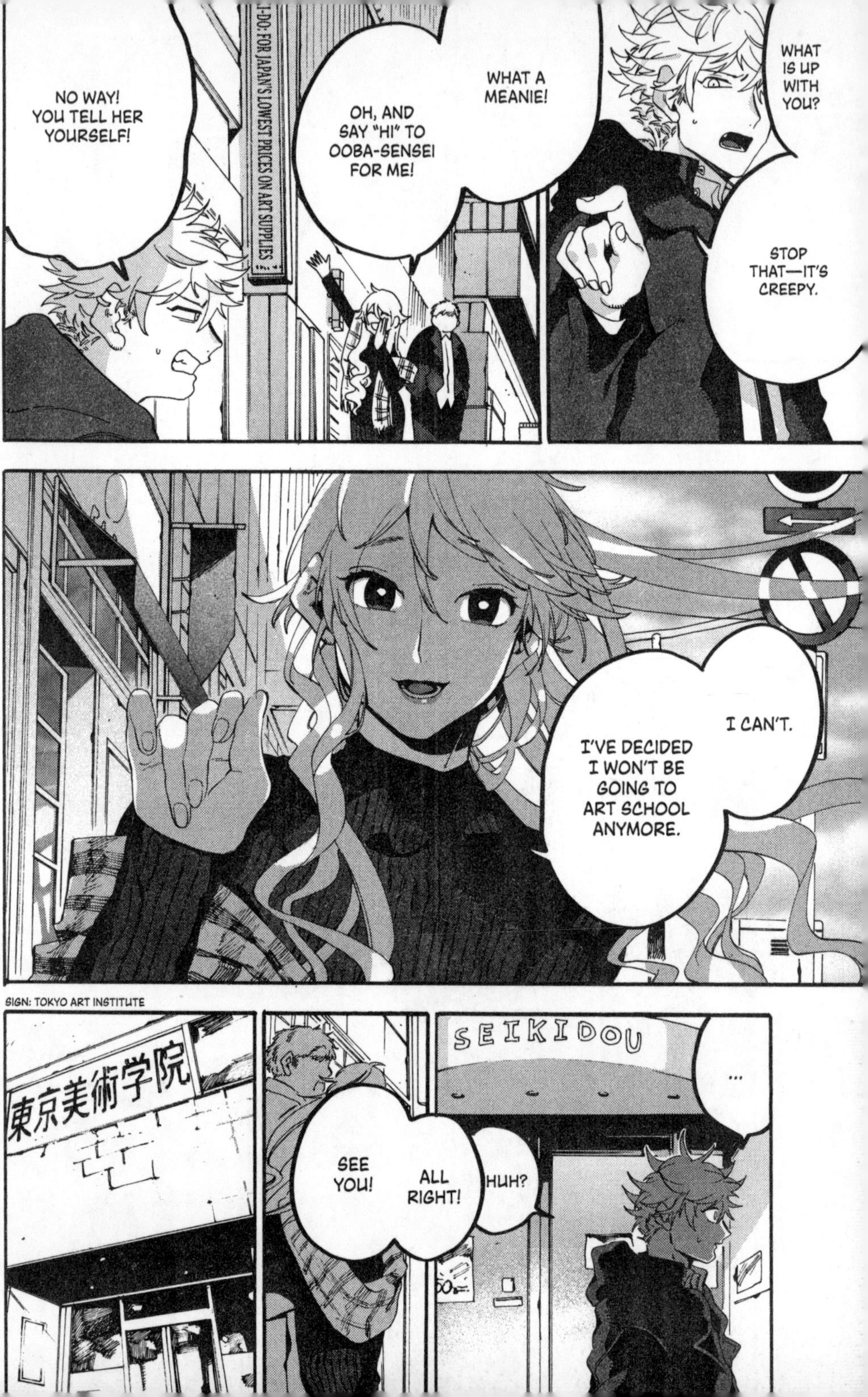
WHAT IS UP WITH YOU?
STOP THAT—IT'S CREEPY.
WHAT A MEANIE!
OH, AND SAY "HI" TO OOBA-SENSEI FOR ME!
I-DO: FOR JAPAN'S LOWEST PRICES ON ART SUPPLIES
NO WAY! YOU TELL HER YOURSELF!
I CAN'T.
I'VE DECIDED I WON'T BE GOING TO ART SCHOOL ANYMORE.
SEIKIDOU
...
HUH?
ALL RIGHT!
SEE YOU!
東京美術学院
SIGN: TOKYO ART INSTITUTE

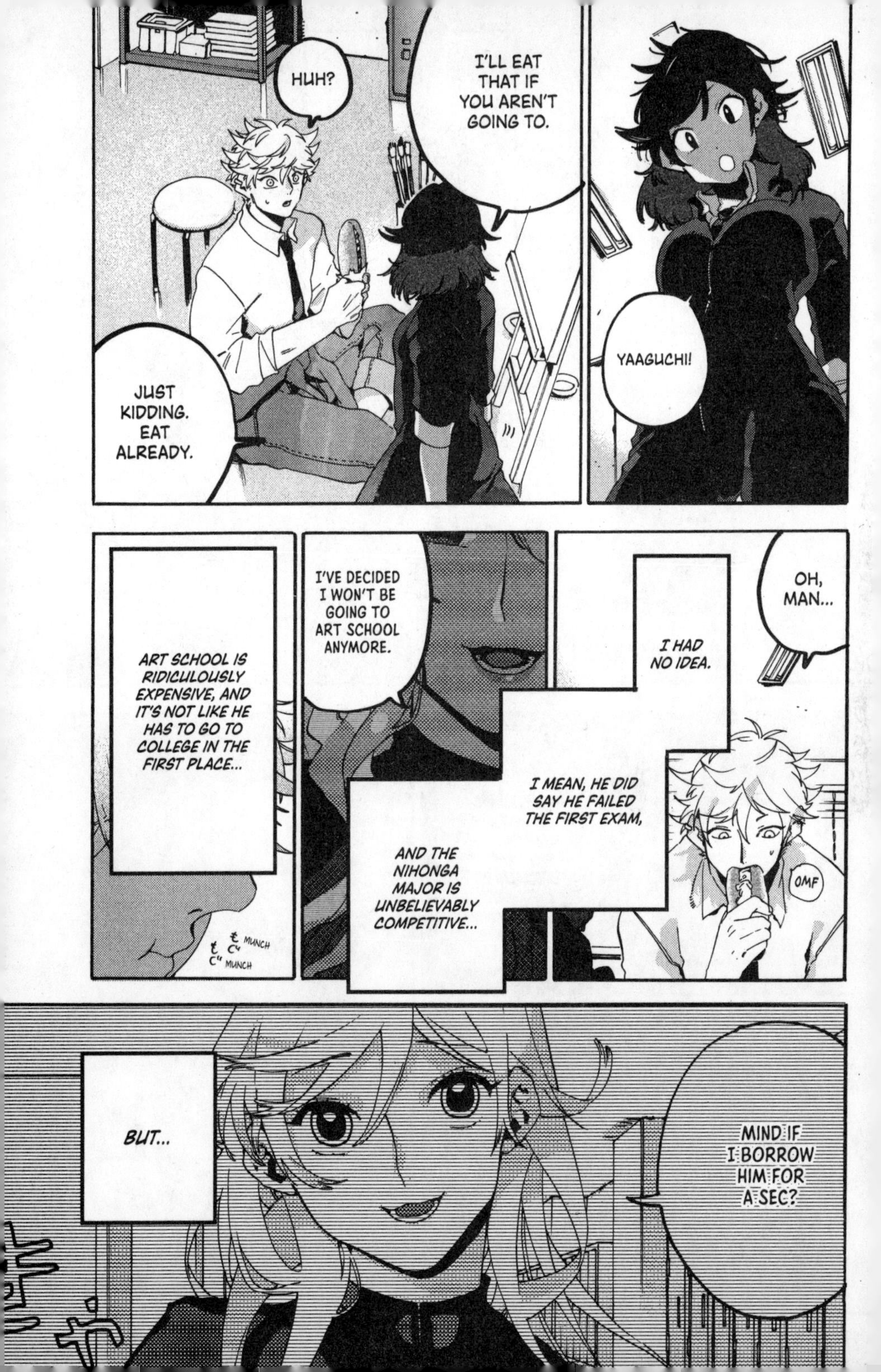
YAAGUCHI!
I'LL EAT THAT IF YOU AREN'T GOING TO.
HUH?
JUST KIDDING. EAT ALREADY.
OH, MAN...
I HAD NO IDEA.
OMF
I MEAN, HE DID SAY HE FAILED THE FIRST EXAM,
AND THE NIHONGA MAJOR IS UNBELIEVABLY COMPETITIVE...
I'VE DECIDED I WON'T BE GOING TO ART SCHOOL ANYMORE.
ART SCHOOL IS RIDICULOUSLY EXPENSIVE, AND IT'S NOT LIKE HE HAS TO GO TO COLLEGE IN THE FIRST PLACE...
MUNCH
MUNCH
MIND IF I BORROW HIM FOR A SEC?
BUT...

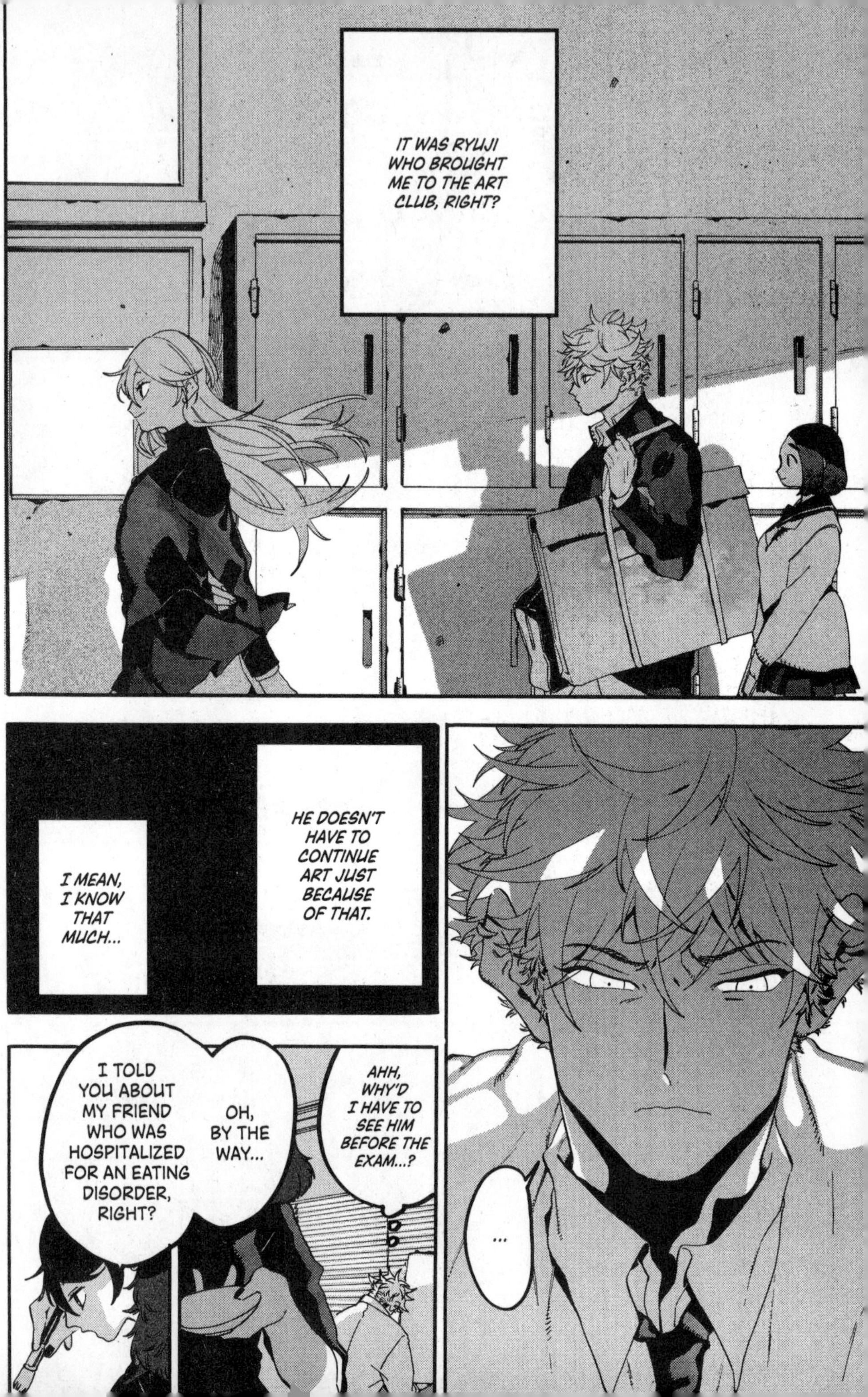
IT WAS RYUJI WHO BROUGHT ME TO THE ART CLUB, RIGHT?
...
HE DOESN'T HAVE TO CONTINUE ART JUST BECAUSE OF THAT.
I MEAN, I KNOW THAT MUCH...
AHH, WHY'D I HAVE TO SEE HIM BEFORE THE EXAM...?
OH, BY THE WAY...
I TOLD YOU ABOUT MY FRIEND WHO WAS HOSPITALIZED FOR AN EATING DISORDER, RIGHT?

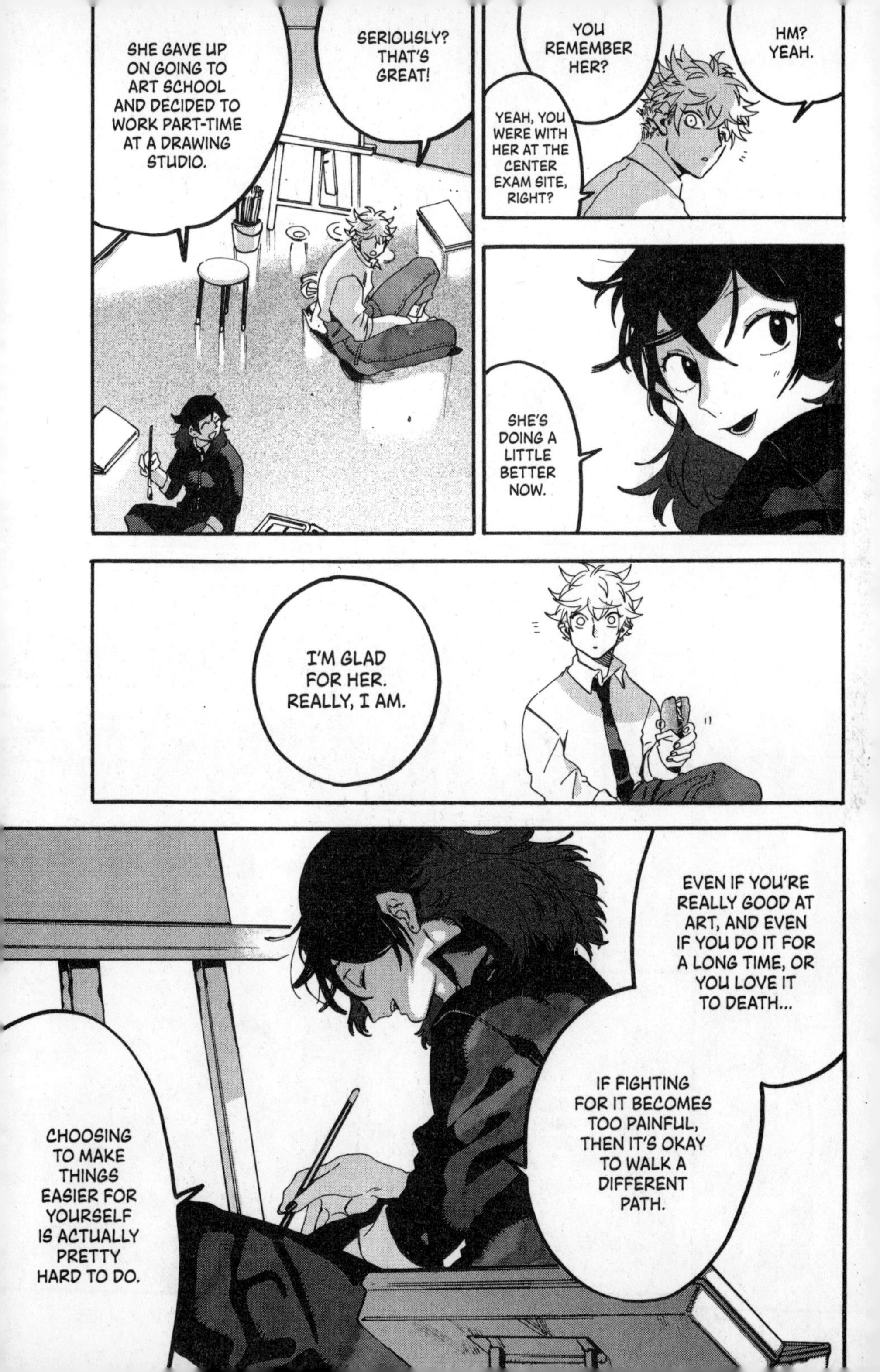
HM? YEAH.
YOU REMEMBER HER?
YEAH, YOU WERE WITH HER AT THE CENTER EXAM SITE, RIGHT?
SHE'S DOING A LITTLE BETTER NOW.
SERIOUSLY? THAT'S GREAT!
SHE GAVE UP ON GOING TO ART SCHOOL AND DECIDED TO WORK PART-TIME AT A DRAWING STUDIO.
I'M GLAD FOR HER. REALLY, I AM.
EVEN IF YOU'RE REALLY GOOD AT ART, AND EVEN IF YOU DO IT FOR A LONG TIME, OR YOU LOVE IT TO DEATH...
IF FIGHTING FOR IT BECOMES TOO PAINFUL, THEN IT'S OKAY TO WALK A DIFFERENT PATH.
CHOOSING TO MAKE THINGS EASIER FOR YOURSELF IS ACTUALLY PRETTY HARD TO DO.

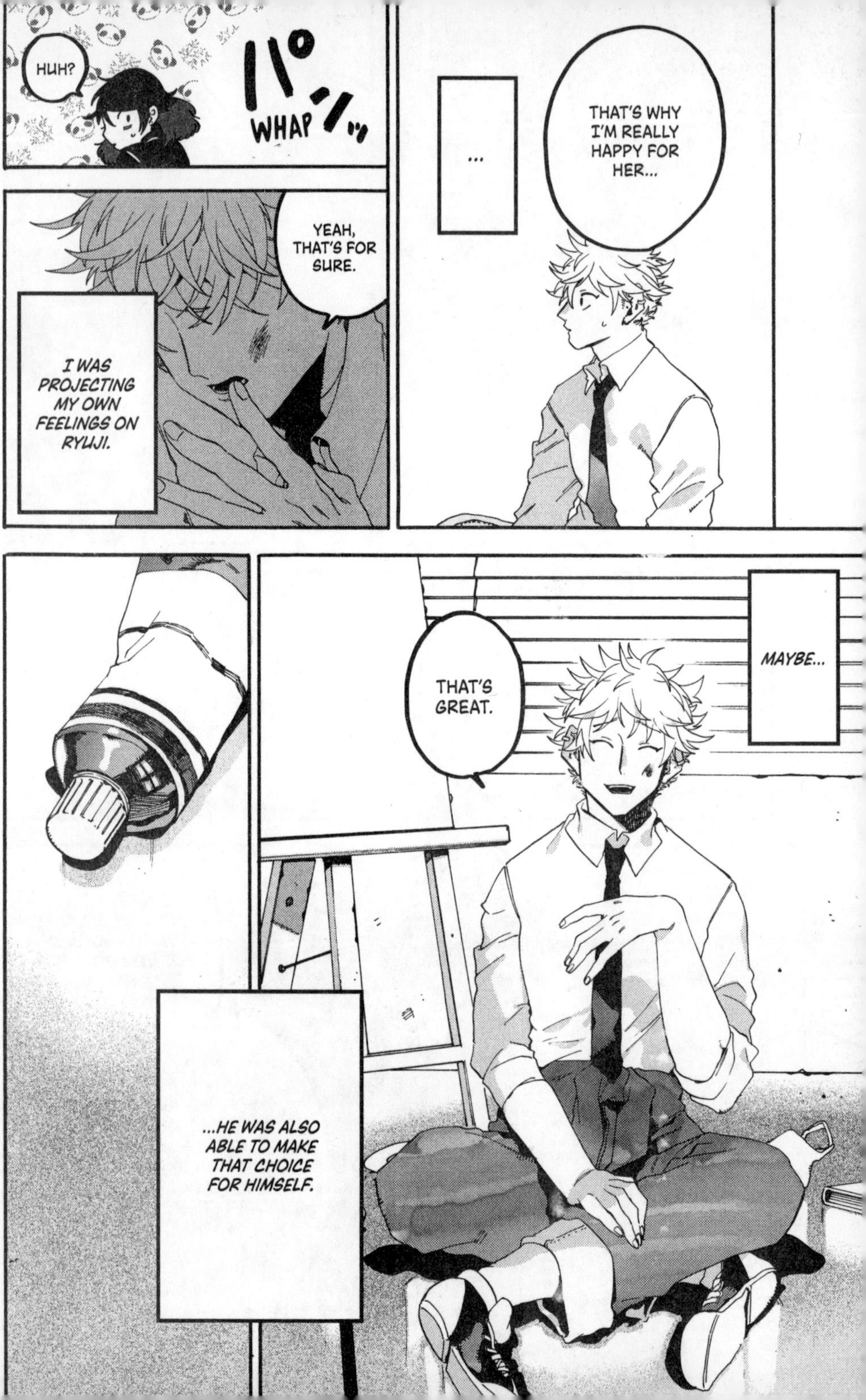
THAT'S WHY I'M REALLY HAPPY FOR HER...
...
HUH?
WHAP
YEAH, THAT'S FOR SURE.
I WAS PROJECTING MY OWN FEELINGS ON RYUJI.
MAYBE...
THAT'S GREAT.
...HE WAS ALSO ABLE TO MAKE THAT CHOICE FOR HIMSELF.

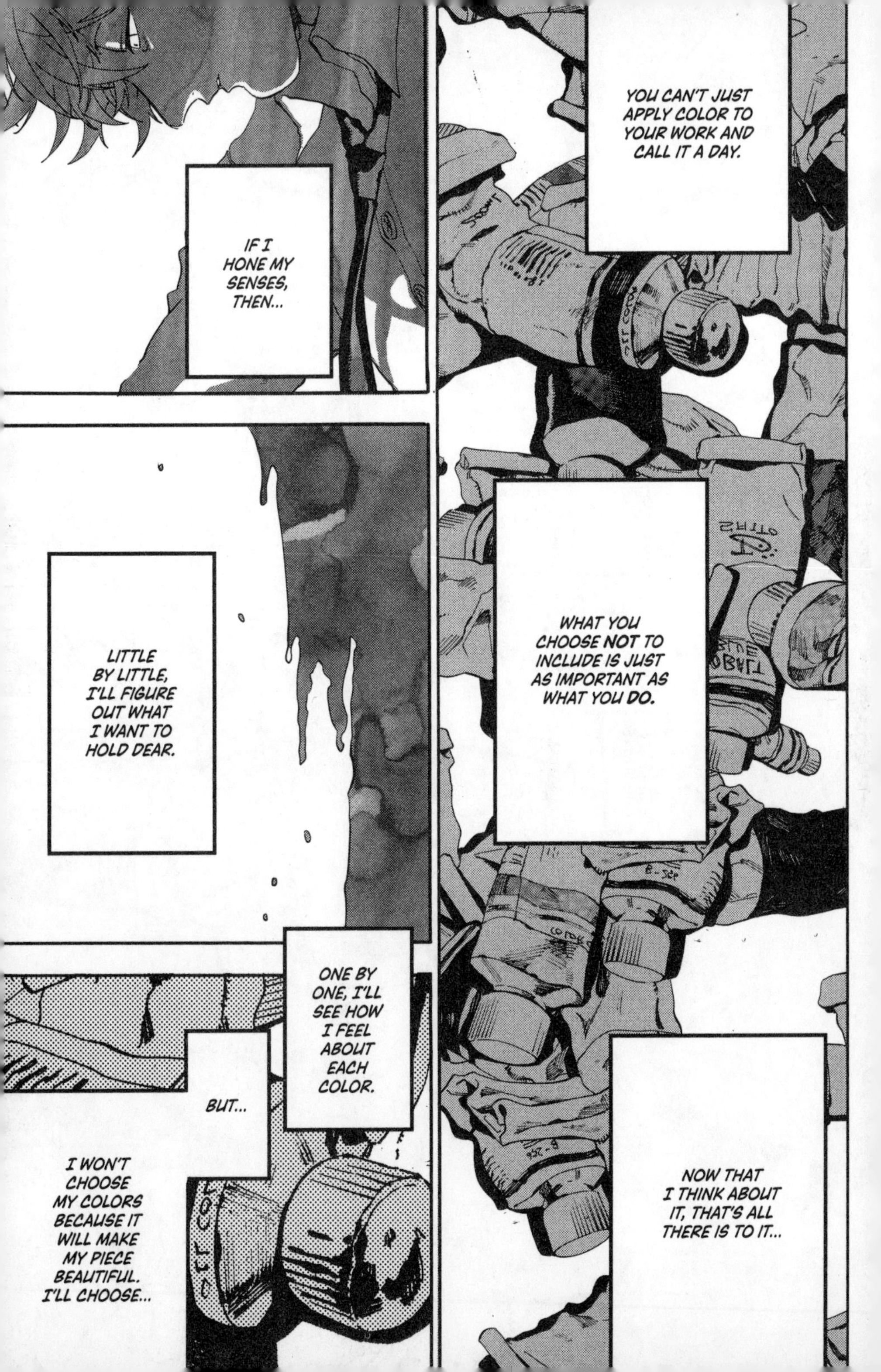

YOU CAN'T JUST APPLY COLOR TO YOUR WORK AND CALL IT A DAY.
WHAT YOU CHOOSE **NOT** TO INCLUDE IS JUST AS IMPORTANT AS WHAT YOU **DO**.
NOW THAT I THINK ABOUT IT, THAT'S ALL THERE IS TO IT...
IF I HONE MY SENSES, THEN...
LITTLE BY LITTLE, I'LL FIGURE OUT WHAT I WANT TO HOLD DEAR.
ONE BY ONE, I'LL SEE HOW I FEEL ABOUT EACH COLOR.
BUT...
I WON'T CHOOSE MY COLORS BECAUSE IT WILL MAKE MY PIECE BEAUTIFUL. I'LL CHOOSE...

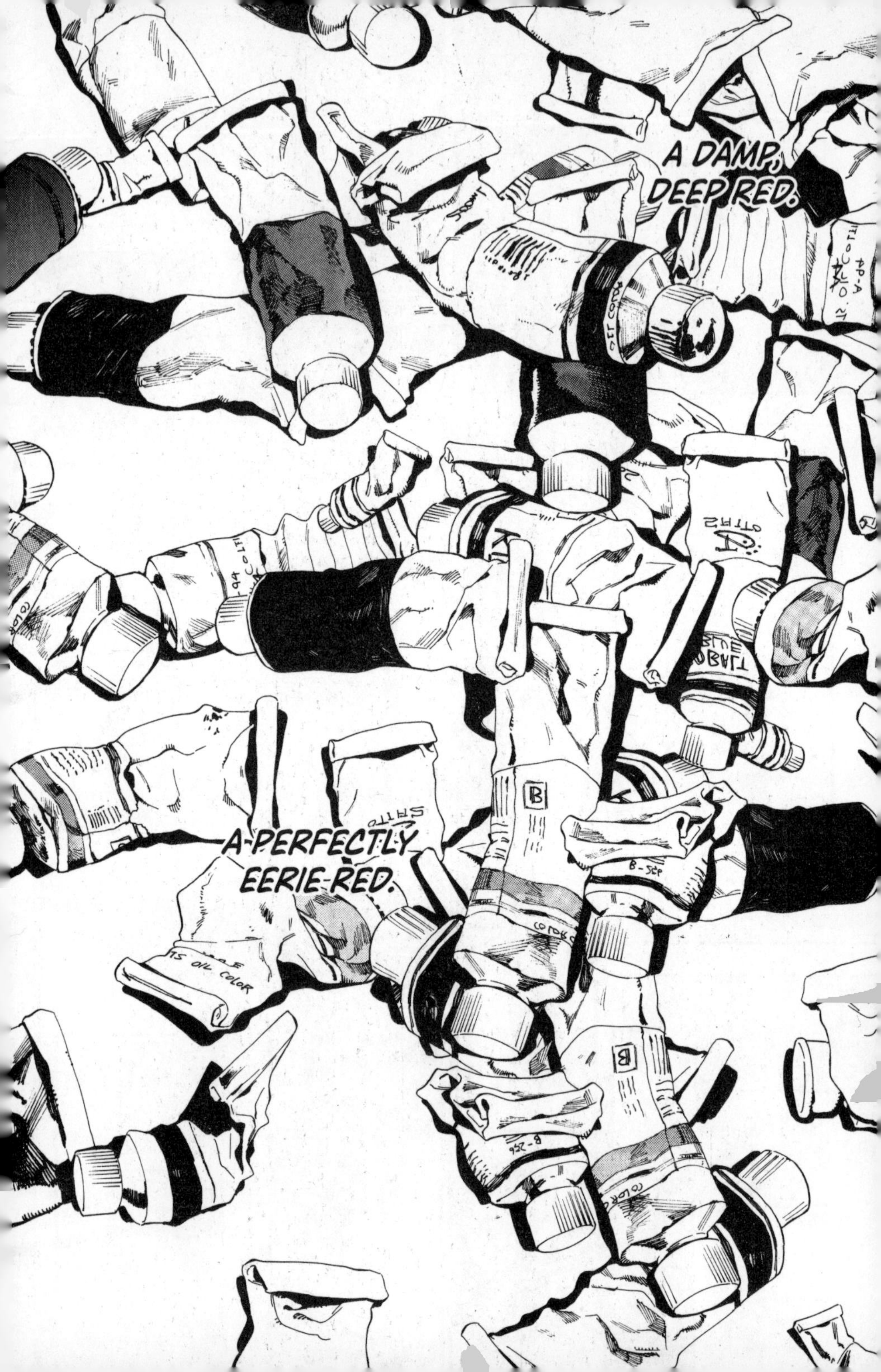
A DAMP, DEEP RED.
A PERFECTLY EERIE RED.

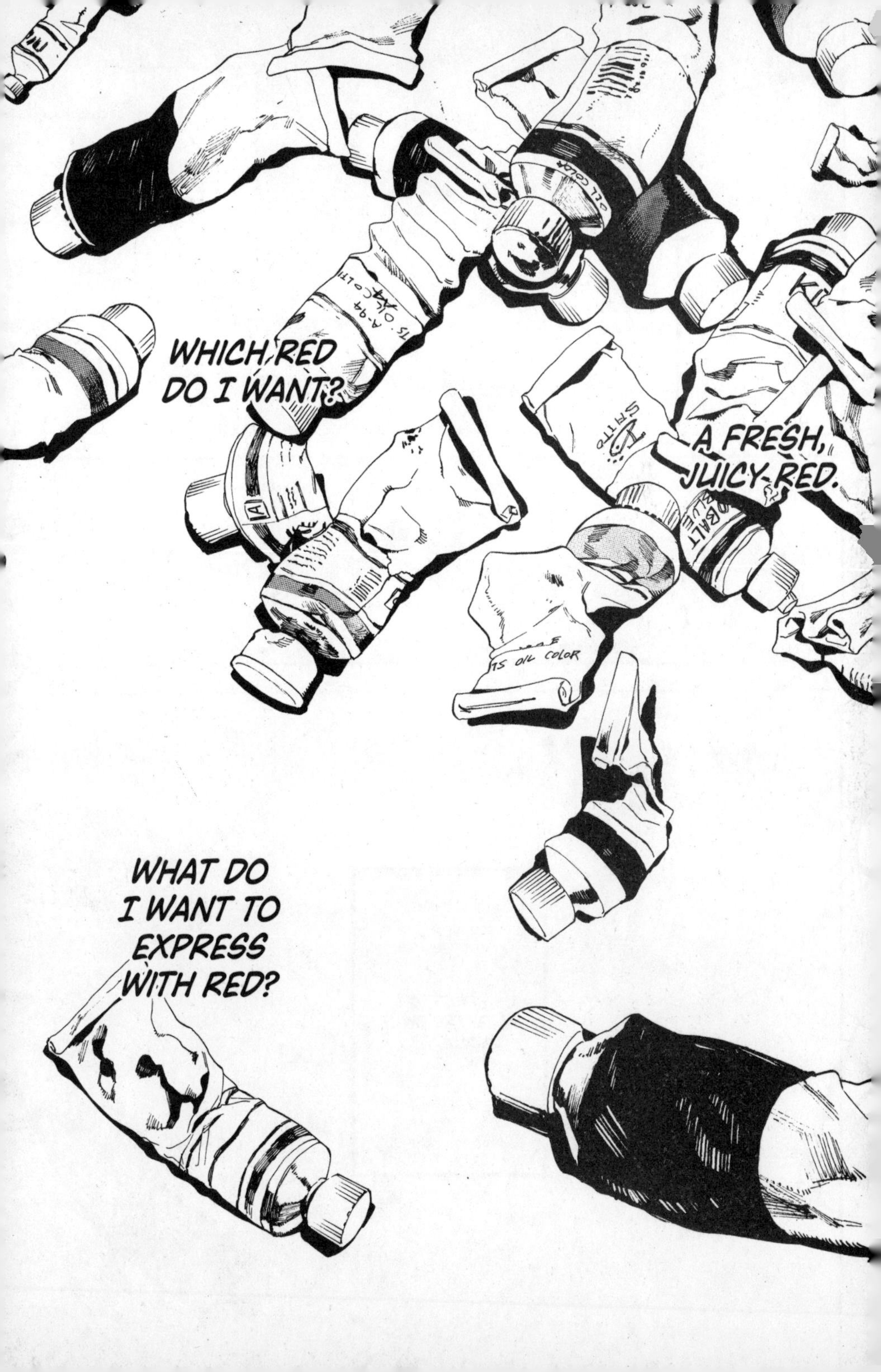
WHICH RED DO I WANT?
A FRESH, JUICY RED.
WHAT DO I WANT TO EXPRESS WITH RED?

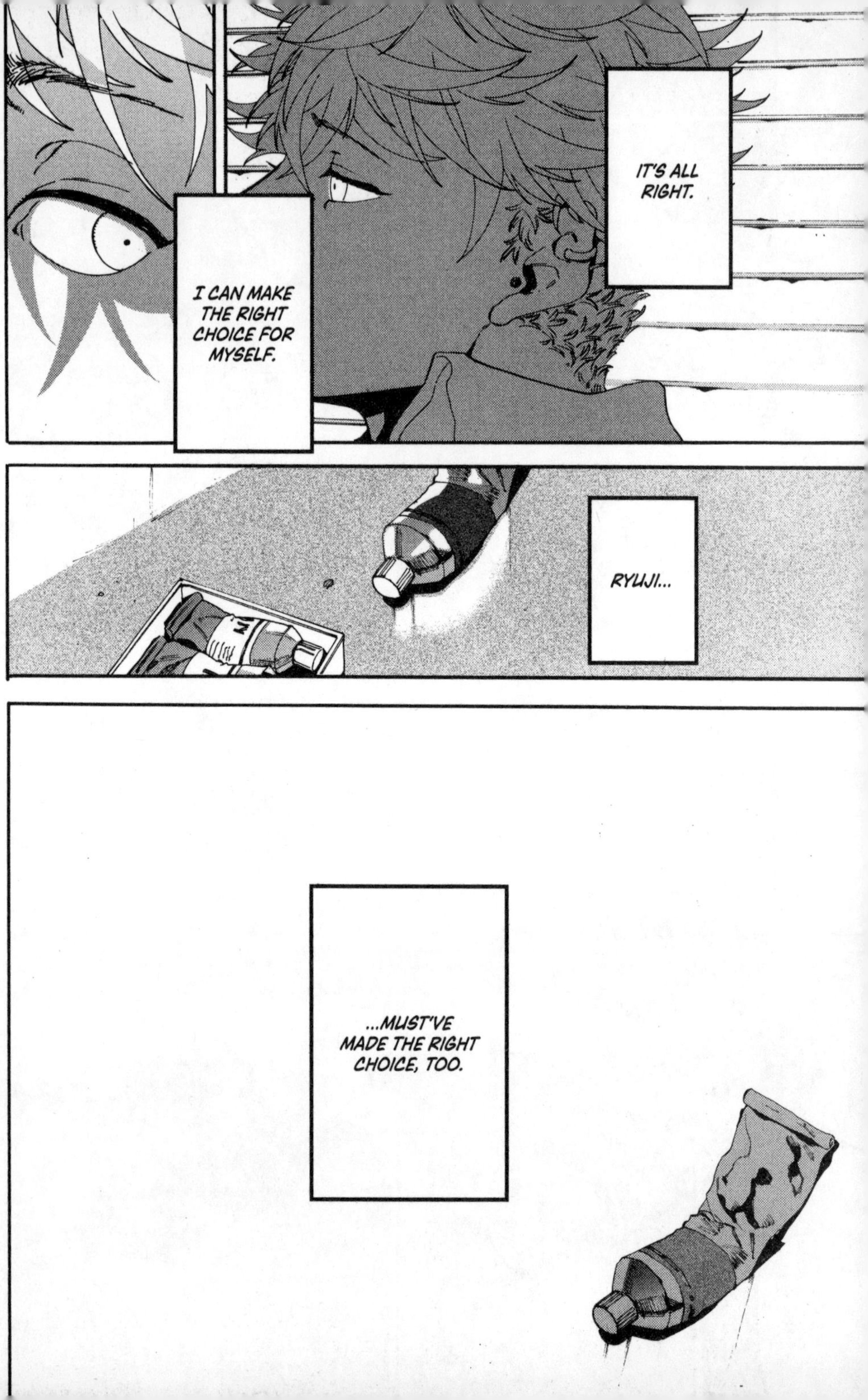
IT'S ALL RIGHT.
I CAN MAKE THE RIGHT CHOICE FOR MYSELF.
RYUJI...
...MUST'VE MADE THE RIGHT CHOICE, TOO.

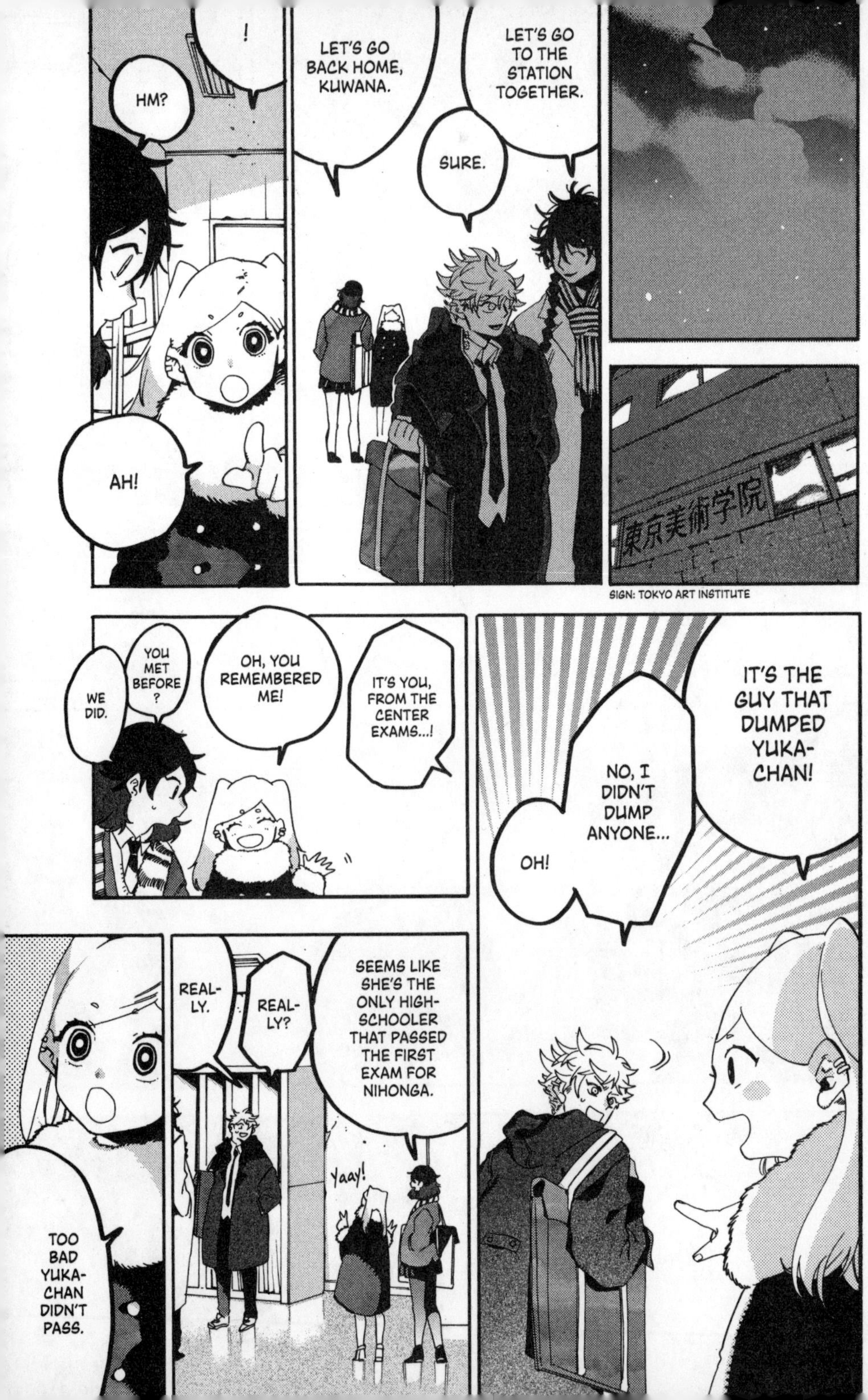
東京美術学院
LET'S GO TO THE STATION TOGETHER.
LET'S GO BACK HOME, KUWANA.
SURE.
!
HM?
AH!
SIGN: TOKYO ART INSTITUTE
IT'S THE GUY THAT DUMPED YUKA-CHAN!
NO, I DIDN'T DUMP ANYONE...
OH!
IT'S YOU, FROM THE CENTER EXAMS...!
OH, YOU REMEMBERED ME!
YOU MET BEFORE?
WE DID.
SEEMS LIKE SHE'S THE ONLY HIGH-SCHOOLER THAT PASSED THE FIRST EXAM FOR NIHONGA.
REAL-LY?
REAL-LY.
Yaay!
TOO BAD YUKA-CHAN DIDN'T PASS.

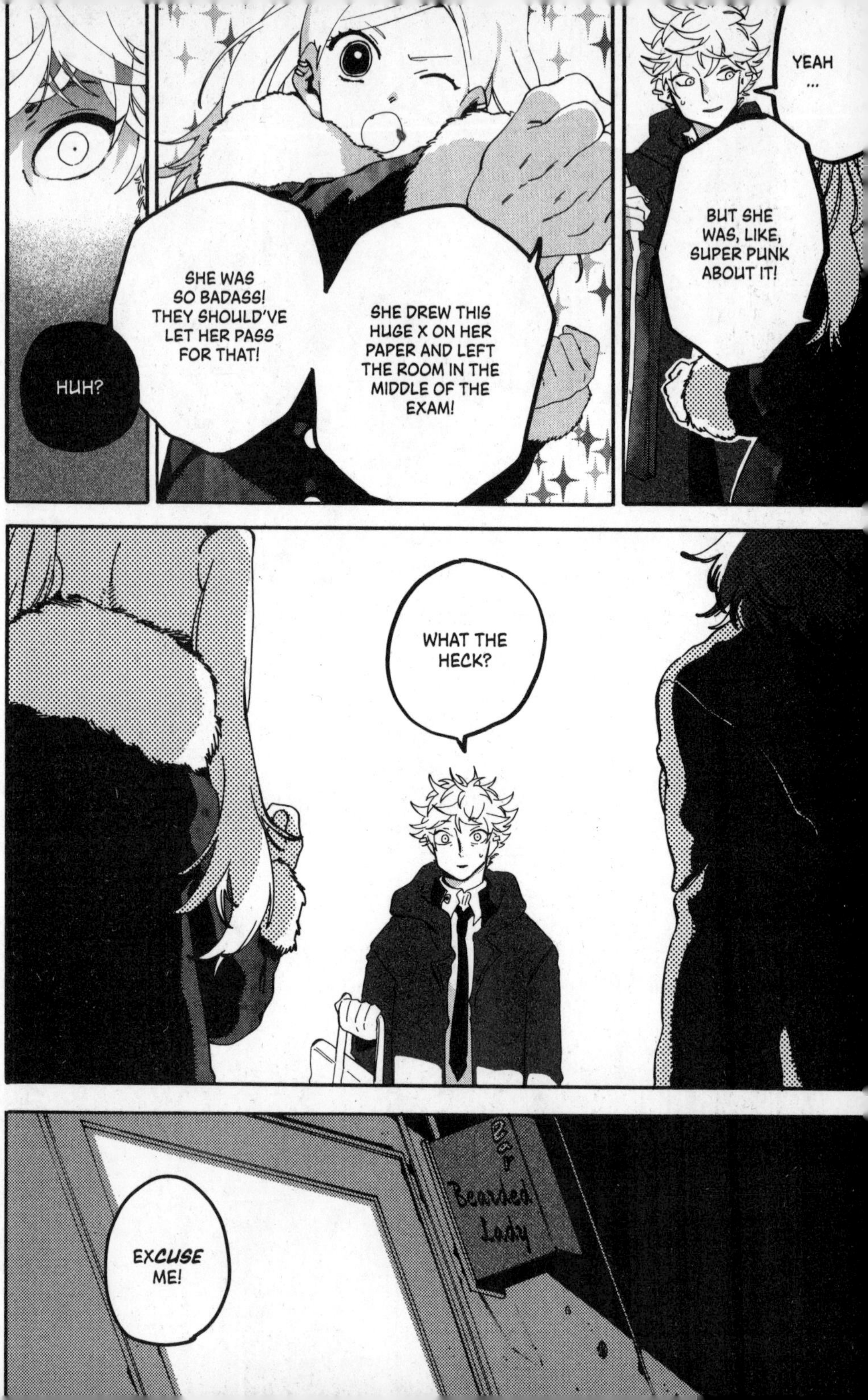
YEAH ...
BUT SHE WAS, LIKE, SUPER PUNK ABOUT IT!
SHE DREW THIS HUGE X ON HER PAPER AND LEFT THE ROOM IN THE MIDDLE OF THE EXAM!
SHE WAS SO BADASS! THEY SHOULD'VE LET HER PASS FOR THAT!
HUH?
WHAT THE HECK?
Bar
Bearded Lady
EXCUSE ME!

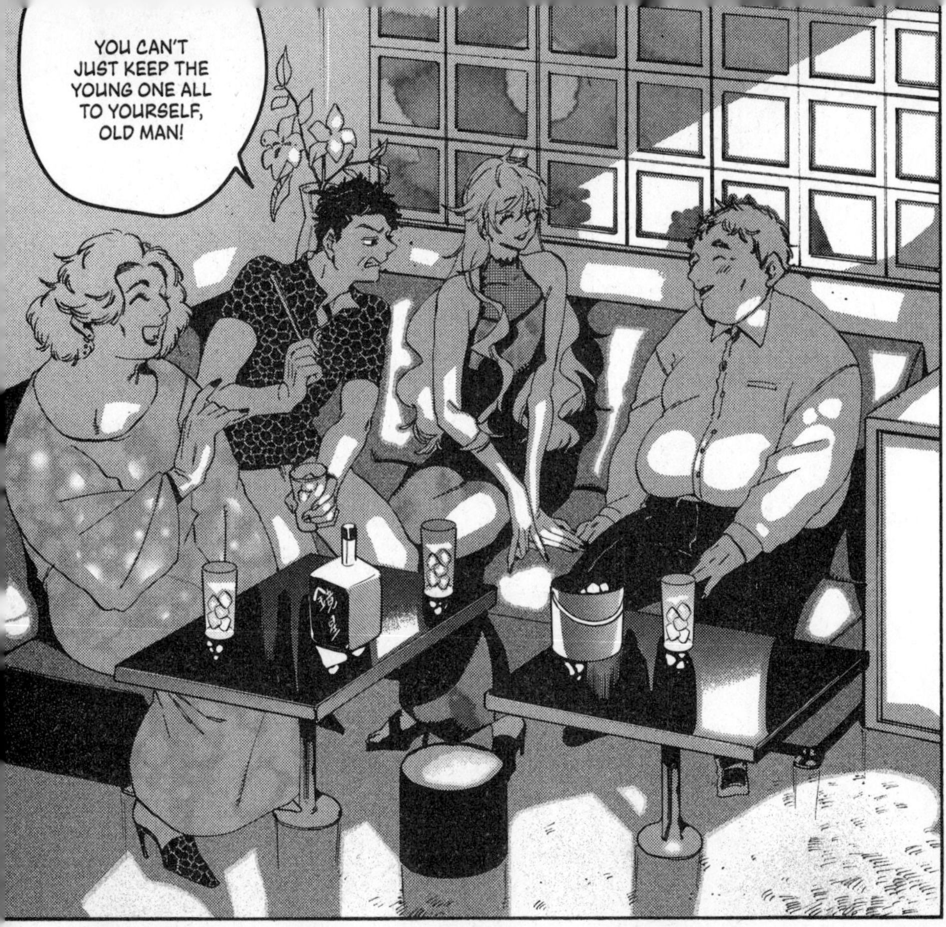
YOU CAN'T JUST KEEP THE YOUNG ONE ALL TO YOURSELF, OLD MAN!

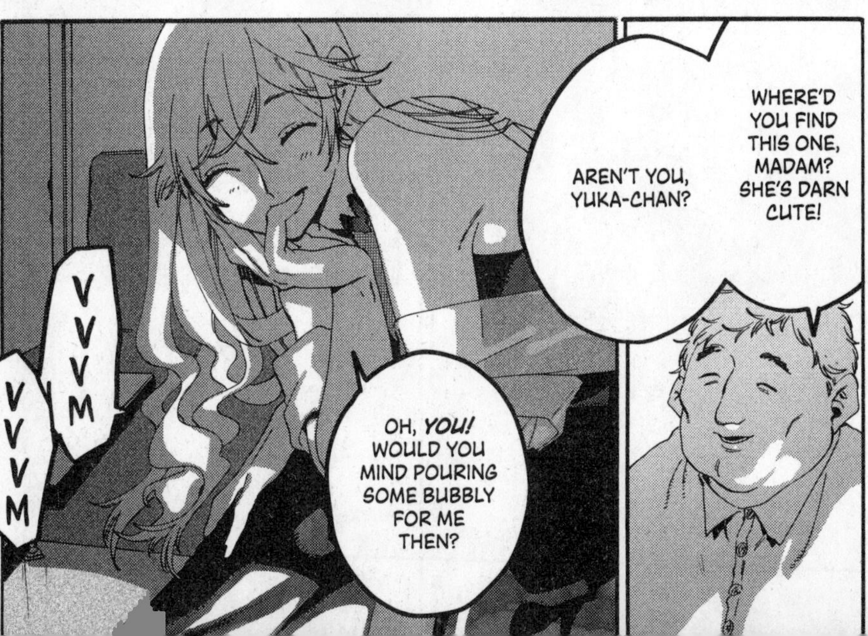
WHERE'D YOU FIND THIS ONE, MADAM? SHE'S DARN CUTE!
AREN'T YOU, YUKA-CHAN?
OH, *YOU!* WOULD YOU MIND POURING SOME BUBBLY FOR ME THEN?
VVVM
VVVM

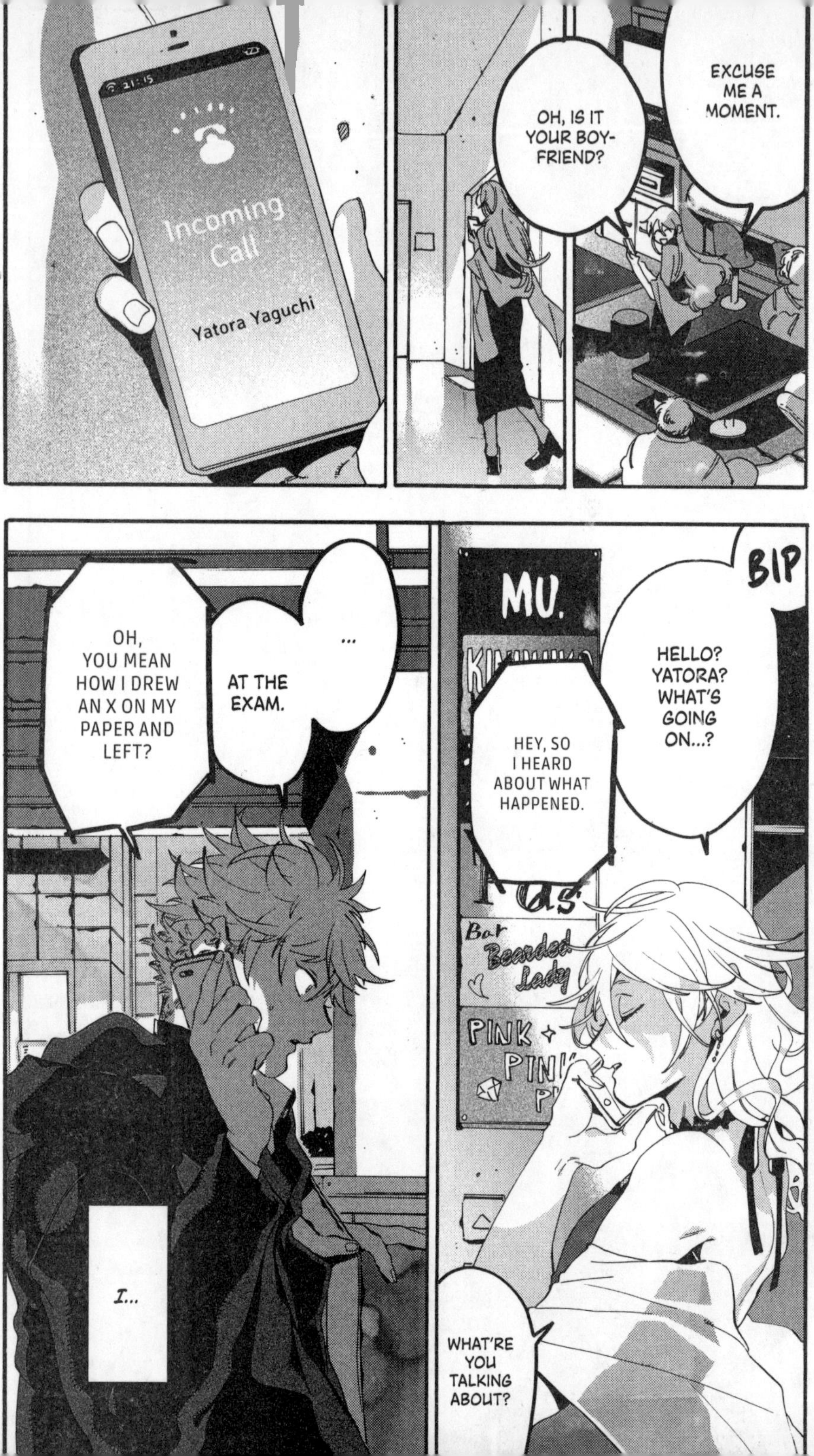
EXCUSE ME A MOMENT.
OH, IS IT YOUR BOY-FRIEND?
21:15
Incoming Call
Yatora Yaguchi
BIP
HELLO? YATORA? WHAT'S GOING ON...?
MU.
HEY, SO I HEARD ABOUT WHAT HAPPENED.
Bar Bearded Lady
WHAT'RE YOU TALKING ABOUT?
...
AT THE EXAM.
OH, YOU MEAN HOW I DREW AN X ON MY PAPER AND LEFT?
I...

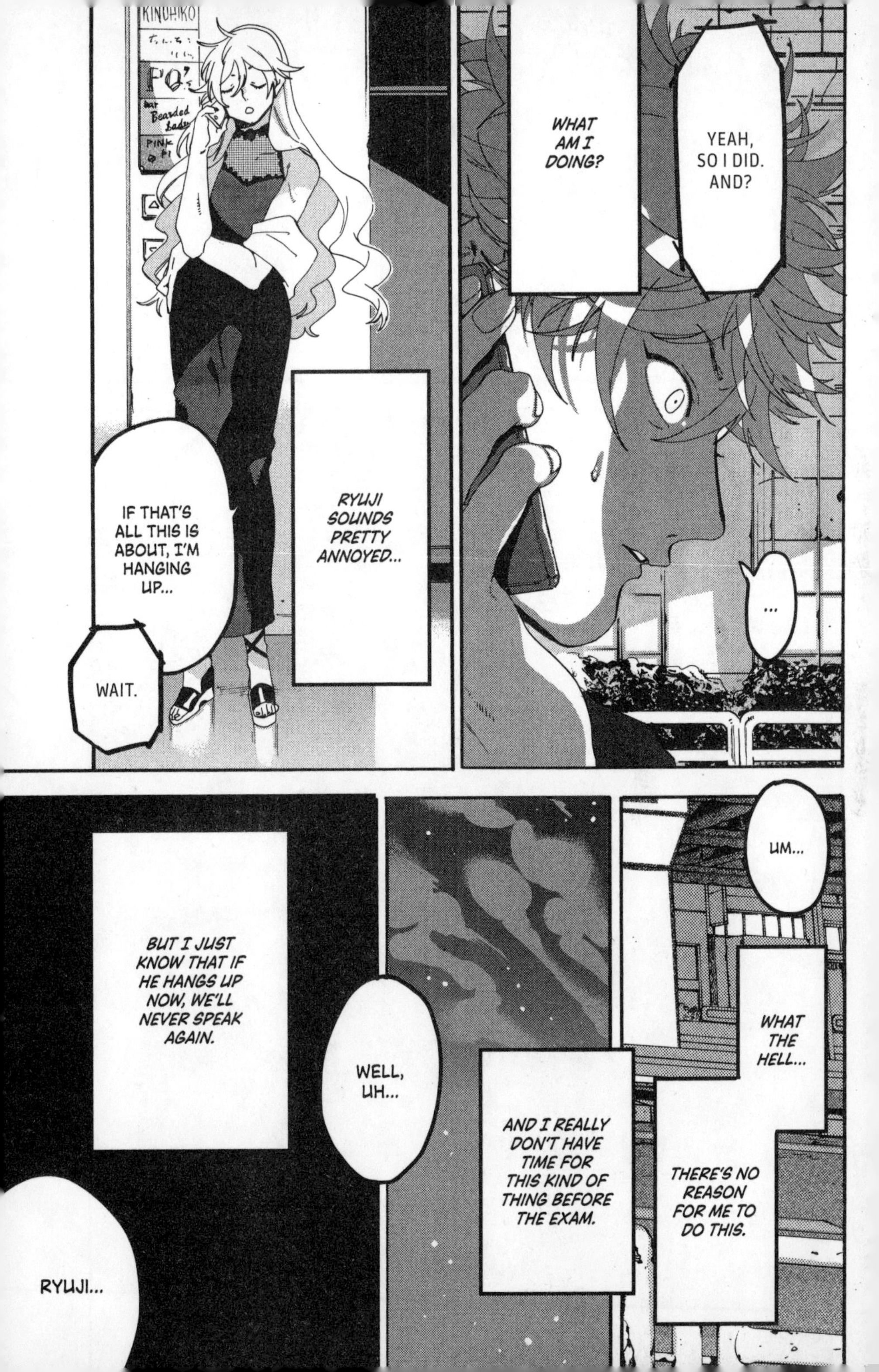
YEAH, SO I DID. AND?
WHAT AM I DOING?
...
RYUJI SOUNDS PRETTY ANNOYED...
IF THAT'S ALL THIS IS ABOUT, I'M HANGING UP...
WAIT.
UM...
WHAT THE HELL...
THERE'S NO REASON FOR ME TO DO THIS.
AND I REALLY DON'T HAVE TIME FOR THIS KIND OF THING BEFORE THE EXAM.
WELL, UH...
BUT I JUST KNOW THAT IF HE HANGS UP NOW, WE'LL NEVER SPEAK AGAIN.
RYUJI...

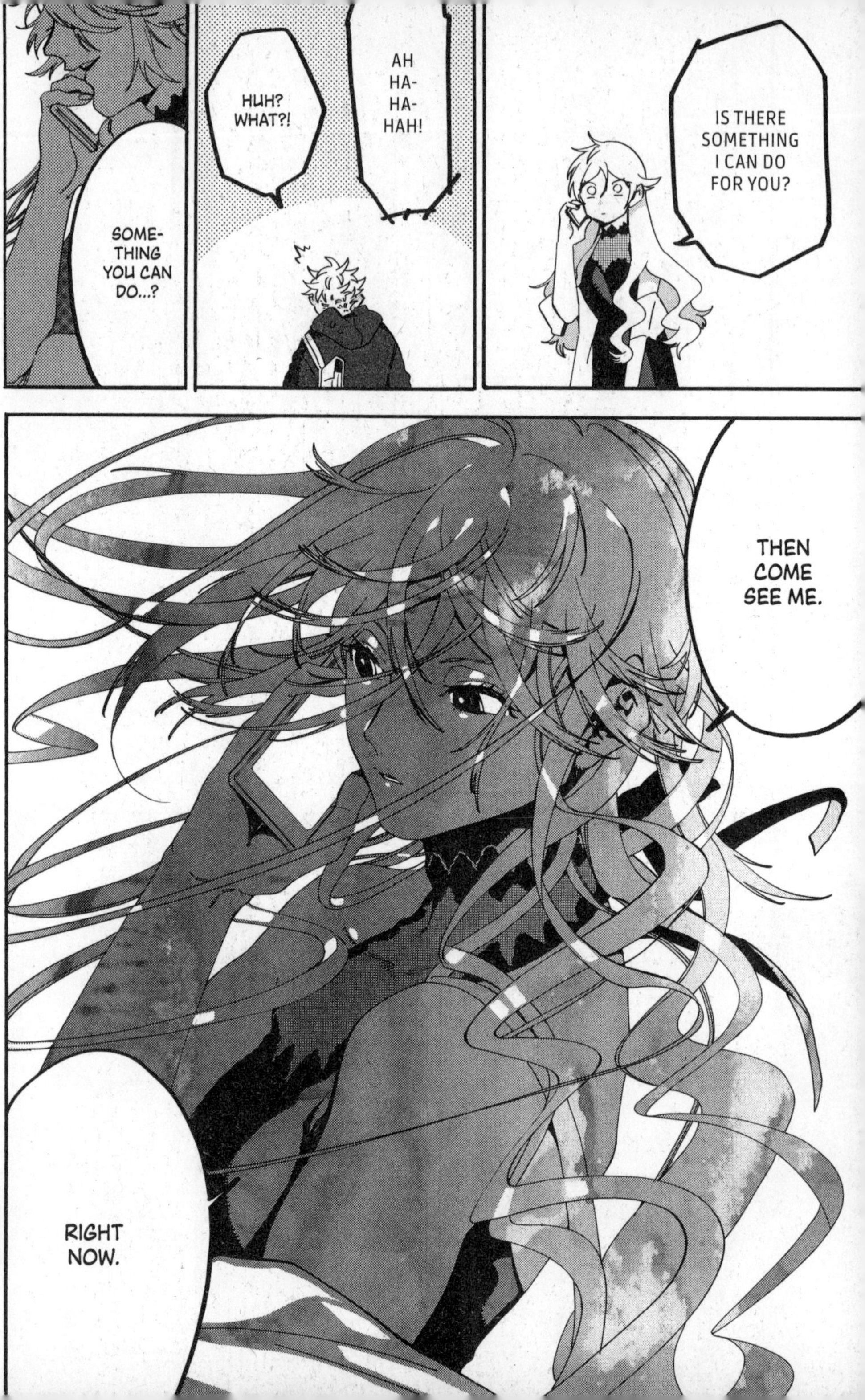
IS THERE SOMETHING I CAN DO FOR YOU?
AH HA-HA-HAH!
HUH? WHAT?!
SOME-THING YOU CAN DO...?
THEN COME SEE ME.
RIGHT NOW.

STROKE 19 END

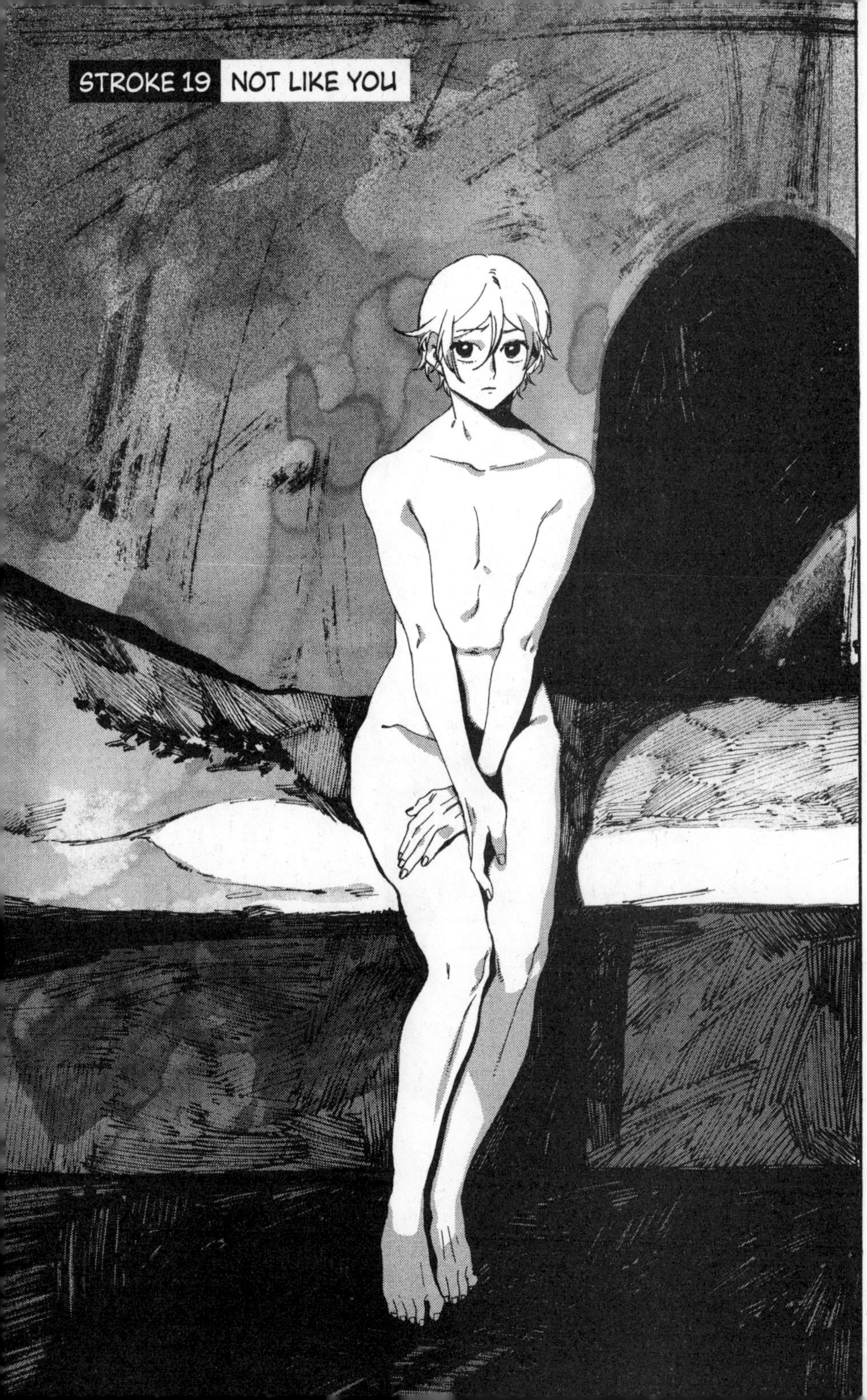
STROKE 19
NOT LIKE YOU

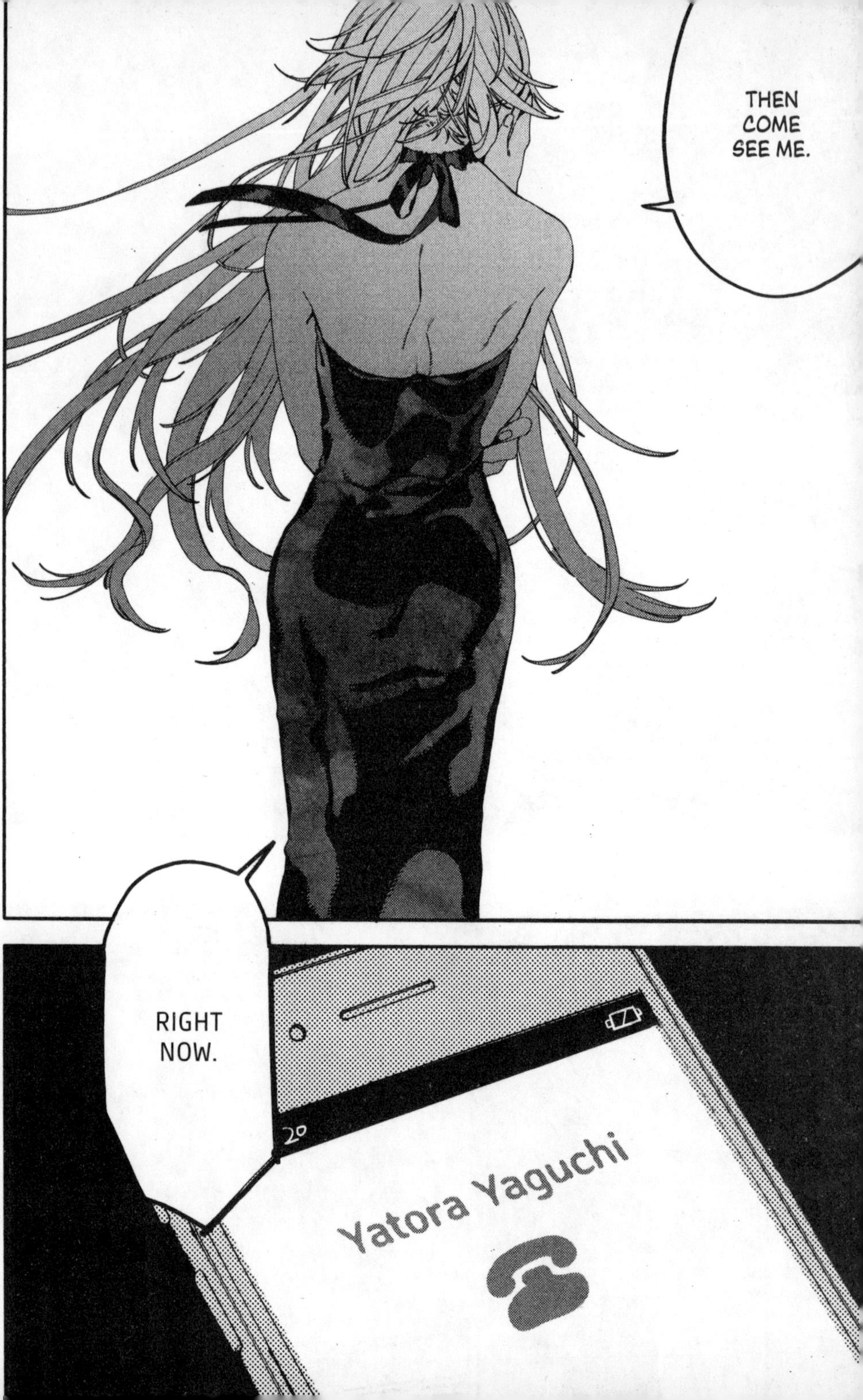
THEN COME SEE ME.
RIGHT NOW.
20
Yatora Yaguchi

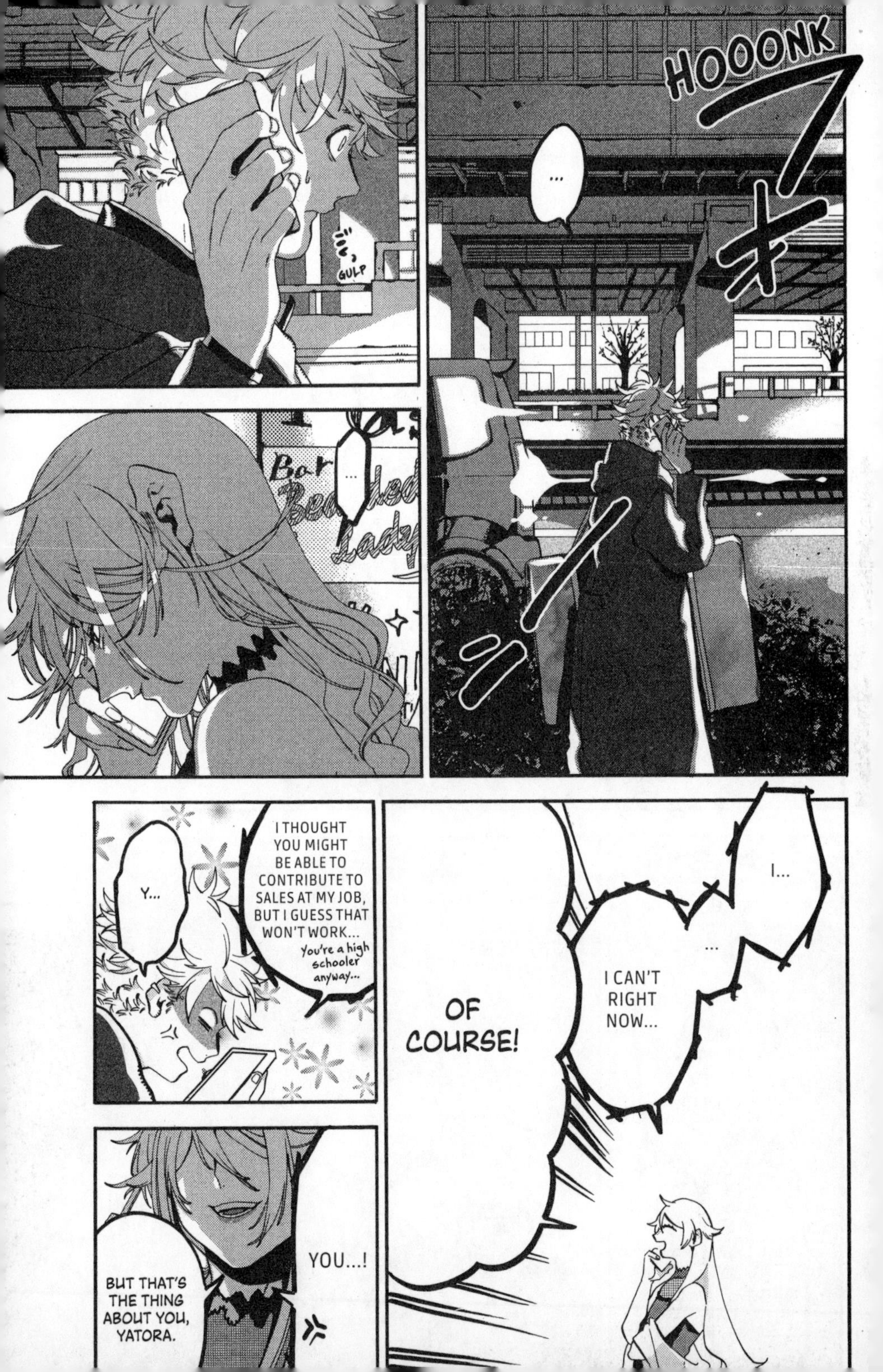
HOOONK
…
GULP
…
Bar
I…
…
I CAN'T RIGHT NOW…
OF COURSE!
I THOUGHT YOU MIGHT BE ABLE TO CONTRIBUTE TO SALES AT MY JOB, BUT I GUESS THAT WON'T WORK…
You're a high schooler anyway…
Y…
YOU…!
BUT THAT'S THE THING ABOUT YOU, YATORA.

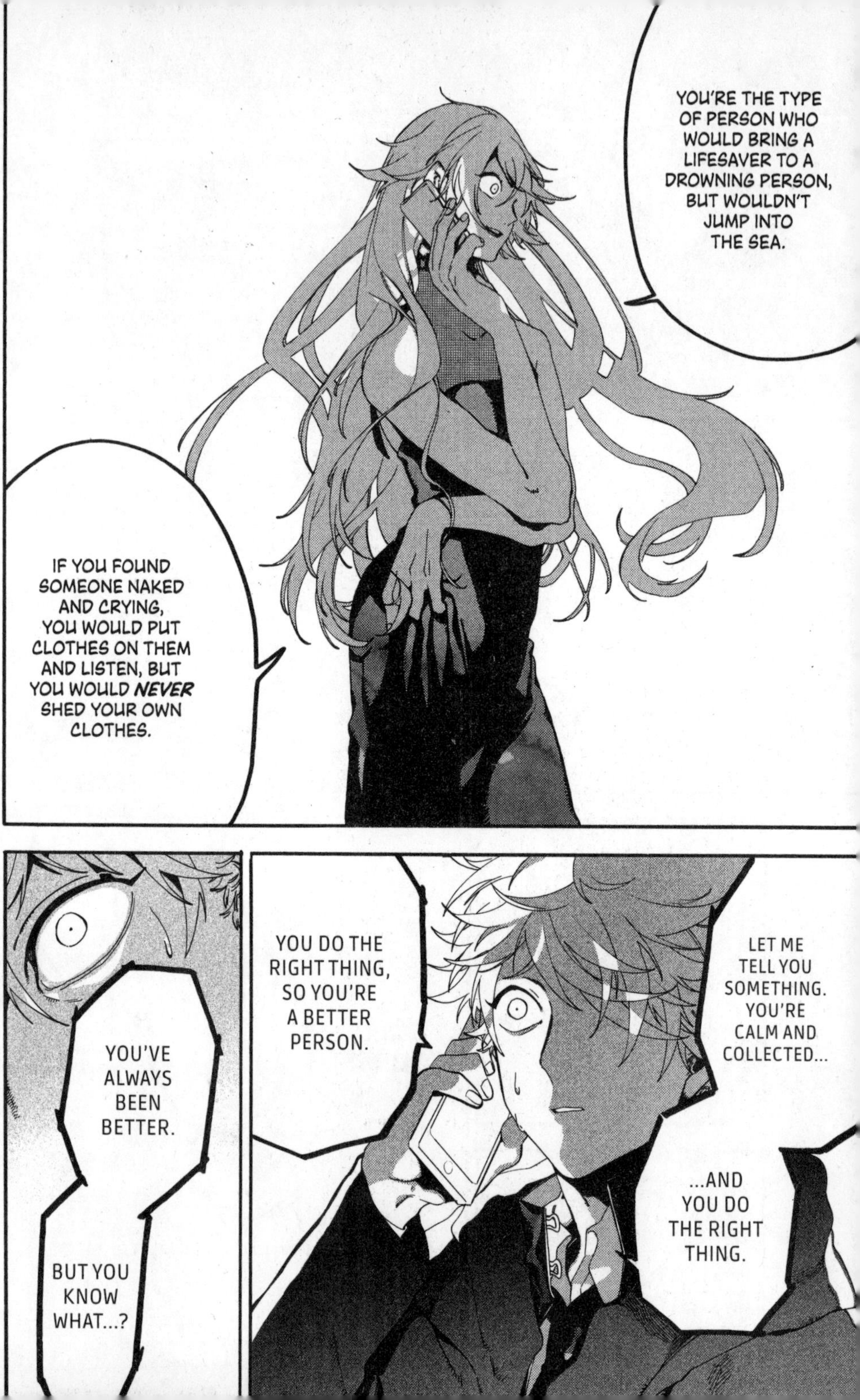
YOU'RE THE TYPE OF PERSON WHO WOULD BRING A LIFESAVER TO A DROWNING PERSON, BUT WOULDN'T JUMP INTO THE SEA.
IF YOU FOUND SOMEONE NAKED AND CRYING, YOU WOULD PUT CLOTHES ON THEM AND LISTEN, BUT YOU WOULD *NEVER* SHED YOUR OWN CLOTHES.
LET ME TELL YOU SOMETHING. YOU'RE CALM AND COLLECTED...
...AND YOU DO THE RIGHT THING.
YOU DO THE RIGHT THING, SO YOU'RE A BETTER PERSON.
YOU'VE ALWAYS BEEN BETTER.
BUT YOU KNOW WHAT...?

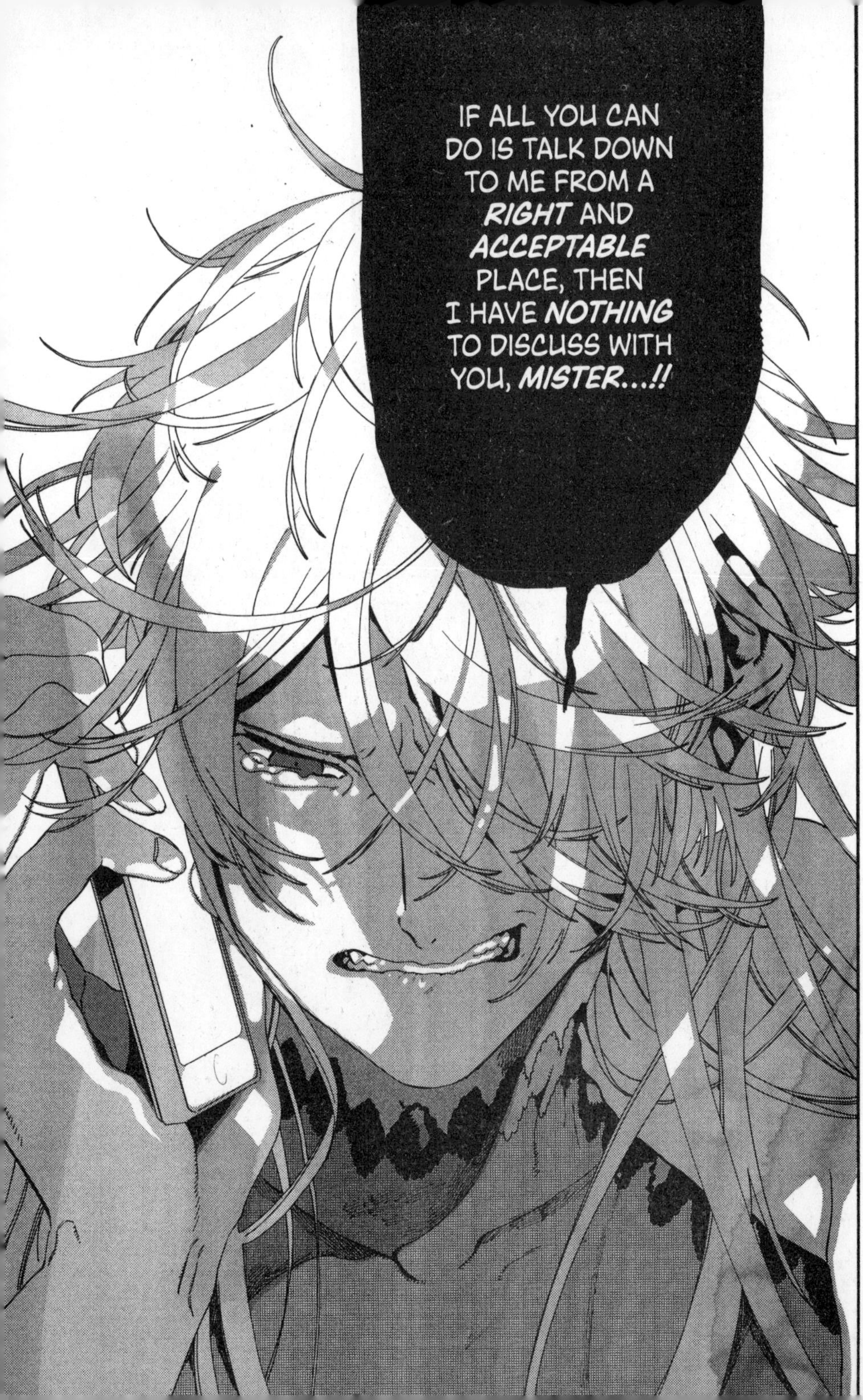
IF ALL YOU CAN DO IS TALK DOWN TO ME FROM A RIGHT AND ACCEPTABLE PLACE, THEN I HAVE NOTHING TO DISCUSS WITH YOU, MISTER...!!

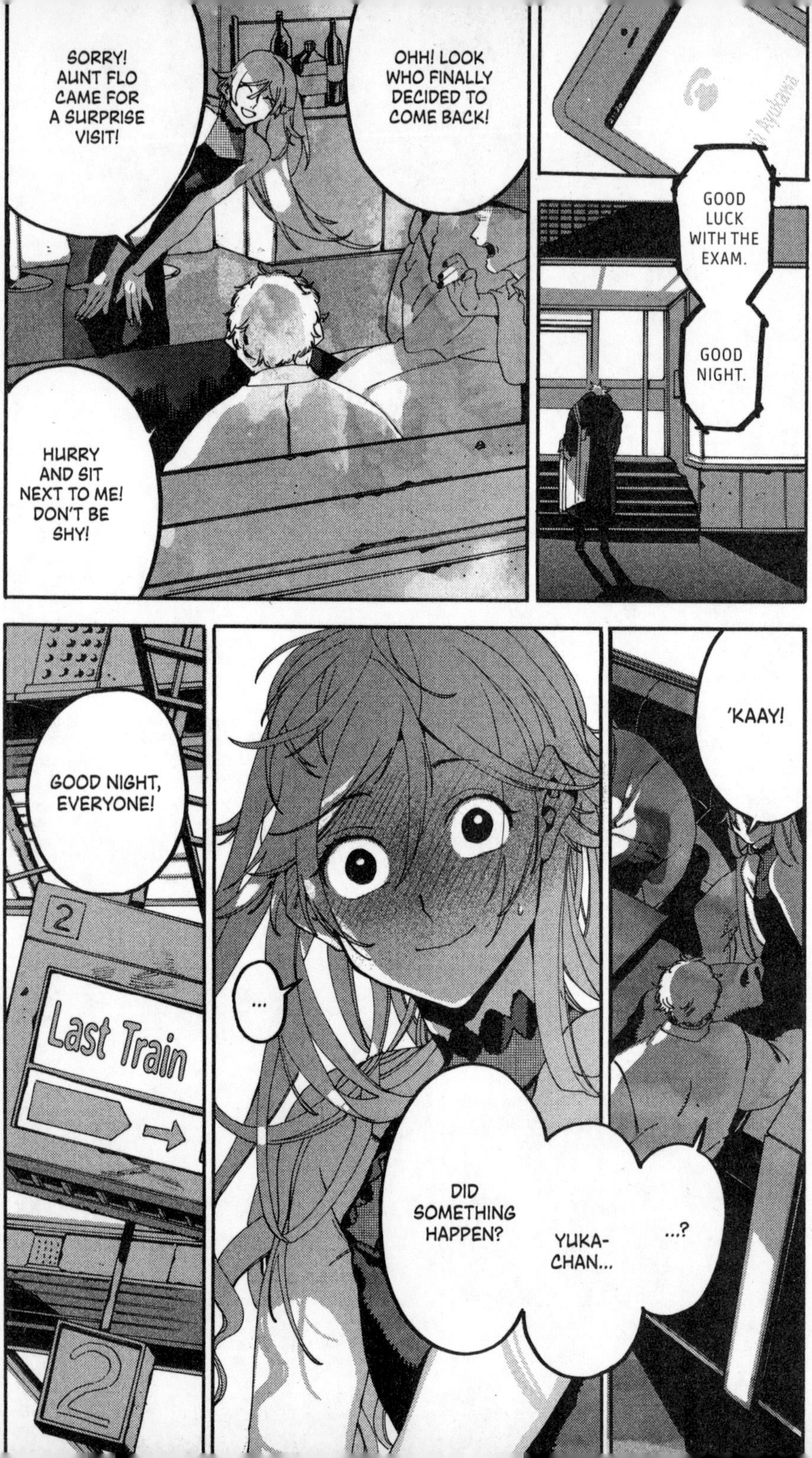
GOOD LUCK WITH THE EXAM.
GOOD NIGHT.
OHH! LOOK WHO FINALLY DECIDED TO COME BACK!
SORRY! AUNT FLO CAME FOR A SURPRISE VISIT!
HURRY AND SIT NEXT TO ME! DON'T BE SHY!
'KAAY!
...?
YUKA-CHAN...
DID SOMETHING HAPPEN?
...
GOOD NIGHT, EVERYONE!
2
Last Train
2

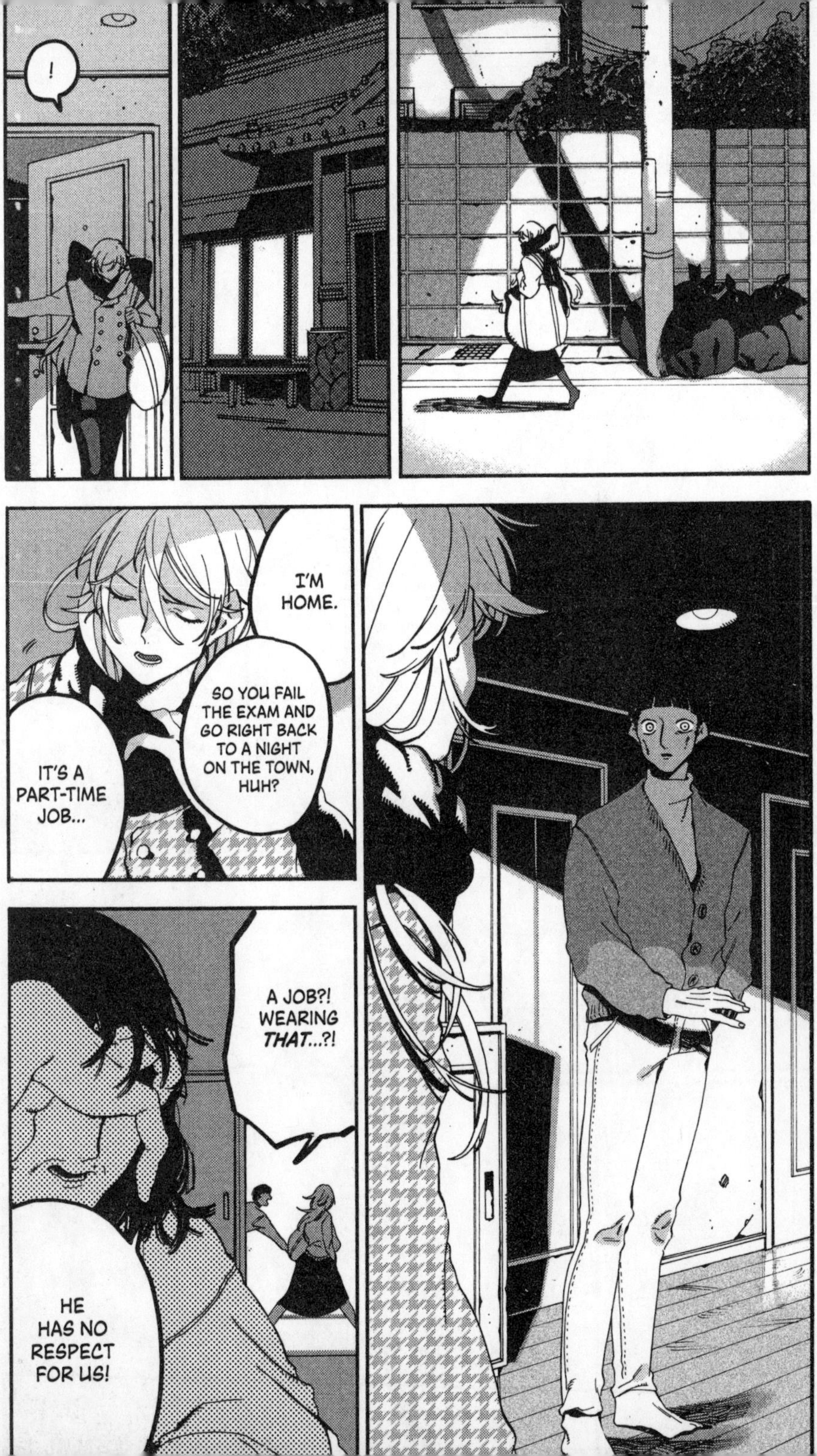
!
I'M HOME.
SO YOU FAIL THE EXAM AND GO RIGHT BACK TO A NIGHT ON THE TOWN, HUH?
IT'S A PART-TIME JOB...
A JOB?! WEARING *THAT*...?!
HE HAS NO RESPECT FOR US!

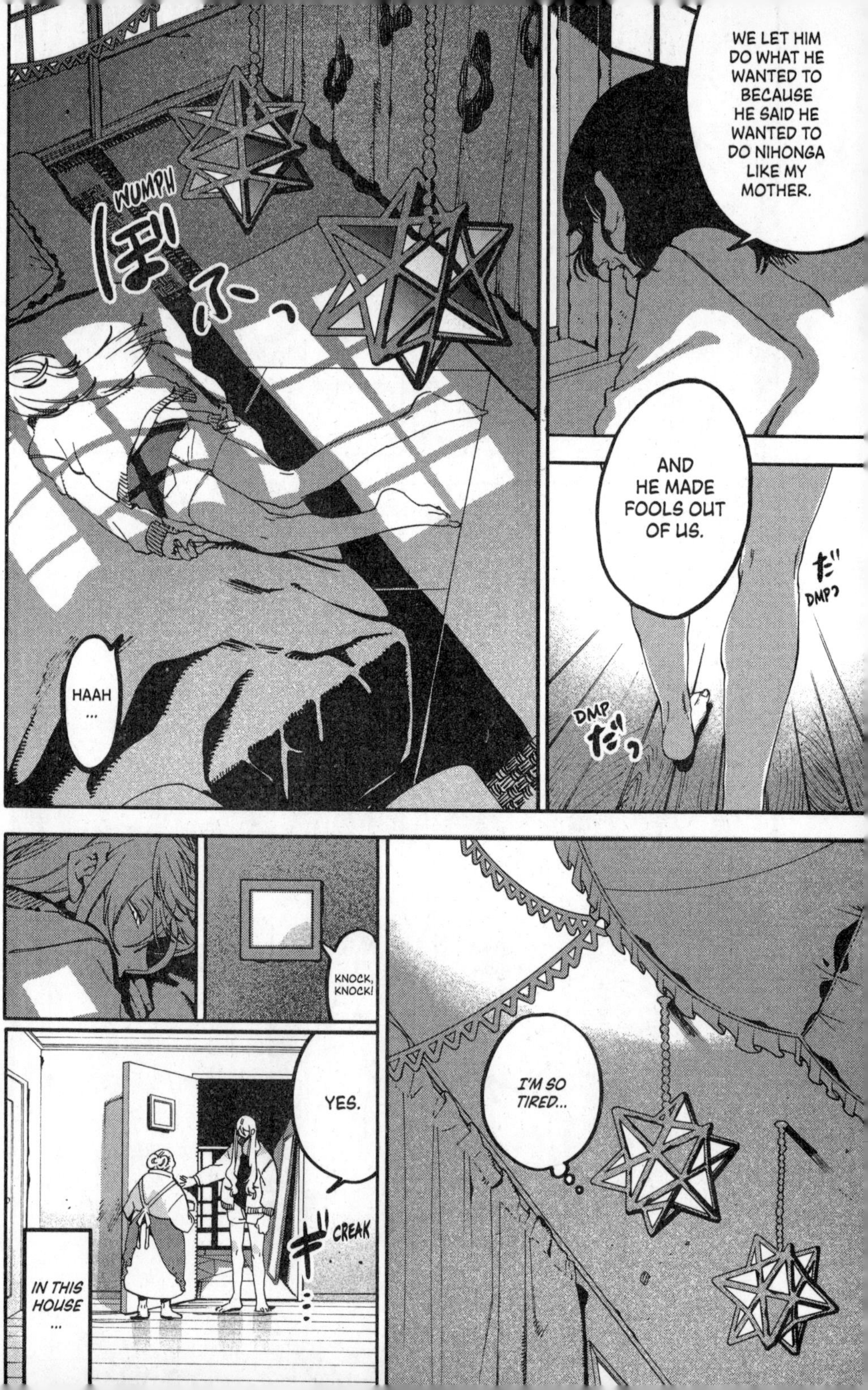
WE LET HIM DO WHAT HE WANTED TO BECAUSE HE SAID HE WANTED TO DO NIHONGA LIKE MY MOTHER.
AND HE MADE FOOLS OUT OF US.
DMP
DMP
WUMPH
HAAH ...
I'M SO TIRED...
KNOCK, KNOCK!
YES.
CREAK
IN THIS HOUSE ...

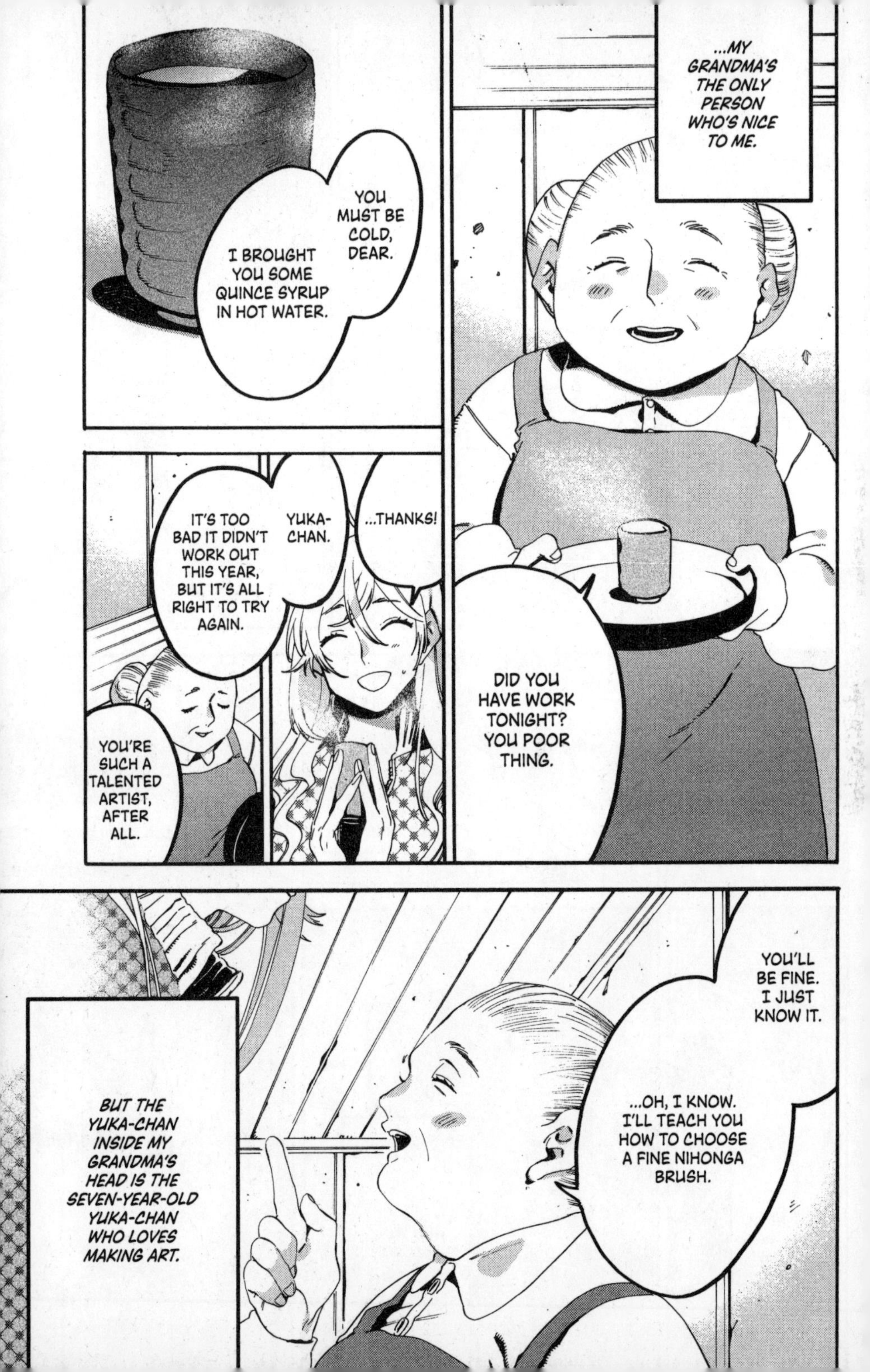
...MY GRANDMA'S THE ONLY PERSON WHO'S NICE TO ME.
DID YOU HAVE WORK TONIGHT? YOU POOR THING.
YOU MUST BE COLD, DEAR.
I BROUGHT YOU SOME QUINCE SYRUP IN HOT WATER.
...THANKS!
YUKA-CHAN.
IT'S TOO BAD IT DIDN'T WORK OUT THIS YEAR, BUT IT'S ALL RIGHT TO TRY AGAIN.
YOU'RE SUCH A TALENTED ARTIST, AFTER ALL.
YOU'LL BE FINE. I JUST KNOW IT.
...OH, I KNOW. I'LL TEACH YOU HOW TO CHOOSE A FINE NIHONGA BRUSH.
BUT THE YUKA-CHAN INSIDE MY GRANDMA'S HEAD IS THE SEVEN-YEAR-OLD YUKA-CHAN WHO LOVES MAKING ART.

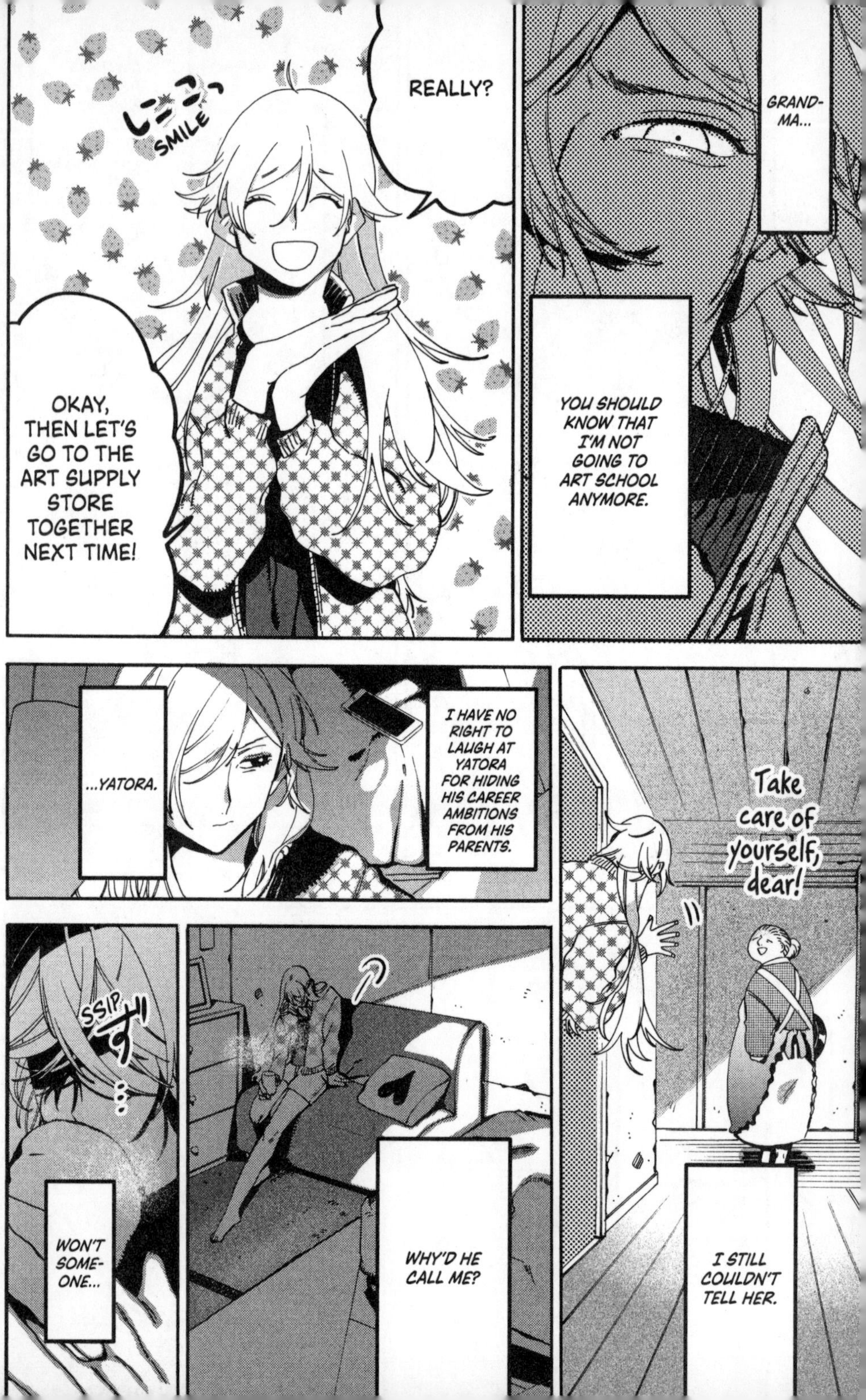
GRAND-MA...
YOU SHOULD KNOW THAT I'M NOT GOING TO ART SCHOOL ANYMORE.
REALLY?
SMILE
OKAY, THEN LET'S GO TO THE ART SUPPLY STORE TOGETHER NEXT TIME!
Take care of yourself, dear!
I STILL COULDN'T TELL HER.
I HAVE NO RIGHT TO LAUGH AT YATORA FOR HIDING HIS CAREER AMBITIONS FROM HIS PARENTS.
...YATORA.
WHY'D HE CALL ME?
SSIP
WON'T SOME-ONE...

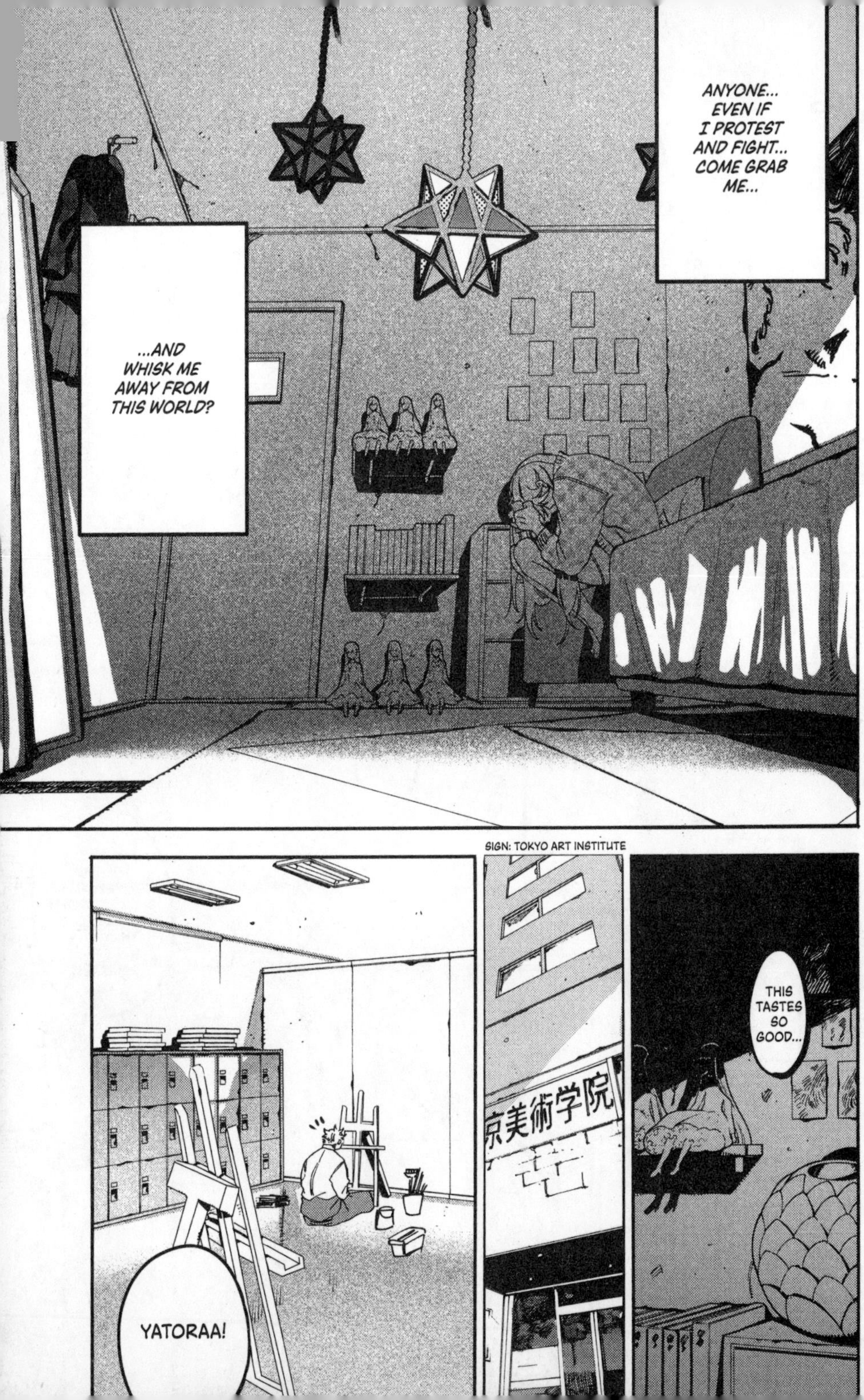
ANYONE... EVEN IF I PROTEST AND FIGHT... COME GRAB ME...
...AND WHISK ME AWAY FROM THIS WORLD?
THIS TASTES SO GOOD...
SIGN: TOKYO ART INSTITUTE
京美術学院
YATORAA!

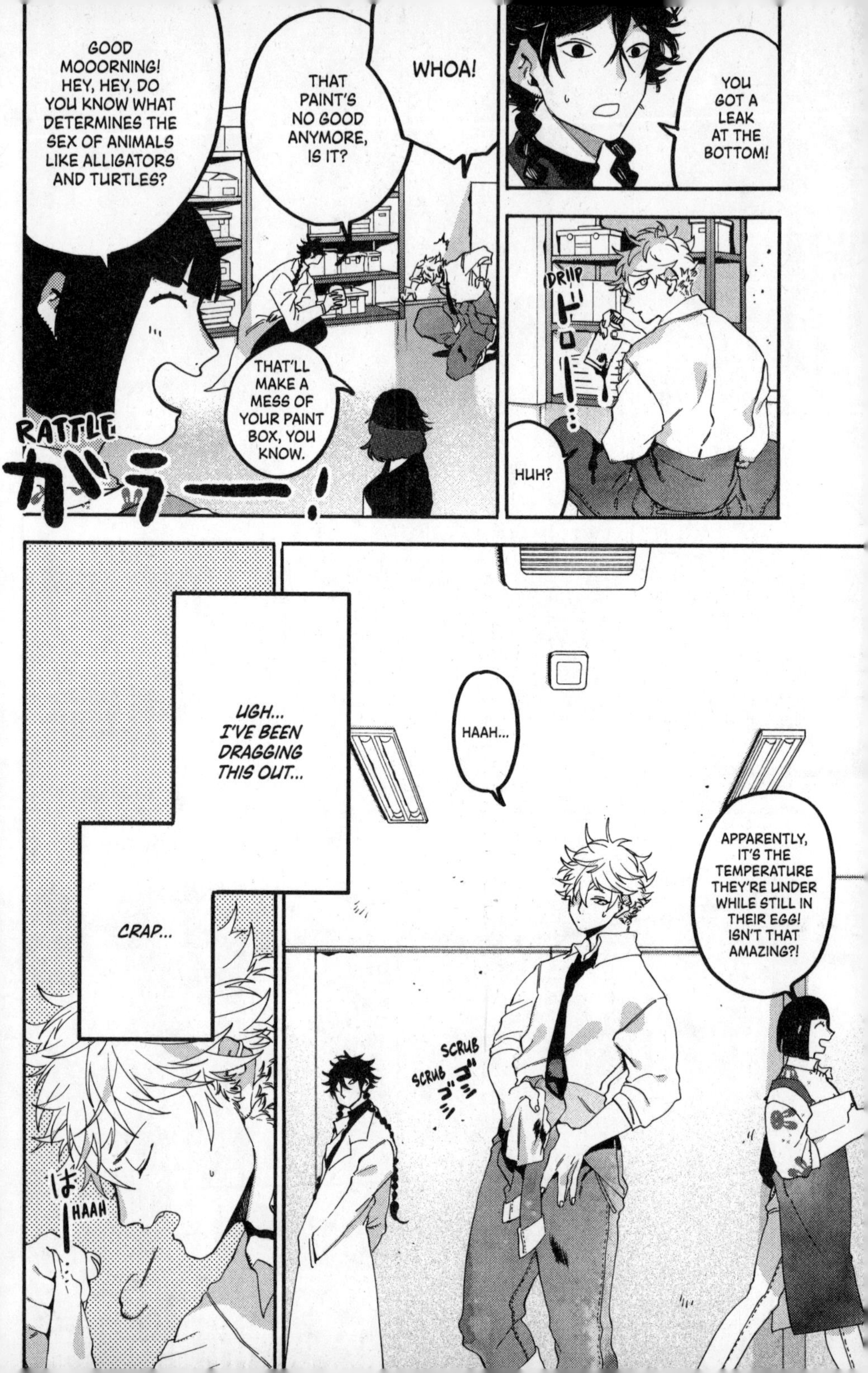
YOU GOT A LEAK AT THE BOTTOM!
DRIIP
ドロー…
HUH?
WHOA!
THAT PAINT'S NO GOOD ANYMORE, IS IT?
GOOD MOOORNING! HEY, HEY, DO YOU KNOW WHAT DETERMINES THE SEX OF ANIMALS LIKE ALLIGATORS AND TURTLES?
THAT'LL MAKE A MESS OF YOUR PAINT BOX, YOU KNOW.
RATTLE
ガラー!
APPARENTLY, IT'S THE TEMPERATURE THEY'RE UNDER WHILE STILL IN THEIR EGG! ISN'T THAT AMAZING?!
HAAH...
SCRUB
SCRUB
ゴシゴシ
UGH... I'VE BEEN DRAGGING THIS OUT...
CRAP...
は
HAAH

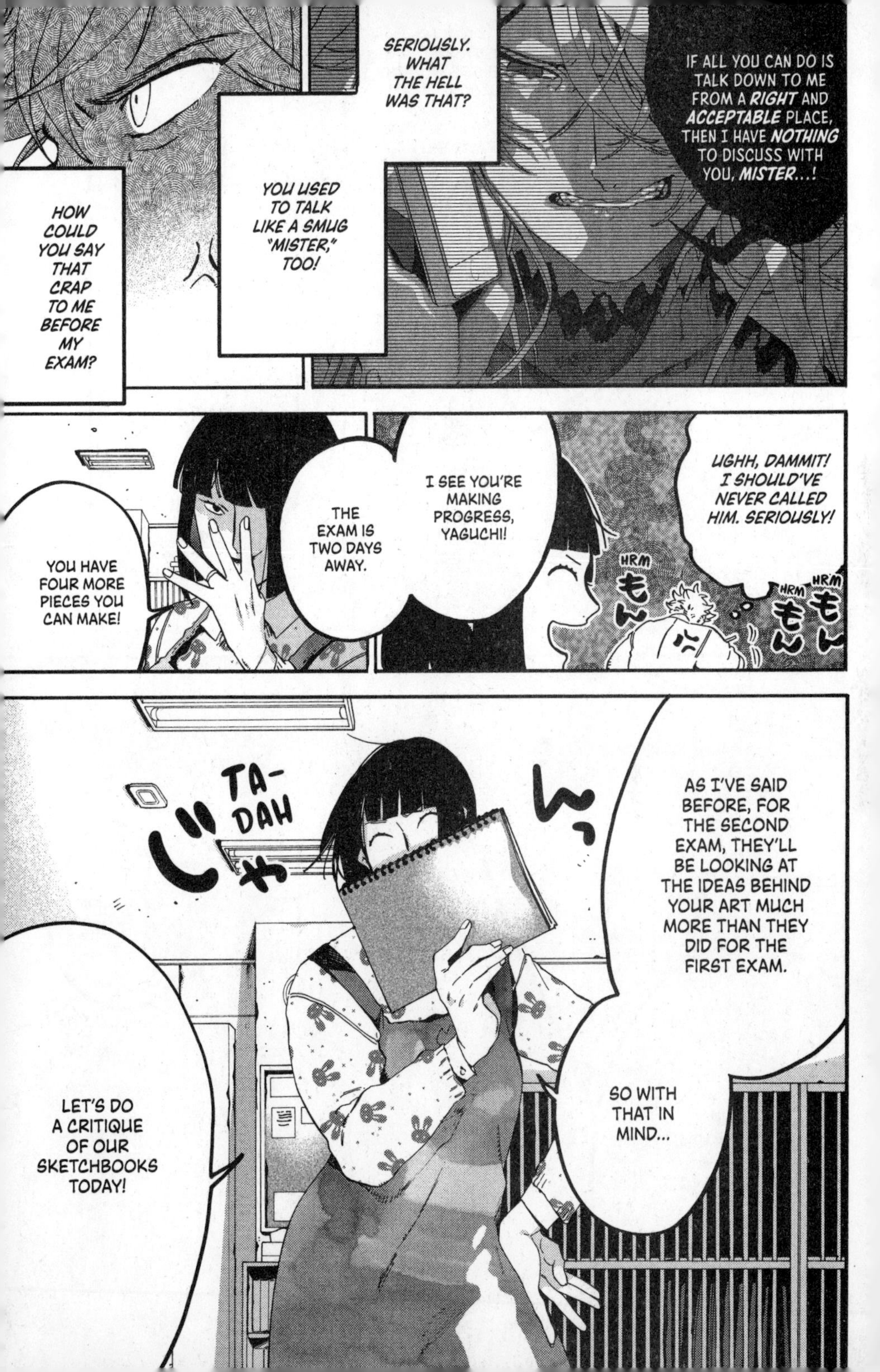
IF ALL YOU CAN DO IS TALK DOWN TO ME FROM A *RIGHT* AND *ACCEPTABLE* PLACE, THEN I HAVE *NOTHING* TO DISCUSS WITH YOU, *MISTER*...!
SERIOUSLY. WHAT THE HELL WAS THAT?
YOU USED TO TALK LIKE A SMUG "MISTER," TOO!
HOW COULD YOU SAY THAT CRAP TO ME BEFORE MY EXAM?
UGHH, DAMMIT! I SHOULD'VE NEVER CALLED HIM. SERIOUSLY!
HRM もん
HRM もん
HRM もん
I SEE YOU'RE MAKING PROGRESS, YAGUCHI!
THE EXAM IS TWO DAYS AWAY.
YOU HAVE FOUR MORE PIECES YOU CAN MAKE!
ん
AS I'VE SAID BEFORE, FOR THE SECOND EXAM, THEY'LL BE LOOKING AT THE IDEAS BEHIND YOUR ART MUCH MORE THAN THEY DID FOR THE FIRST EXAM.
TA-DAH
じゃ
SO WITH THAT IN MIND...
LET'S DO A CRITIQUE OF OUR SKETCHBOOKS TODAY!

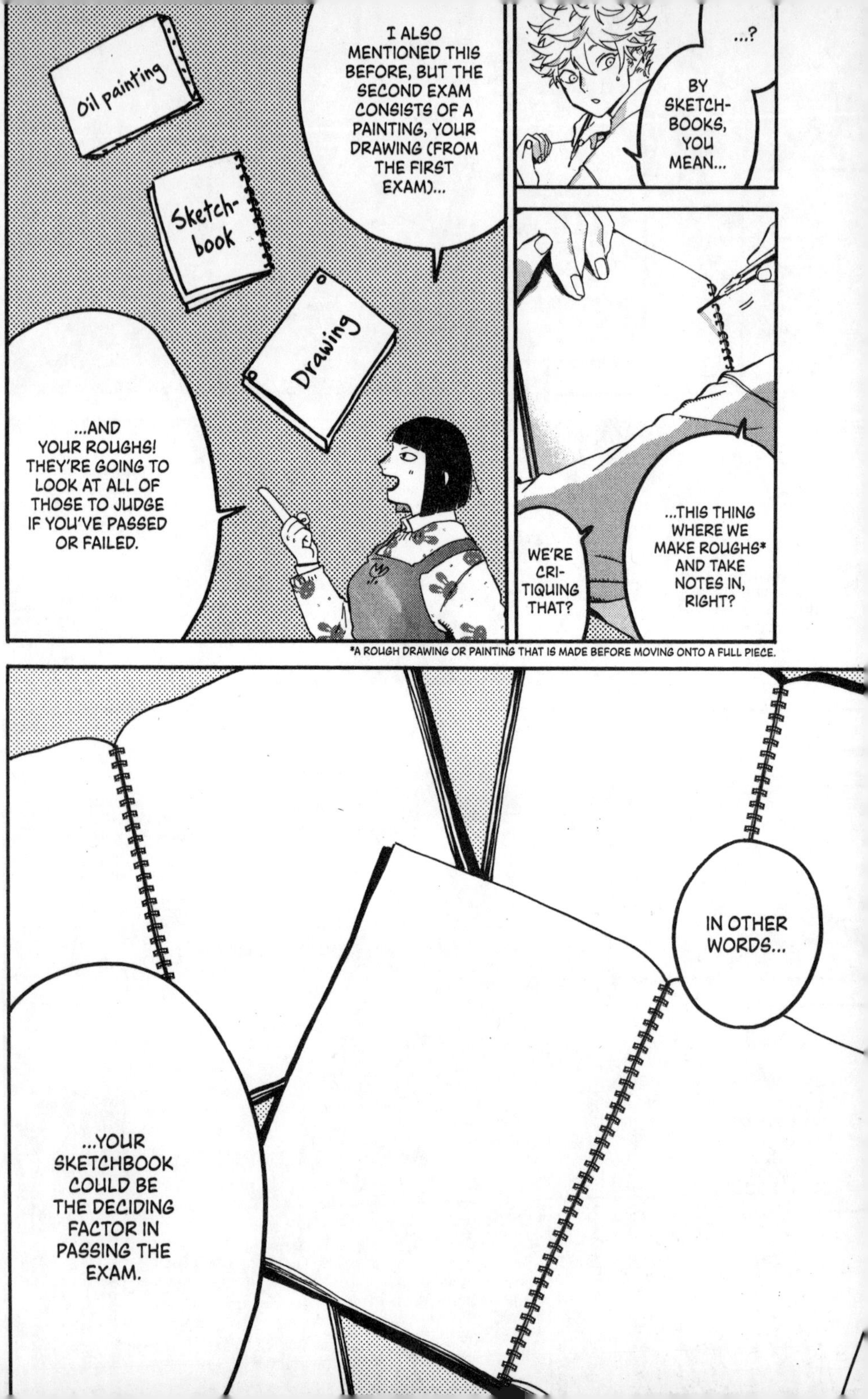
...?
BY SKETCH-BOOKS, YOU MEAN...
...THIS THING WHERE WE MAKE ROUGHS* AND TAKE NOTES IN, RIGHT?
WE'RE CRI-TIQUING THAT?
I ALSO MENTIONED THIS BEFORE, BUT THE SECOND EXAM CONSISTS OF A PAINTING, YOUR DRAWING (FROM THE FIRST EXAM)...
Oil painting
Sketch-book
Drawing
...AND YOUR ROUGHS! THEY'RE GOING TO LOOK AT ALL OF THOSE TO JUDGE IF YOU'VE PASSED OR FAILED.
IN OTHER WORDS...
...YOUR SKETCHBOOK COULD BE THE DECIDING FACTOR IN PASSING THE EXAM.

*A ROUGH DRAWING OR PAINTING THAT IS MADE BEFORE MOVING ONTO A FULL PIECE.

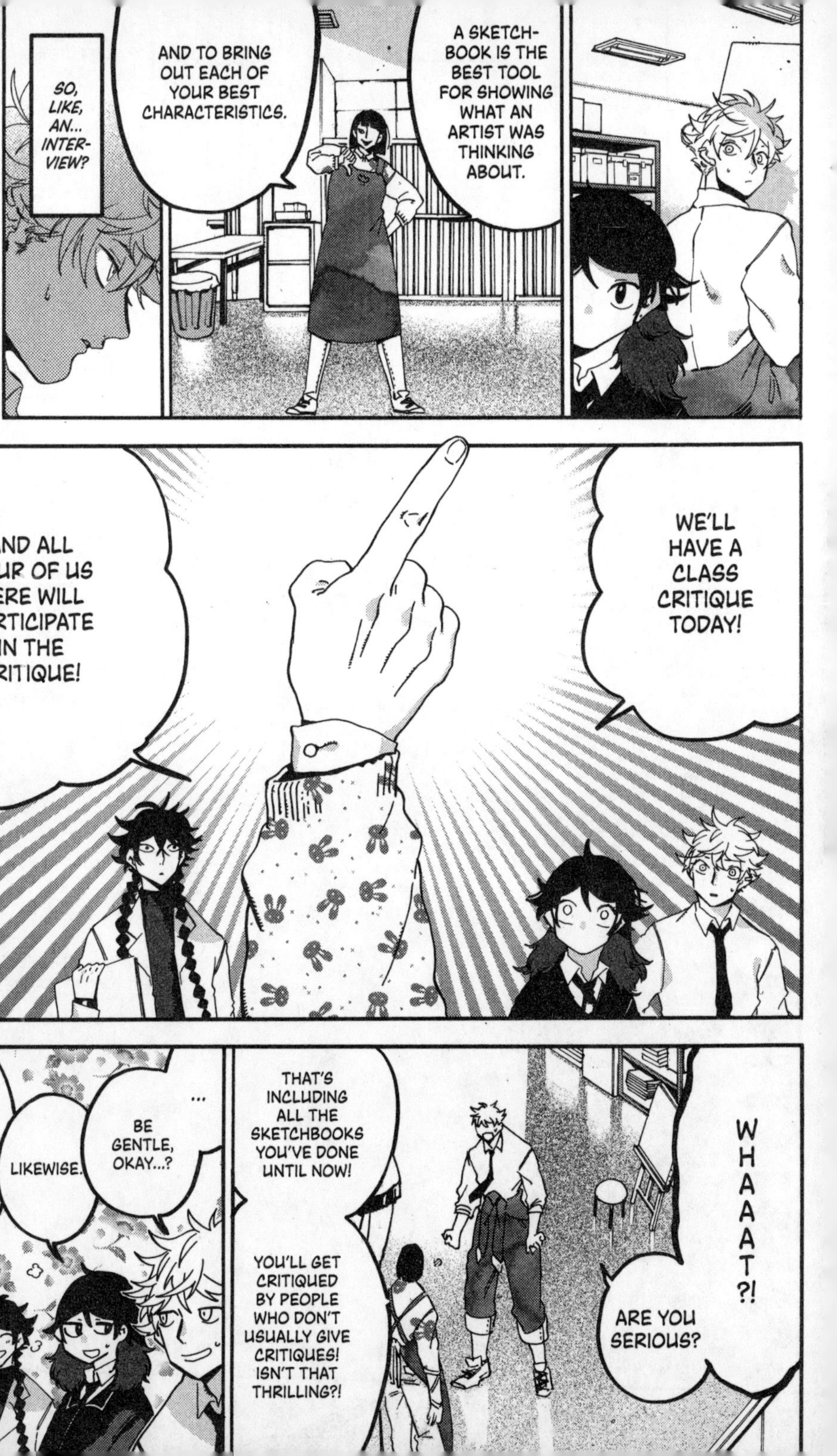
A SKETCHBOOK IS THE BEST TOOL FOR SHOWING WHAT AN ARTIST WAS THINKING ABOUT.
AND TO BRING OUT EACH OF YOUR BEST CHARACTERISTICS.
SO, LIKE, AN... INTERVIEW?
WE'LL HAVE A CLASS CRITIQUE TODAY!
AND ALL FOUR OF US HERE WILL PARTICIPATE IN THE CRITIQUE!
WHAAAT?!
THAT'S INCLUDING ALL THE SKETCHBOOKS YOU'VE DONE UNTIL NOW!
ARE YOU SERIOUS?
YOU'LL GET CRITIQUED BY PEOPLE WHO DON'T USUALLY GIVE CRITIQUES! ISN'T THAT THRILLING?!
...
BE GENTLE, OKAY...?
LIKEWISE.
HOW FUN!

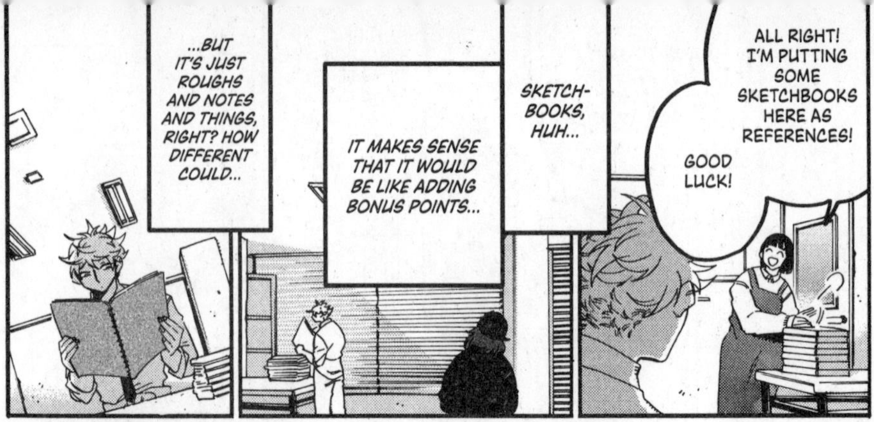
ALL RIGHT! I'M PUTTING SOME SKETCHBOOKS HERE AS REFERENCES!
GOOD LUCK!
SKETCH-BOOKS, HUH...
IT MAKES SENSE THAT IT WOULD BE LIKE ADDING BONUS POINTS...
...BUT IT'S JUST ROUGHS AND NOTES AND THINGS, RIGHT? HOW DIFFERENT COULD...

ART: MATSUBA YACHIGUSA

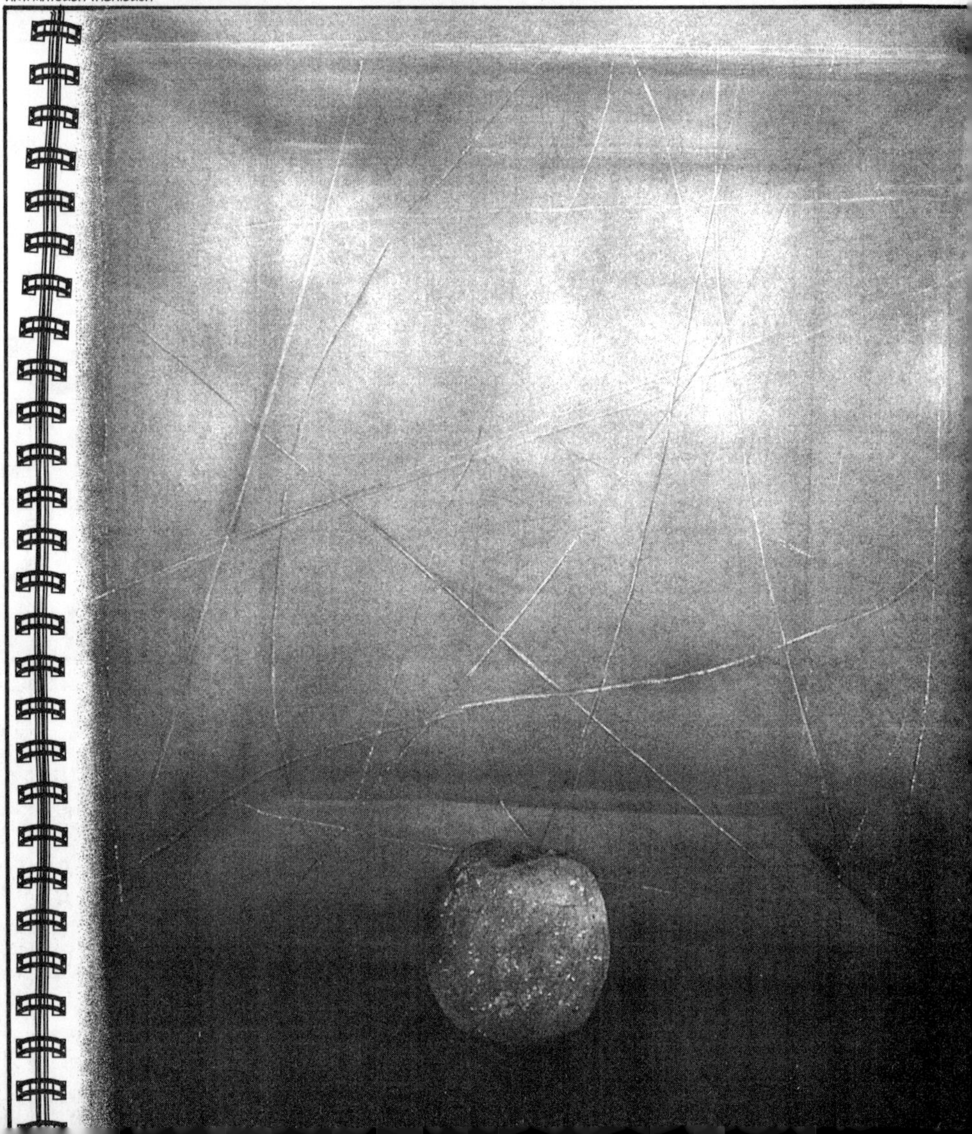

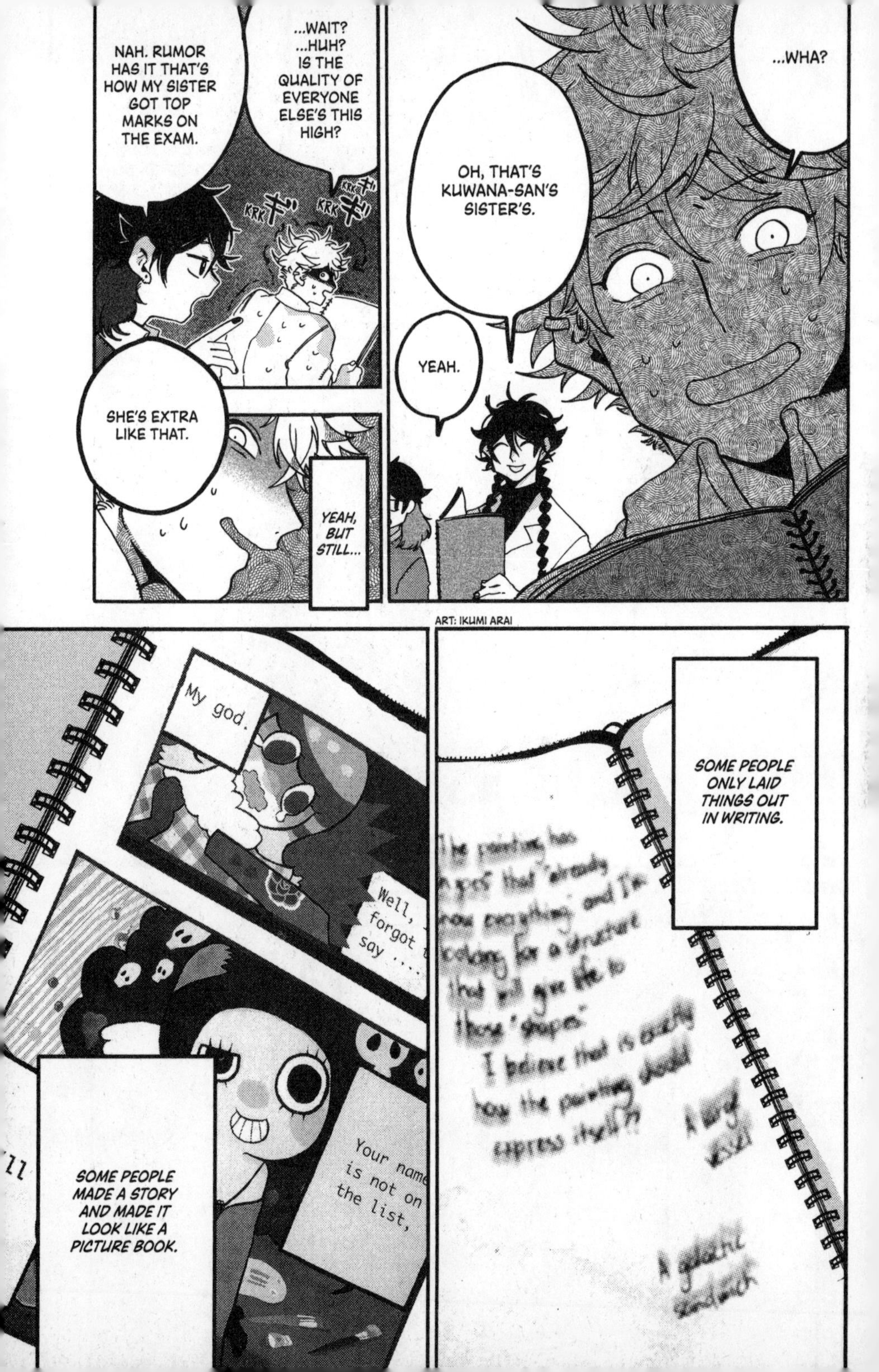
...WHA?
OH, THAT'S KUWANA-SAN'S SISTER'S.
YEAH.
...WAIT? ...HUH? IS THE QUALITY OF EVERYONE ELSE'S THIS HIGH?
NAH. RUMOR HAS IT THAT'S HOW MY SISTER GOT TOP MARKS ON THE EXAM.
KRK KRK KRK
SHE'S EXTRA LIKE THAT.
YEAH, BUT STILL...
ART: IKUMI ARAI
SOME PEOPLE ONLY LAID THINGS OUT IN WRITING.
My god.
SOME PEOPLE MADE A STORY AND MADE IT LOOK LIKE A PICTURE BOOK.

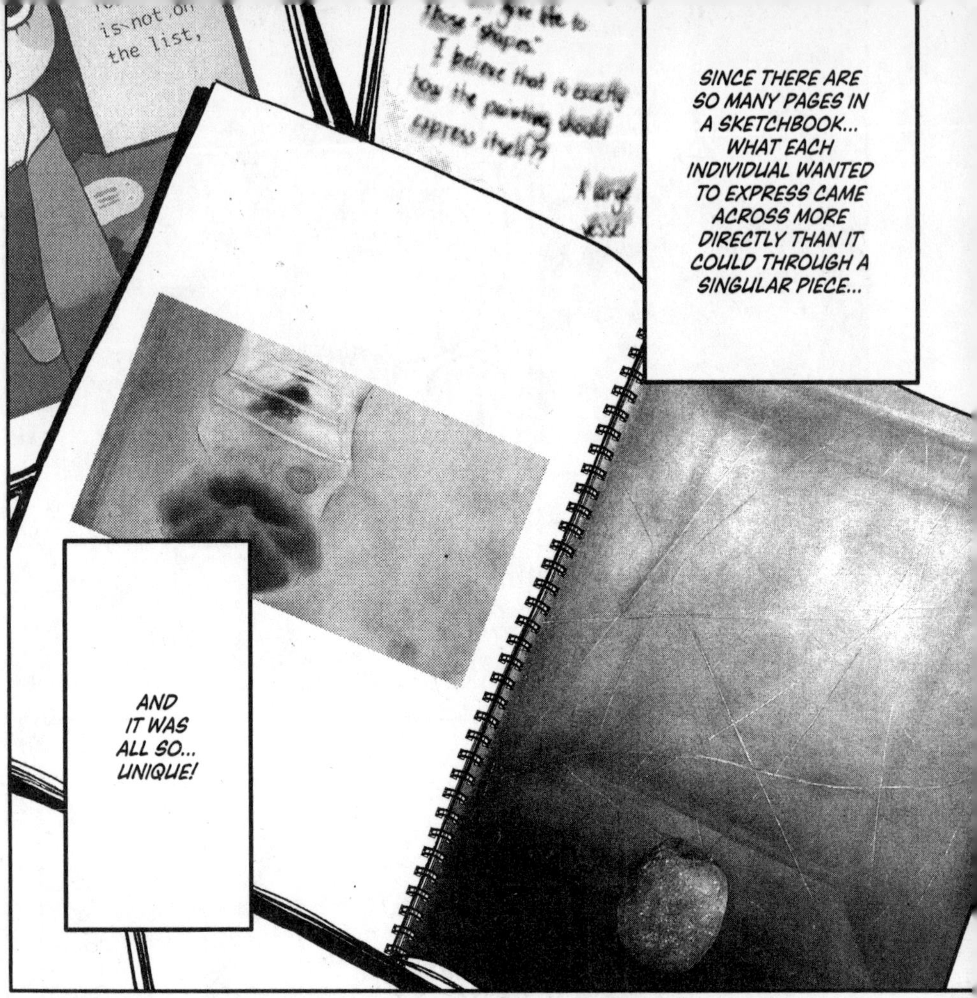
is~not on
the list,
SINCE THERE ARE SO MANY PAGES IN A SKETCHBOOK... WHAT EACH INDIVIDUAL WANTED TO EXPRESS CAME ACROSS MORE DIRECTLY THAN IT COULD THROUGH A SINGULAR PIECE...
AND IT WAS ALL SO... UNIQUE!

ART: SHOTA YAMAMICHI

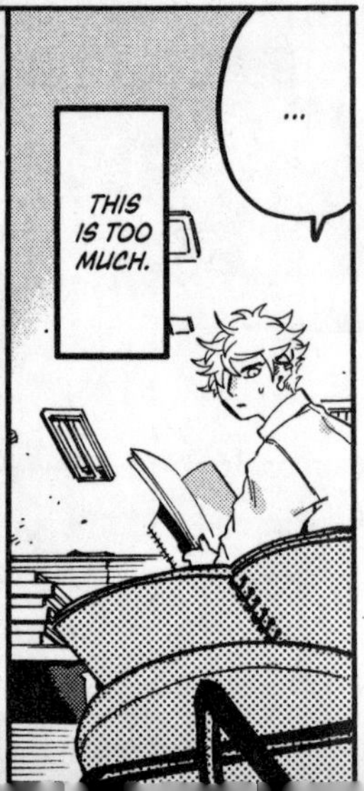
...
THIS IS TOO MUCH.

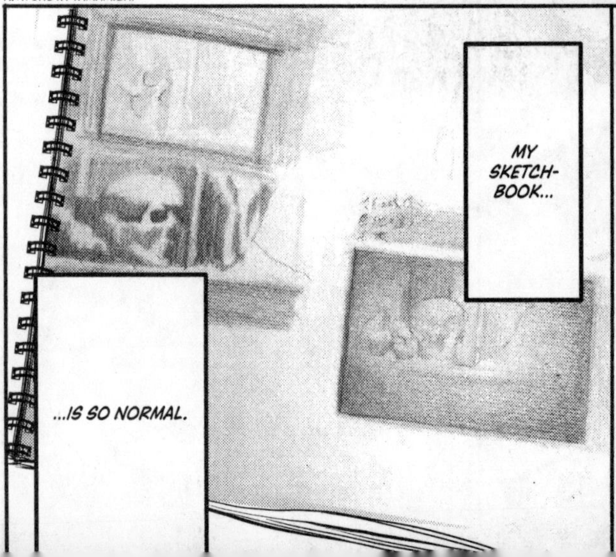
MY SKETCH-BOOK...
...IS SO NORMAL.

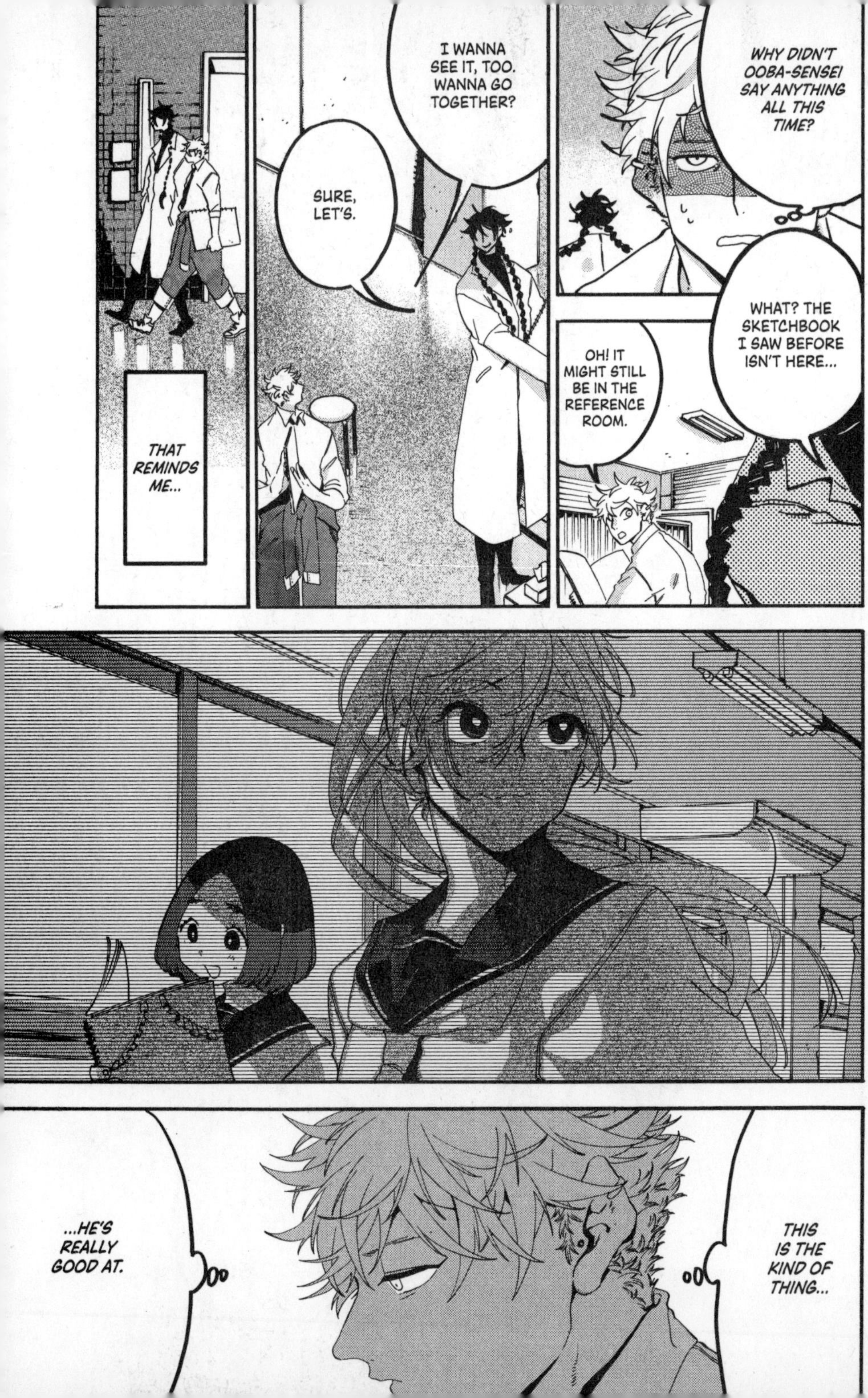
WHY DIDN'T OOBA-SENSEI SAY ANYTHING ALL THIS TIME?
WHAT? THE SKETCHBOOK I SAW BEFORE ISN'T HERE...
OH! IT MIGHT STILL BE IN THE REFERENCE ROOM.
I WANNA SEE IT, TOO. WANNA GO TOGETHER?
SURE, LET'S.
THAT REMINDS ME...
THIS IS THE KIND OF THING...
...HE'S REALLY GOOD AT.

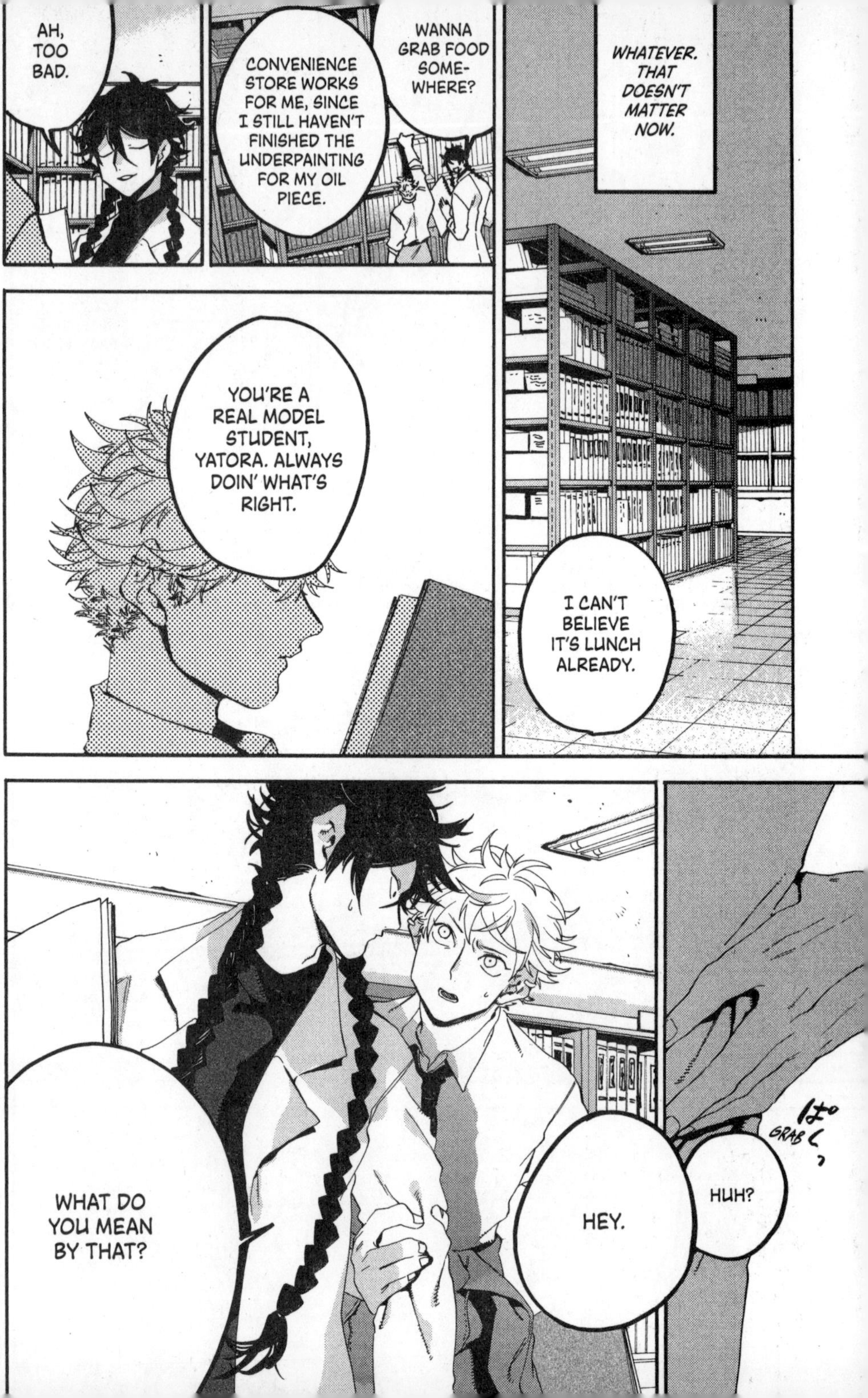
WHATEVER. THAT DOESN'T MATTER NOW.
I CAN'T BELIEVE IT'S LUNCH ALREADY.
WANNA GRAB FOOD SOME-WHERE?
CONVENIENCE STORE WORKS FOR ME, SINCE I STILL HAVEN'T FINISHED THE UNDERPAINTING FOR MY OIL PIECE.
AH, TOO BAD.
YOU'RE A REAL MODEL STUDENT, YATORA. ALWAYS DOIN' WHAT'S RIGHT.
ぱしっ
GRAB
HUH?
HEY.
WHAT DO YOU MEAN BY THAT?

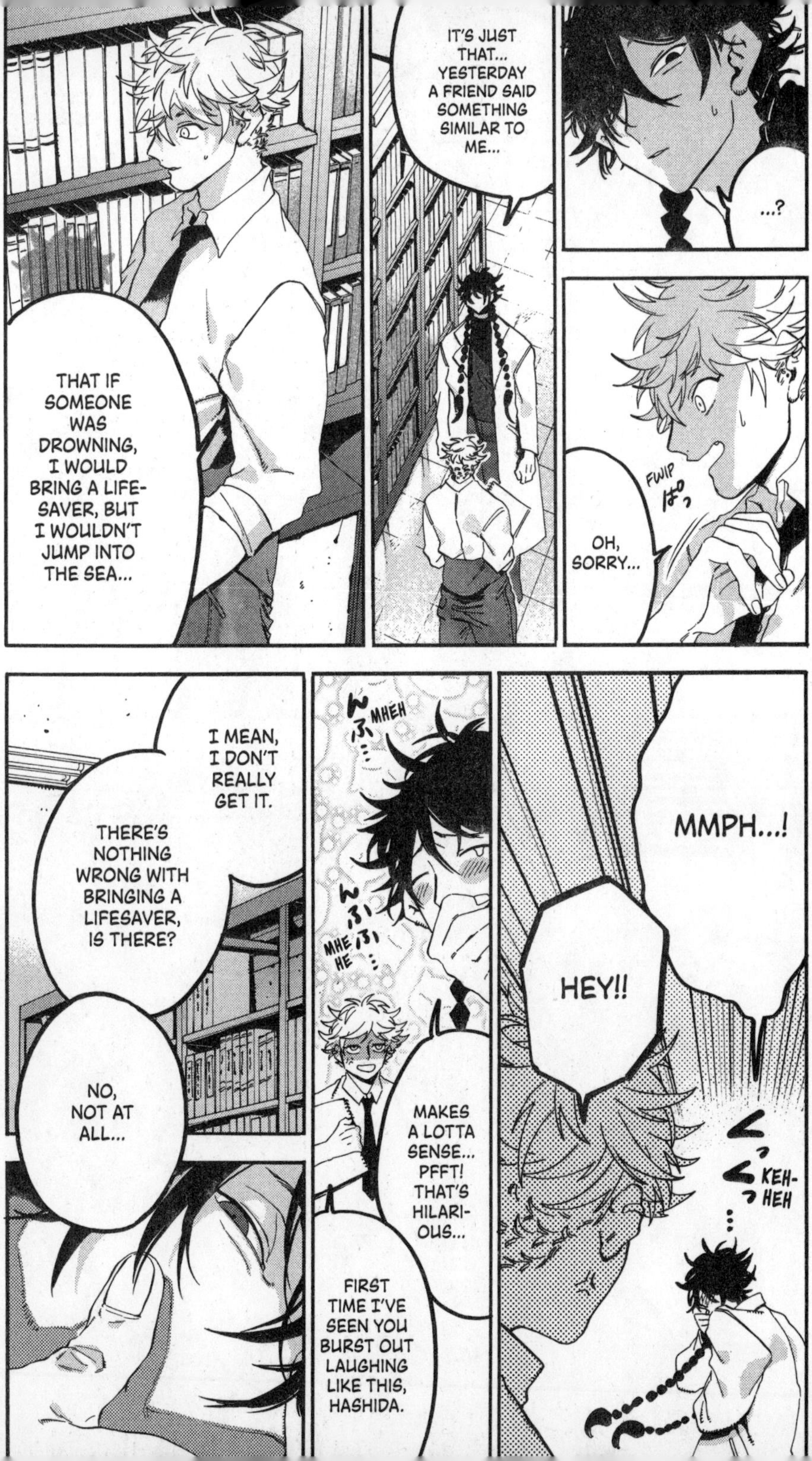
...?
FWIP
OH, SORRY...
IT'S JUST THAT... YESTERDAY A FRIEND SAID SOMETHING SIMILAR TO ME...
THAT IF SOMEONE WAS DROWNING, I WOULD BRING A LIFE-SAVER, BUT I WOULDN'T JUMP INTO THE SEA...
MMPH...!
HEY!!
KEH-HEH
MHEH
MHE HE
MAKES A LOTTA SENSE... PFFT! THAT'S HILARI-OUS...
I MEAN, I DON'T REALLY GET IT.
THERE'S NOTHING WRONG WITH BRINGING A LIFESAVER, IS THERE?
NO, NOT AT ALL...
FIRST TIME I'VE SEEN YOU BURST OUT LAUGHING LIKE THIS, HASHIDA.

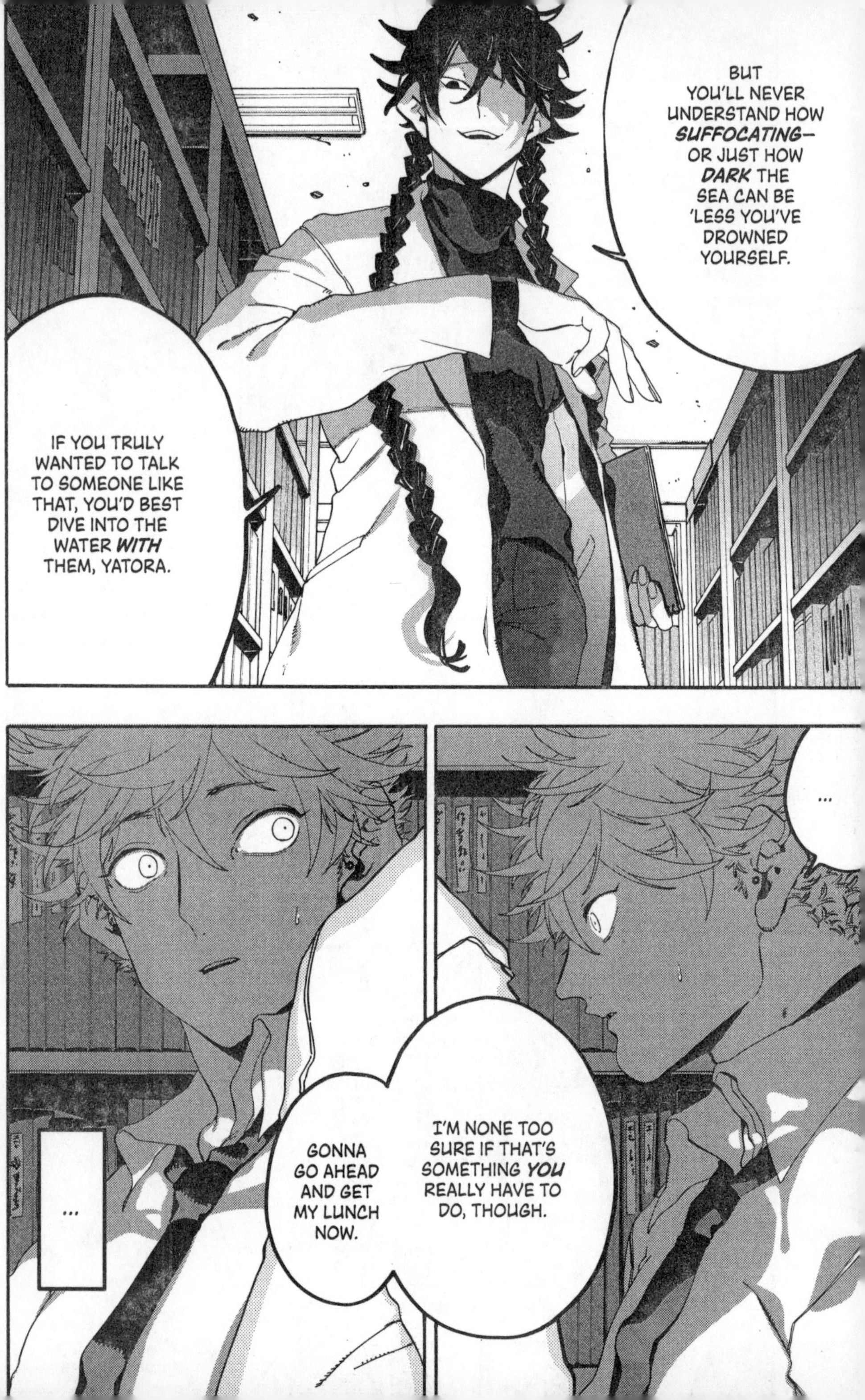
BUT YOU'LL NEVER UNDERSTAND HOW SUFFOCATING— OR JUST HOW DARK THE SEA CAN BE 'LESS YOU'VE DROWNED YOURSELF.
IF YOU TRULY WANTED TO TALK TO SOMEONE LIKE THAT, YOU'D BEST DIVE INTO THE WATER WITH THEM, YATORA.
...
I'M NONE TOO SURE IF THAT'S SOMETHING YOU REALLY HAVE TO DO, THOUGH.
GONNA GO AHEAD AND GET MY LUNCH NOW.
...

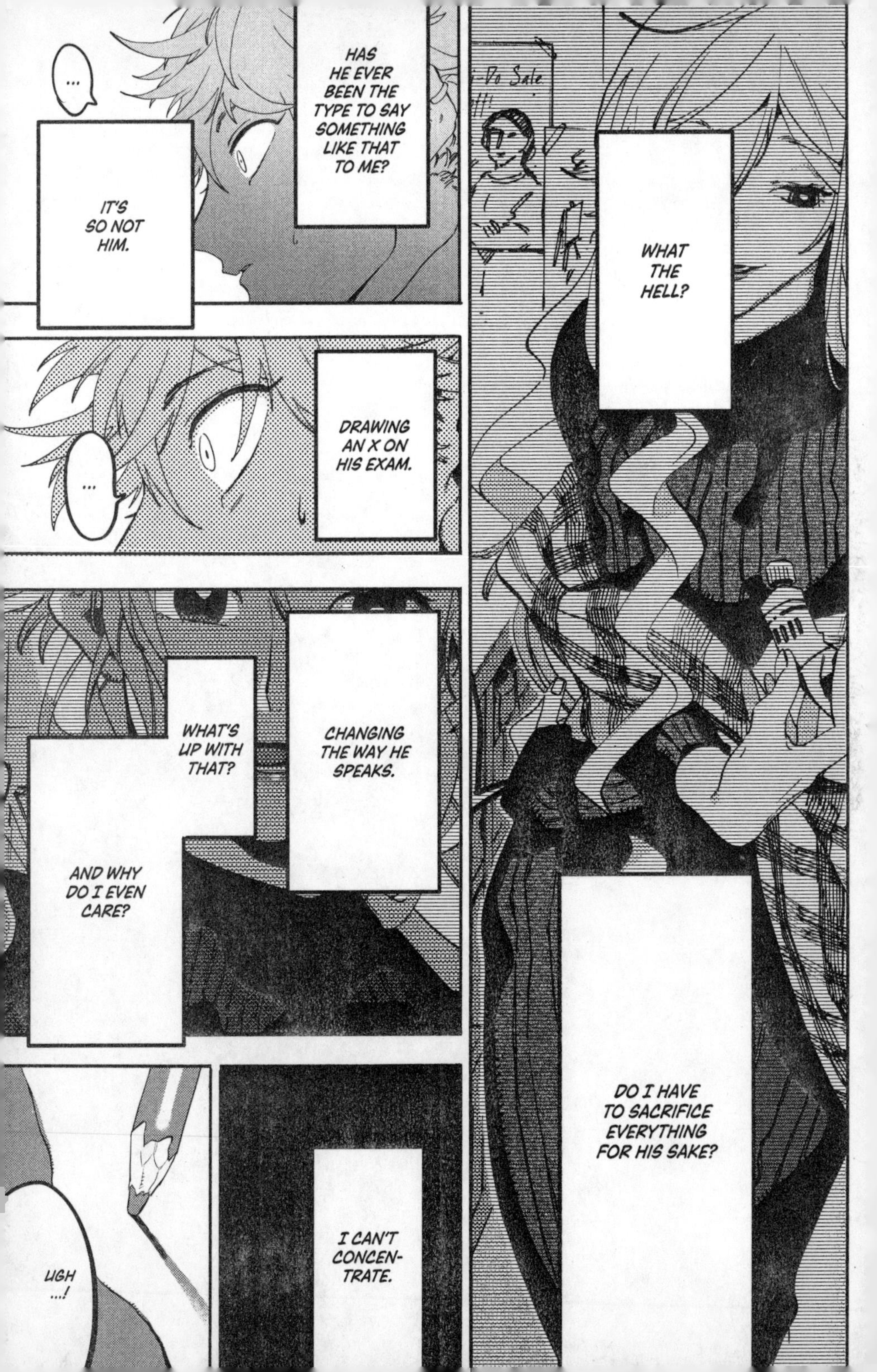
WHAT THE HELL?
DO I HAVE TO SACRIFICE EVERYTHING FOR HIS SAKE?
HAS HE EVER BEEN THE TYPE TO SAY SOMETHING LIKE THAT TO ME?
...
IT'S SO NOT HIM.
DRAWING AN X ON HIS EXAM.
...
CHANGING THE WAY HE SPEAKS.
WHAT'S UP WITH THAT?
AND WHY DO I EVEN CARE?
I CAN'T CONCENTRATE.
UGH ...!

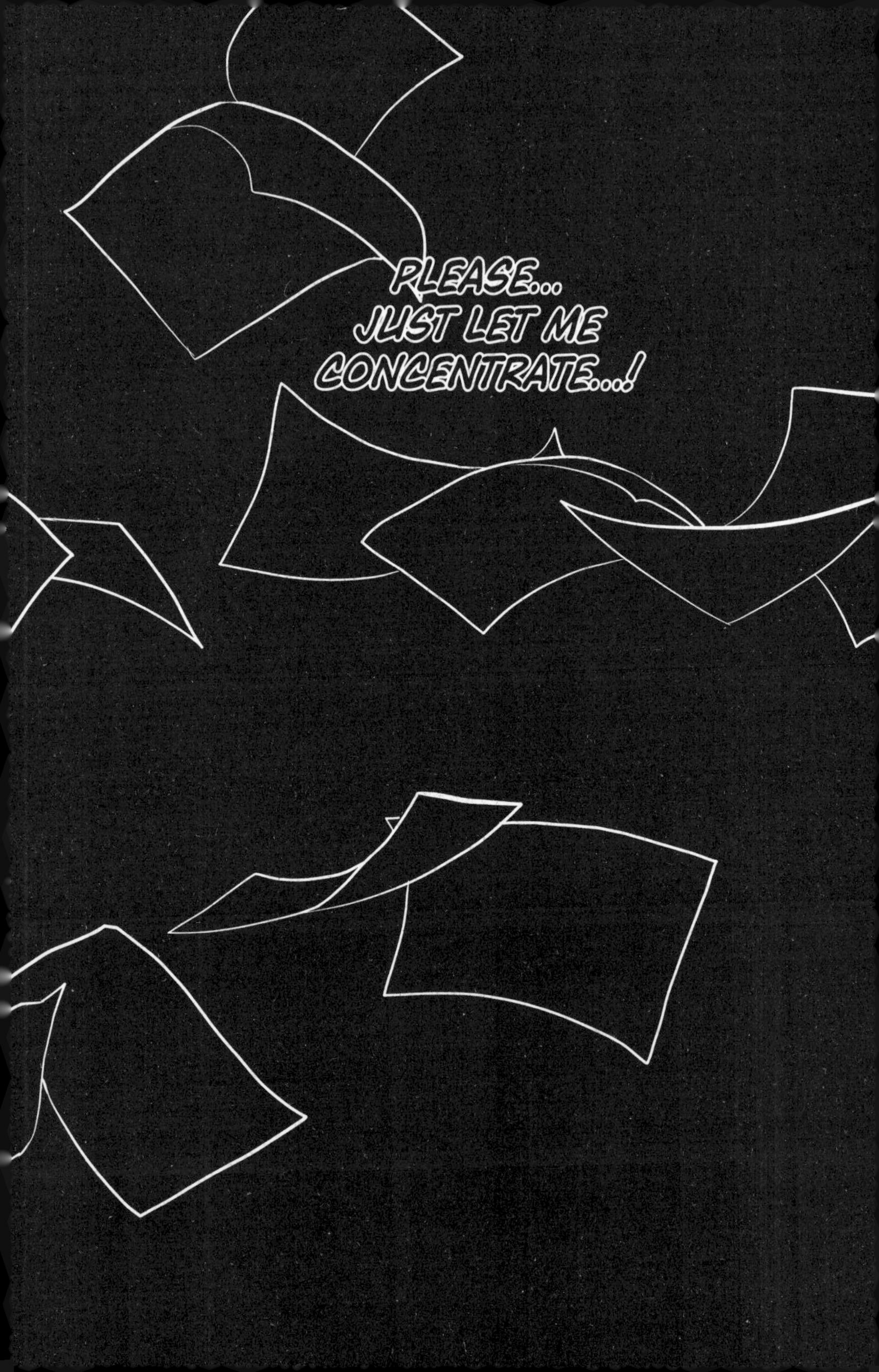
PLEASE... JUST LET ME CONCENTRATE...!

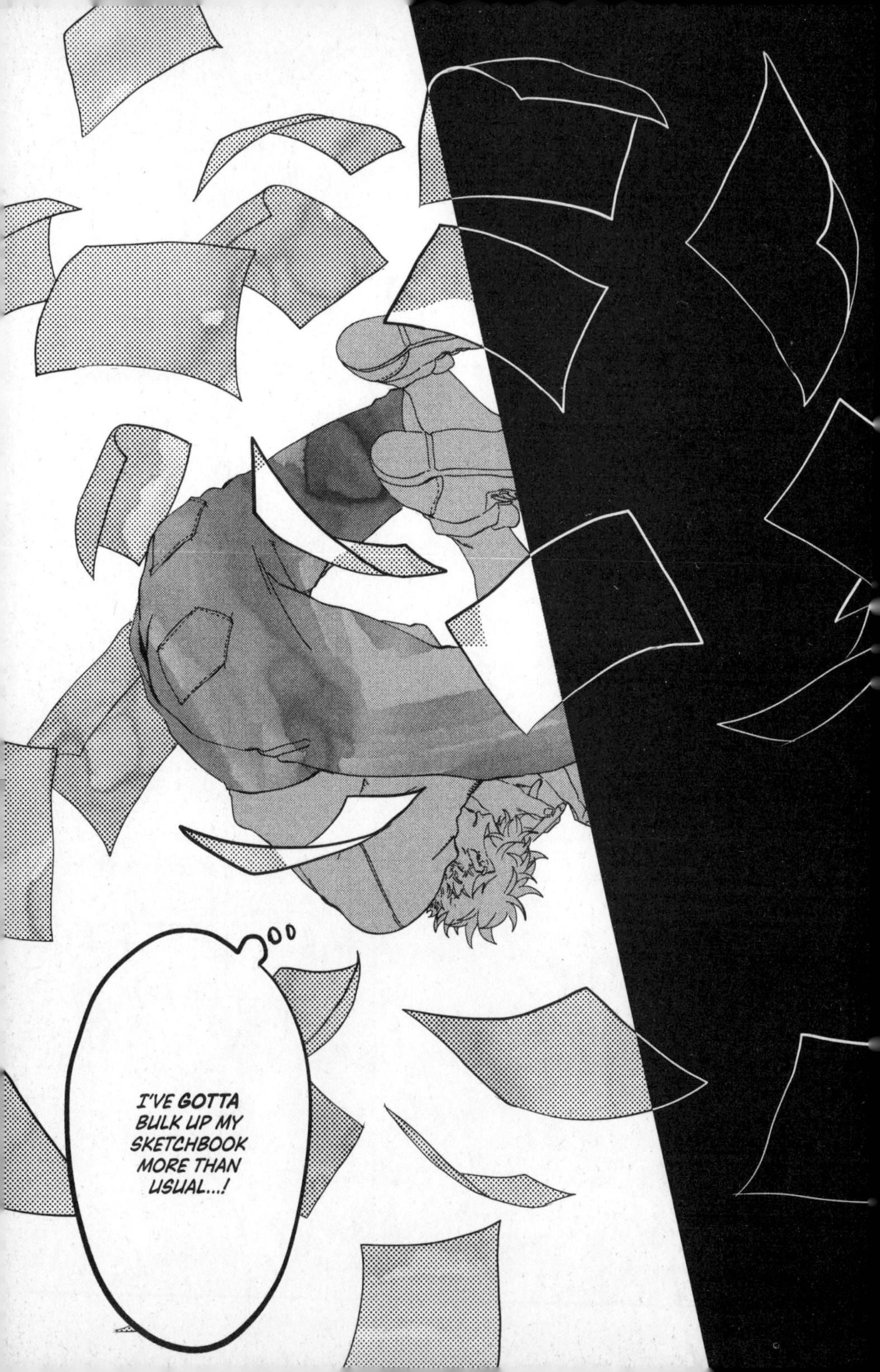
I'VE GOTTA BULK UP MY SKETCHBOOK MORE THAN USUAL...!

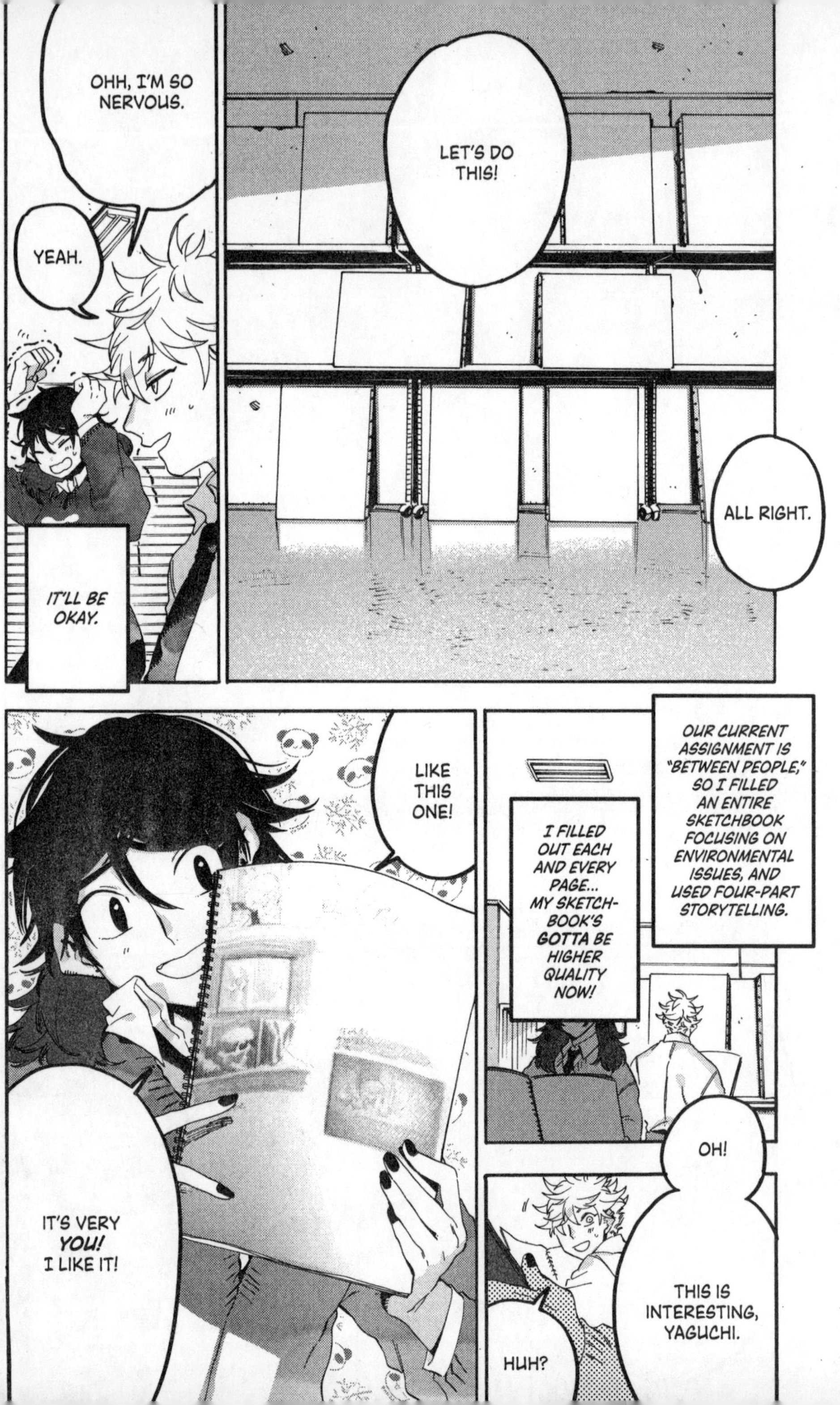
LET'S DO THIS!
ALL RIGHT.
OHH, I'M SO NERVOUS.
YEAH.
IT'LL BE OKAY.
OUR CURRENT ASSIGNMENT IS "BETWEEN PEOPLE," SO I FILLED AN ENTIRE SKETCHBOOK FOCUSING ON ENVIRONMENTAL ISSUES, AND USED FOUR-PART STORYTELLING.
I FILLED OUT EACH AND EVERY PAGE... MY SKETCH-BOOK'S GOTTA BE HIGHER QUALITY NOW!
OH!
THIS IS INTERESTING, YAGUCHI.
HUH?
LIKE THIS ONE!
IT'S VERY YOU! I LIKE IT!

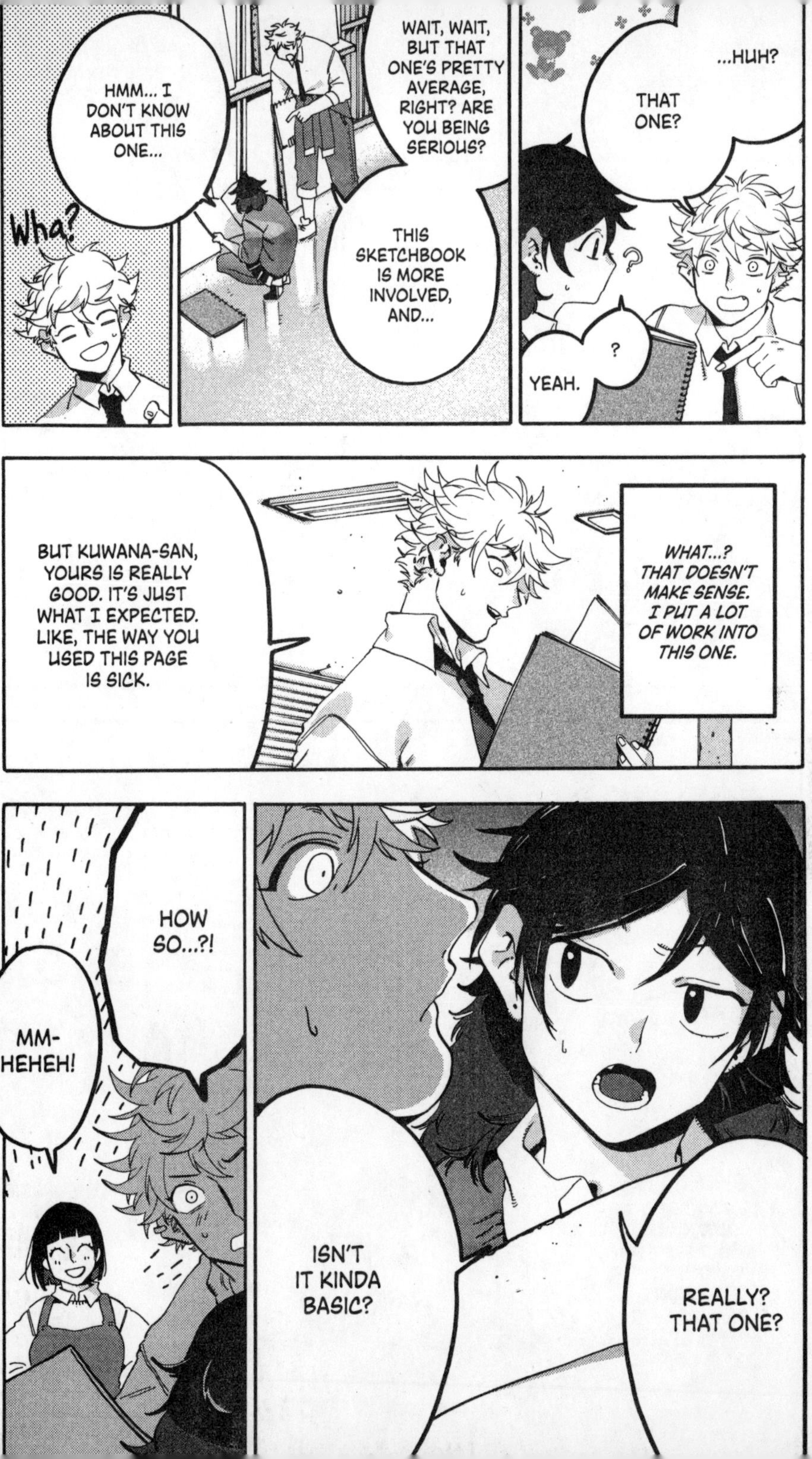
...HUH?
THAT ONE?
?
YEAH.
WAIT, WAIT, BUT THAT ONE'S PRETTY AVERAGE, RIGHT? ARE YOU BEING SERIOUS?
THIS SKETCHBOOK IS MORE INVOLVED, AND...
HMM... I DON'T KNOW ABOUT THIS ONE...
Wha?
WHAT...? THAT DOESN'T MAKE SENSE. I PUT A LOT OF WORK INTO THIS ONE.
BUT KUWANA-SAN, YOURS IS REALLY GOOD. IT'S JUST WHAT I EXPECTED. LIKE, THE WAY YOU USED THIS PAGE IS SICK.
REALLY? THAT ONE?
ISN'T IT KINDA BASIC?
HOW SO...?!
MM-HEHEH!

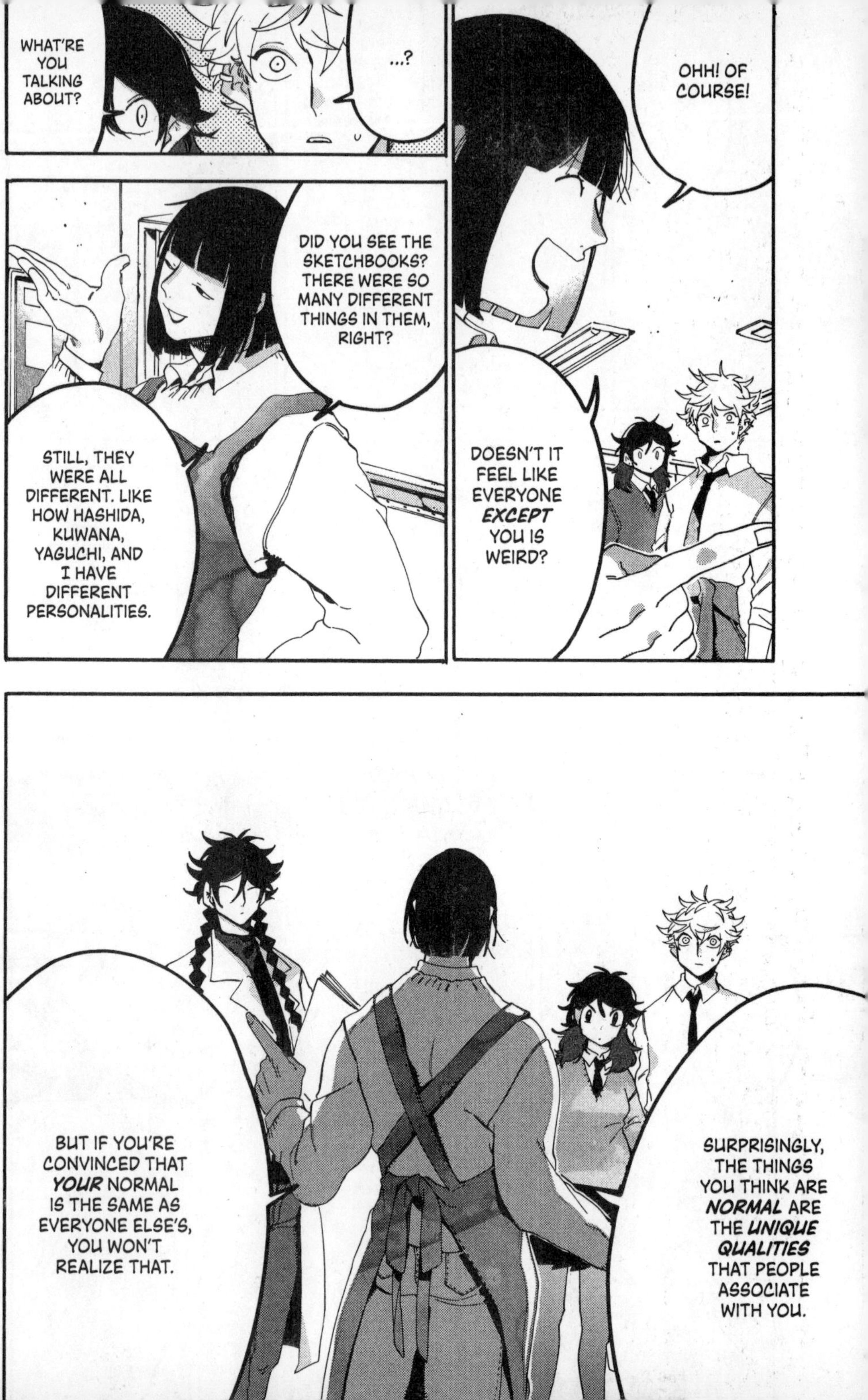
OHH! OF COURSE!
DOESN'T IT FEEL LIKE EVERYONE *EXCEPT* YOU IS WEIRD?
...?
WHAT'RE YOU TALKING ABOUT?
DID YOU SEE THE SKETCHBOOKS? THERE WERE SO MANY DIFFERENT THINGS IN THEM, RIGHT?
STILL, THEY WERE ALL DIFFERENT. LIKE HOW HASHIDA, KUWANA, YAGUCHI, AND I HAVE DIFFERENT PERSONALITIES.
SURPRISINGLY, THE THINGS YOU THINK ARE *NORMAL* ARE THE *UNIQUE QUALITIES* THAT PEOPLE ASSOCIATE WITH YOU.
BUT IF YOU'RE CONVINCED THAT *YOUR* NORMAL IS THE SAME AS EVERYONE ELSE'S, YOU WON'T REALIZE THAT.

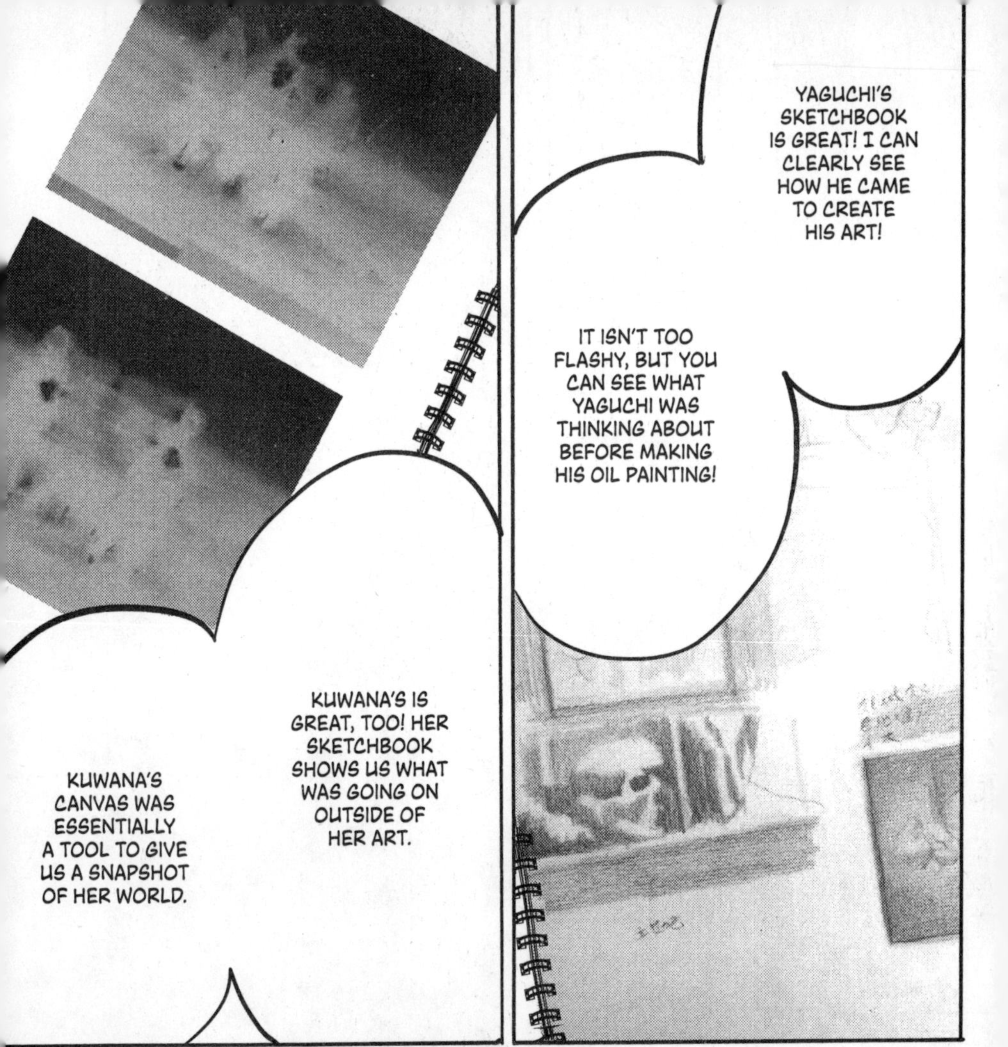
YAGUCHI'S SKETCHBOOK IS GREAT! I CAN CLEARLY SEE HOW HE CAME TO CREATE HIS ART!
IT ISN'T TOO FLASHY, BUT YOU CAN SEE WHAT YAGUCHI WAS THINKING ABOUT BEFORE MAKING HIS OIL PAINTING!
KUWANA'S IS GREAT, TOO! HER SKETCHBOOK SHOWS US WHAT WAS GOING ON OUTSIDE OF HER ART.
KUWANA'S CANVAS WAS ESSENTIALLY A TOOL TO GIVE US A SNAPSHOT OF HER WORLD.
ART: MOEKO NATSUI

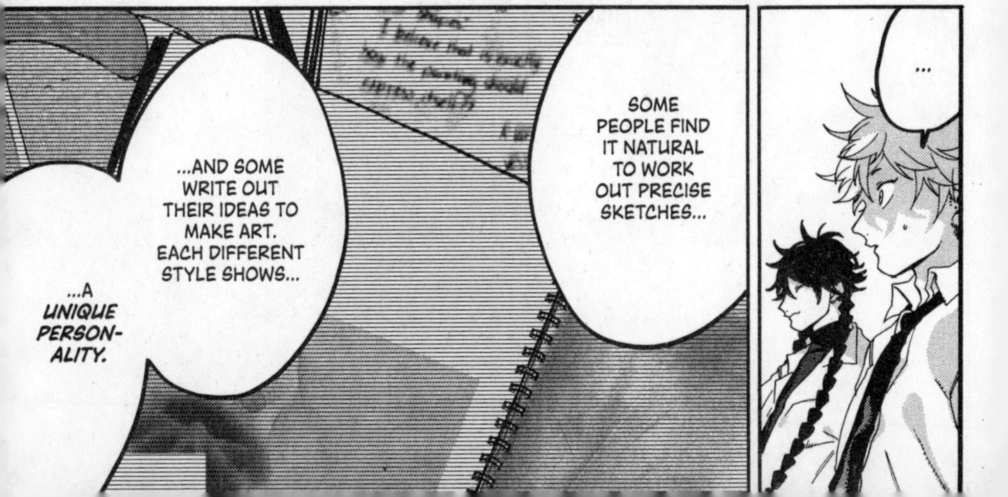
...
SOME PEOPLE FIND IT NATURAL TO WORK OUT PRECISE SKETCHES...
...AND SOME WRITE OUT THEIR IDEAS TO MAKE ART. EACH DIFFERENT STYLE SHOWS...
...A *UNIQUE PERSON-ALITY.*

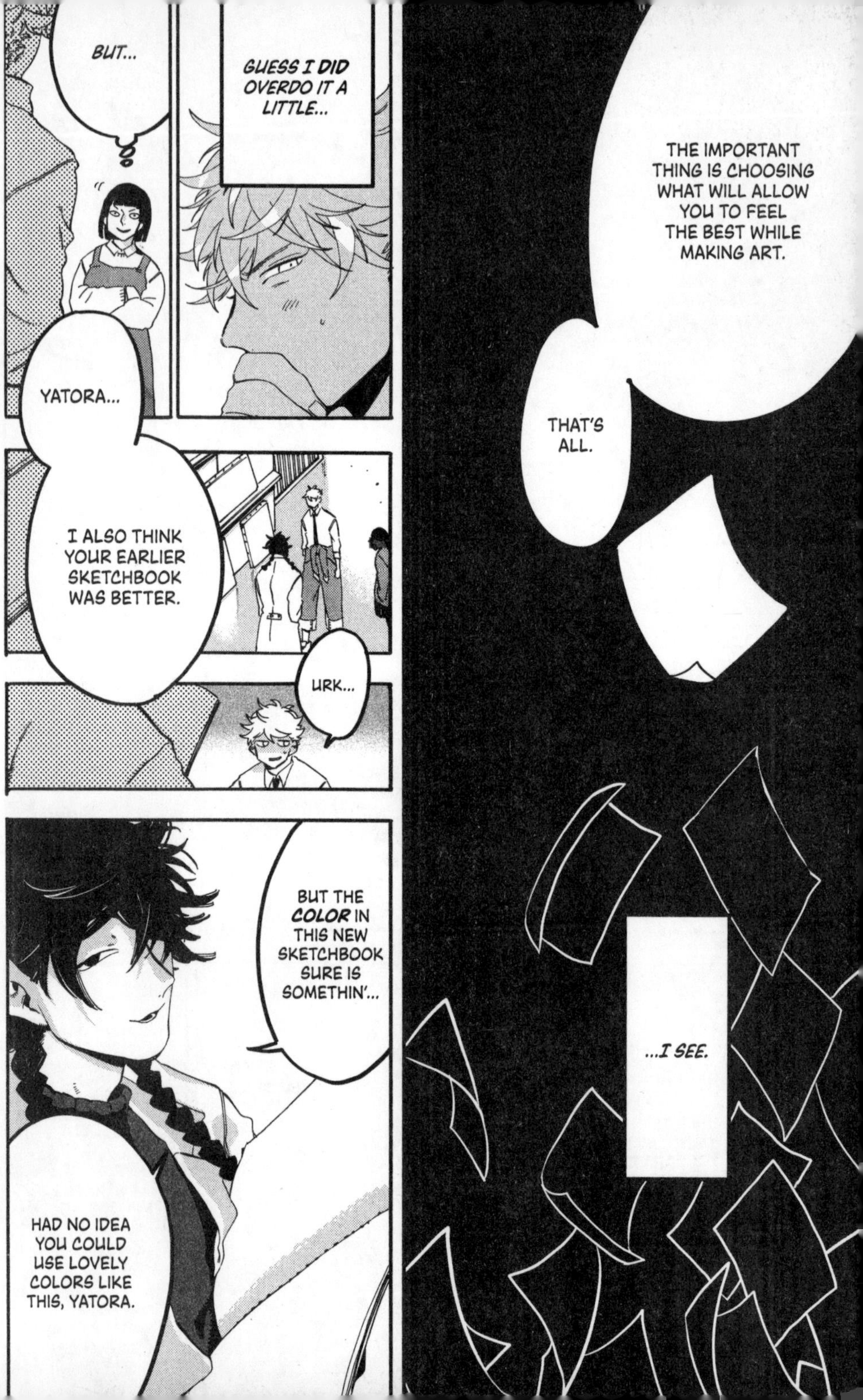
THE IMPORTANT THING IS CHOOSING WHAT WILL ALLOW YOU TO FEEL THE BEST WHILE MAKING ART.
THAT'S ALL.
...I SEE.
GUESS I DID OVERDO IT A LITTLE...
BUT...
YATORA...
I ALSO THINK YOUR EARLIER SKETCHBOOK WAS BETTER.
URK...
BUT THE COLOR IN THIS NEW SKETCHBOOK SURE IS SOMETHIN'...
HAD NO IDEA YOU COULD USE LOVELY COLORS LIKE THIS, YATORA.

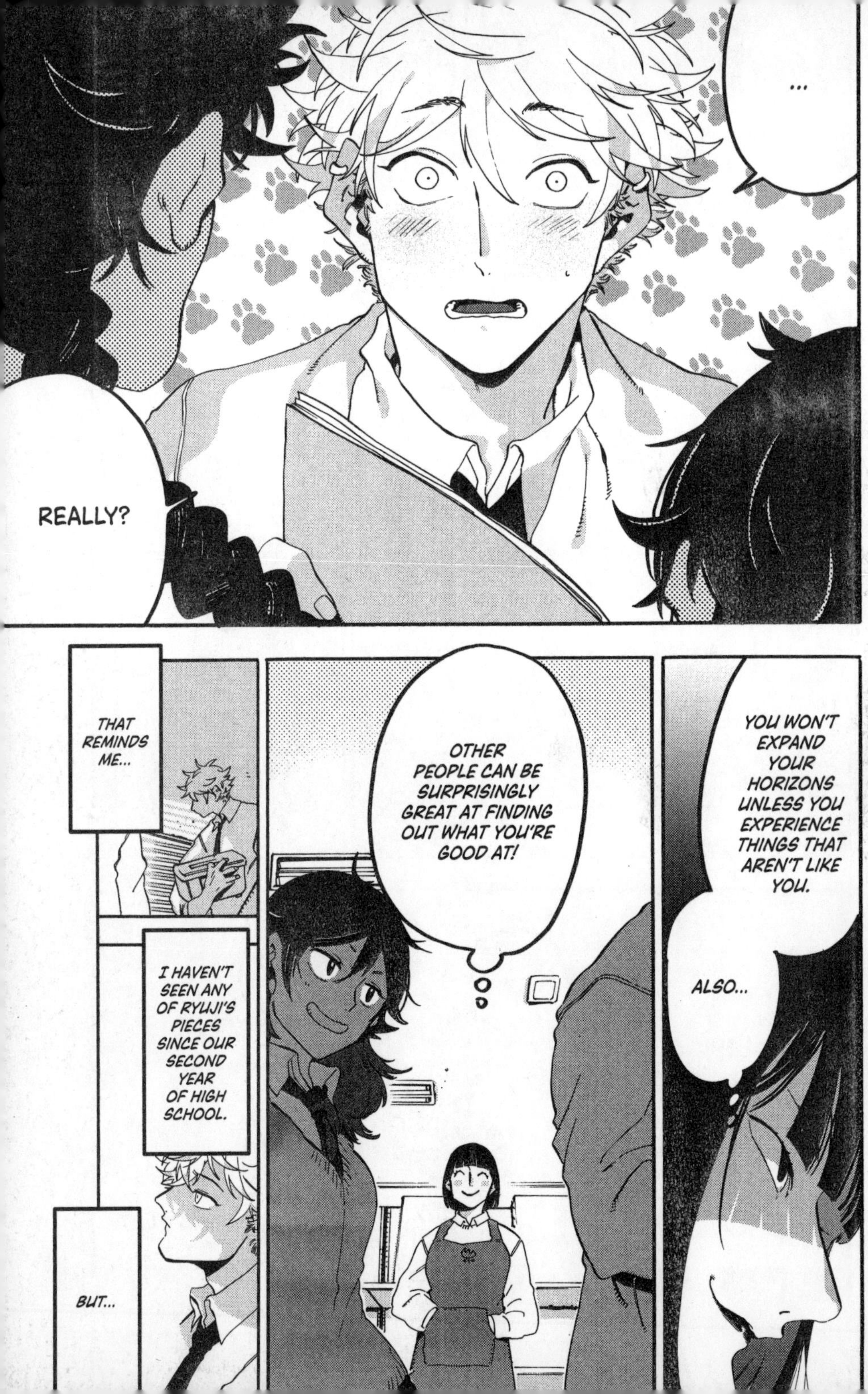
...
REALLY?
YOU WON'T EXPAND YOUR HORIZONS UNLESS YOU EXPERIENCE THINGS THAT AREN'T LIKE YOU.
ALSO...
OTHER PEOPLE CAN BE SURPRISINGLY GREAT AT FINDING OUT WHAT YOU'RE GOOD AT!
THAT REMINDS ME...
I HAVEN'T SEEN ANY OF RYUJI'S PIECES SINCE OUR SECOND YEAR OF HIGH SCHOOL.
BUT...

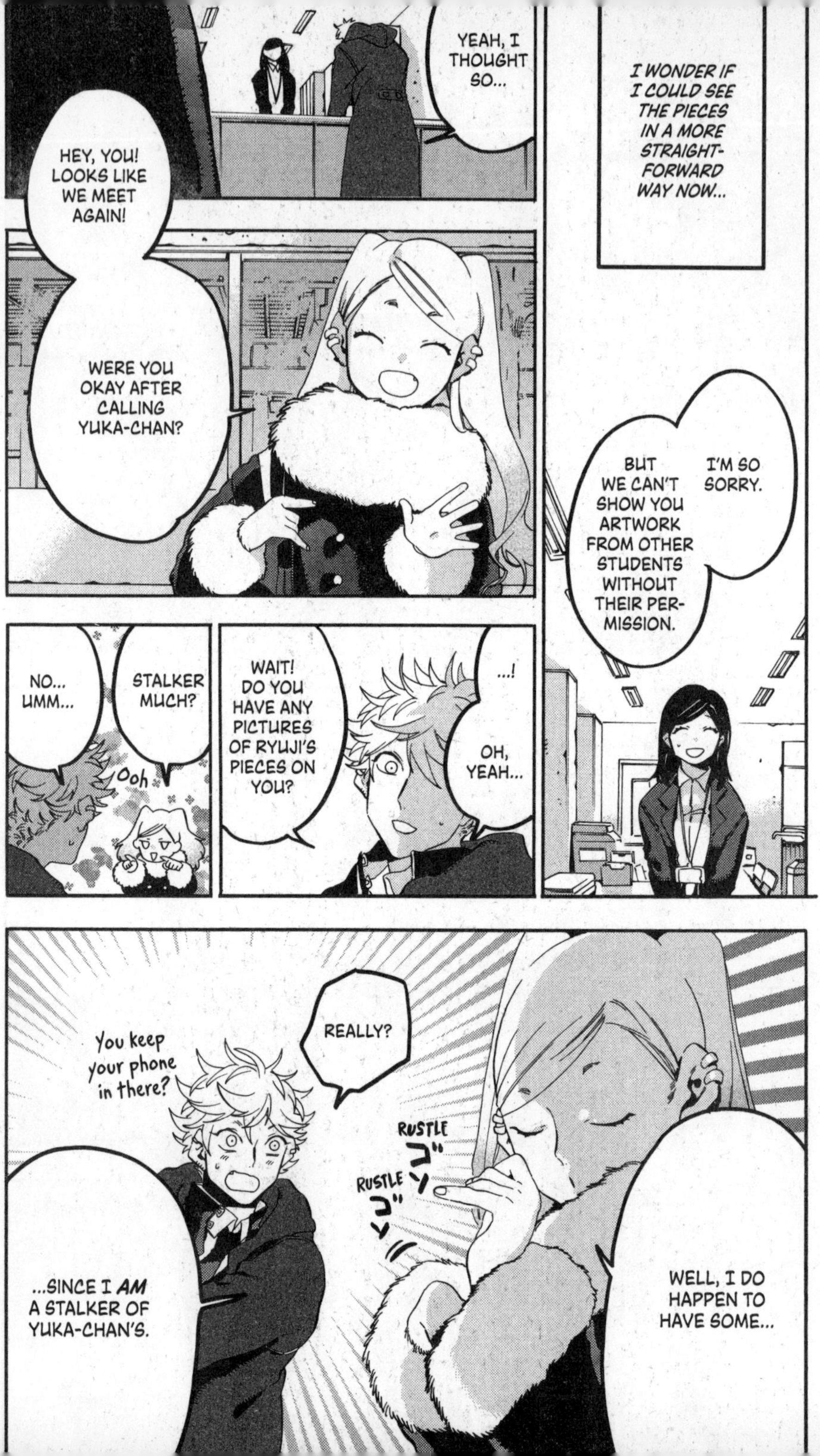
I WONDER IF I COULD SEE THE PIECES IN A MORE STRAIGHT-FORWARD WAY NOW...
I'M SO SORRY.
BUT WE CAN'T SHOW YOU ARTWORK FROM OTHER STUDENTS WITHOUT THEIR PER-MISSION.
YEAH, I THOUGHT SO...
HEY, YOU! LOOKS LIKE WE MEET AGAIN!
WERE YOU OKAY AFTER CALLING YUKA-CHAN?
...!
OH, YEAH...
WAIT! DO YOU HAVE ANY PICTURES OF RYUJI'S PIECES ON YOU?
STALKER MUCH?
Ooh
NO... UMM...
REALLY?
You keep your phone in there?
RUSTLE
RUSTLE
WELL, I DO HAPPEN TO HAVE SOME...
...SINCE I *AM* A STALKER OF YUKA-CHAN'S.

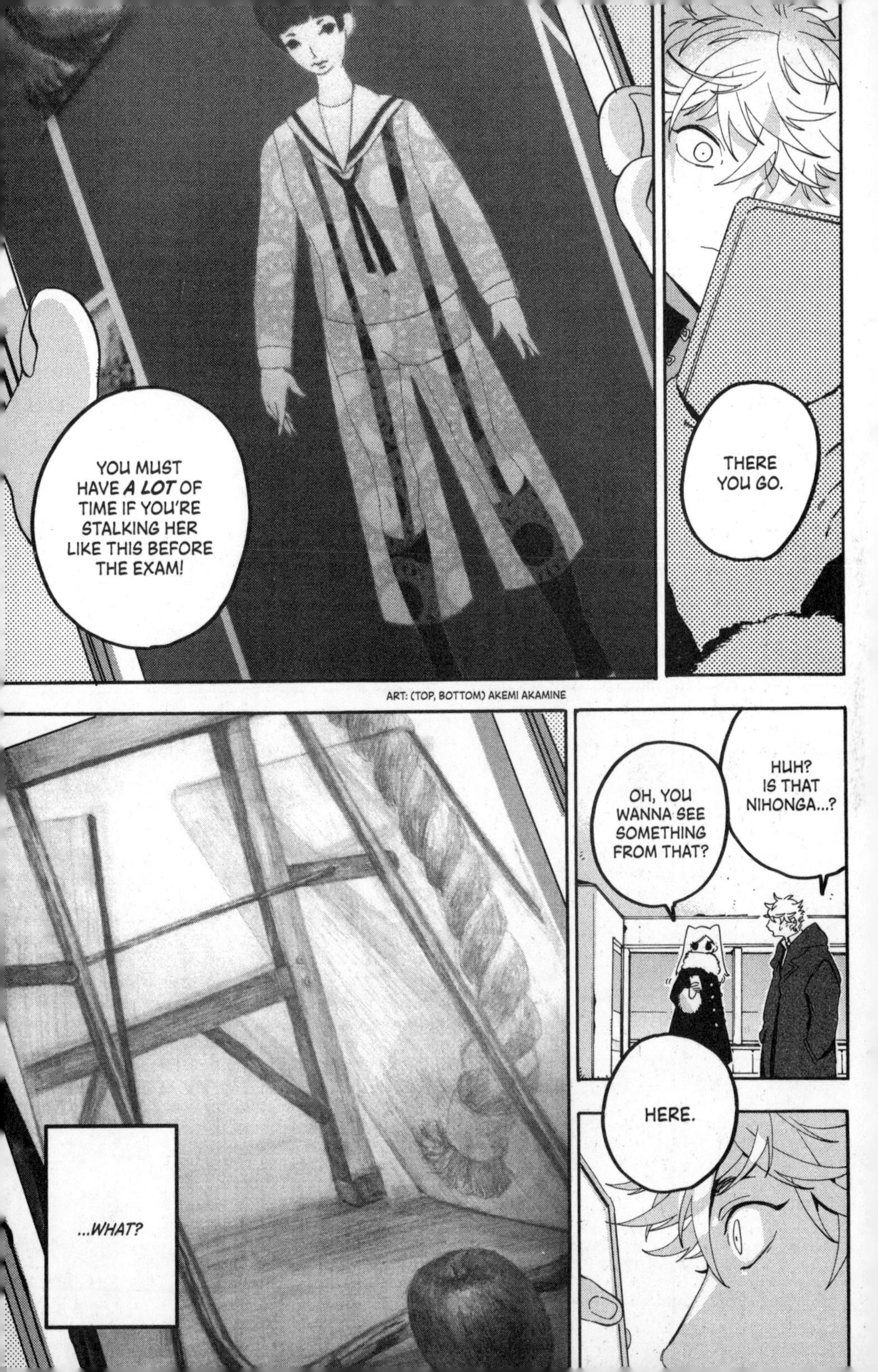
THERE YOU GO.
YOU MUST HAVE ***A LOT*** OF TIME IF YOU'RE STALKING HER LIKE THIS BEFORE THE EXAM!
HUH? IS THAT NIHONGA...?
OH, YOU WANNA SEE SOMETHING FROM THAT?
HERE.
*...WHAT?*
ART: (TOP, BOTTOM) AKEMI AKAMINE

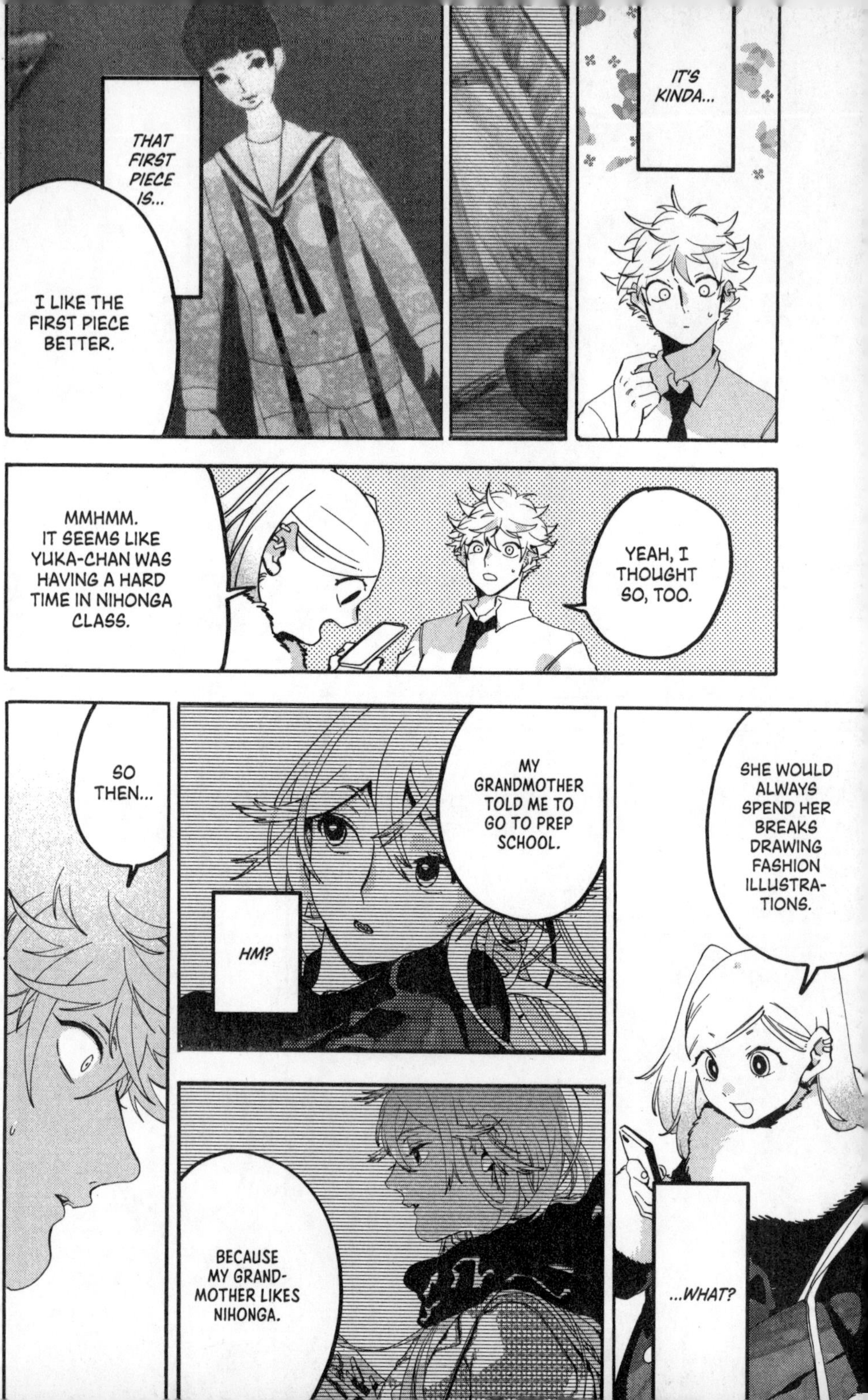
IT'S KINDA...
THAT FIRST PIECE IS...
I LIKE THE FIRST PIECE BETTER.
YEAH, I THOUGHT SO, TOO.
MMHMM. IT SEEMS LIKE YUKA-CHAN WAS HAVING A HARD TIME IN NIHONGA CLASS.
SHE WOULD ALWAYS SPEND HER BREAKS DRAWING FASHION ILLUSTRA-TIONS.
...WHAT?
MY GRANDMOTHER TOLD ME TO GO TO PREP SCHOOL.
HM?
BECAUSE MY GRAND-MOTHER LIKES NIHONGA.
SO THEN...

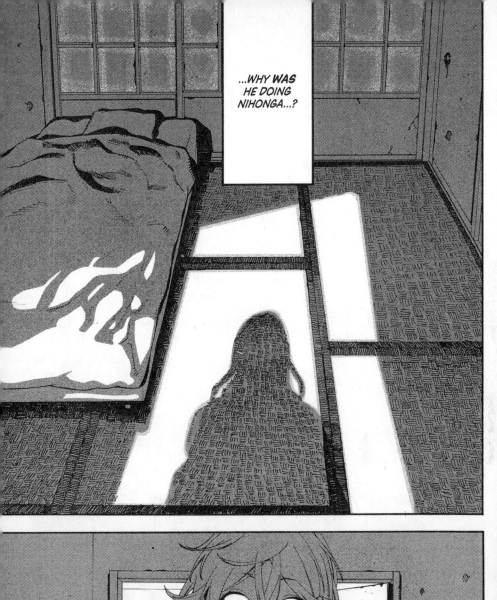

...WHY WAS
HE DOING
NIHONGA...?

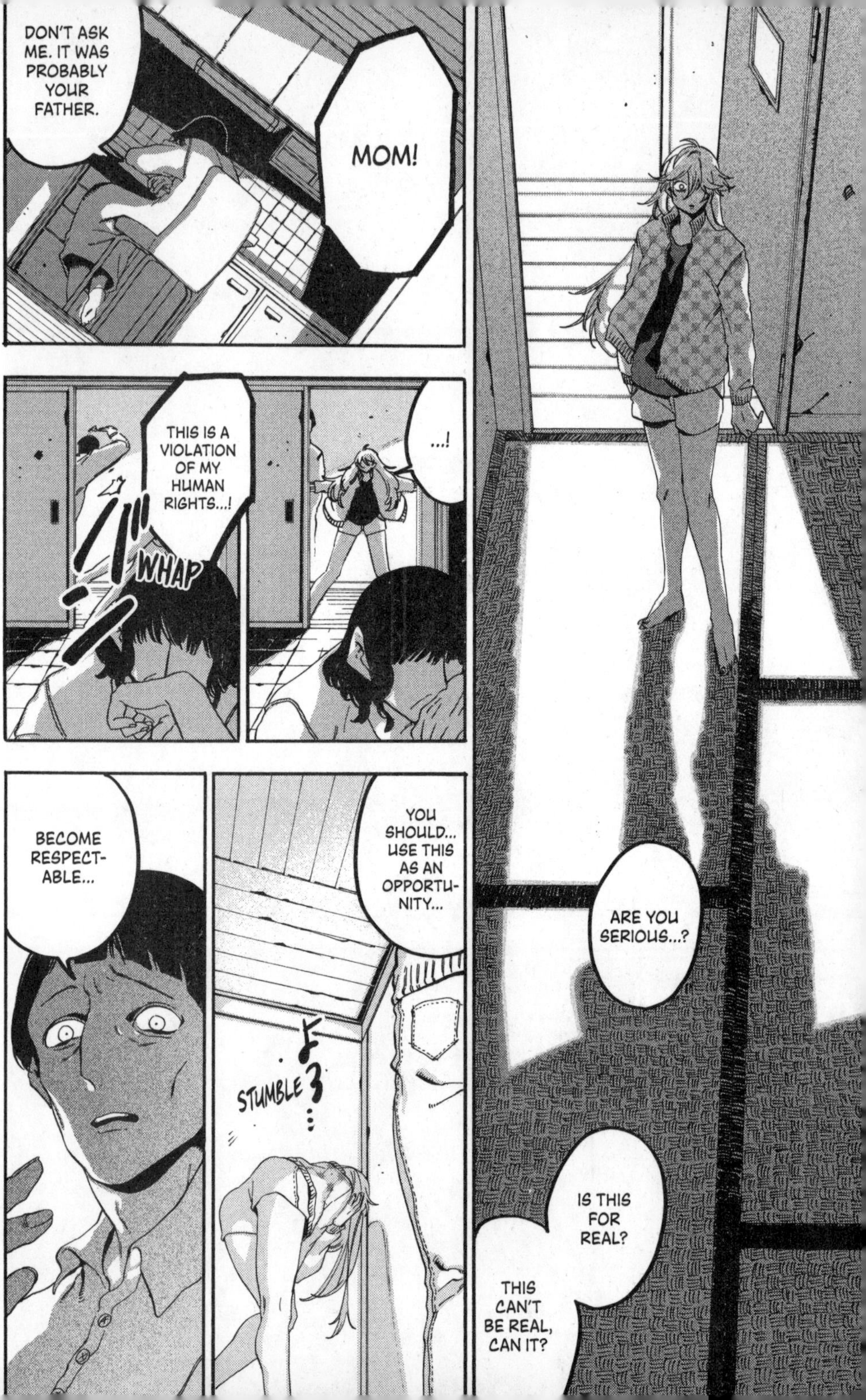
ARE YOU SERIOUS...?
IS THIS FOR REAL?
THIS CAN'T BE REAL, CAN IT?
MOM!
DON'T ASK ME. IT WAS PROBABLY YOUR FATHER.
...!
THIS IS A VIOLATION OF MY HUMAN RIGHTS...!
WHAP
YOU SHOULD... USE THIS AS AN OPPORTUNITY...
STUMBLE
BECOME RESPECTABLE...

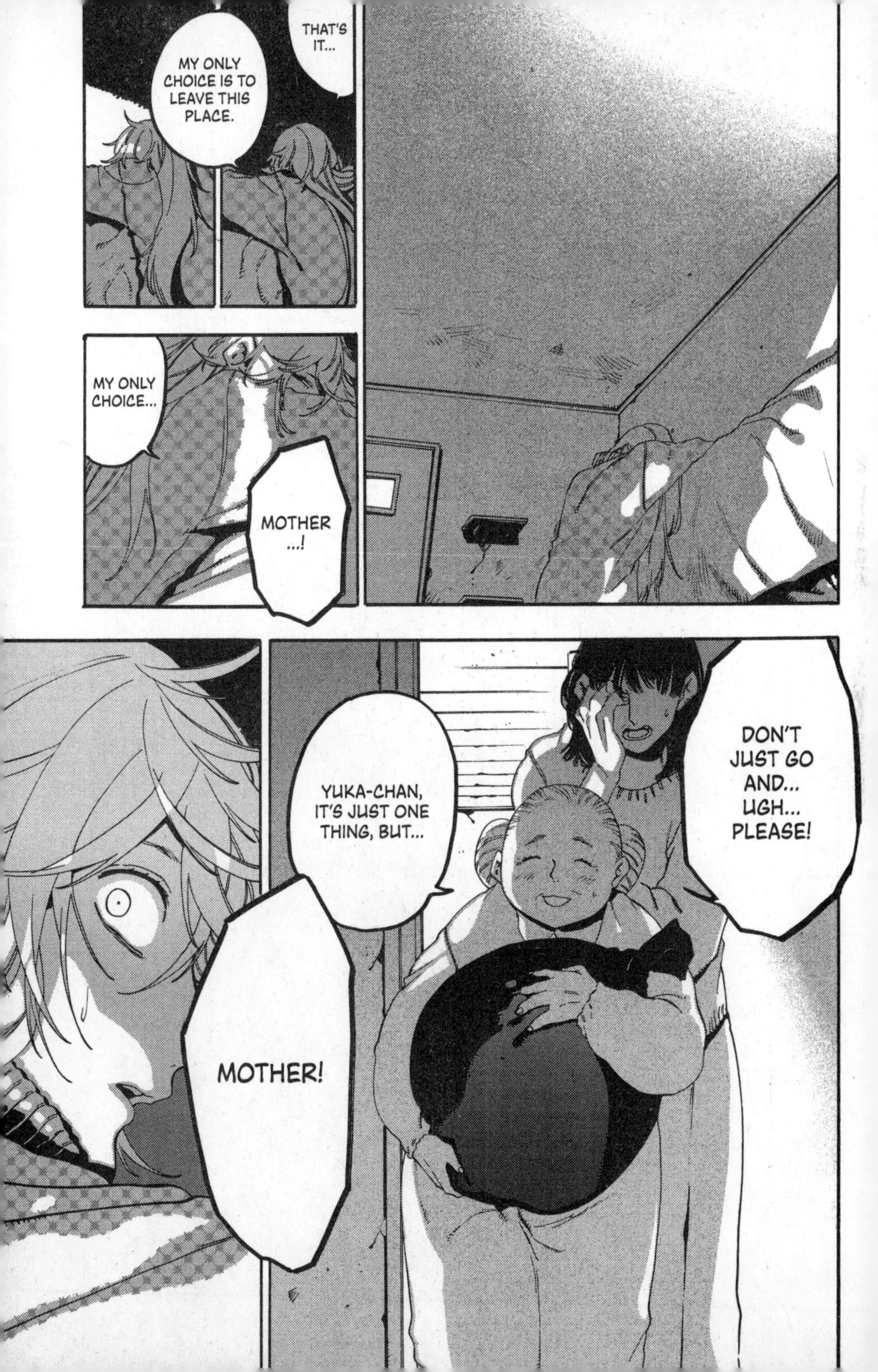
THAT'S IT...
MY ONLY CHOICE IS TO LEAVE THIS PLACE.
MY ONLY CHOICE...
MOTHER ...!
DON'T JUST GO AND... UGH... PLEASE!
YUKA-CHAN, IT'S JUST ONE THING, BUT...
MOTHER!

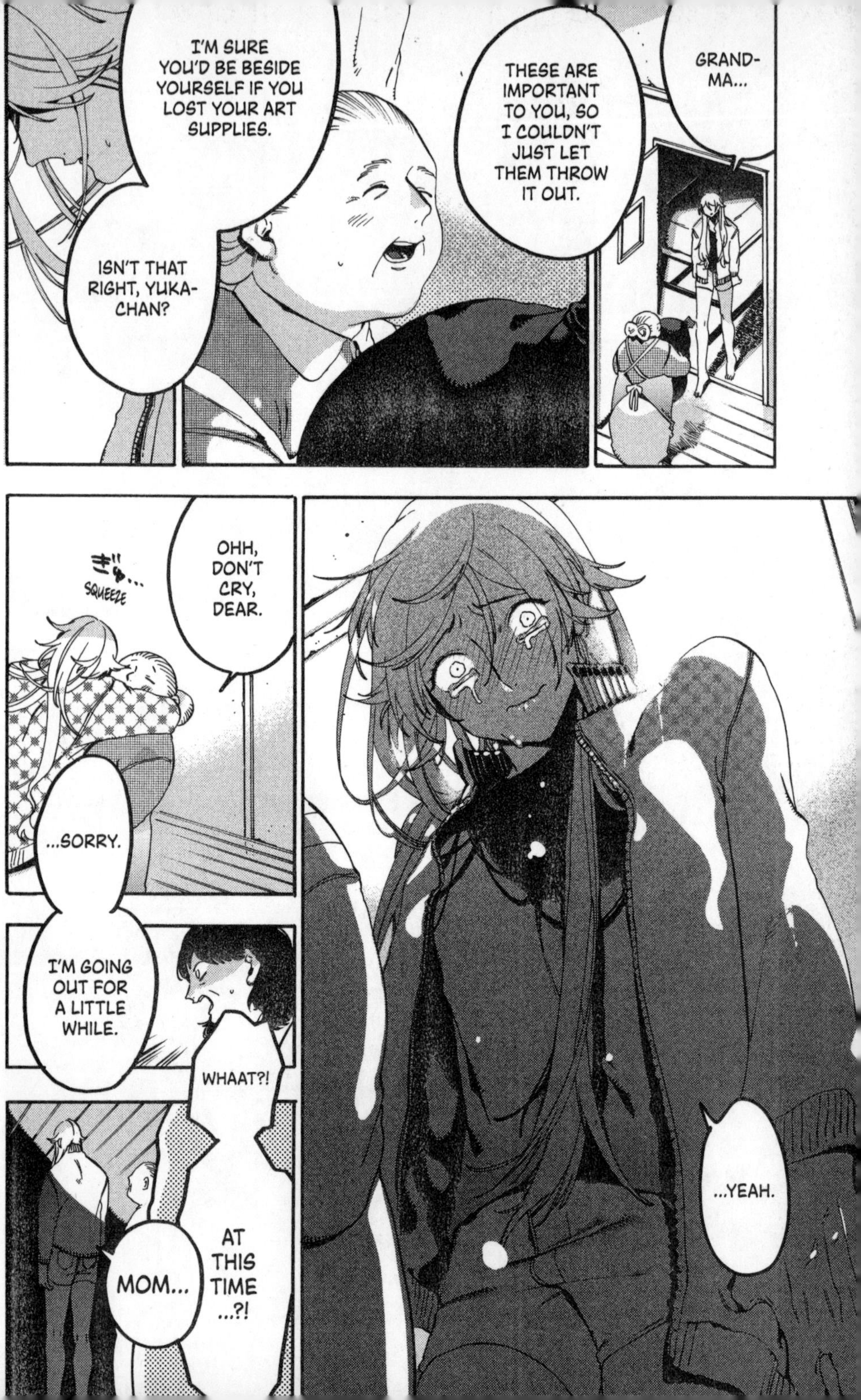
GRAND-MA...
THESE ARE IMPORTANT TO YOU, SO I COULDN'T JUST LET THEM THROW IT OUT.
I'M SURE YOU'D BE BESIDE YOURSELF IF YOU LOST YOUR ART SUPPLIES.
ISN'T THAT RIGHT, YUKA-CHAN?
...YEAH.
OHH, DON'T CRY, DEAR.
ぎゅ…
SQUEEZE
...SORRY.
I'M GOING OUT FOR A LITTLE WHILE.
WHAAT?!
AT THIS TIME ...?!
MOM...

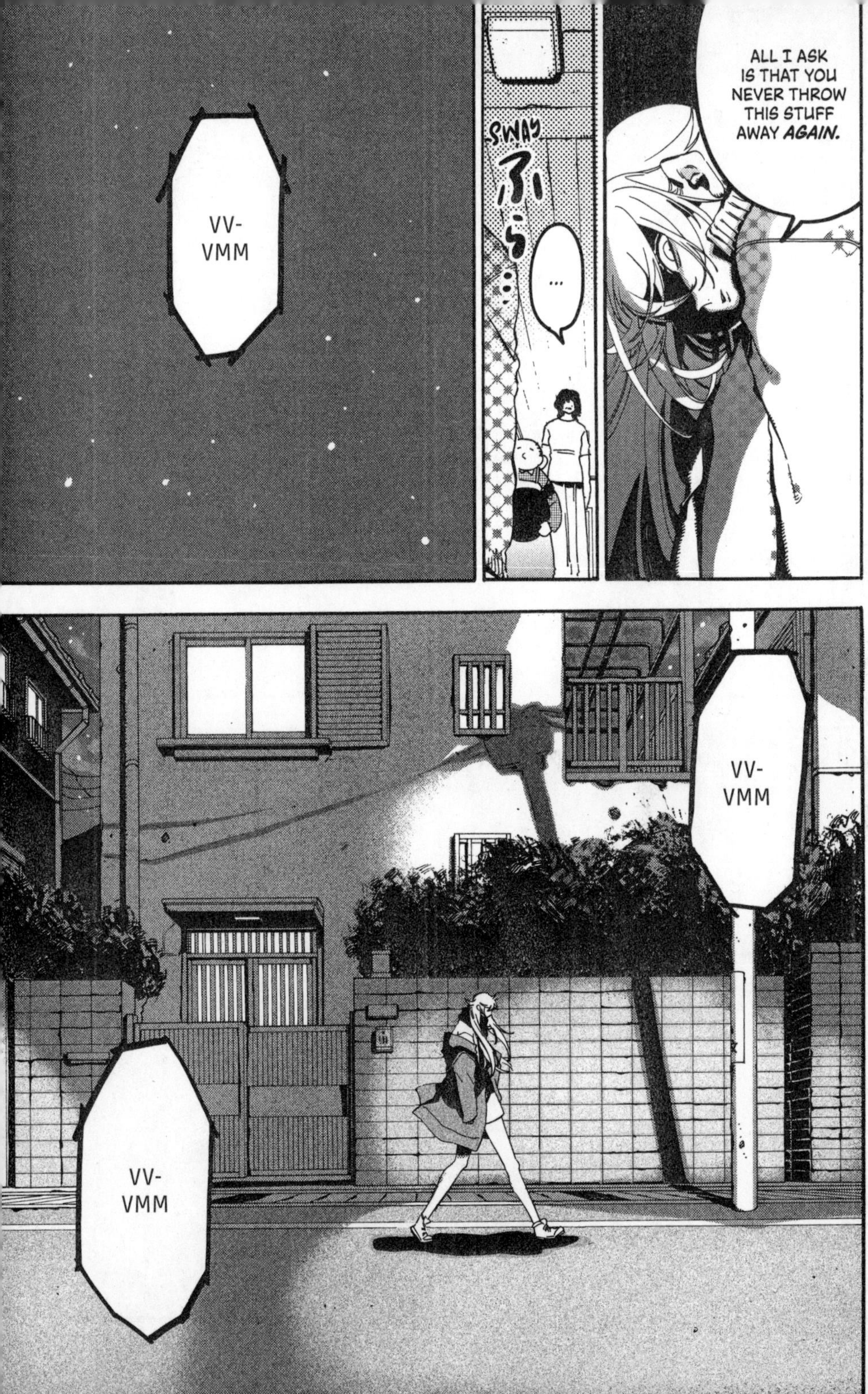
ALL I ASK IS THAT YOU NEVER THROW THIS STUFF AWAY *AGAIN.*
SWAY
ふら…
...
VV-VMM
VV-VMM
VV-VMM

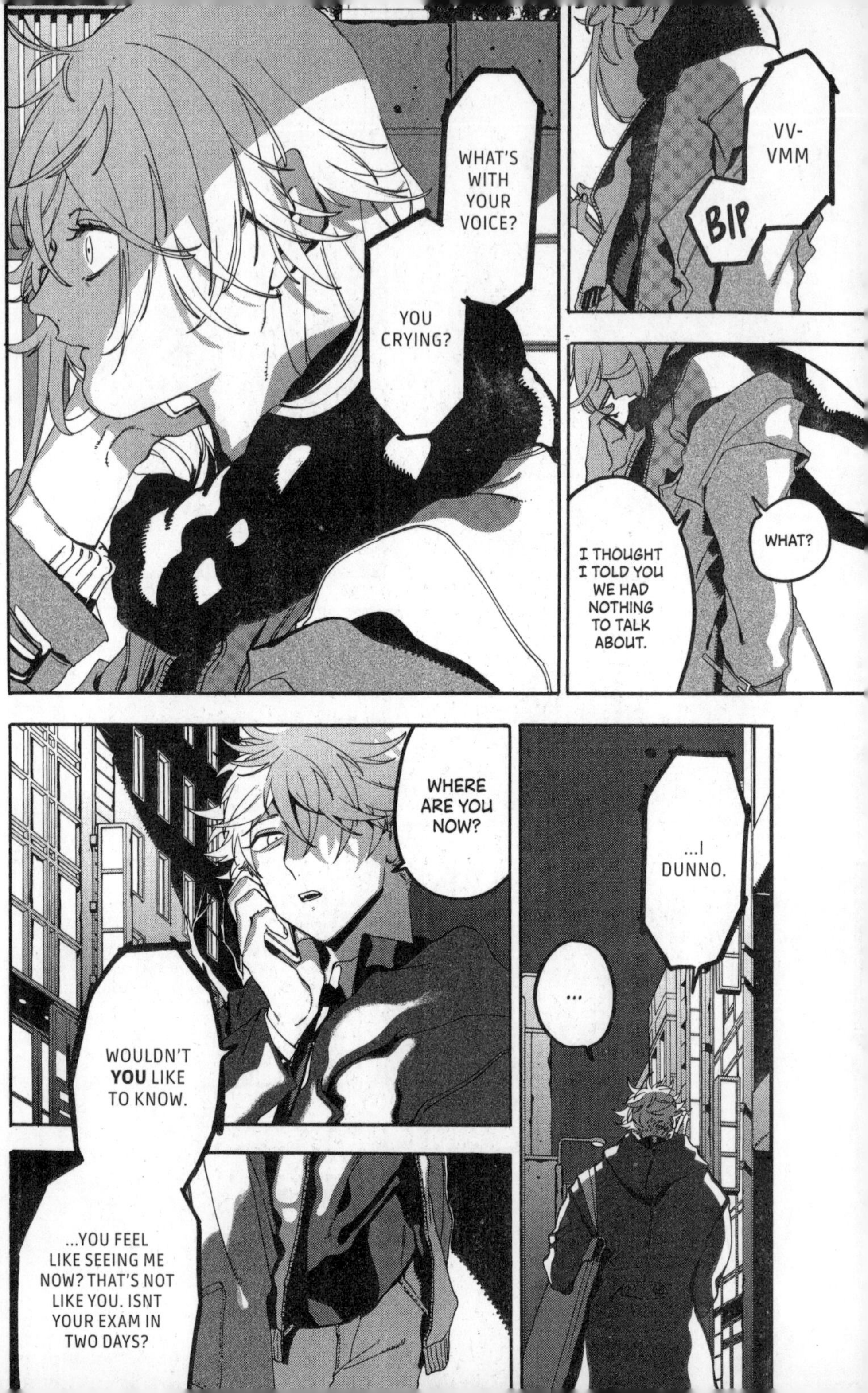
VV-VMM
BIP
WHAT?
I THOUGHT I TOLD YOU WE HAD NOTHING TO TALK ABOUT.
WHAT'S WITH YOUR VOICE?
YOU CRYING?
...I DUNNO.
...
WHERE ARE YOU NOW?
WOULDN'T **YOU** LIKE TO KNOW.
...YOU FEEL LIKE SEEING ME NOW? THAT'S NOT LIKE YOU. ISNT YOUR EXAM IN TWO DAYS?

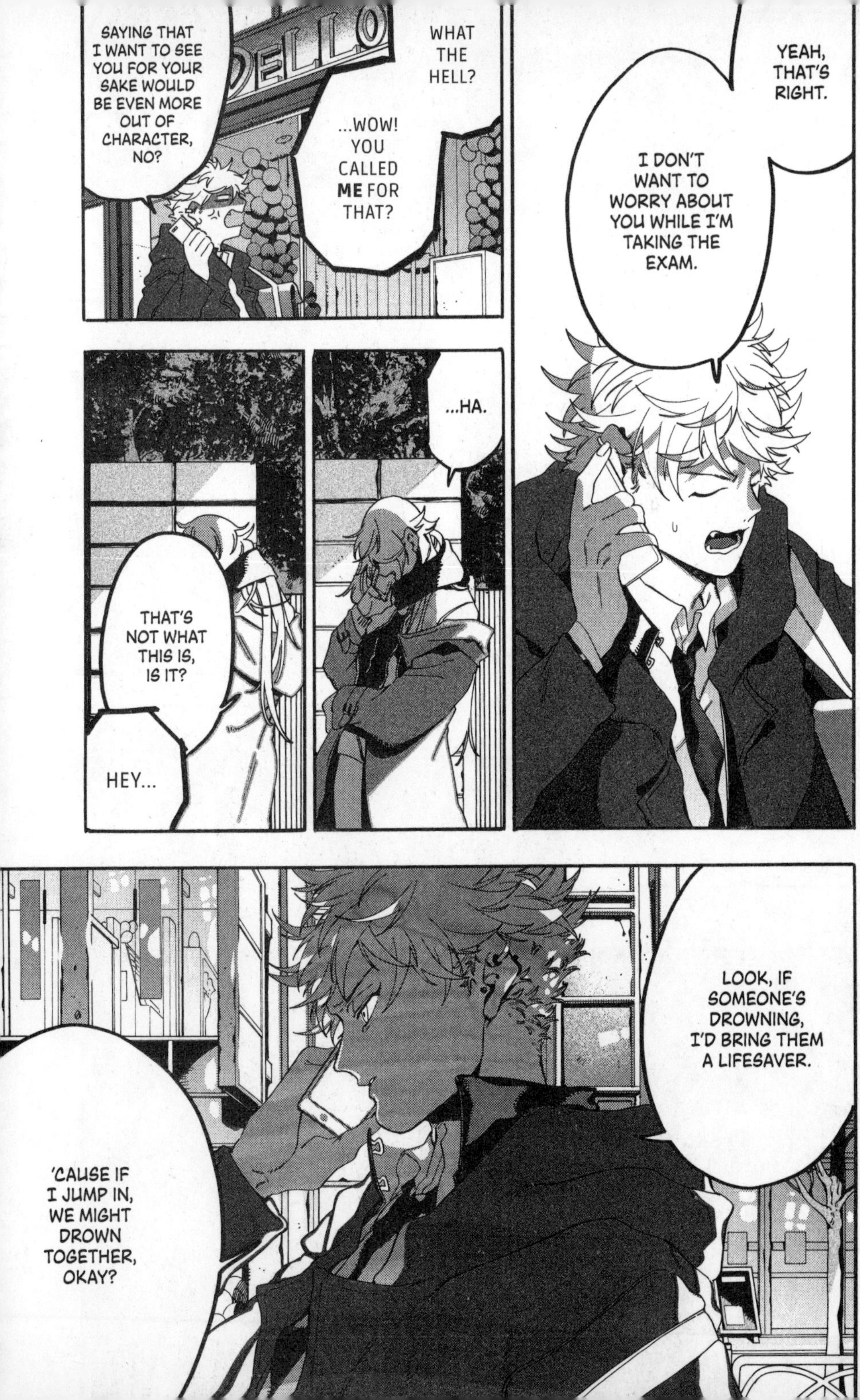
YEAH, THAT'S RIGHT.
I DON'T WANT TO WORRY ABOUT YOU WHILE I'M TAKING THE EXAM.
WHAT THE HELL?
...WOW! YOU CALLED **ME** FOR THAT?
SAYING THAT I WANT TO SEE YOU FOR YOUR SAKE WOULD BE EVEN MORE OUT OF CHARACTER, NO?
...HA.
THAT'S NOT WHAT THIS IS, IS IT?
HEY...
LOOK, IF SOMEONE'S DROWNING, I'D BRING THEM A LIFESAVER.
'CAUSE IF I JUMP IN, WE MIGHT DROWN TOGETHER, OKAY?

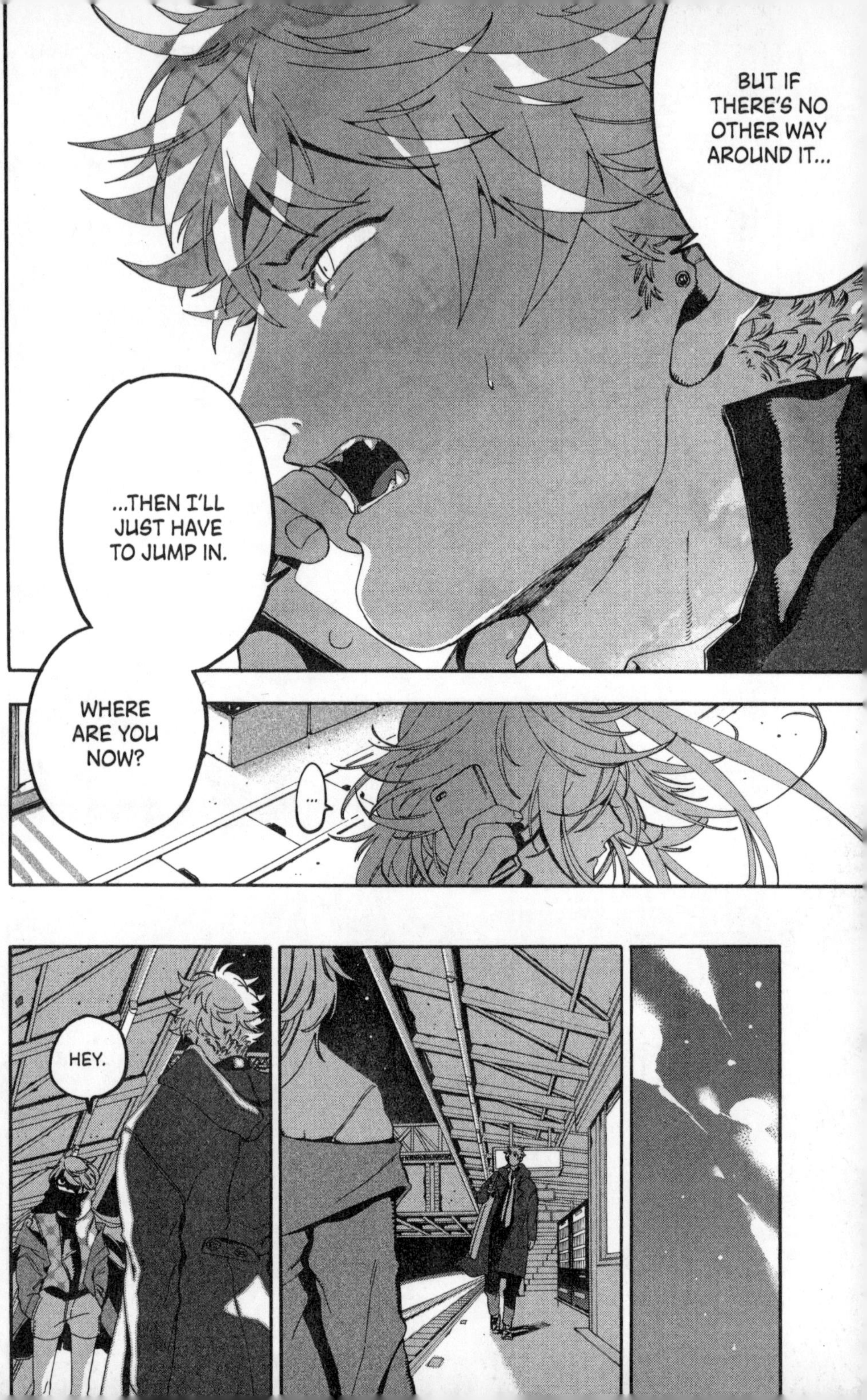
BUT IF THERE'S NO OTHER WAY AROUND IT...
...THEN I'LL JUST HAVE TO JUMP IN.
WHERE ARE YOU NOW?
...
HEY.

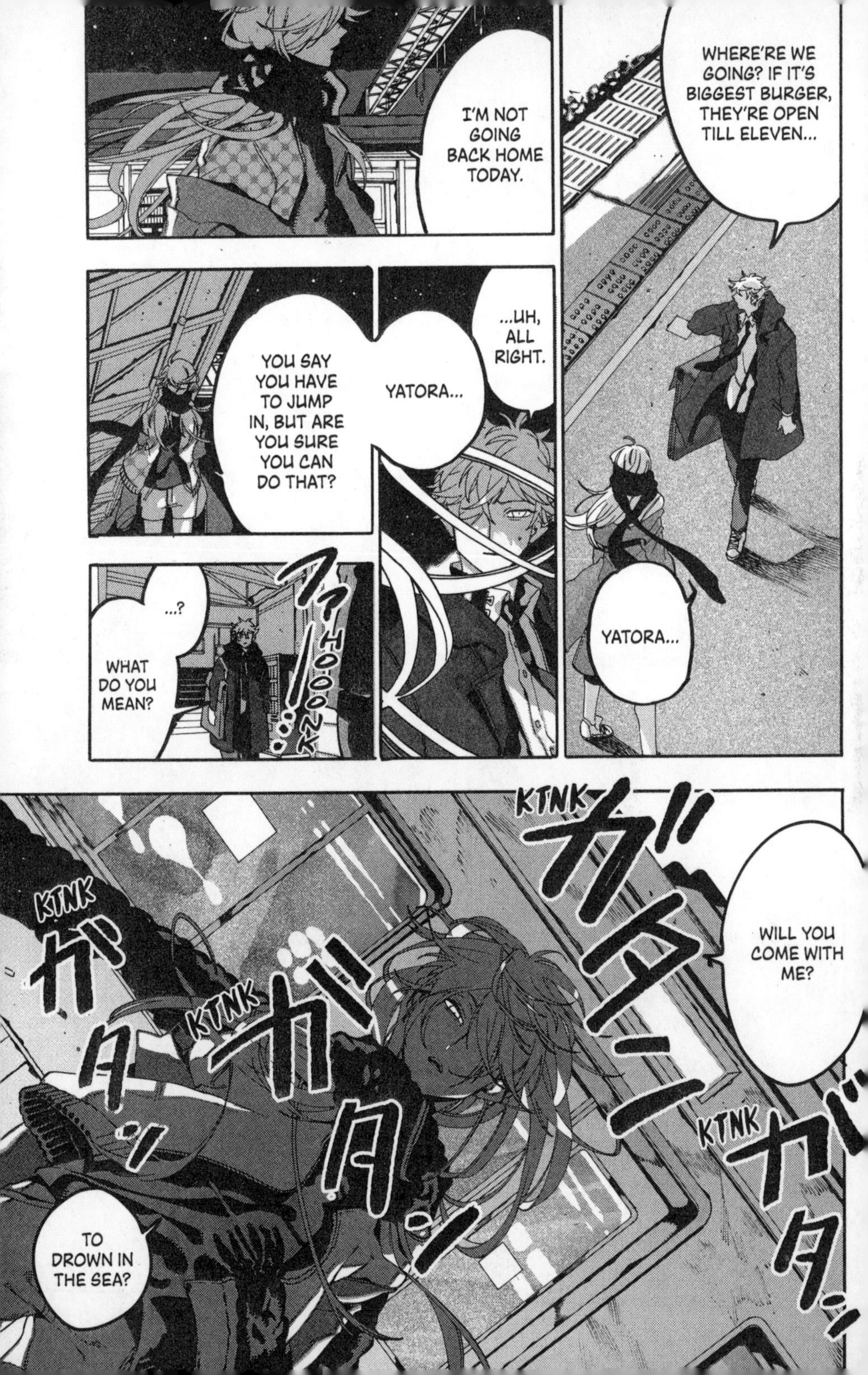
WHERE'RE WE GOING? IF IT'S BIGGEST BURGER, THEY'RE OPEN TILL ELEVEN...
YATORA...
I'M NOT GOING BACK HOME TODAY.
...UH, ALL RIGHT.
YATORA...
YOU SAY YOU HAVE TO JUMP IN, BUT ARE YOU SURE YOU CAN DO THAT?
HOOOONK...
...?
WHAT DO YOU MEAN?
WILL YOU COME WITH ME?
KTNK
KTNK
KTNK
KTNK
TO DROWN IN THE SEA?

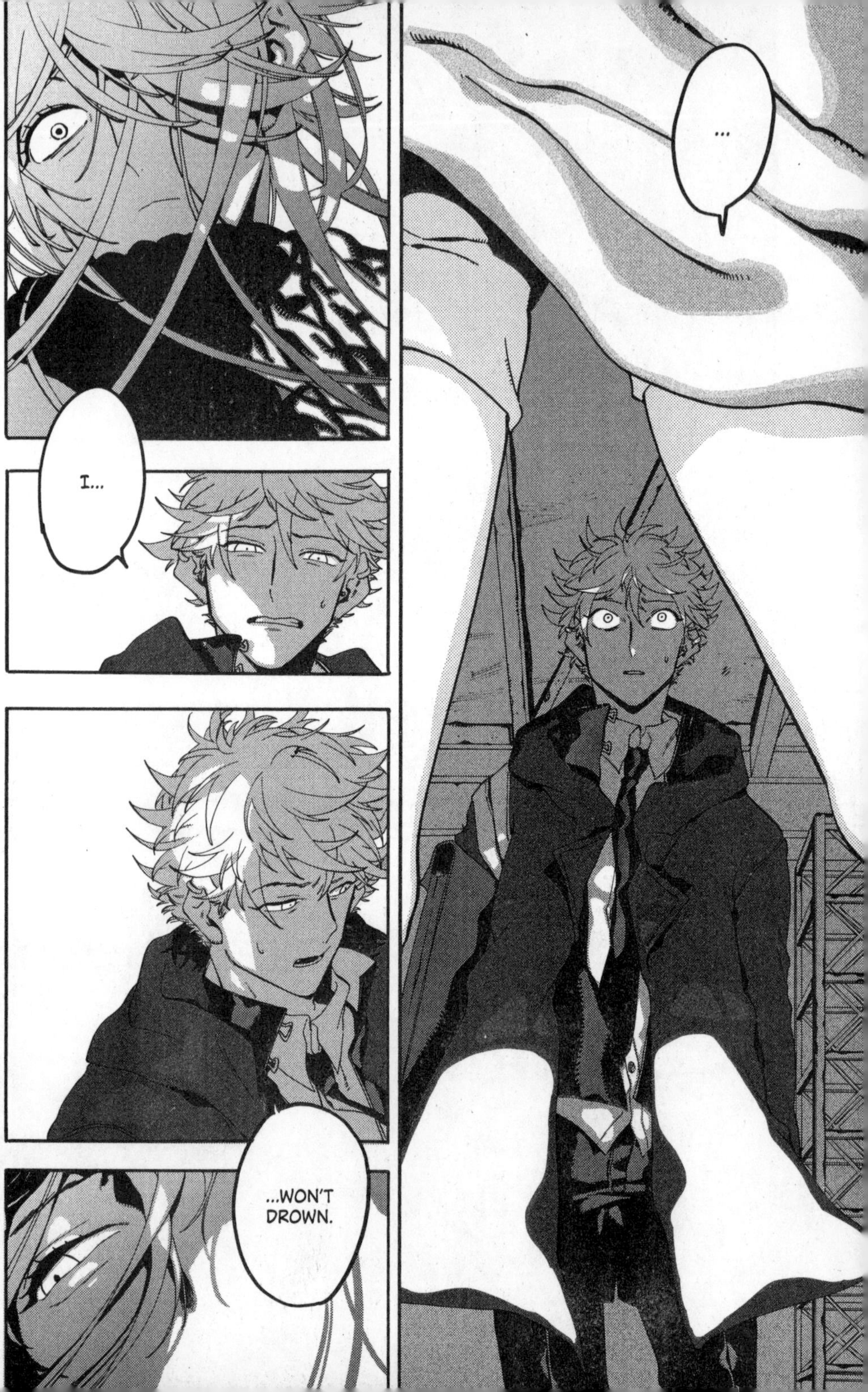
...
I...
...WON'T DROWN.

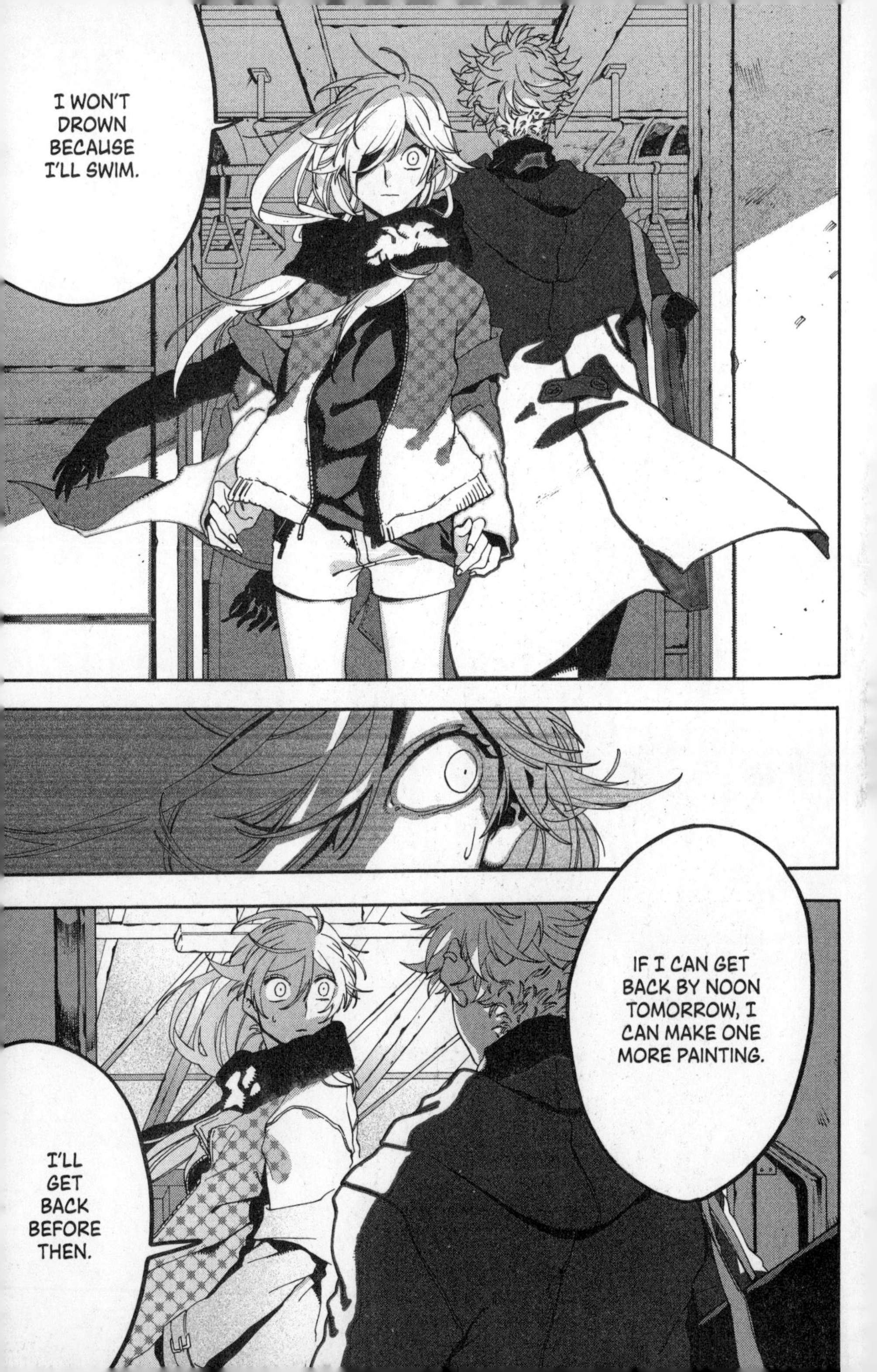
I WON'T DROWN BECAUSE I'LL SWIM.
IF I CAN GET BACK BY NOON TOMORROW, I CAN MAKE ONE MORE PAINTING.
I'LL GET BACK BEFORE THEN.

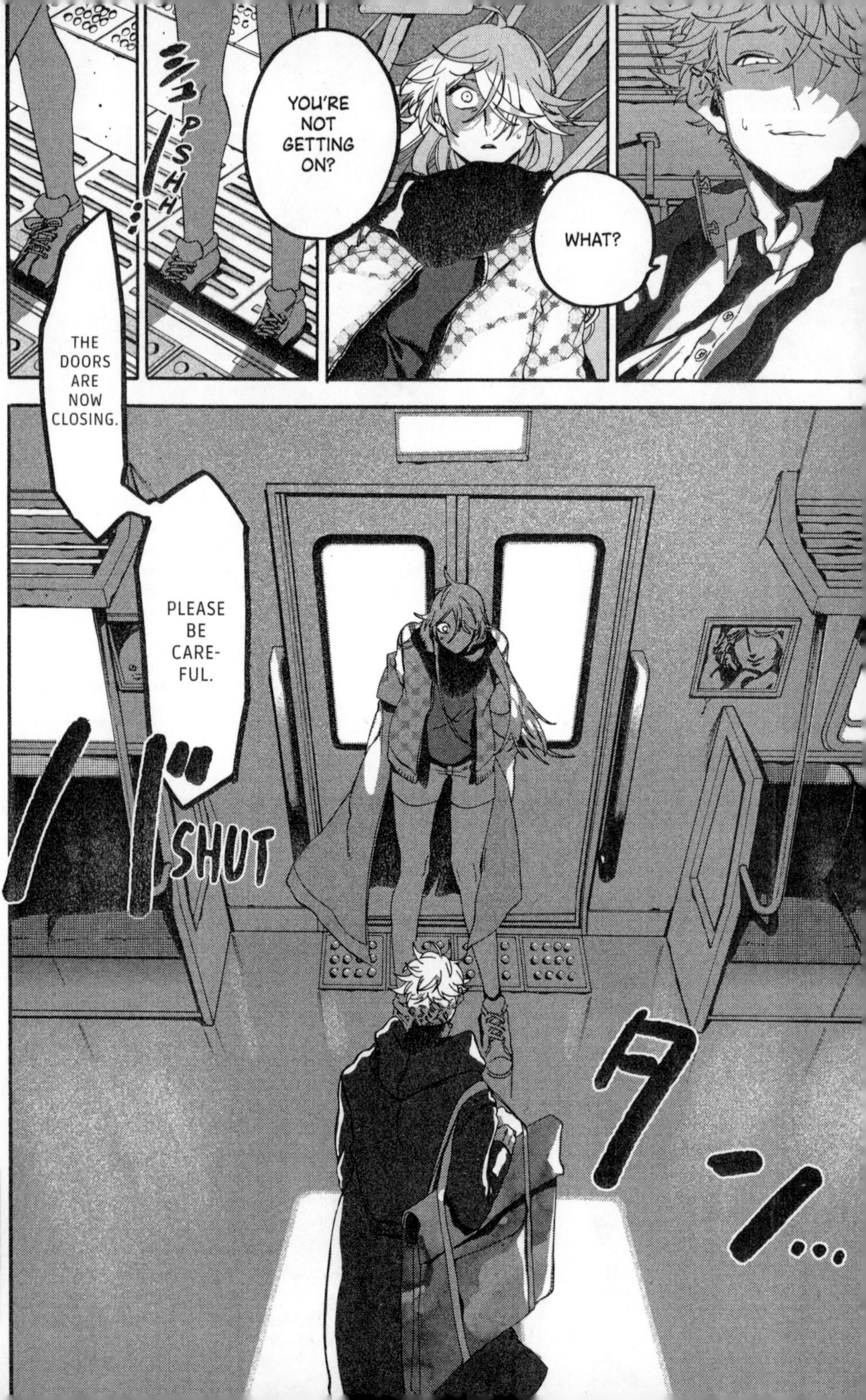

WHAT?
YOU'RE NOT GETTING ON?
PSHH
THE DOORS ARE NOW CLOSING.
PLEASE BE CARE-FUL.
SHUT

STORY 19 END

# BLUE PERIOD

## GETTING EXCITED

MORI-SENPAI AND YUKA-CHAN...
...LOVE JAPANESE SWEETS.
AH... I WANNA EAT SOME *ANMITSU* FROM MIHASHI.
WANNA GO NEXT TIME?
OH, IN THAT CASE, I'D LIKE TO TRY GOING TO KAMEJUU IN ASAKUSA.
AH, THAT SOUNDS NICE... JAPANESE SWEETS... I SURE COULD GO FOR SOME NOW...
WOULD YOU CARE FOR SOME YAOTSU *KURI-KINTON*?
POP
HUH?! WHOA! IT'S THE REAL THING!!
OH, WOW! SO IT'S ALREADY IN SEASON!
They were a gift.


## ABOUT THE PREP-SCHOOL STUDENTS

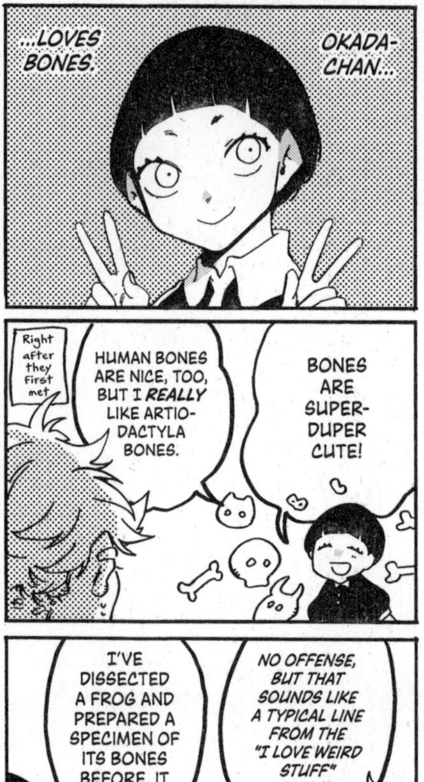

OKADA-CHAN...
...LOVES BONES.
BONES ARE SUPER-DUPER CUTE!
HUMAN BONES ARE NICE, TOO, BUT I *REALLY* LIKE ARTIO-DACTYLA BONES.
Right after they first met
NO OFFENSE, BUT THAT SOUNDS LIKE A TYPICAL LINE FROM THE "I LOVE WEIRD STUFF" CROWD.
I'VE DISSECTED A FROG AND PREPARED A SPECIMEN OF ITS BONES BEFORE. IT WAS FUN!
OH, SHE'S THE REAL DEAL...
I'D LIKE TO TRY FEEDING MEAT TO MAGGOTS TO HAVE THEM EAT IT CLEAN TO THE BONE!

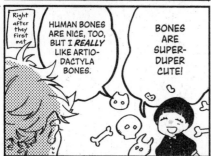

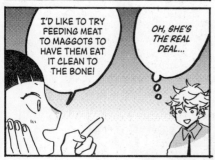

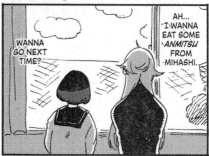

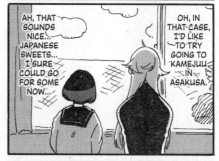

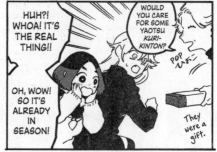

HOW THEY COMPLIMENT A BEAUTY

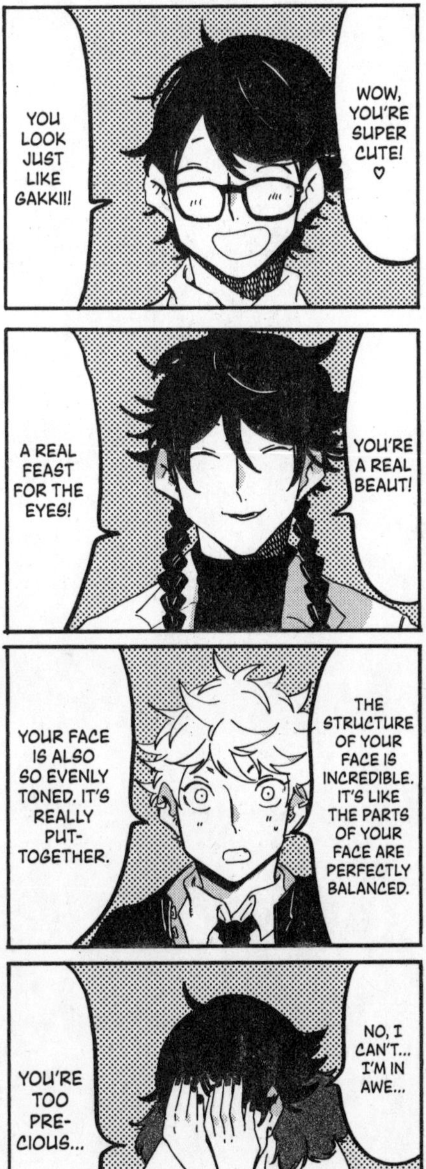
WOW, YOU'RE SUPER CUTE! ♡
YOU LOOK JUST LIKE GAKKII!
YOU'RE A REAL BEAUT!
A REAL FEAST FOR THE EYES!
THE STRUCTURE OF YOUR FACE IS INCREDIBLE. IT'S LIKE THE PARTS OF YOUR FACE ARE PERFECTLY BALANCED.
YOUR FACE IS ALSO SO EVENLY TONED. IT'S REALLY PUT-TOGETHER.
NO, I CAN'T... I'M IN AWE...
YOU'RE TOO PRECIOUS...

IT'S KINDA EMBARRASSING FOR OTHERS TO SEE YOUR ART

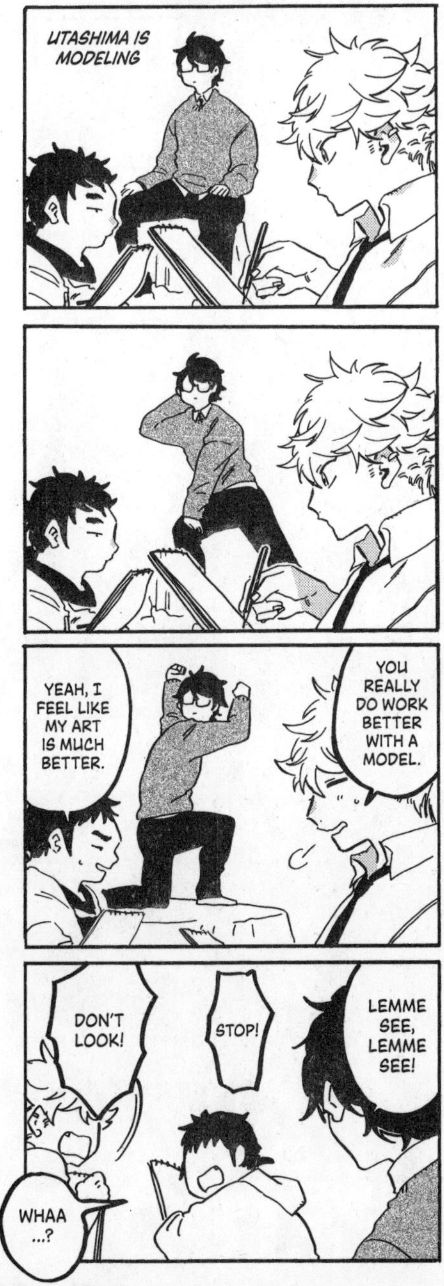
UTASHIMA IS MODELING
YOU REALLY DO WORK BETTER WITH A MODEL.
YEAH, I FEEL LIKE MY ART IS MUCH BETTER.
LEMME SEE, LEMME SEE!
STOP!
DON'T LOOK!
WHAA ...?

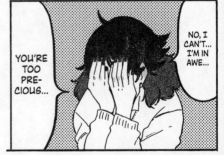

# BLUE PERIOD

# STROKE 20

## OUR BLUE

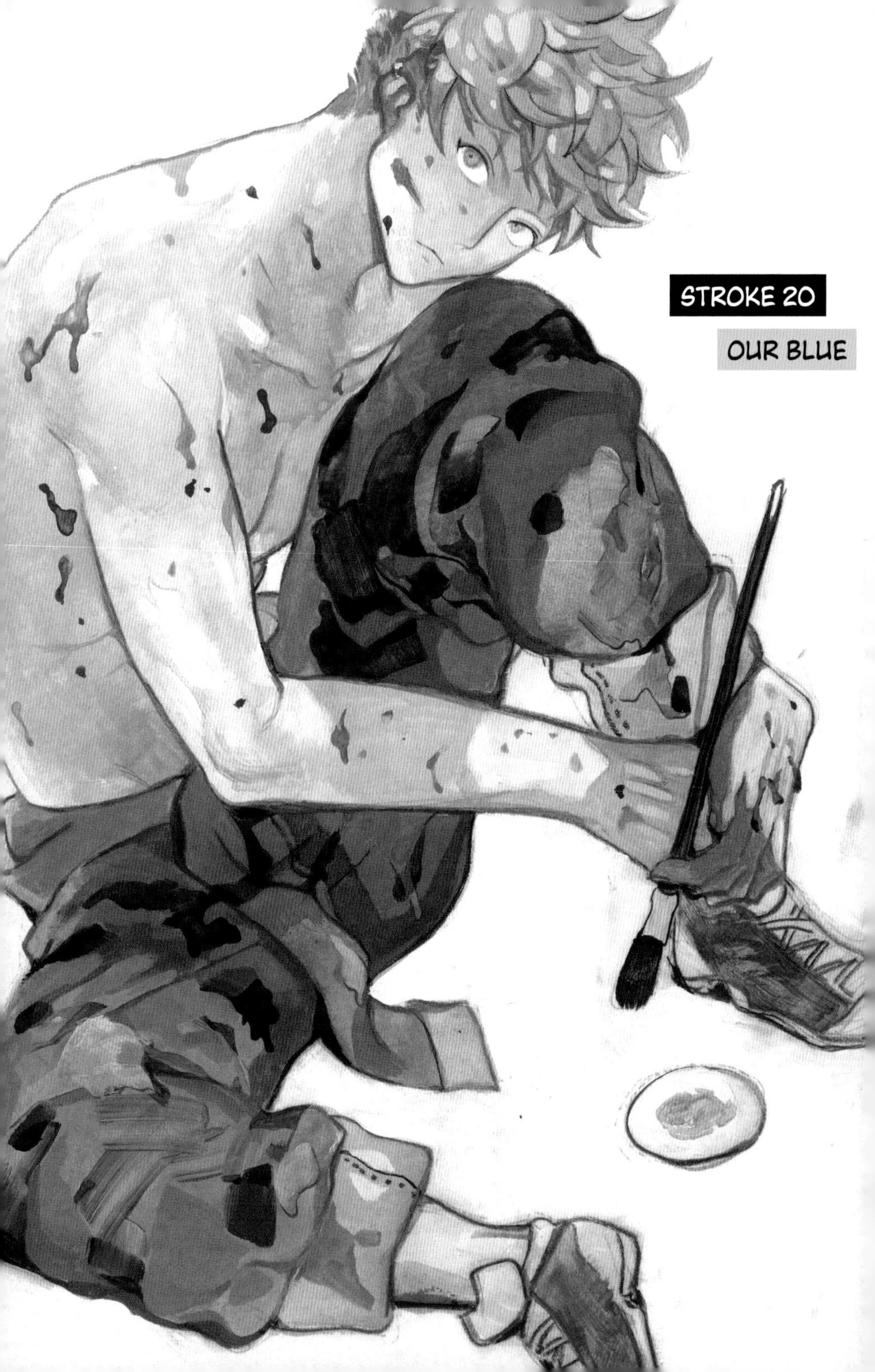

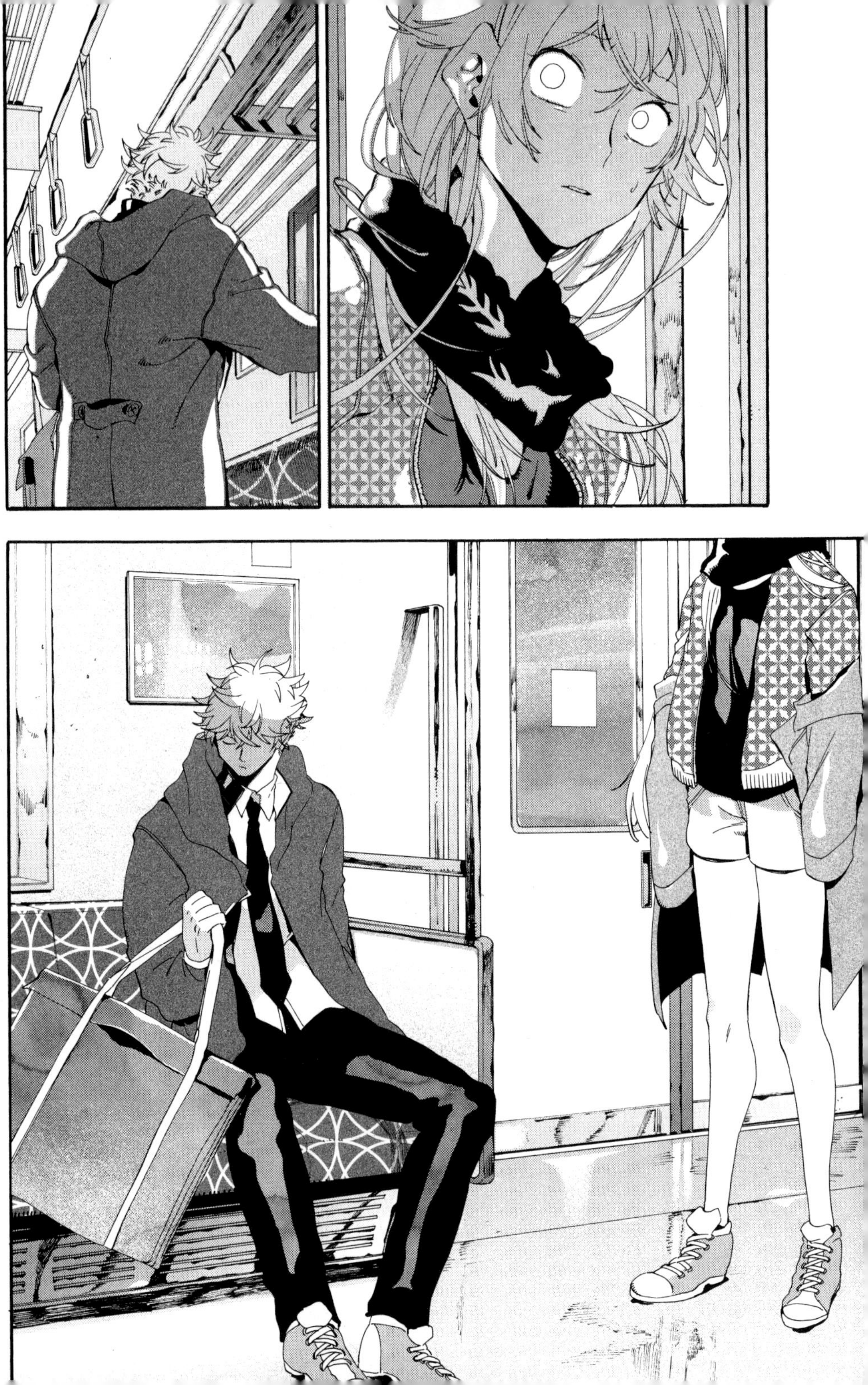

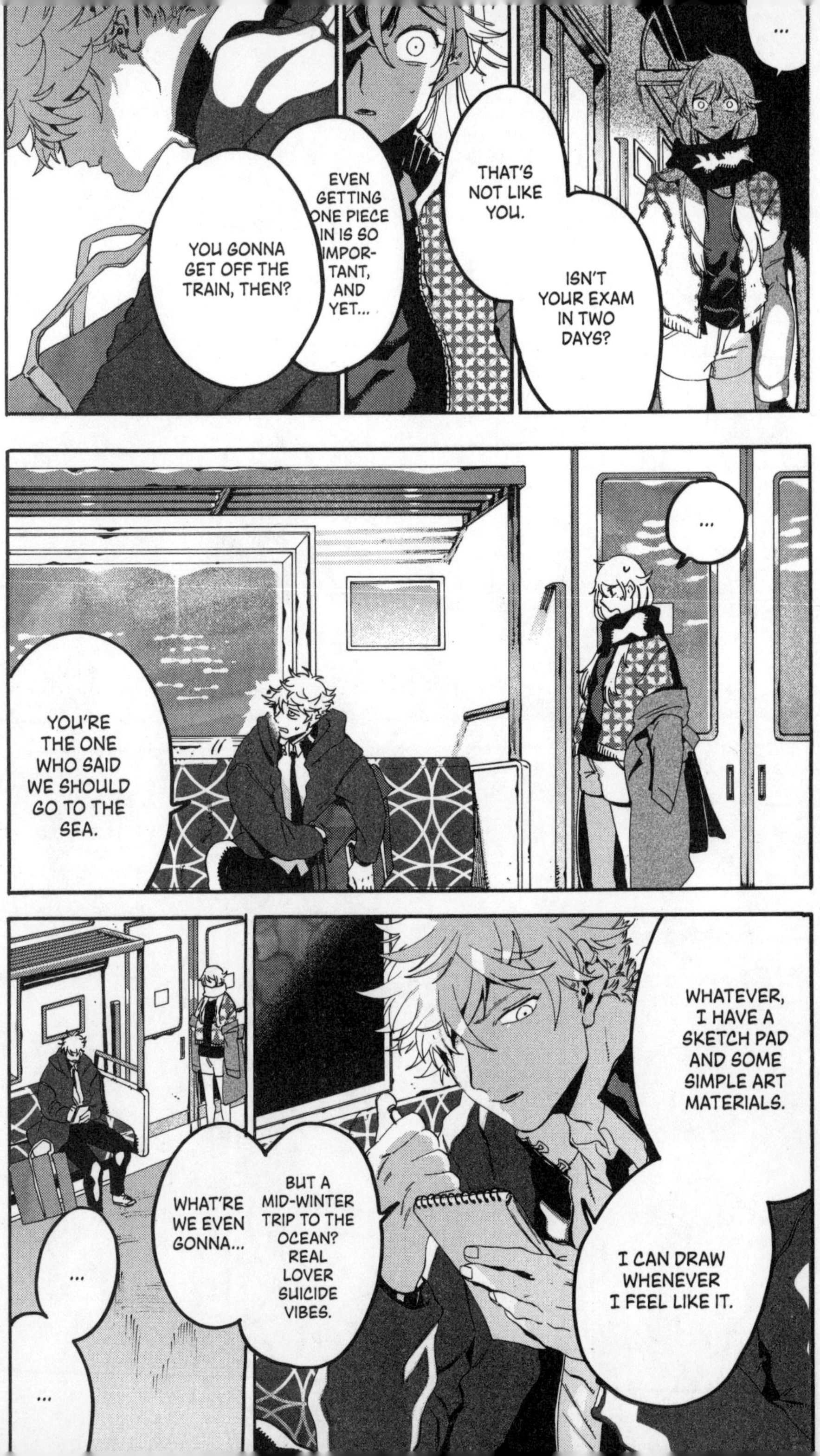
...
THAT'S NOT LIKE YOU.
ISN'T YOUR EXAM IN TWO DAYS?
EVEN GETTING ONE PIECE IN IS SO IMPORTANT, AND YET...
YOU GONNA GET OFF THE TRAIN, THEN?
...
YOU'RE THE ONE WHO SAID WE SHOULD GO TO THE SEA.
WHATEVER, I HAVE A SKETCH PAD AND SOME SIMPLE ART MATERIALS.
I CAN DRAW WHENEVER I FEEL LIKE IT.
BUT A MID-WINTER TRIP TO THE OCEAN? REAL LOVER SUICIDE VIBES.
WHAT'RE WE EVEN GONNA...
...
...

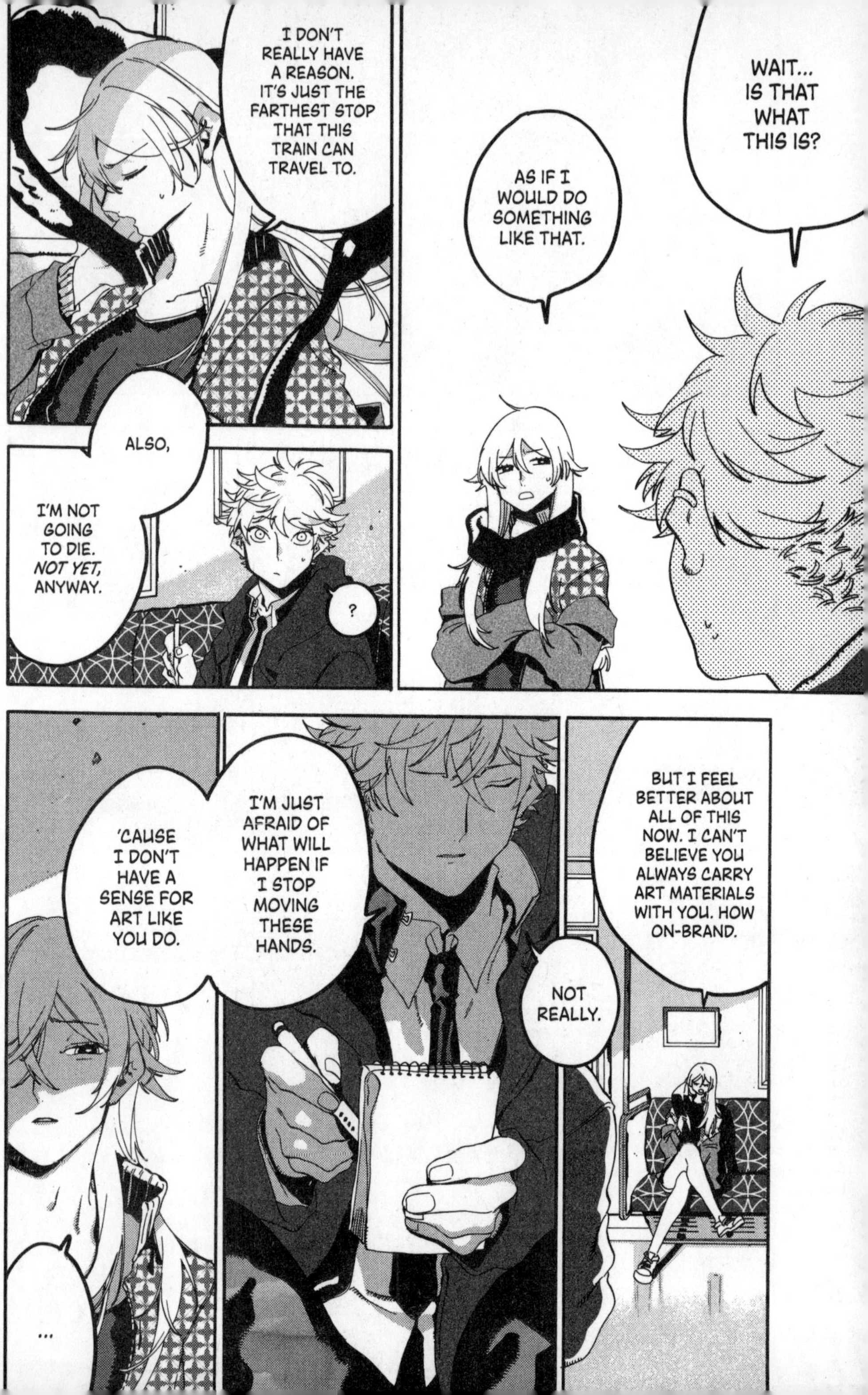
WAIT... IS THAT WHAT THIS IS?
AS IF I WOULD DO SOMETHING LIKE THAT.
I DON'T REALLY HAVE A REASON. IT'S JUST THE FARTHEST STOP THAT THIS TRAIN CAN TRAVEL TO.
ALSO,
I'M NOT GOING TO DIE. *NOT YET,* ANYWAY.
?
BUT I FEEL BETTER ABOUT ALL OF THIS NOW. I CAN'T BELIEVE YOU ALWAYS CARRY ART MATERIALS WITH YOU. HOW ON-BRAND.
NOT REALLY.
I'M JUST AFRAID OF WHAT WILL HAPPEN IF I STOP MOVING THESE HANDS.
'CAUSE I DON'T HAVE A SENSE FOR ART LIKE YOU DO.
...

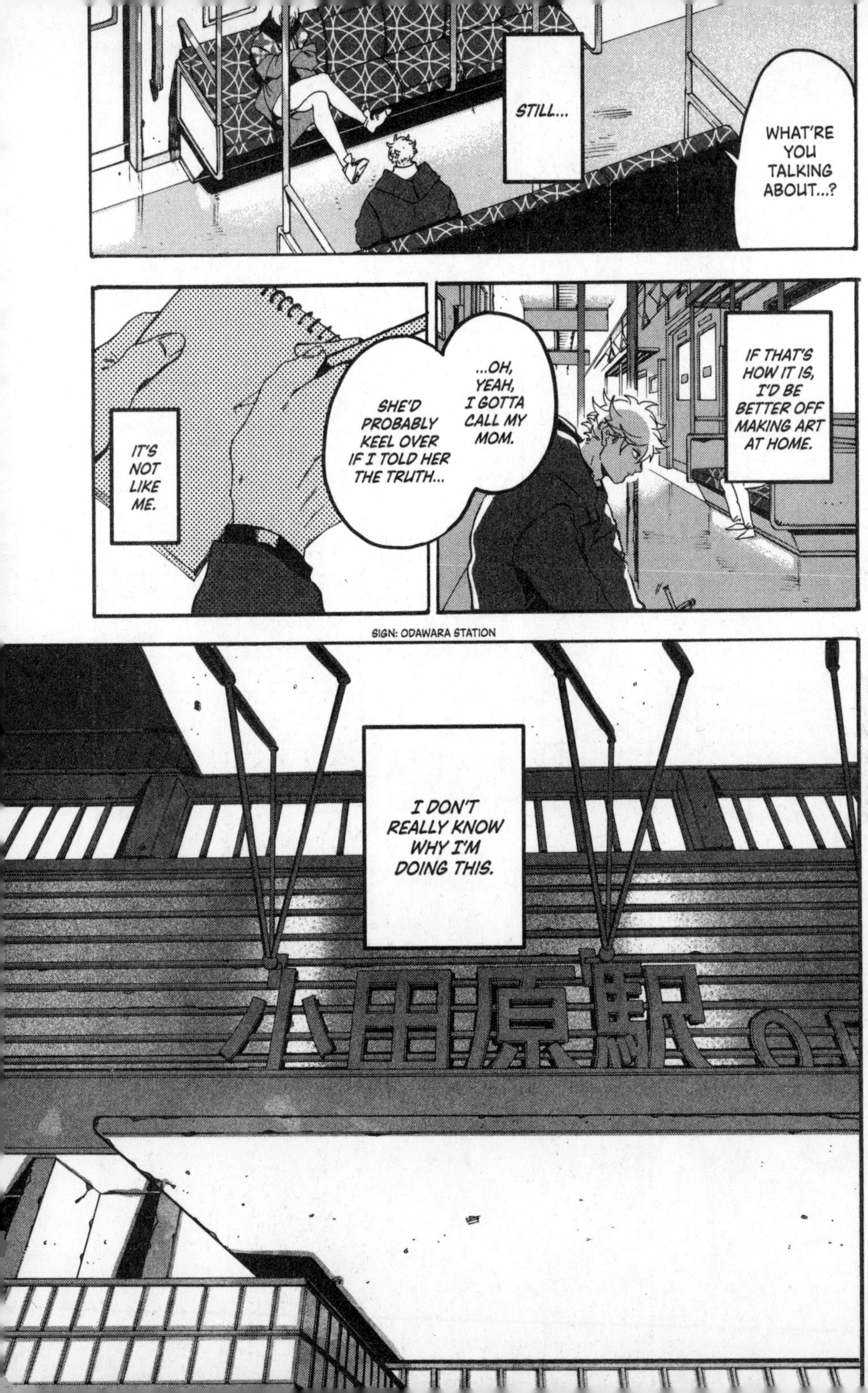
WHAT'RE YOU TALKING ABOUT...?
STILL...
IF THAT'S HOW IT IS, I'D BE BETTER OFF MAKING ART AT HOME.
...OH, YEAH, I GOTTA CALL MY MOM.
SHE'D PROBABLY KEEL OVER IF I TOLD HER THE TRUTH...
IT'S NOT LIKE ME.
SIGN: ODAWARA STATION
I DON'T REALLY KNOW WHY I'M DOING THIS.
小田原駅

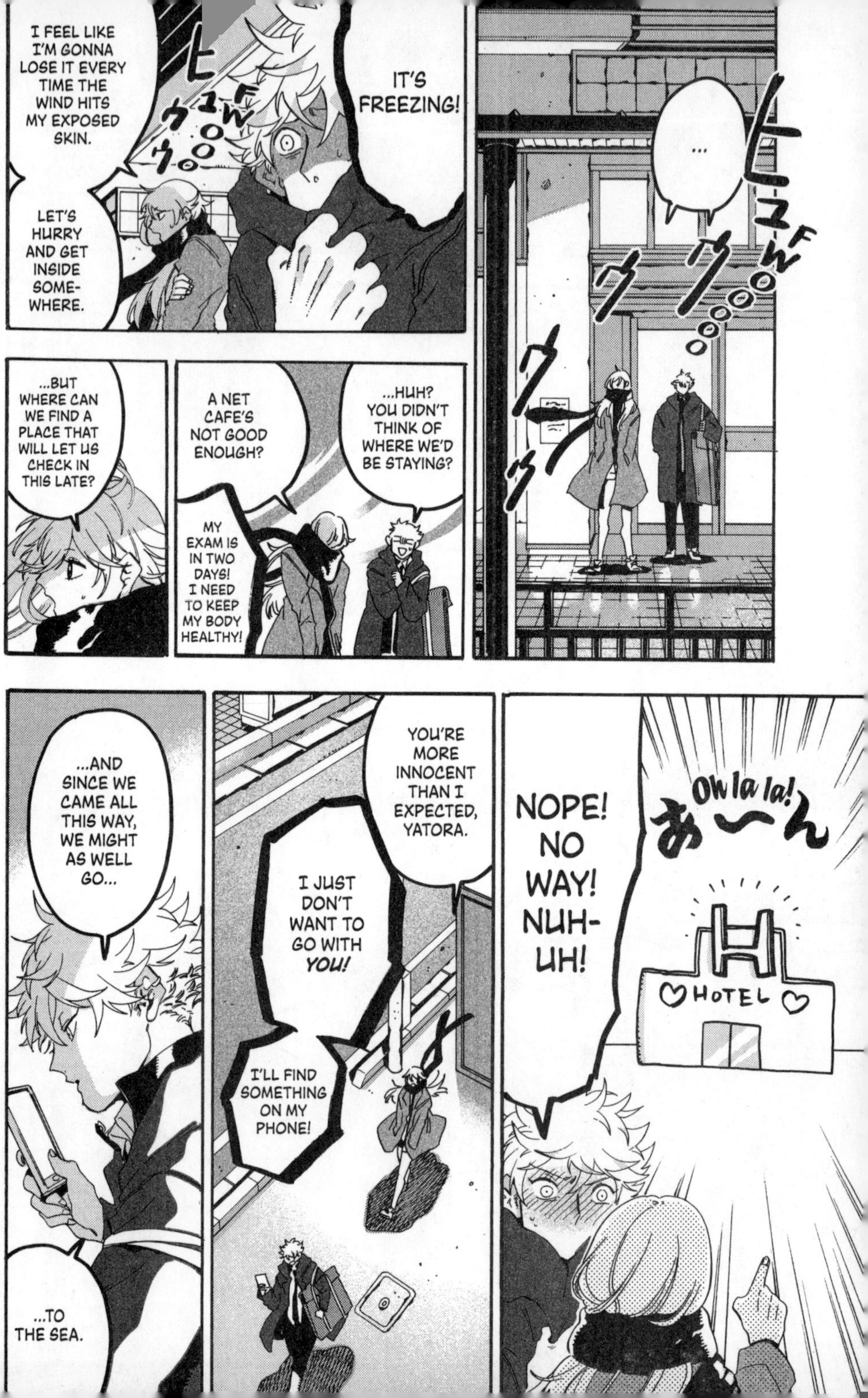
...
ヒュウウウ FWOOO
ウウウ
IT'S FREEZING!
ヒュウウ FWOOO
I FEEL LIKE I'M GONNA LOSE IT EVERY TIME THE WIND HITS MY EXPOSED SKIN.
LET'S HURRY AND GET INSIDE SOME-WHERE.
...HUH? YOU DIDN'T THINK OF WHERE WE'D BE STAYING?
A NET CAFE'S NOT GOOD ENOUGH?
MY EXAM IS IN TWO DAYS! I NEED TO KEEP MY BODY HEALTHY!
...BUT WHERE CAN WE FIND A PLACE THAT WILL LET US CHECK IN THIS LATE?
Ow la la! おーん
HOTEL
NOPE! NO WAY! NUH-UH!
YOU'RE MORE INNOCENT THAN I EXPECTED, YATORA.
I JUST DON'T WANT TO GO WITH YOU!
I'LL FIND SOMETHING ON MY PHONE!
...AND SINCE WE CAME ALL THIS WAY, WE MIGHT AS WELL GO...
...TO THE SEA.

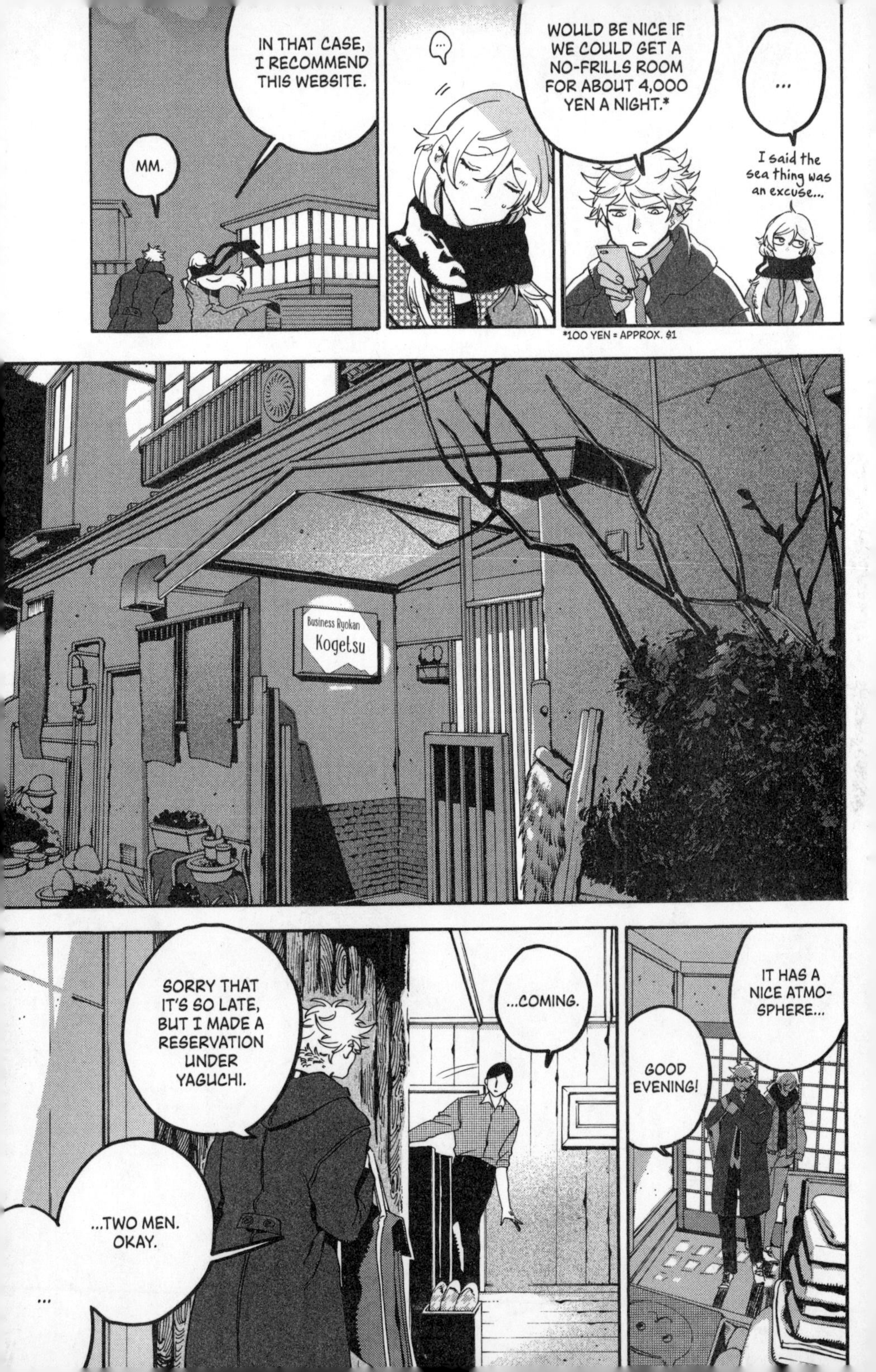
...
WOULD BE NICE IF WE COULD GET A NO-FRILLS ROOM FOR ABOUT 4,000 YEN A NIGHT.*
I said the sea thing was an excuse...
...
IN THAT CASE, I RECOMMEND THIS WEBSITE.
MM.
*100 YEN = APPROX. $1
Business Ryokan
Kogetsu
IT HAS A NICE ATMOSPHERE...
GOOD EVENING!
...COMING.
SORRY THAT IT'S SO LATE, BUT I MADE A RESERVATION UNDER YAGUCHI.
...
...TWO MEN. OKAY.
...

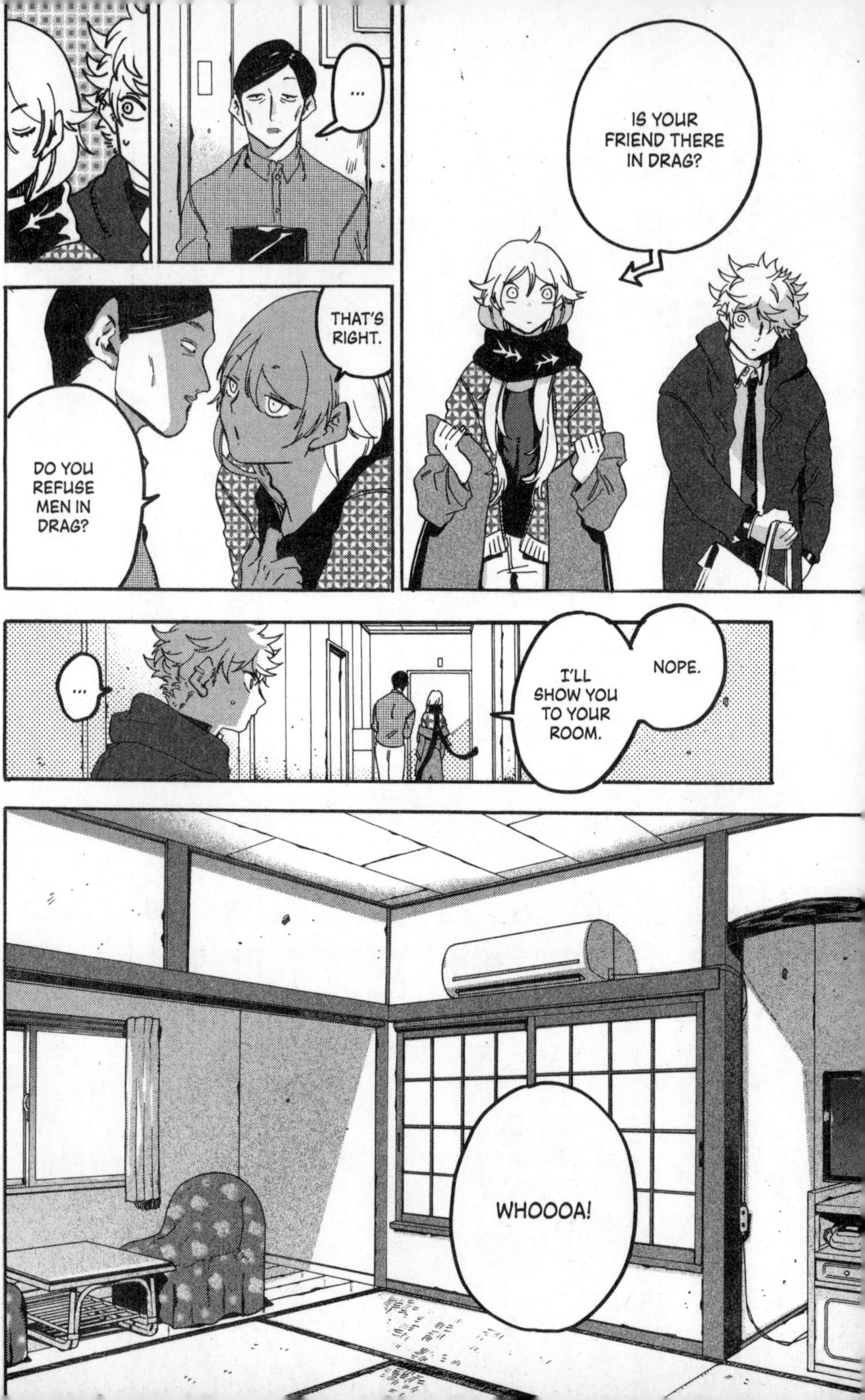
IS YOUR FRIEND THERE IN DRAG?
...
THAT'S RIGHT.
DO YOU REFUSE MEN IN DRAG?
NOPE.
I'LL SHOW YOU TO YOUR ROOM.
...
WHOOOA!

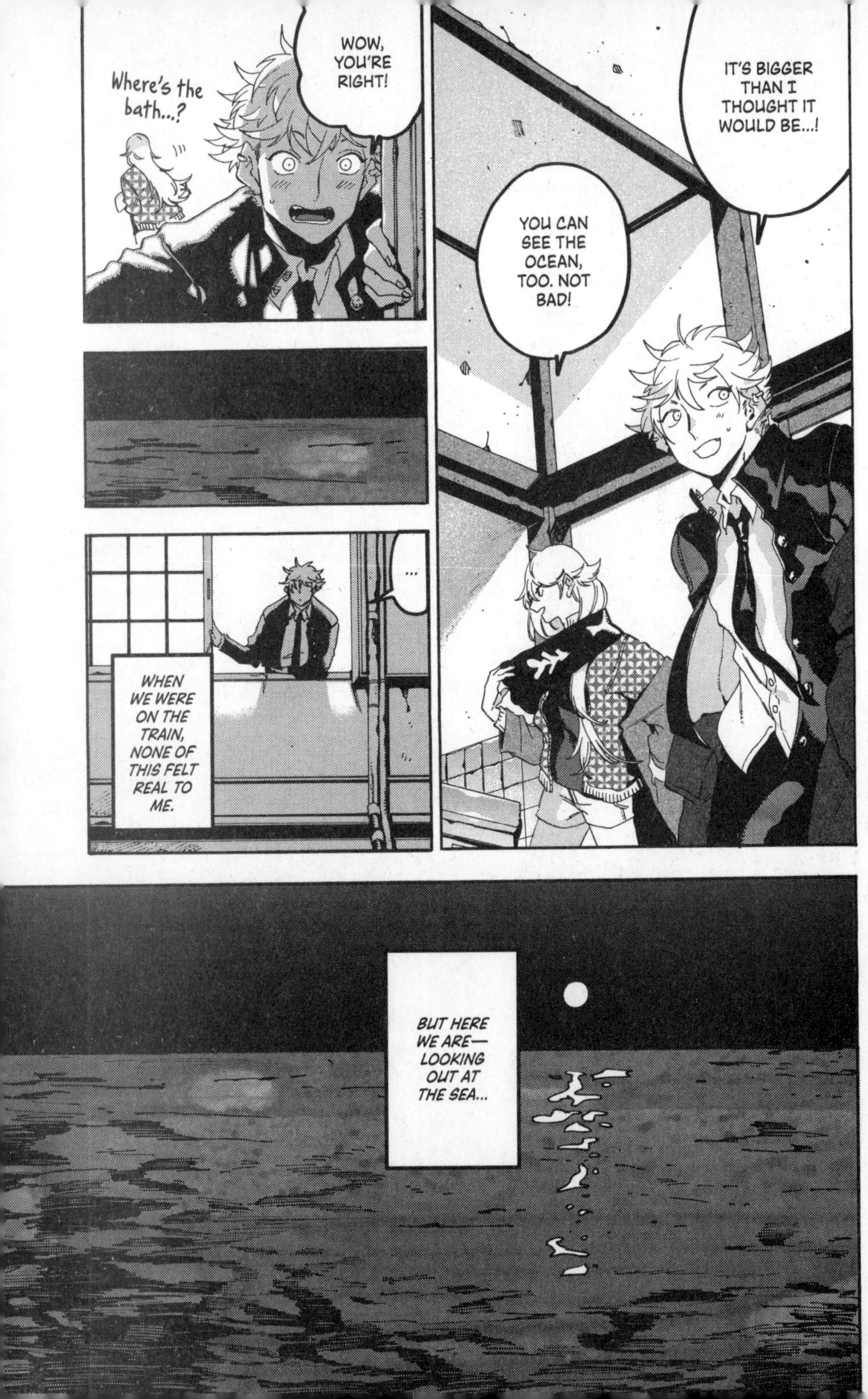
IT'S BIGGER THAN I THOUGHT IT WOULD BE...!
YOU CAN SEE THE OCEAN, TOO. NOT BAD!
WOW, YOU'RE RIGHT!
Where's the bath...?
...
WHEN WE WERE ON THE TRAIN, NONE OF THIS FELT REAL TO ME.
BUT HERE WE ARE— LOOKING OUT AT THE SEA...

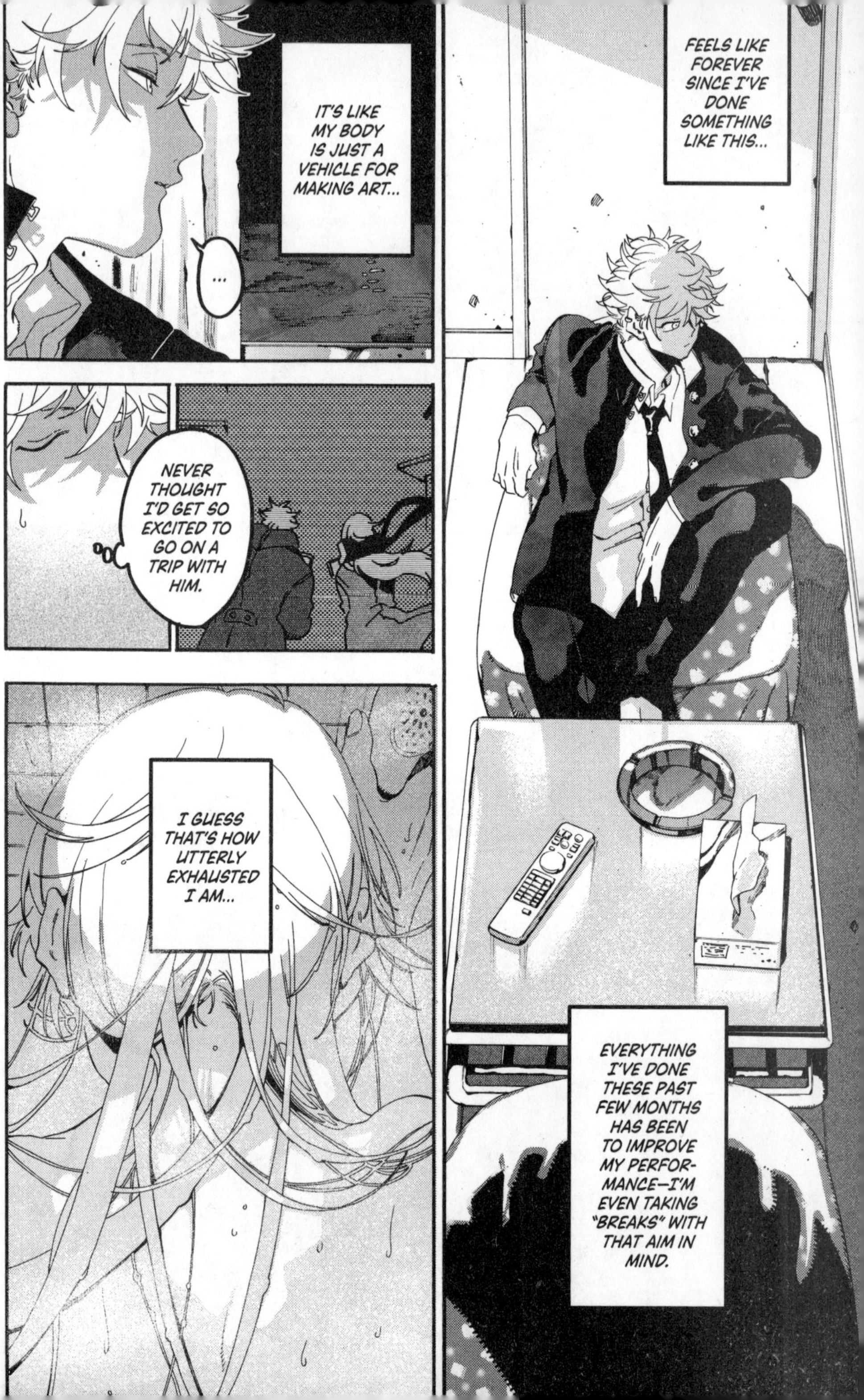
FEELS LIKE FOREVER SINCE I'VE DONE SOMETHING LIKE THIS...
EVERYTHING I'VE DONE THESE PAST FEW MONTHS HAS BEEN TO IMPROVE MY PERFOR-MANCE—I'M EVEN TAKING "BREAKS" WITH THAT AIM IN MIND.
IT'S LIKE MY BODY IS JUST A VEHICLE FOR MAKING ART...
...
NEVER THOUGHT I'D GET SO EXCITED TO GO ON A TRIP WITH HIM.
I GUESS THAT'S HOW UTTERLY EXHAUSTED I AM...

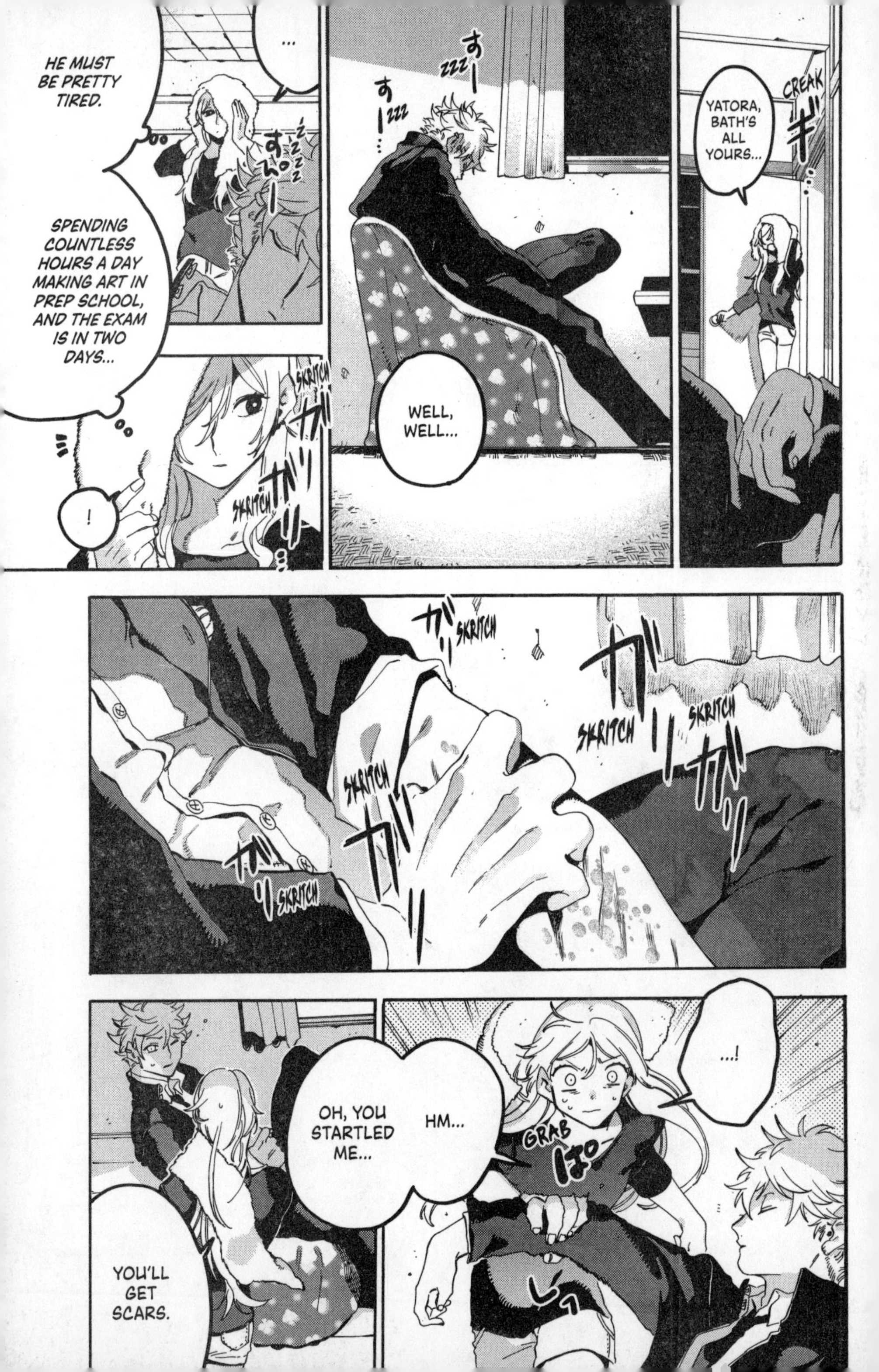
CREAK
YATORA, BATH'S ALL YOURS...
ZZZ
ZZZ
WELL, WELL...
...
HE MUST BE PRETTY TIRED.
SPENDING COUNTLESS HOURS A DAY MAKING ART IN PREP SCHOOL, AND THE EXAM IS IN TWO DAYS...
SKRITCH
SKRITCH
!
SKRITCH
SKRITCH
SKRITCH
SKRITCH
SKRITCH
...!
GRAB
HM...
OH, YOU STARTLED ME...
YOU'LL GET SCARS.

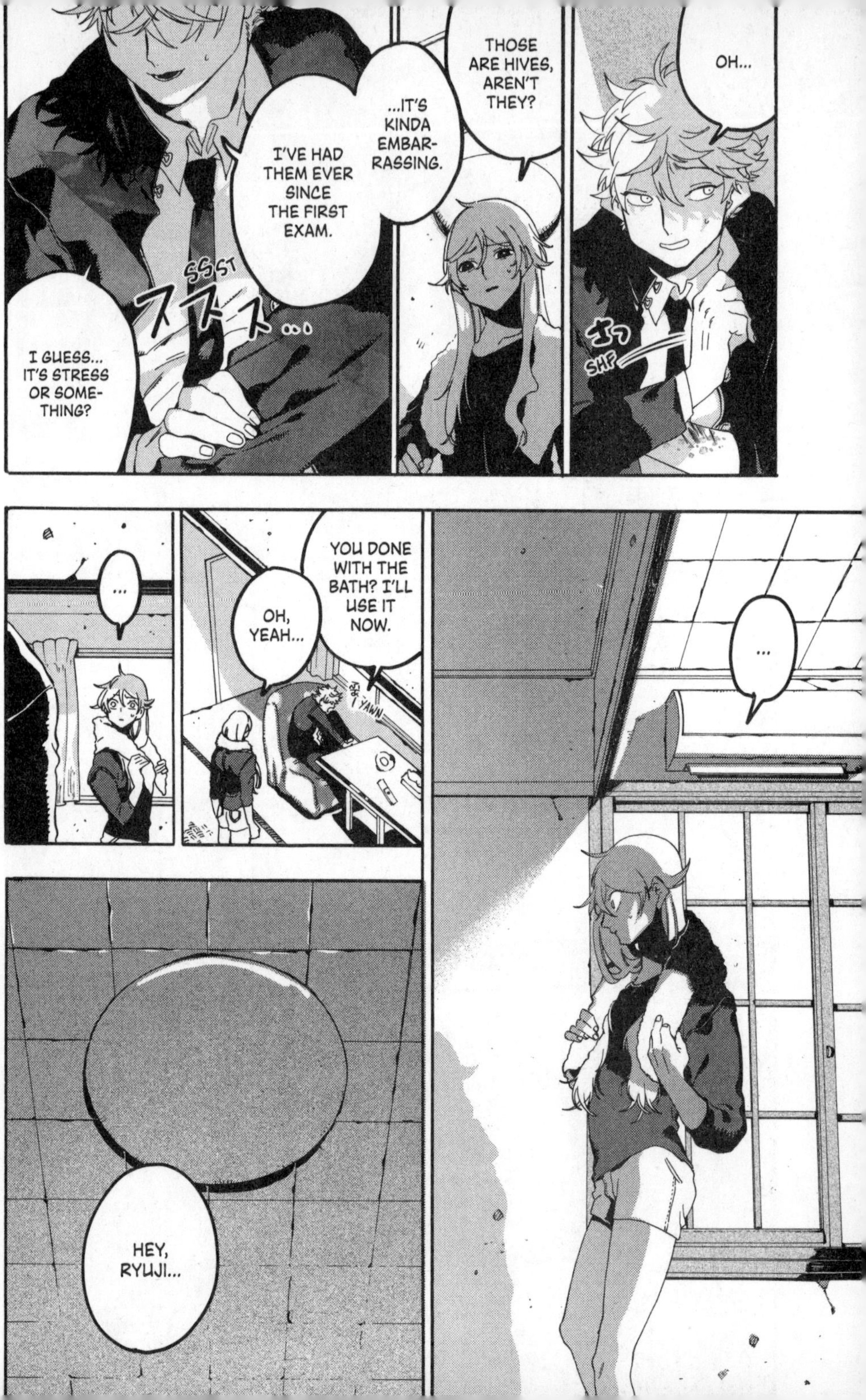
OH...
さっ
SHF
THOSE ARE HIVES, AREN'T THEY?
...IT'S KINDA EMBARRASSING.
I'VE HAD THEM EVER SINCE THE FIRST EXAM.
スススッ
SSSST
I GUESS... IT'S STRESS OR SOMETHING?
...
YOU DONE WITH THE BATH? I'LL USE IT NOW.
YAWN
OH, YEAH...
...
HEY, RYUJI...

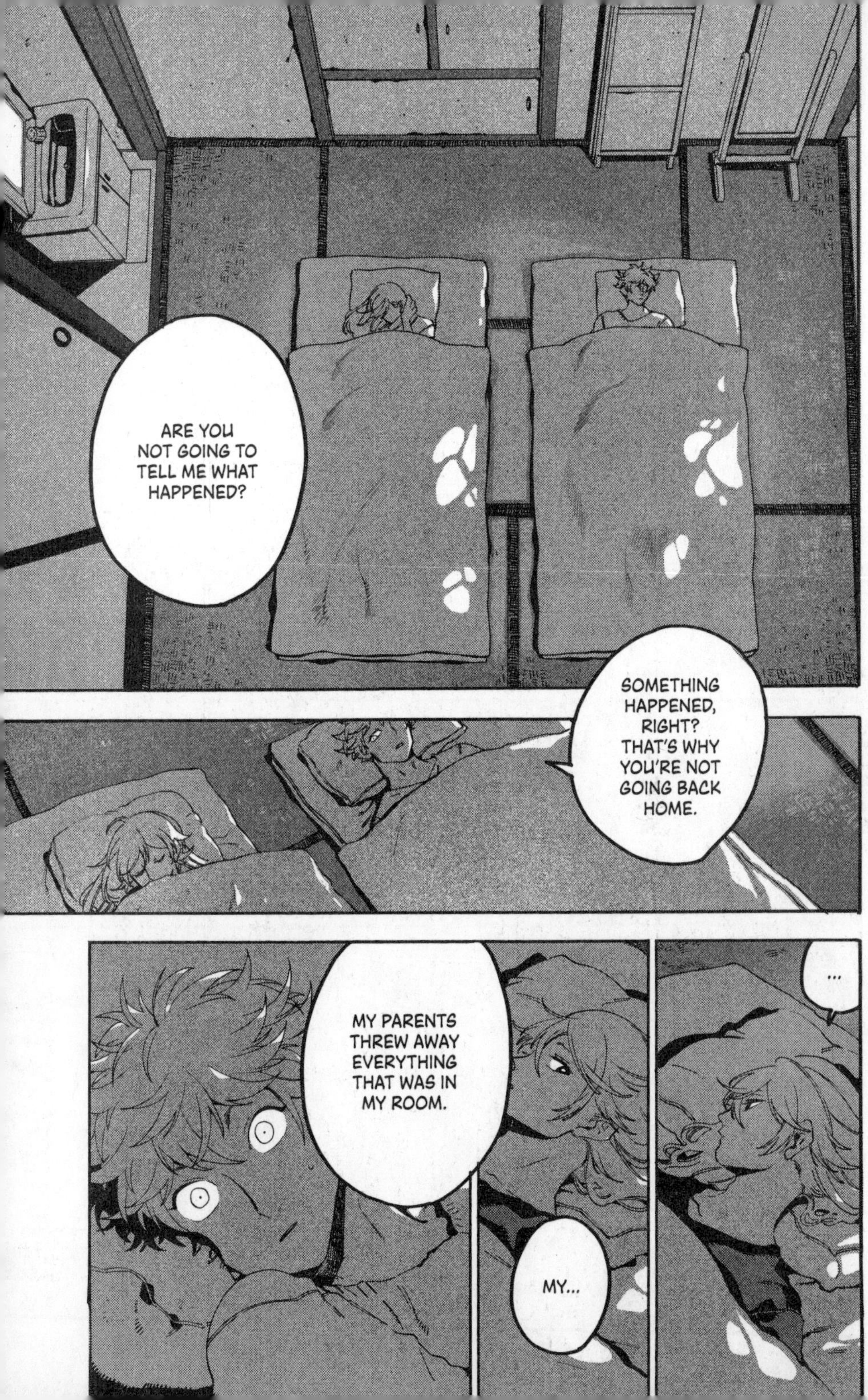
ARE YOU NOT GOING TO TELL ME WHAT HAPPENED?
SOMETHING HAPPENED, RIGHT? THAT'S WHY YOU'RE NOT GOING BACK HOME.
...
MY...
MY PARENTS THREW AWAY EVERYTHING THAT WAS IN MY ROOM.

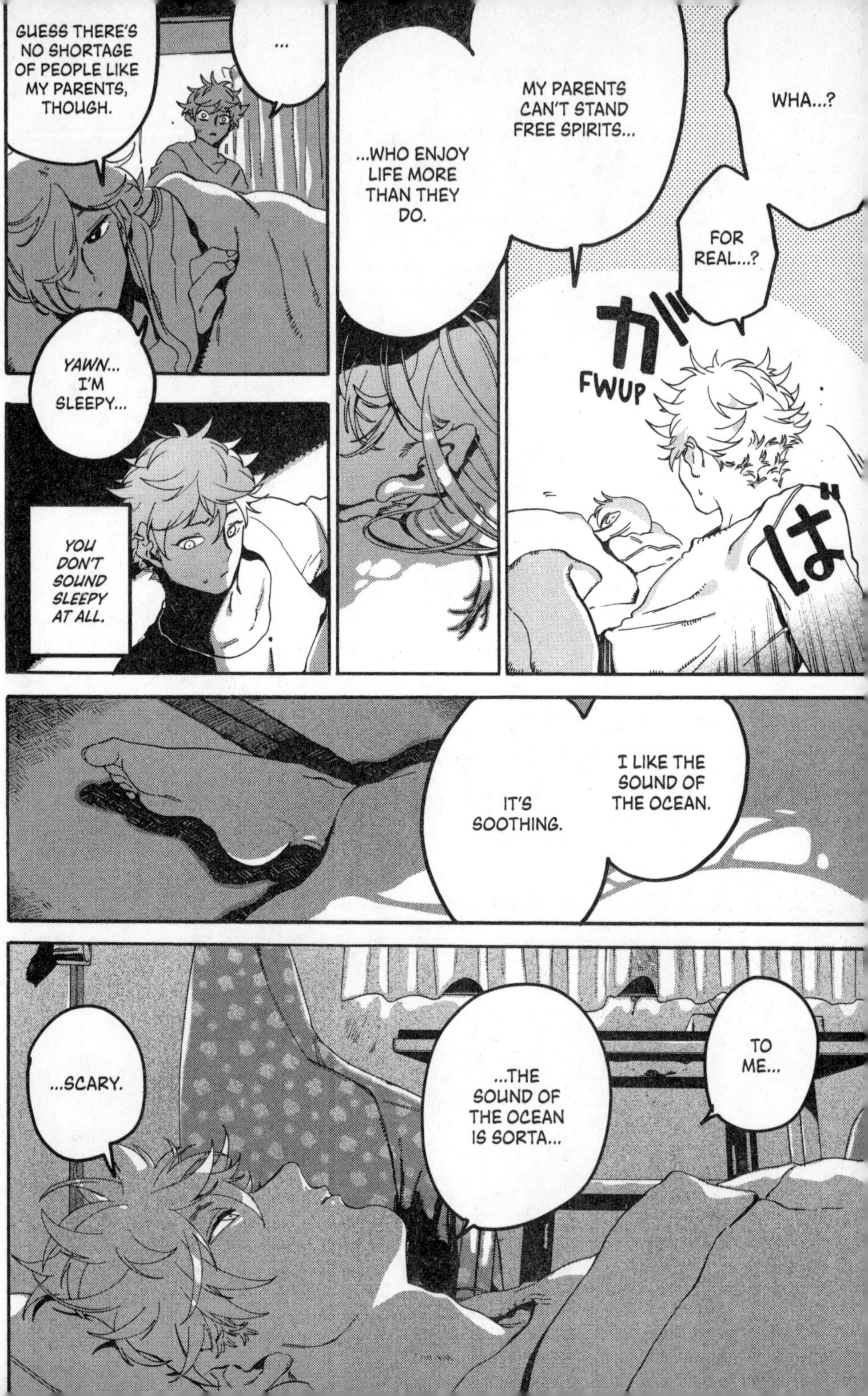
WHA...?
MY PARENTS CAN'T STAND FREE SPIRITS...
FOR REAL...?
カ゛
FWUP
ば
...WHO ENJOY LIFE MORE THAN THEY DO.
GUESS THERE'S NO SHORTAGE OF PEOPLE LIKE MY PARENTS, THOUGH.
...
YAWN... I'M SLEEPY...
YOU DON'T SOUND SLEEPY AT ALL.
I LIKE THE SOUND OF THE OCEAN.
IT'S SOOTHING.
TO ME...
...THE SOUND OF THE OCEAN IS SORTA...
...SCARY.

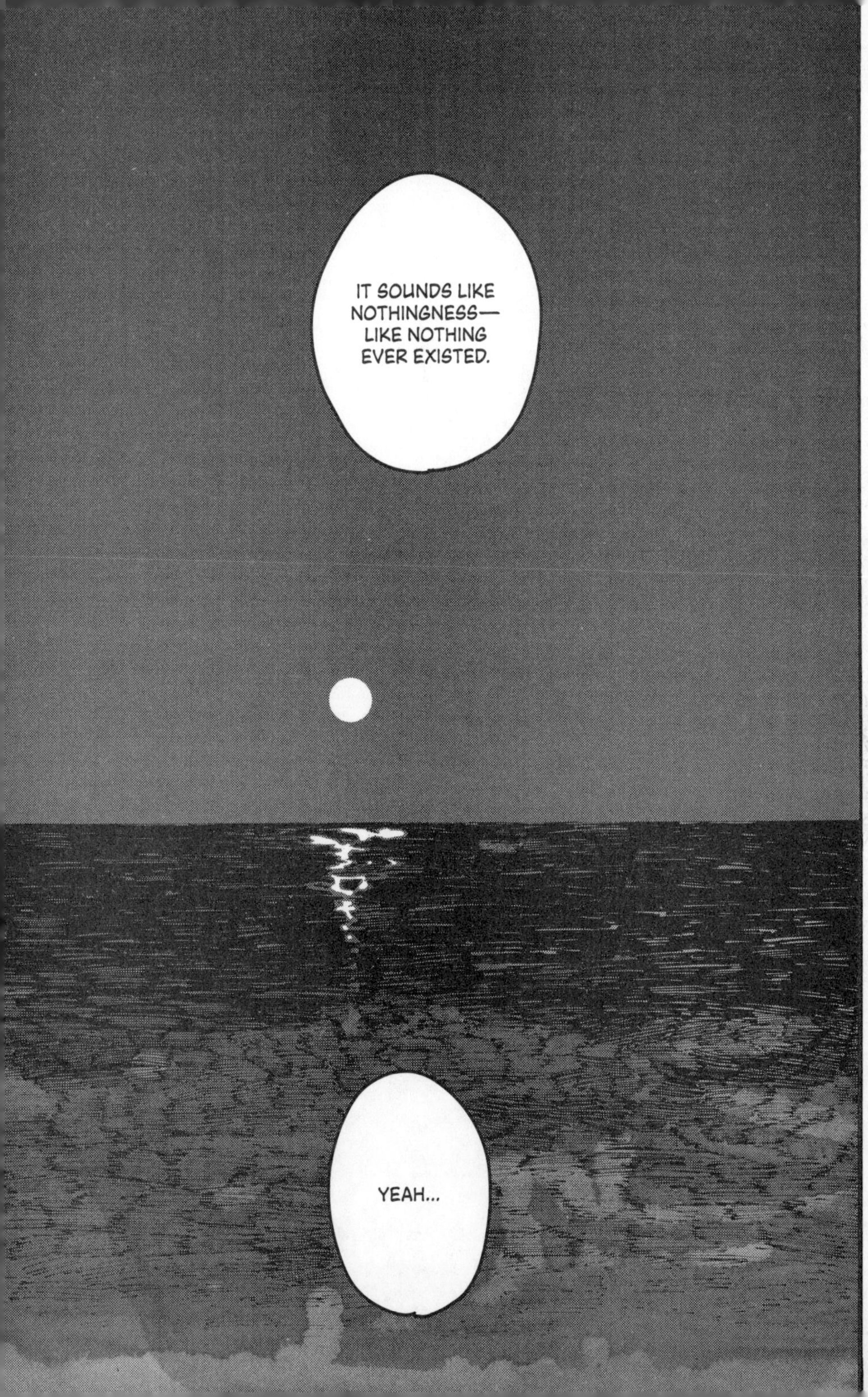
IT SOUNDS LIKE NOTHINGNESS— LIKE NOTHING EVER EXISTED.
YEAH...

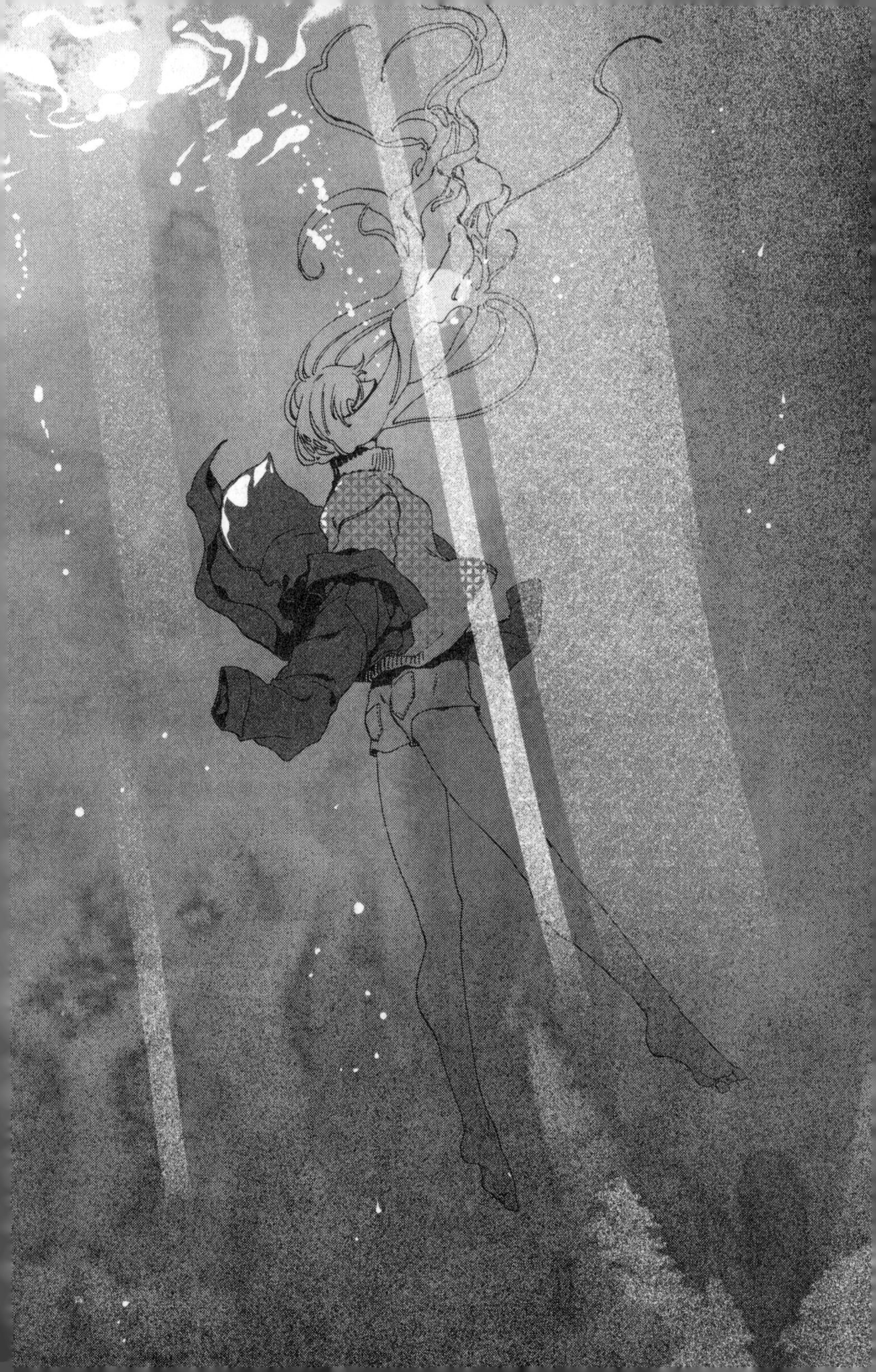

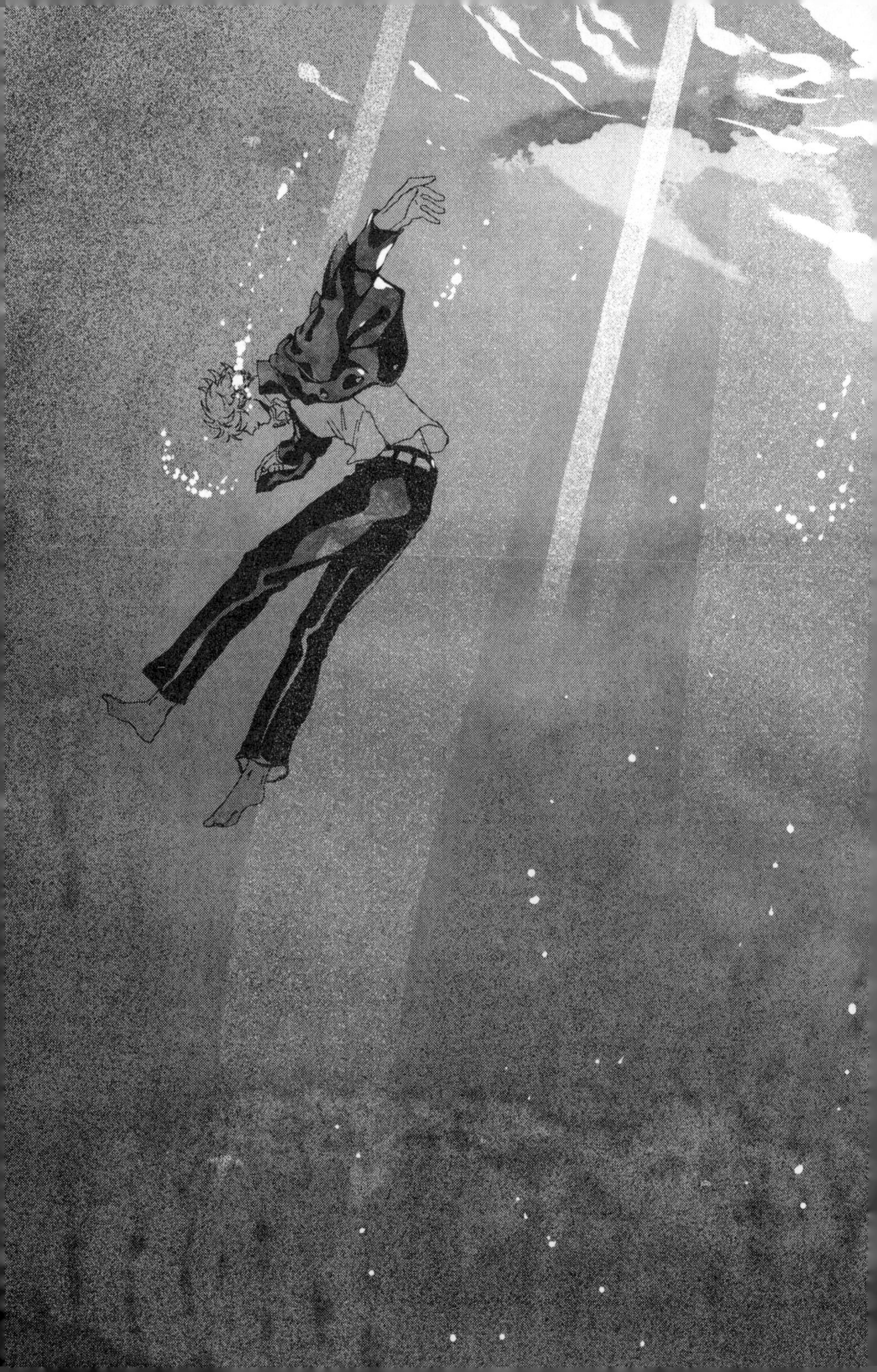

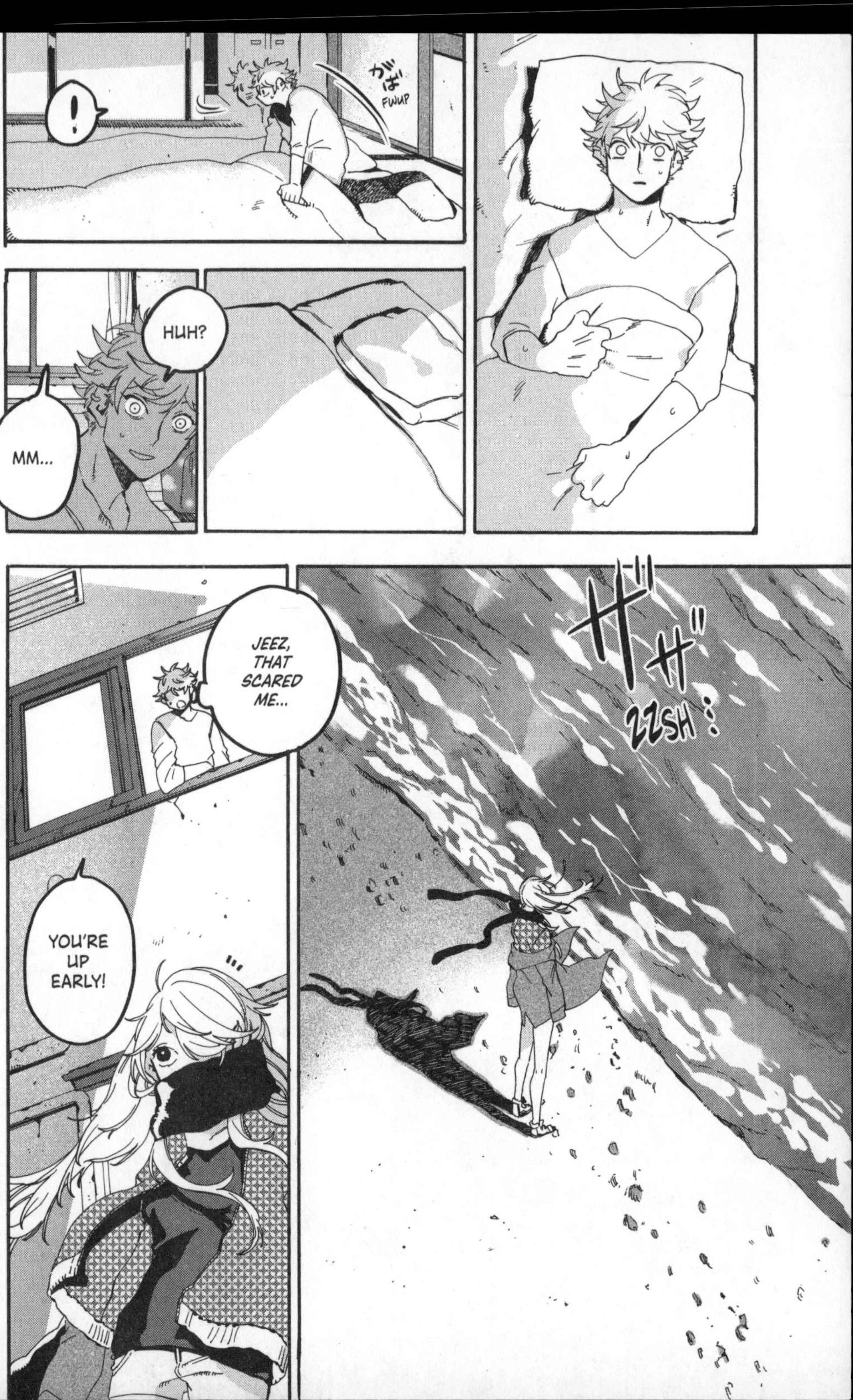
!
がば
FWUP
HUH?
MM...
ザザ
ZZSH
JEEZ, THAT SCARED ME...
YOU'RE UP EARLY!

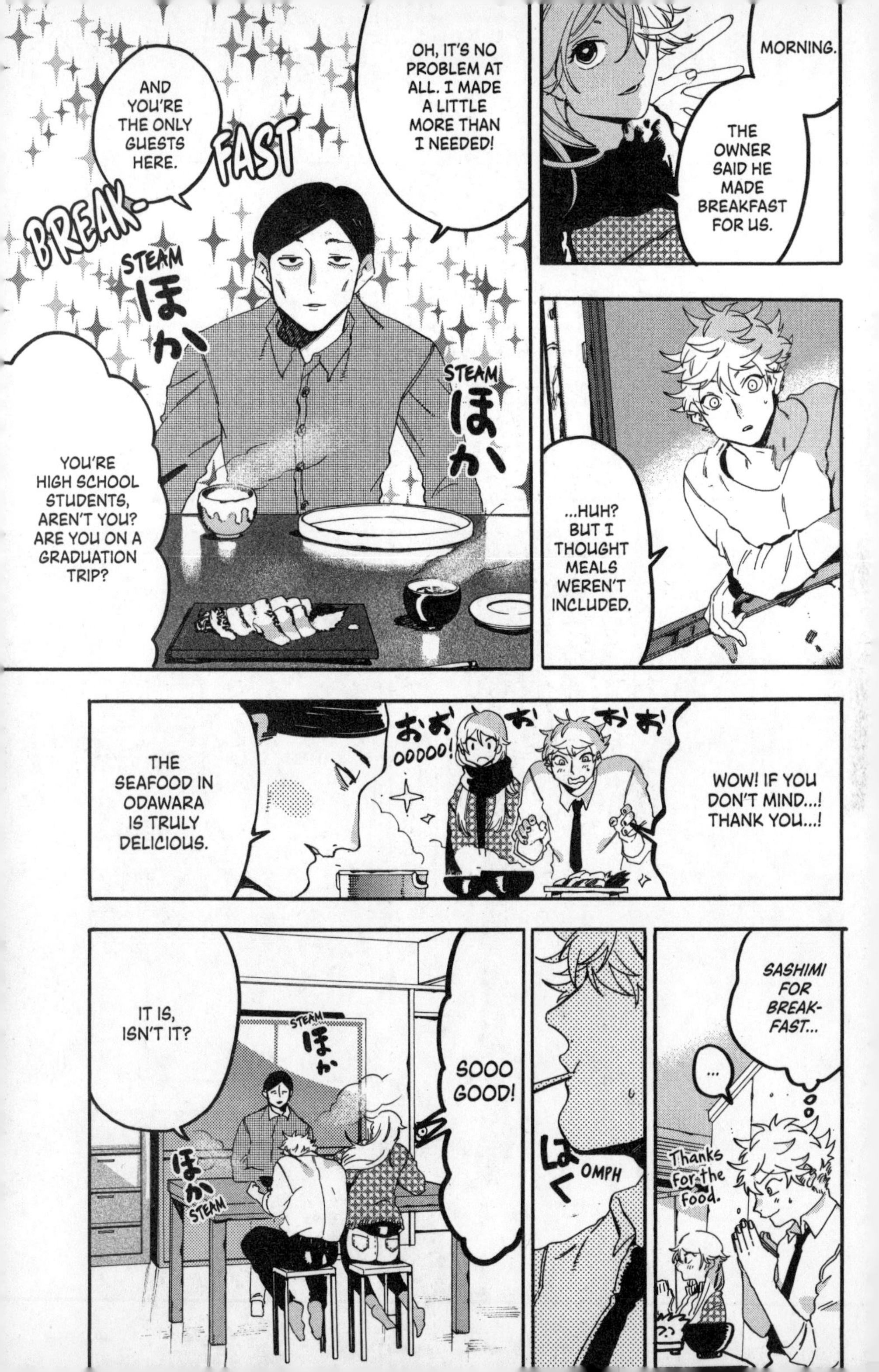
MORNING.
THE OWNER SAID HE MADE BREAKFAST FOR US.
...HUH? BUT I THOUGHT MEALS WEREN'T INCLUDED.
OH, IT'S NO PROBLEM AT ALL. I MADE A LITTLE MORE THAN I NEEDED!
AND YOU'RE THE ONLY GUESTS HERE.
BREAK-FAST
STEAM ほか
STEAM ほか
YOU'RE HIGH SCHOOL STUDENTS, AREN'T YOU? ARE YOU ON A GRADUATION TRIP?
WOW! IF YOU DON'T MIND...! THANK YOU...!
おお お おお OOOOO!
THE SEAFOOD IN ODAWARA IS TRULY DELICIOUS.
SASHIMI FOR BREAK-FAST...
...
Thanks for the food.
OMPH
SOOO GOOD!
IT IS, ISN'T IT?
STEAM ほか
ほか STEAM

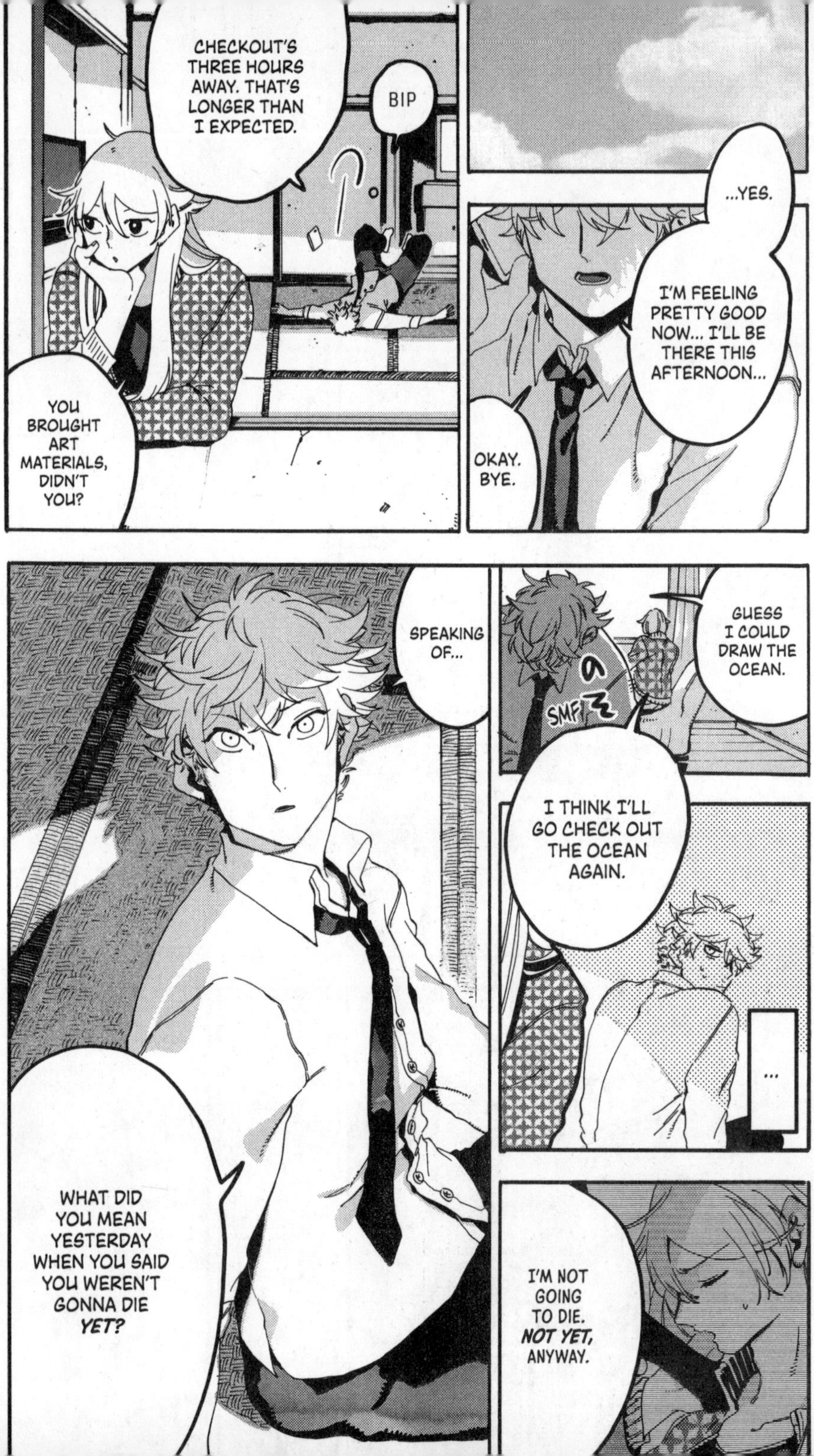
...YES.
I'M FEELING PRETTY GOOD NOW... I'LL BE THERE THIS AFTERNOON...
OKAY. BYE.
BIP
CHECKOUT'S THREE HOURS AWAY. THAT'S LONGER THAN I EXPECTED.
YOU BROUGHT ART MATERIALS, DIDN'T YOU?
GUESS I COULD DRAW THE OCEAN.
SMF
I THINK I'LL GO CHECK OUT THE OCEAN AGAIN.
...
I'M NOT GOING TO DIE. *NOT YET*, ANYWAY.
SPEAKING OF...
WHAT DID YOU MEAN YESTERDAY WHEN YOU SAID YOU WEREN'T GONNA DIE *YET*?

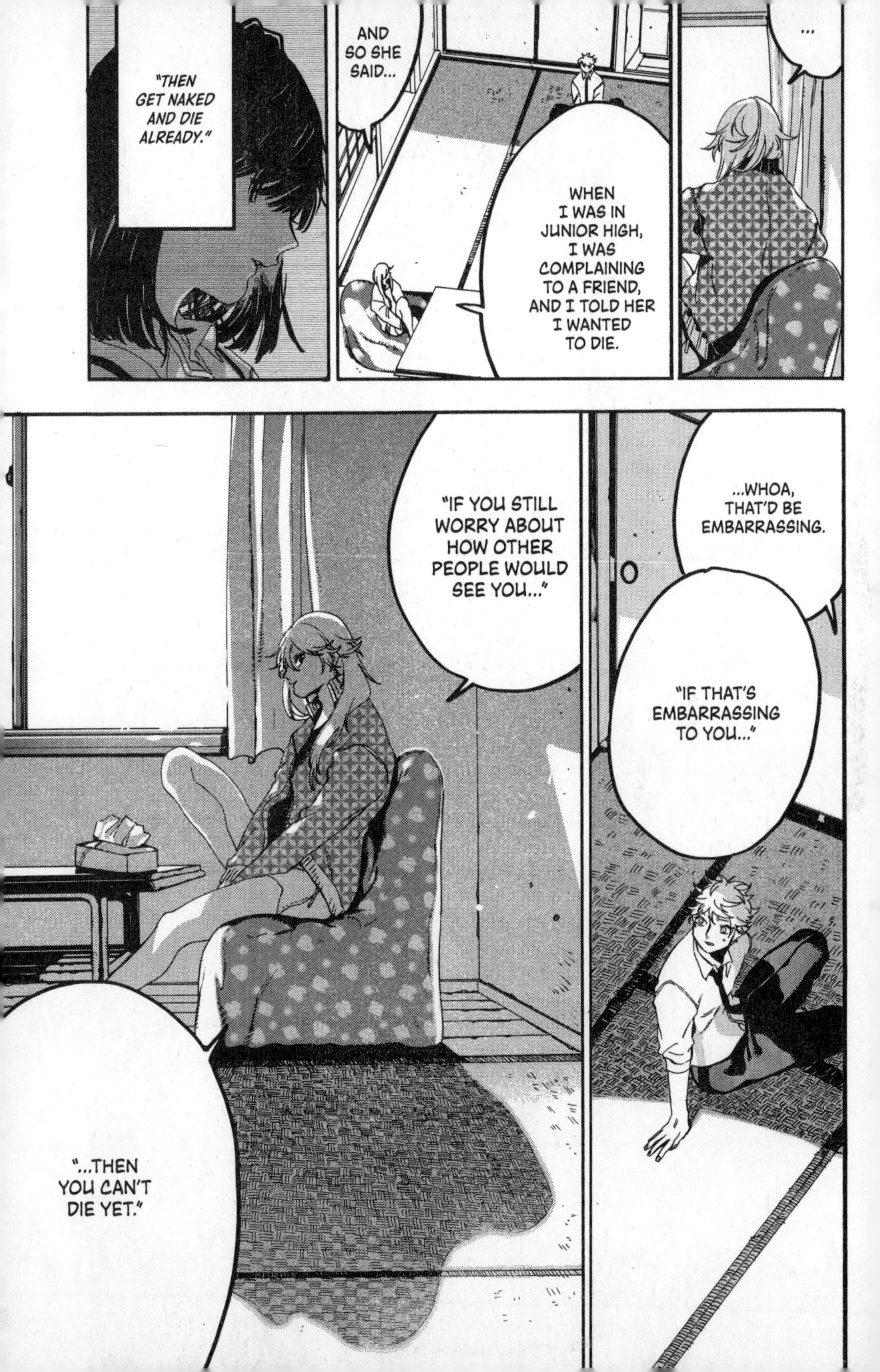
...
WHEN I WAS IN JUNIOR HIGH, I WAS COMPLAINING TO A FRIEND, AND I TOLD HER I WANTED TO DIE.
AND SO SHE SAID...
"THEN GET NAKED AND DIE ALREADY."
...WHOA, THAT'D BE EMBARRASSING.
"IF THAT'S EMBARRASSING TO YOU..."
"IF YOU STILL WORRY ABOUT HOW OTHER PEOPLE WOULD SEE YOU..."
"...THEN YOU CAN'T DIE YET."

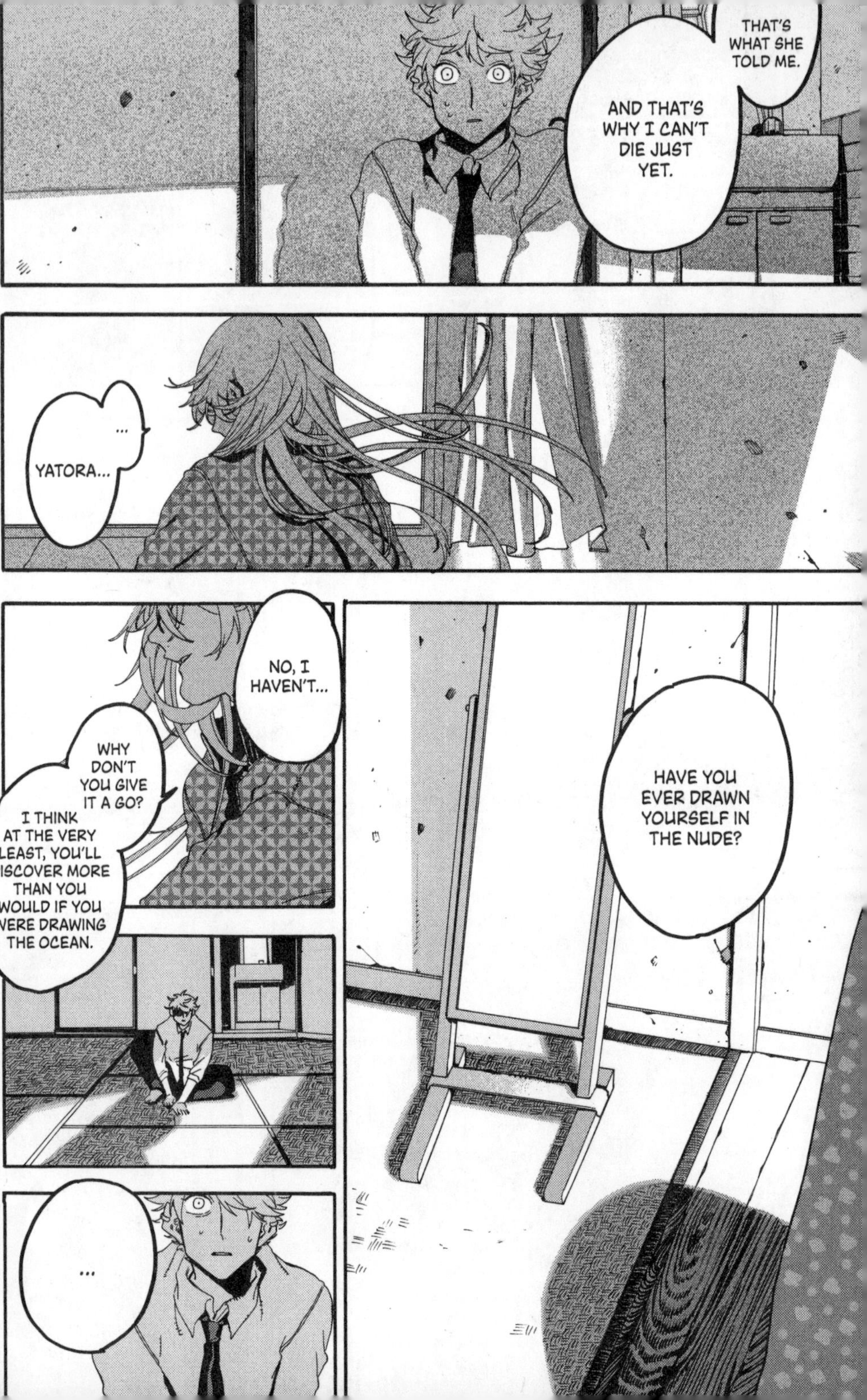
THAT'S WHAT SHE TOLD ME.
AND THAT'S WHY I CAN'T DIE JUST YET.
... YATORA...
HAVE YOU EVER DRAWN YOURSELF IN THE NUDE?
NO, I HAVEN'T...
WHY DON'T YOU GIVE IT A GO?
I THINK AT THE VERY LEAST, YOU'LL DISCOVER MORE THAN YOU WOULD IF YOU WERE DRAWING THE OCEAN.
...

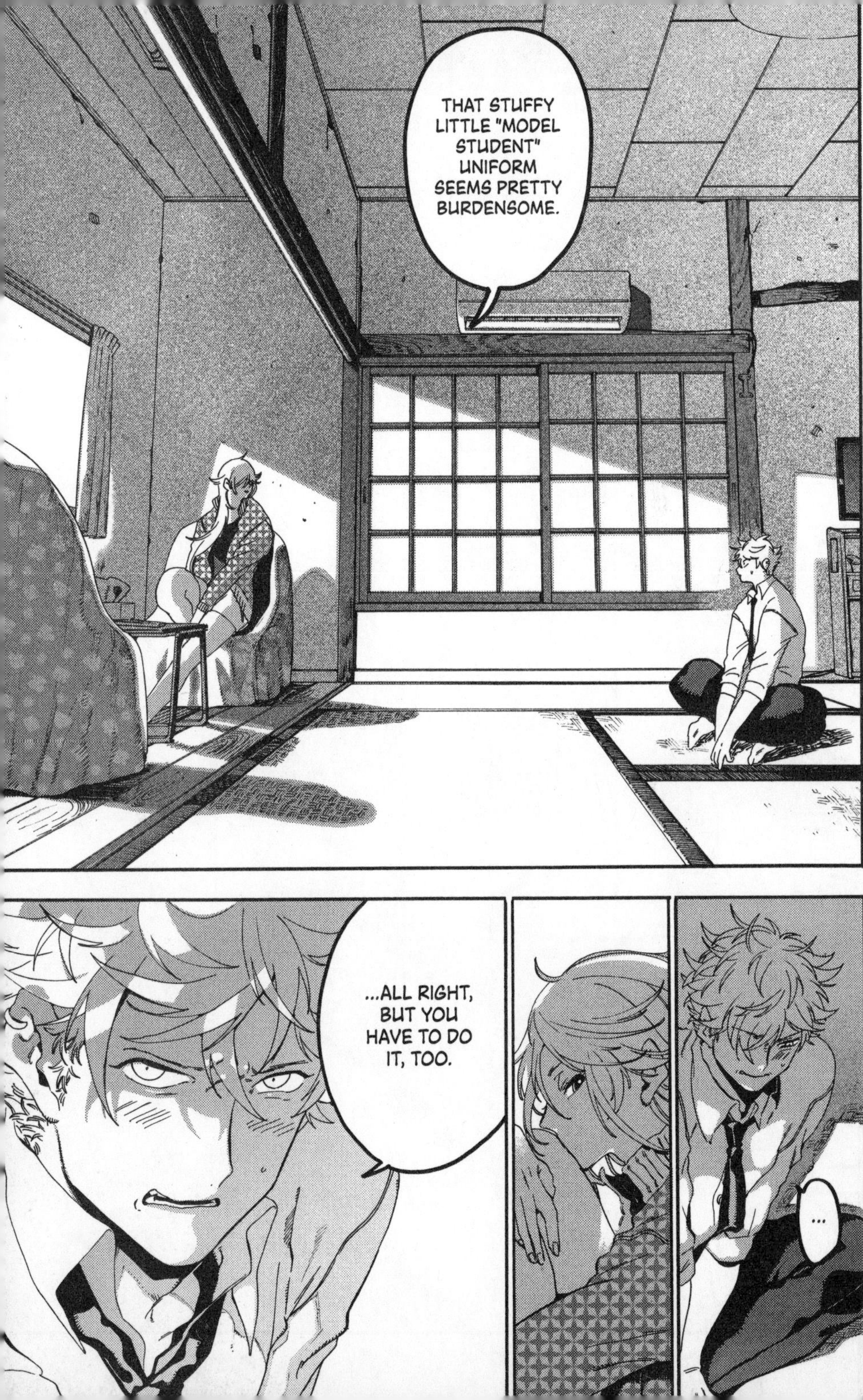
THAT STUFFY LITTLE "MODEL STUDENT" UNIFORM SEEMS PRETTY BURDENSOME.
...
...ALL RIGHT, BUT YOU HAVE TO DO IT, TOO.

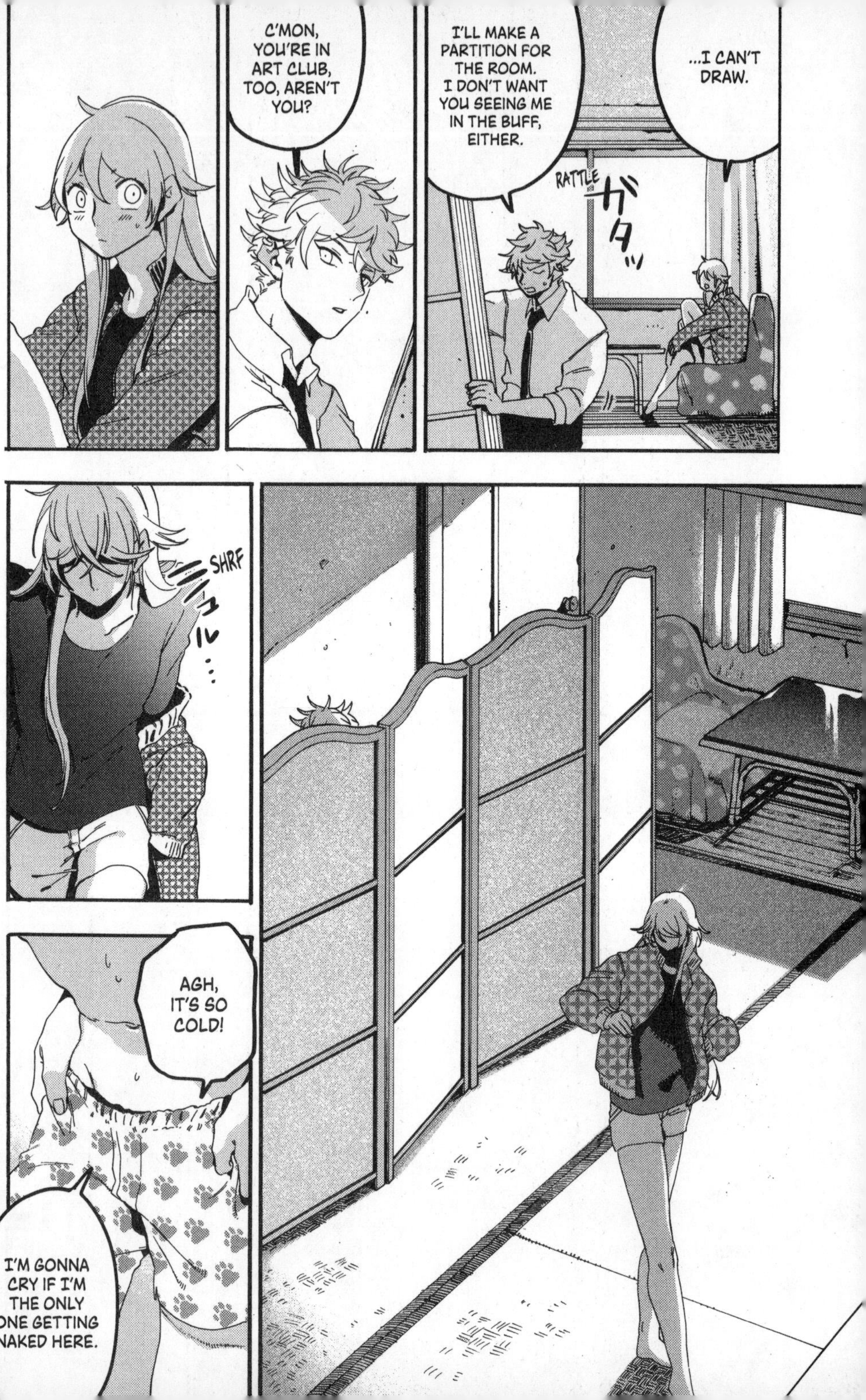
...I CAN'T DRAW.
I'LL MAKE A PARTITION FOR THE ROOM. I DON'T WANT YOU SEEING ME IN THE BUFF, EITHER.
RATTLE
ガタッ
C'MON, YOU'RE IN ART CLUB, TOO, AREN'T YOU?
SHRF
AGH, IT'S SO COLD!
I'M GONNA CRY IF I'M THE ONLY ONE GETTING NAKED HERE.

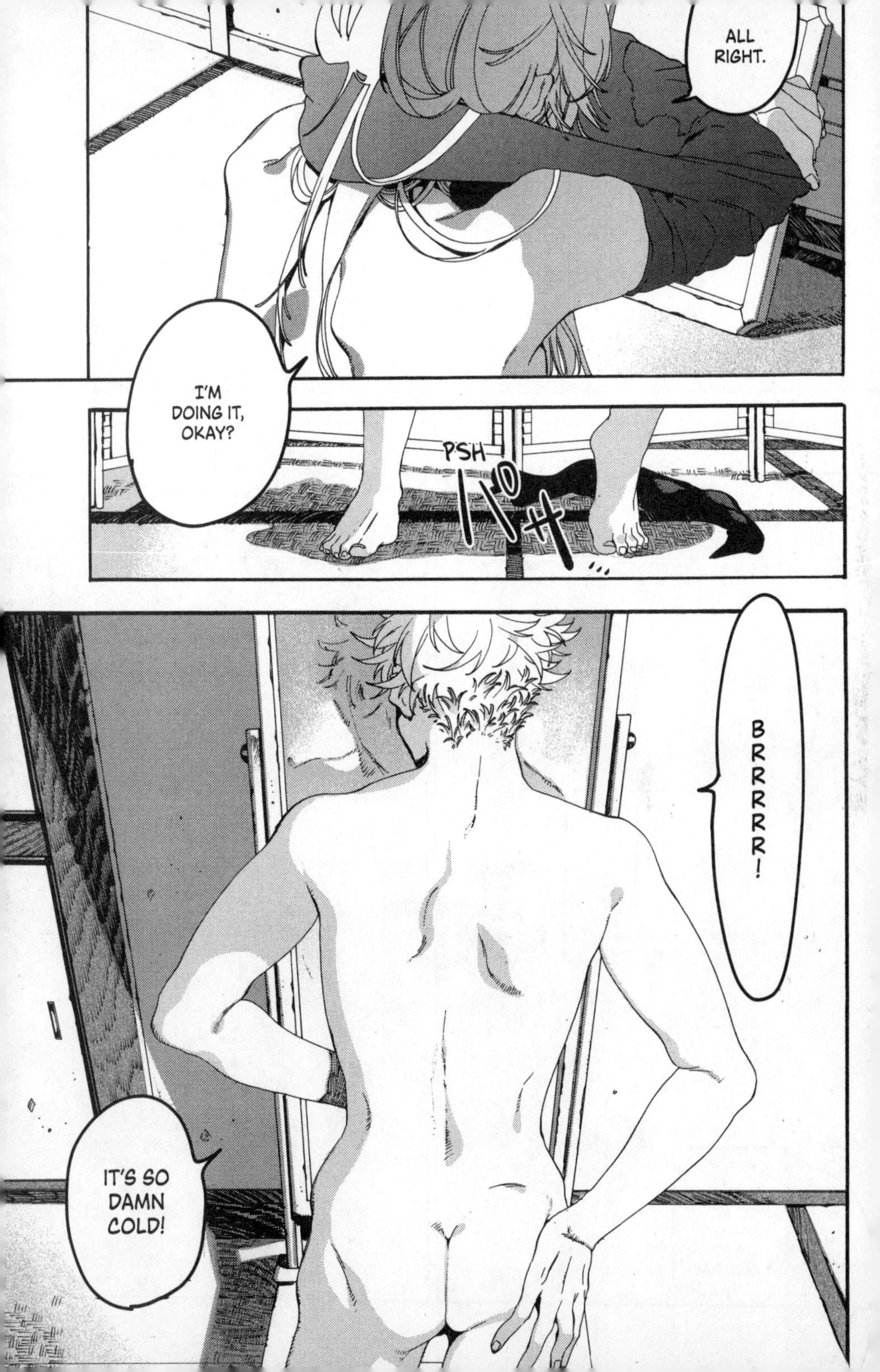
ALL RIGHT.
I'M DOING IT, OKAY?
PSH
BRRRRR!
IT'S SO DAMN COLD!

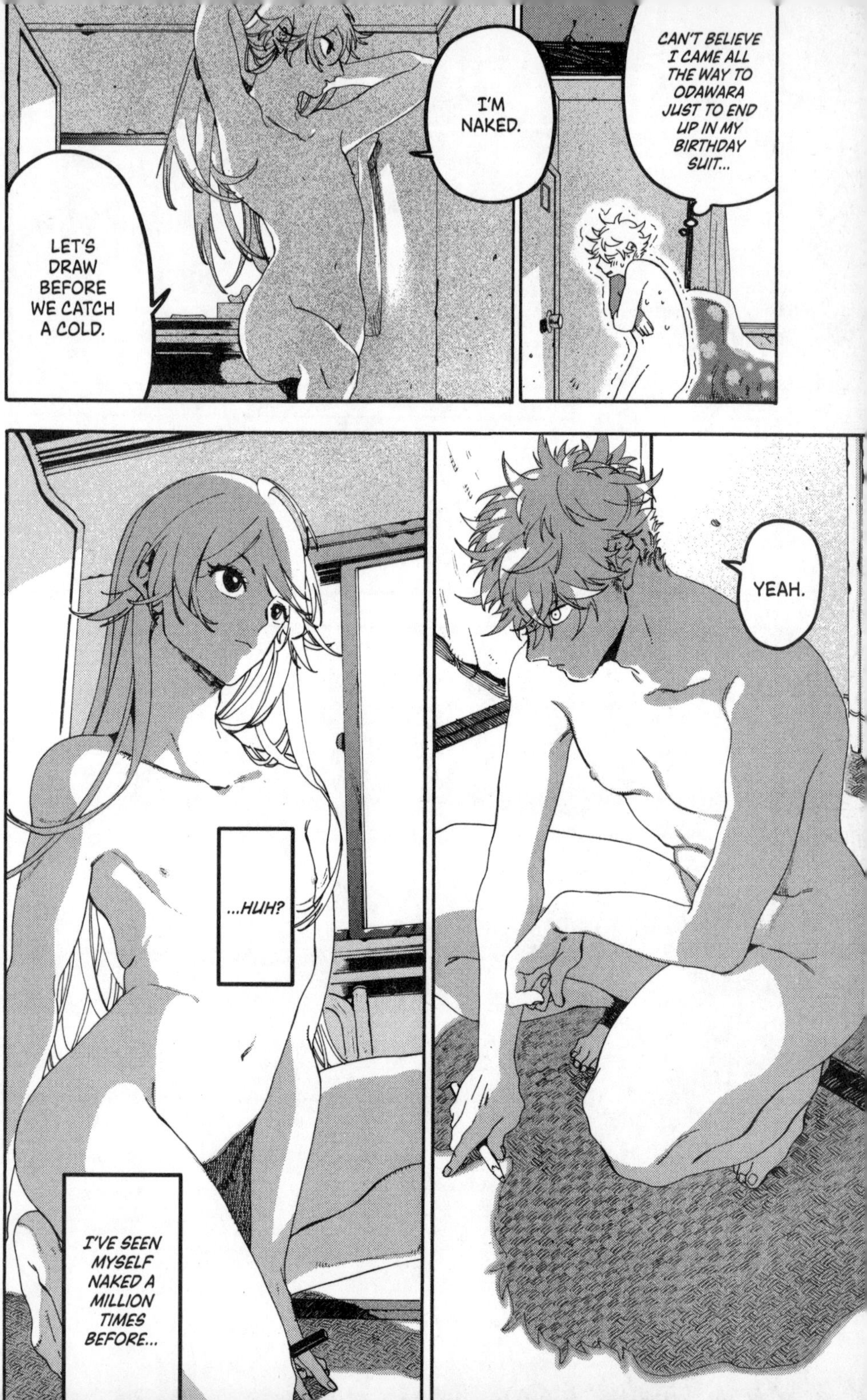
CAN'T BELIEVE I CAME ALL THE WAY TO ODAWARA JUST TO END UP IN MY BIRTHDAY SUIT...
I'M NAKED.
LET'S DRAW BEFORE WE CATCH A COLD.
YEAH.
...HUH?
I'VE SEEN MYSELF NAKED A MILLION TIMES BEFORE...

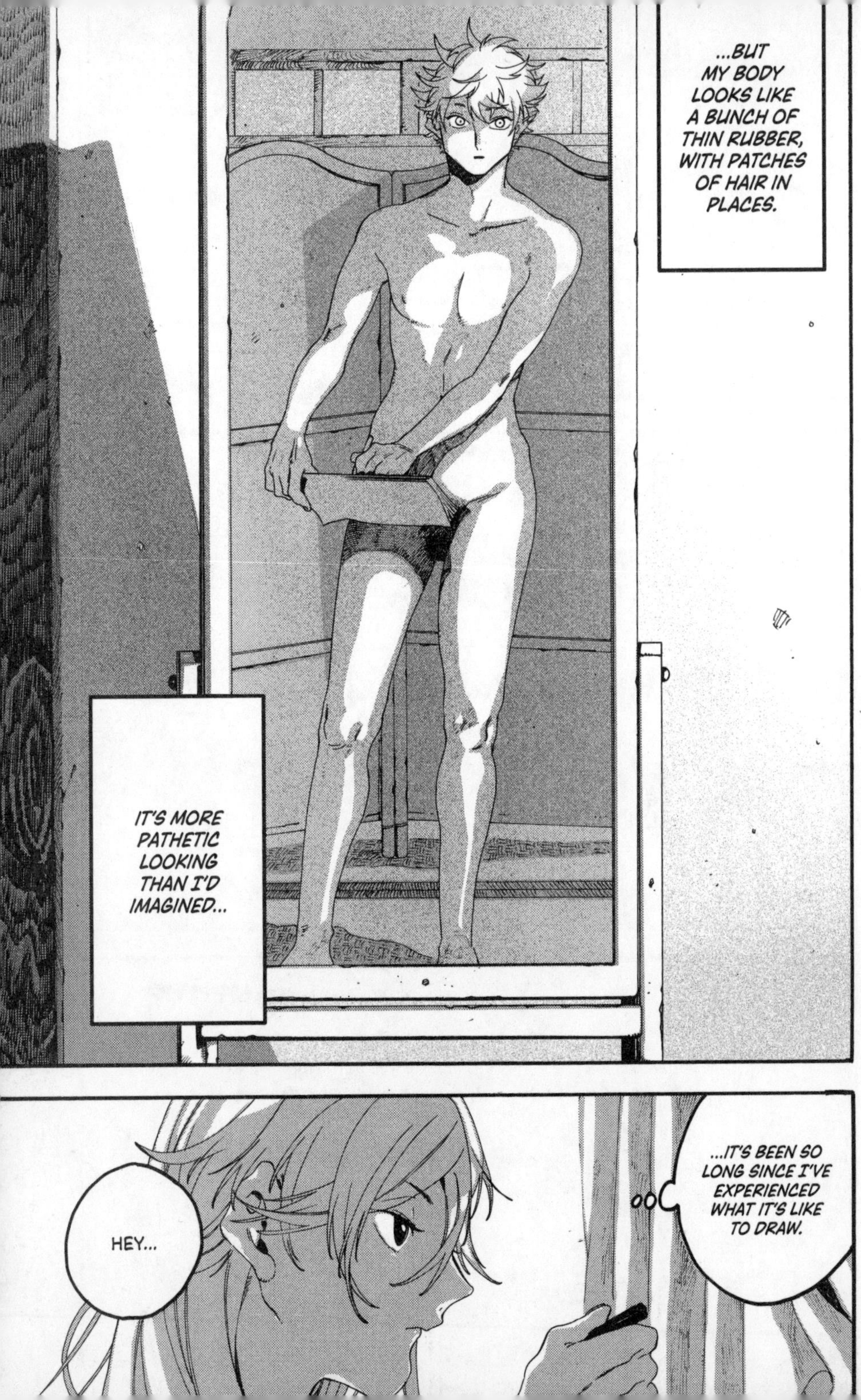
...BUT MY BODY LOOKS LIKE A BUNCH OF THIN RUBBER, WITH PATCHES OF HAIR IN PLACES.
IT'S MORE PATHETIC LOOKING THAN I'D IMAGINED...
...IT'S BEEN SO LONG SINCE I'VE EXPERIENCED WHAT IT'S LIKE TO DRAW.
HEY...

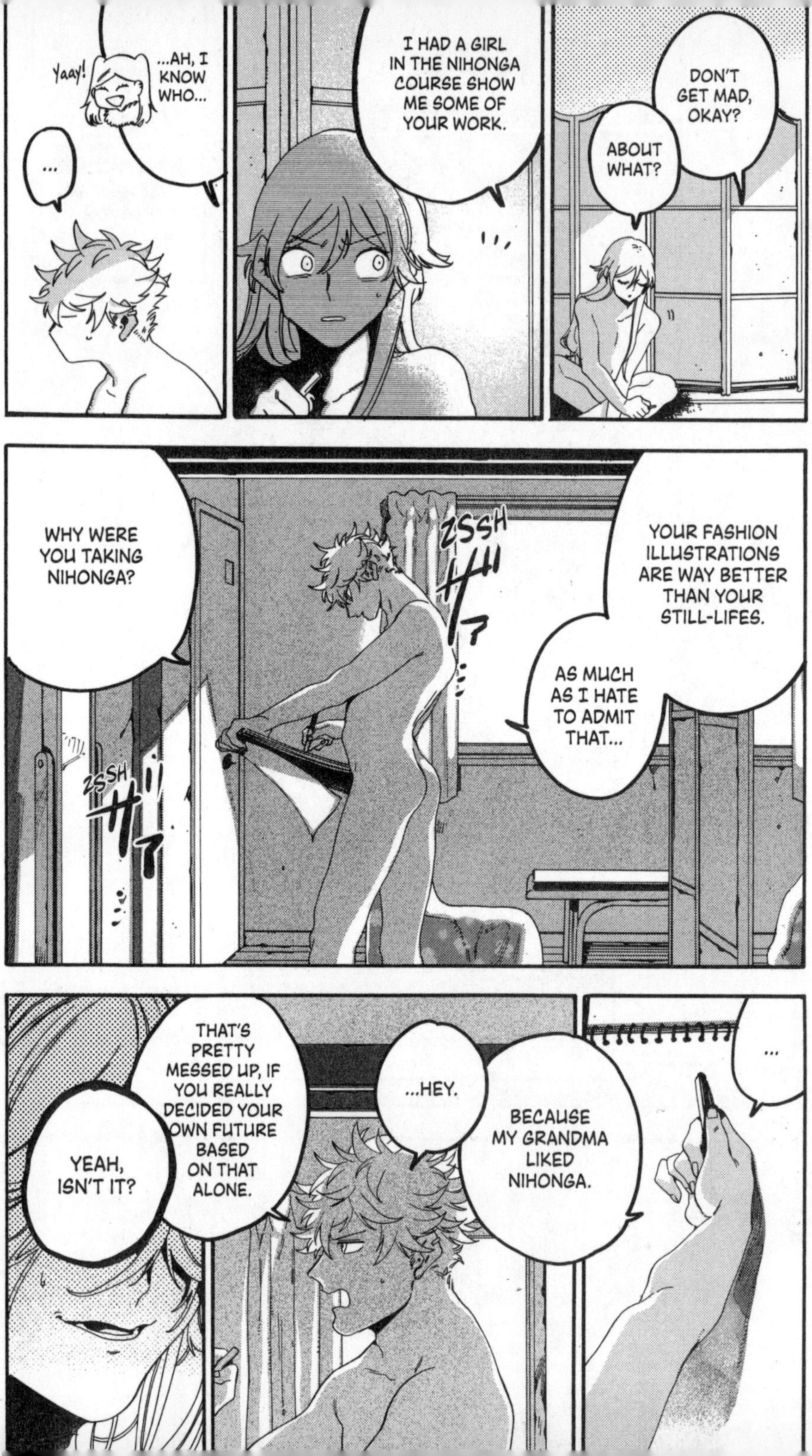
DON'T GET MAD, OKAY?
ABOUT WHAT?
I HAD A GIRL IN THE NIHONGA COURSE SHOW ME SOME OF YOUR WORK.
...AH, I KNOW WHO...
Yaay!
...
YOUR FASHION ILLUSTRATIONS ARE WAY BETTER THAN YOUR STILL-LIFES.
AS MUCH AS I HATE TO ADMIT THAT...
ZSSH
WHY WERE YOU TAKING NIHONGA?
ZSSH
...
BECAUSE MY GRANDMA LIKED NIHONGA.
...HEY.
THAT'S PRETTY MESSED UP, IF YOU REALLY DECIDED YOUR OWN FUTURE BASED ON THAT ALONE.
YEAH, ISN'T IT?

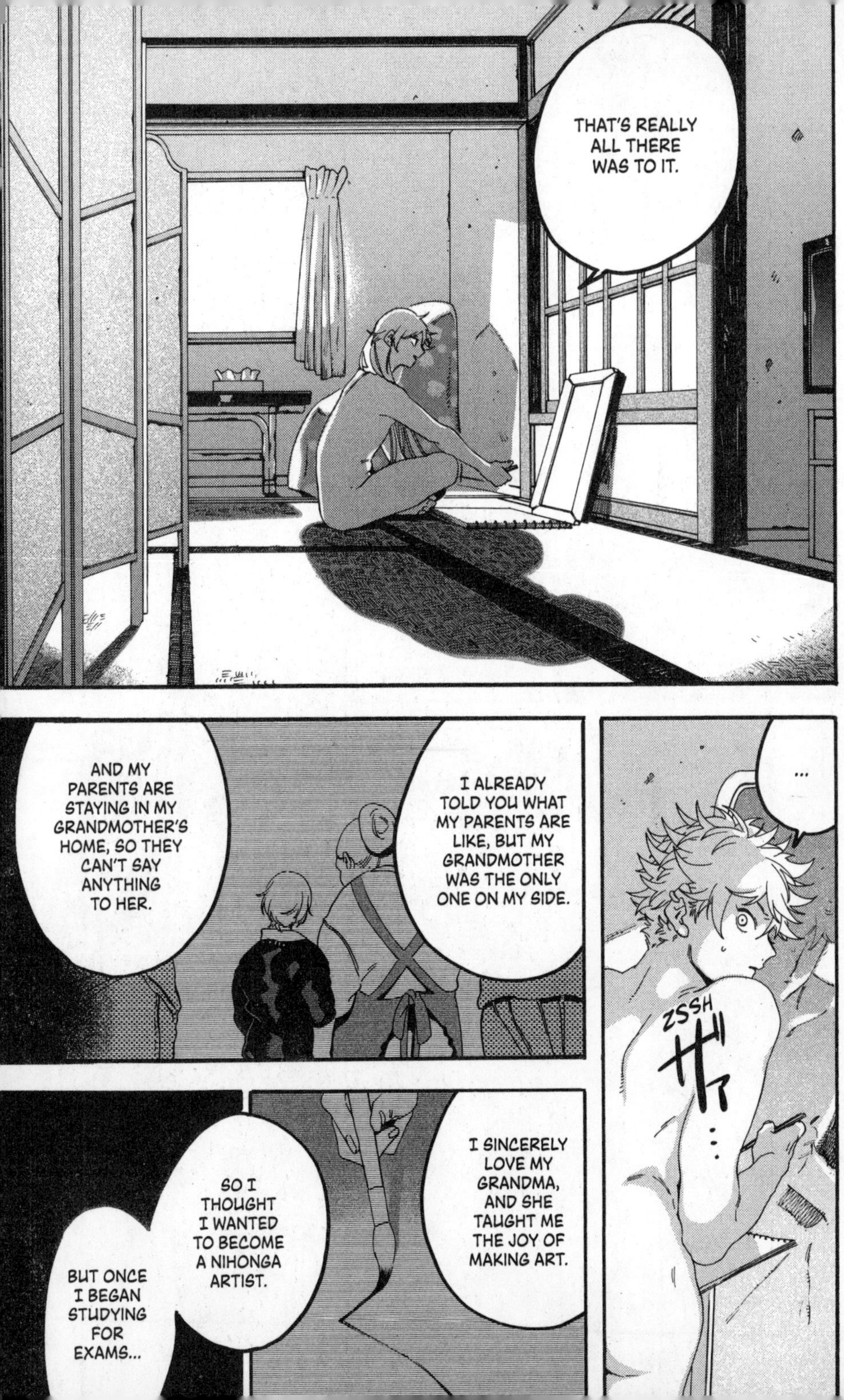
THAT'S REALLY ALL THERE WAS TO IT.
...
ZSSH
ザァ
...
I ALREADY TOLD YOU WHAT MY PARENTS ARE LIKE, BUT MY GRANDMOTHER WAS THE ONLY ONE ON MY SIDE.
AND MY PARENTS ARE STAYING IN MY GRANDMOTHER'S HOME, SO THEY CAN'T SAY ANYTHING TO HER.
I SINCERELY LOVE MY GRANDMA, AND SHE TAUGHT ME THE JOY OF MAKING ART.
SO I THOUGHT I WANTED TO BECOME A NIHONGA ARTIST.
BUT ONCE I BEGAN STUDYING FOR EXAMS...

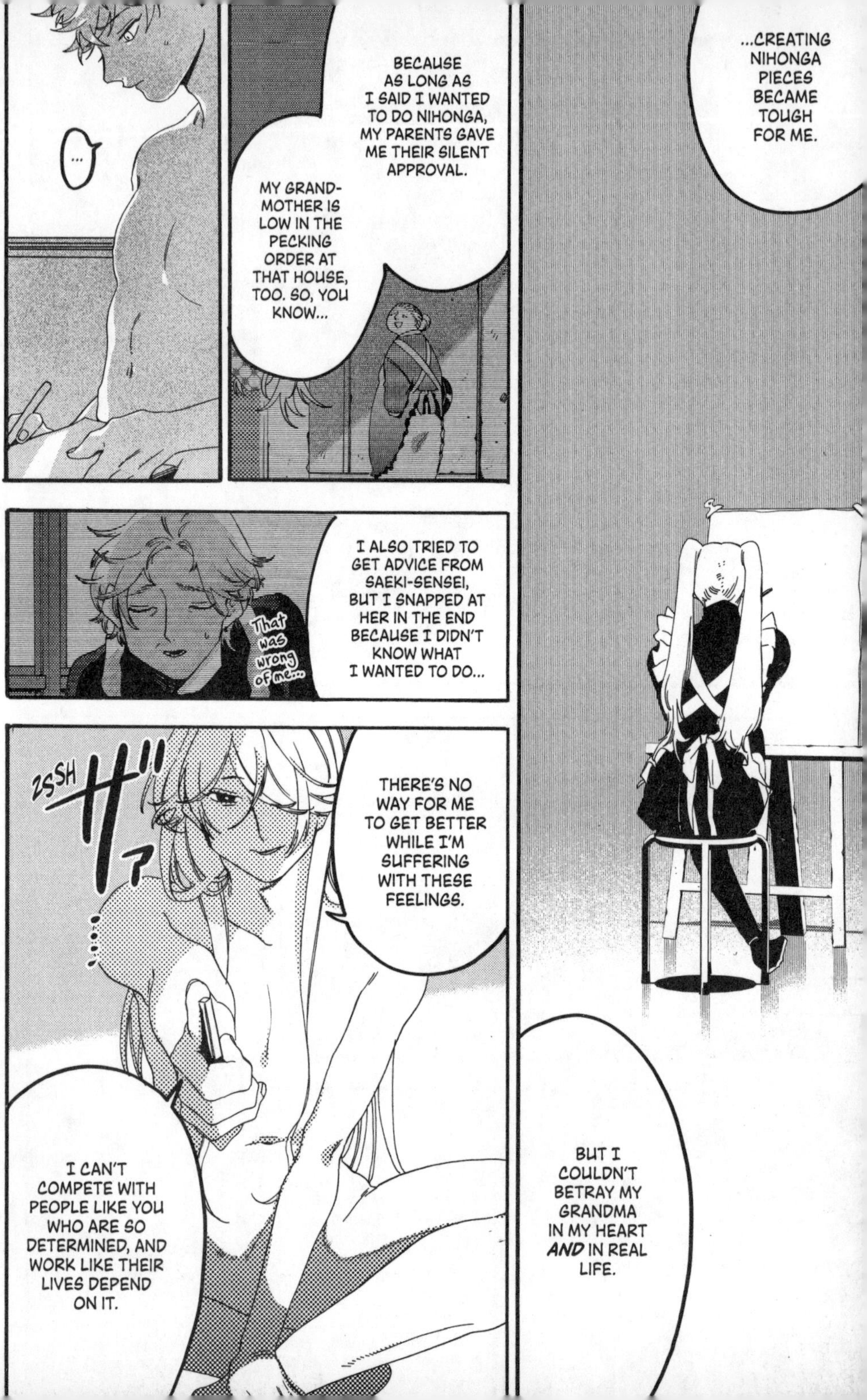

...CREATING NIHONGA PIECES BECAME TOUGH FOR ME.
BUT I COULDN'T BETRAY MY GRANDMA IN MY HEART *AND* IN REAL LIFE.
BECAUSE AS LONG AS I SAID I WANTED TO DO NIHONGA, MY PARENTS GAVE ME THEIR SILENT APPROVAL.
MY GRAND-MOTHER IS LOW IN THE PECKING ORDER AT THAT HOUSE, TOO. SO, YOU KNOW...
...
I ALSO TRIED TO GET ADVICE FROM SAEKI-SENSEI, BUT I SNAPPED AT HER IN THE END BECAUSE I DIDN'T KNOW WHAT I WANTED TO DO...
That was wrong of me...
ZSSH
THERE'S NO WAY FOR ME TO GET BETTER WHILE I'M SUFFERING WITH THESE FEELINGS.
I CAN'T COMPETE WITH PEOPLE LIKE YOU WHO ARE SO DETERMINED, AND WORK LIKE THEIR LIVES DEPEND ON IT.

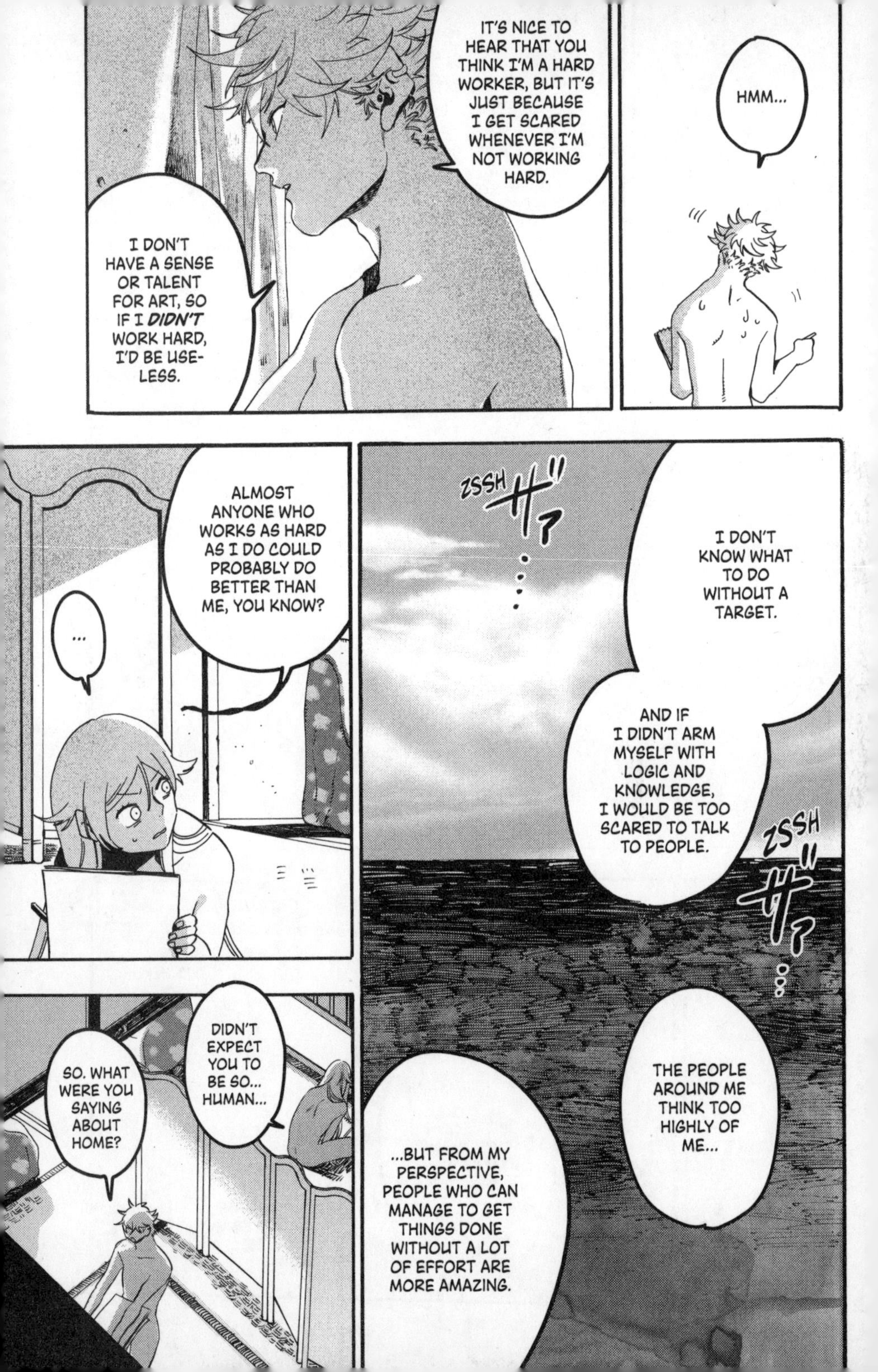
HMM...
IT'S NICE TO HEAR THAT YOU THINK I'M A HARD WORKER, BUT IT'S JUST BECAUSE I GET SCARED WHENEVER I'M NOT WORKING HARD.
I DON'T HAVE A SENSE OR TALENT FOR ART, SO IF I *DIDN'T* WORK HARD, I'D BE USE-LESS.
ZSSH
I DON'T KNOW WHAT TO DO WITHOUT A TARGET.
AND IF I DIDN'T ARM MYSELF WITH LOGIC AND KNOWLEDGE, I WOULD BE TOO SCARED TO TALK TO PEOPLE.
ZSSH
THE PEOPLE AROUND ME THINK TOO HIGHLY OF ME...
...BUT FROM MY PERSPECTIVE, PEOPLE WHO CAN MANAGE TO GET THINGS DONE WITHOUT A LOT OF EFFORT ARE MORE AMAZING.
ALMOST ANYONE WHO WORKS AS HARD AS I DO COULD PROBABLY DO BETTER THAN ME, YOU KNOW?
...
DIDN'T EXPECT YOU TO BE SO... HUMAN...
SO. WHAT WERE YOU SAYING ABOUT HOME?

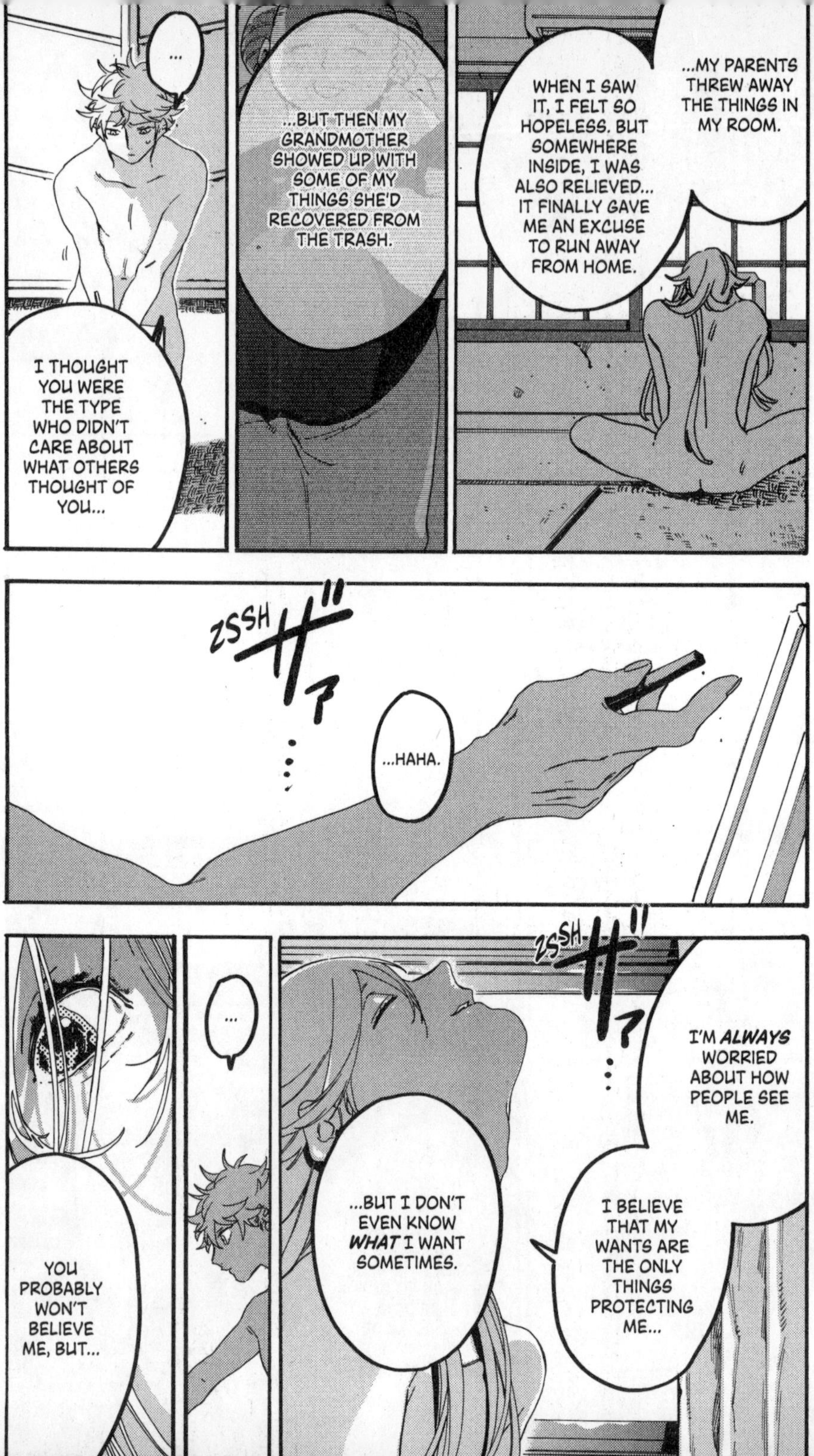
...MY PARENTS THREW AWAY THE THINGS IN MY ROOM.
WHEN I SAW IT, I FELT SO HOPELESS. BUT SOMEWHERE INSIDE, I WAS ALSO RELIEVED... IT FINALLY GAVE ME AN EXCUSE TO RUN AWAY FROM HOME.
...BUT THEN MY GRANDMOTHER SHOWED UP WITH SOME OF MY THINGS SHE'D RECOVERED FROM THE TRASH.
...
I THOUGHT YOU WERE THE TYPE WHO DIDN'T CARE ABOUT WHAT OTHERS THOUGHT OF YOU...
ZSSH
...
...HAHA.
ZSSH
...
I'M *ALWAYS* WORRIED ABOUT HOW PEOPLE SEE ME.
I BELIEVE THAT MY WANTS ARE THE ONLY THINGS PROTECTING ME...
...BUT I DON'T EVEN KNOW *WHAT* I WANT SOMETIMES.
...
YOU PROBABLY WON'T BELIEVE ME, BUT...

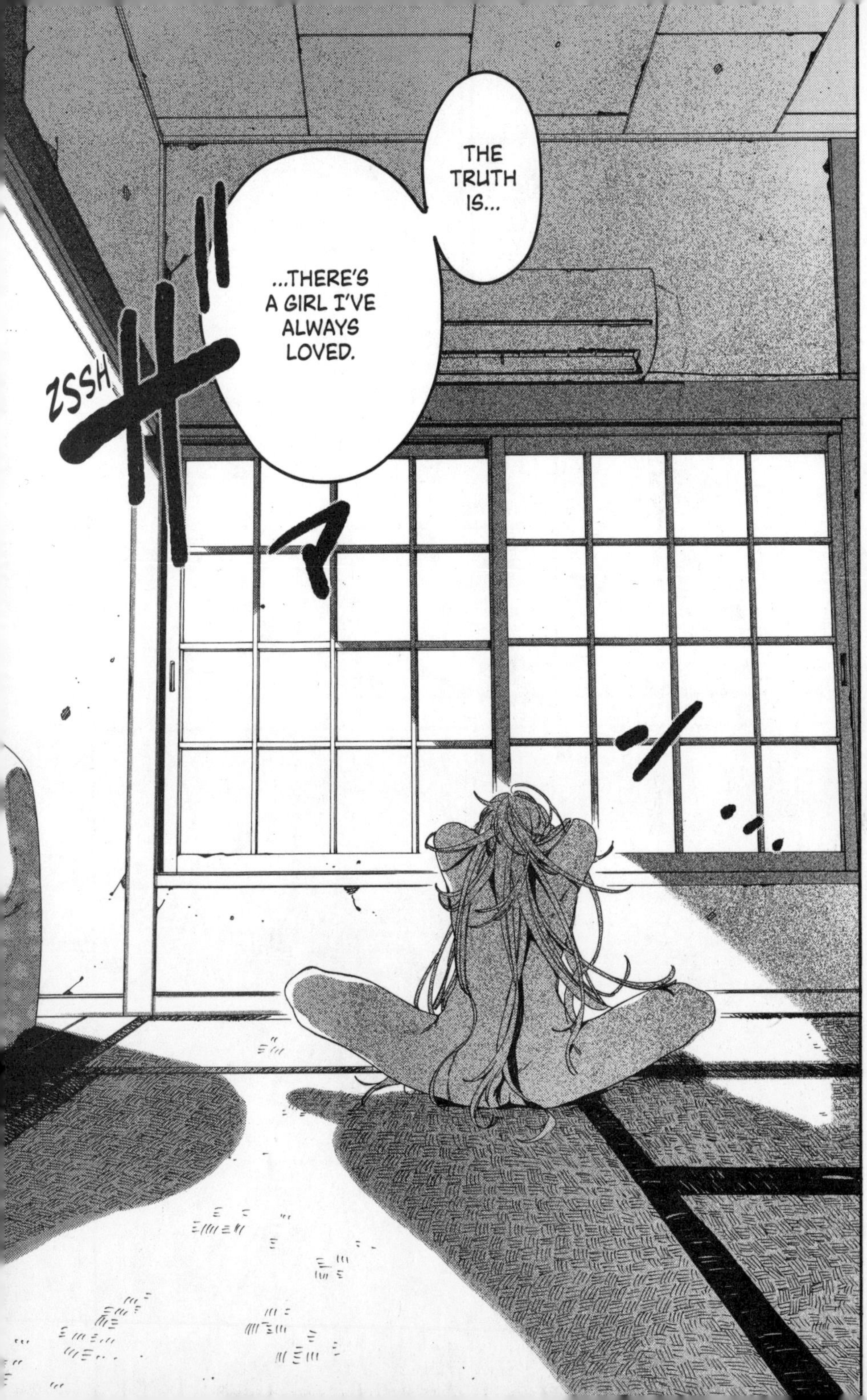
THE TRUTH IS...
...THERE'S A GIRL I'VE ALWAYS LOVED.
ZSSH

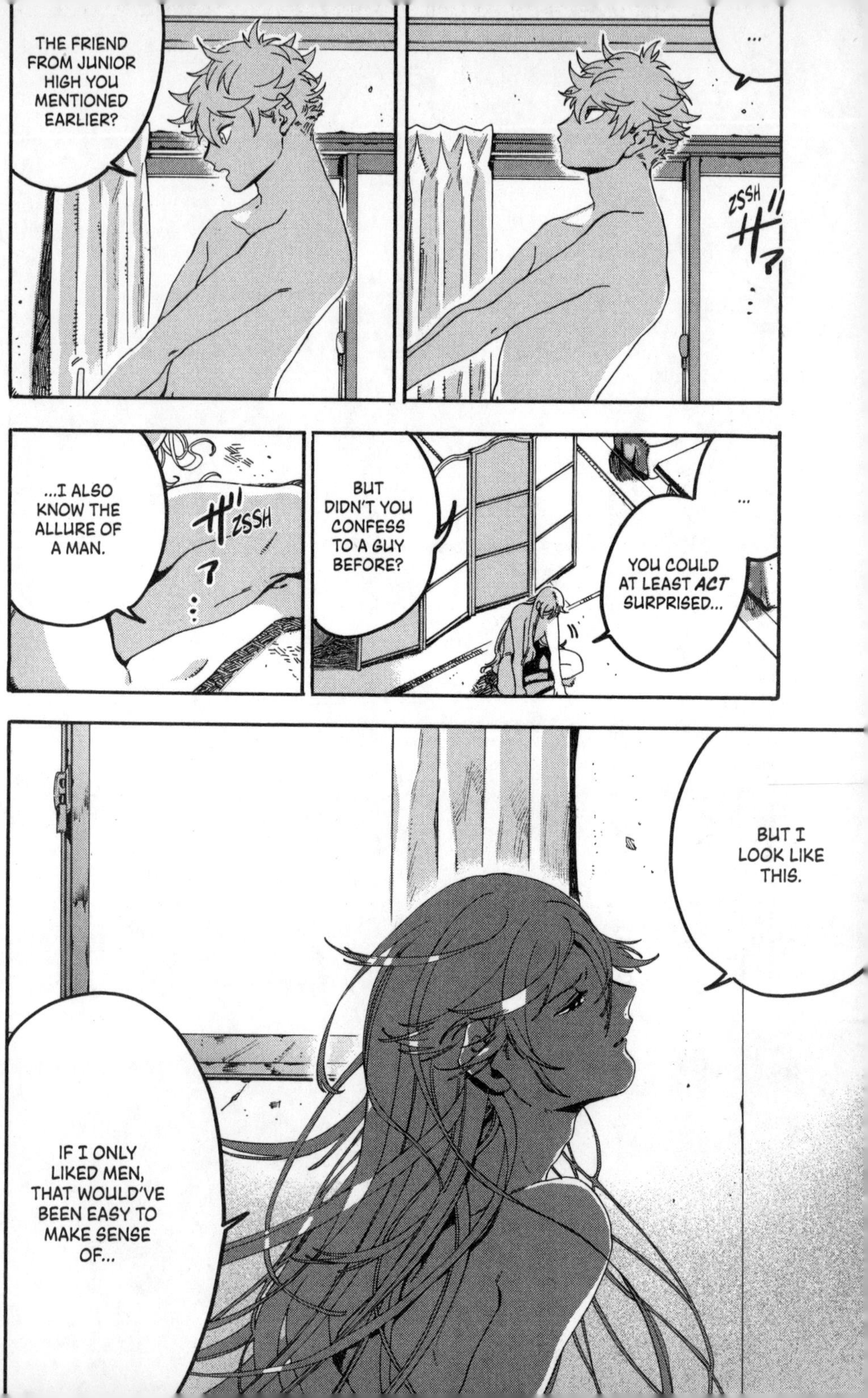
...
ZSSH
THE FRIEND FROM JUNIOR HIGH YOU MENTIONED EARLIER?
...
YOU COULD AT LEAST *ACT* SURPRISED...
BUT DIDN'T YOU CONFESS TO A GUY BEFORE?
...I ALSO KNOW THE ALLURE OF A MAN.
ZSSH
BUT I LOOK LIKE THIS.
IF I ONLY LIKED MEN, THAT WOULD'VE BEEN EASY TO MAKE SENSE OF...

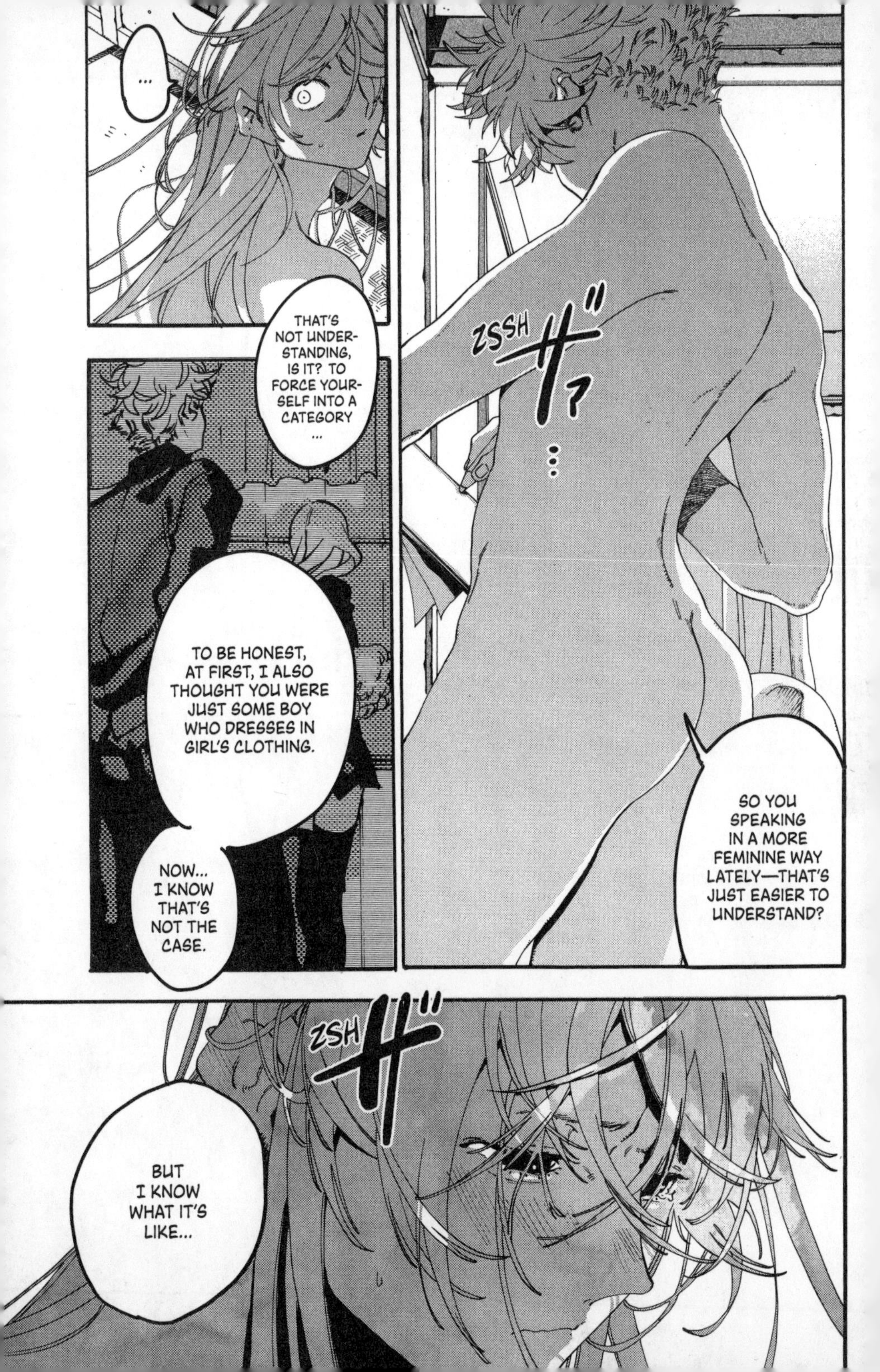
ZSSH
?
...
SO YOU SPEAKING IN A MORE FEMININE WAY LATELY—THAT'S JUST EASIER TO UNDERSTAND?
...
THAT'S NOT UNDER-STANDING, IS IT? TO FORCE YOUR-SELF INTO A CATEGORY ...
TO BE HONEST, AT FIRST, I ALSO THOUGHT YOU WERE JUST SOME BOY WHO DRESSES IN GIRL'S CLOTHING.
NOW... I KNOW THAT'S NOT THE CASE.
ZSH
BUT I KNOW WHAT IT'S LIKE...

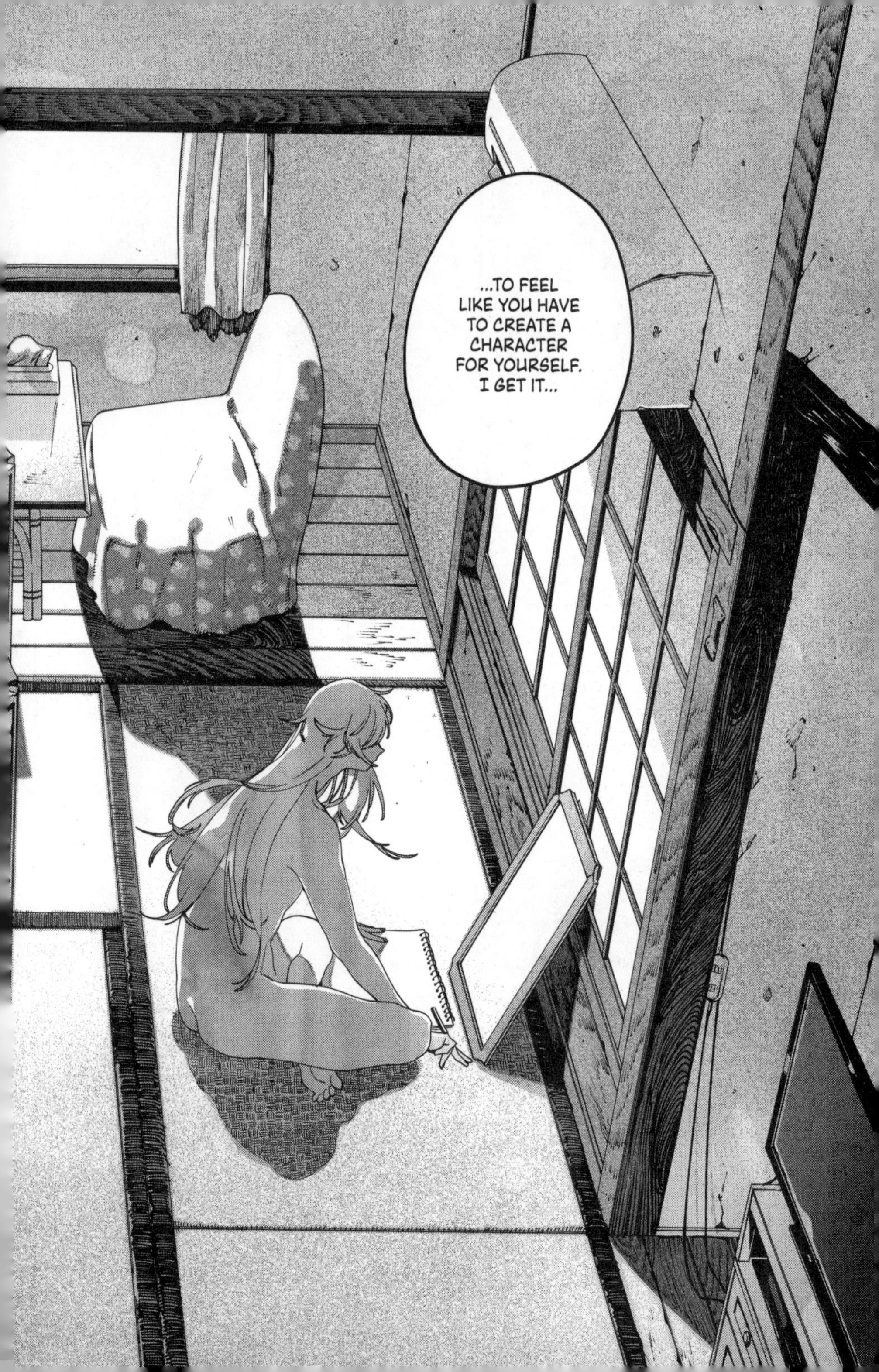
...TO FEEL LIKE YOU HAVE TO CREATE A CHARACTER FOR YOURSELF. I GET IT...

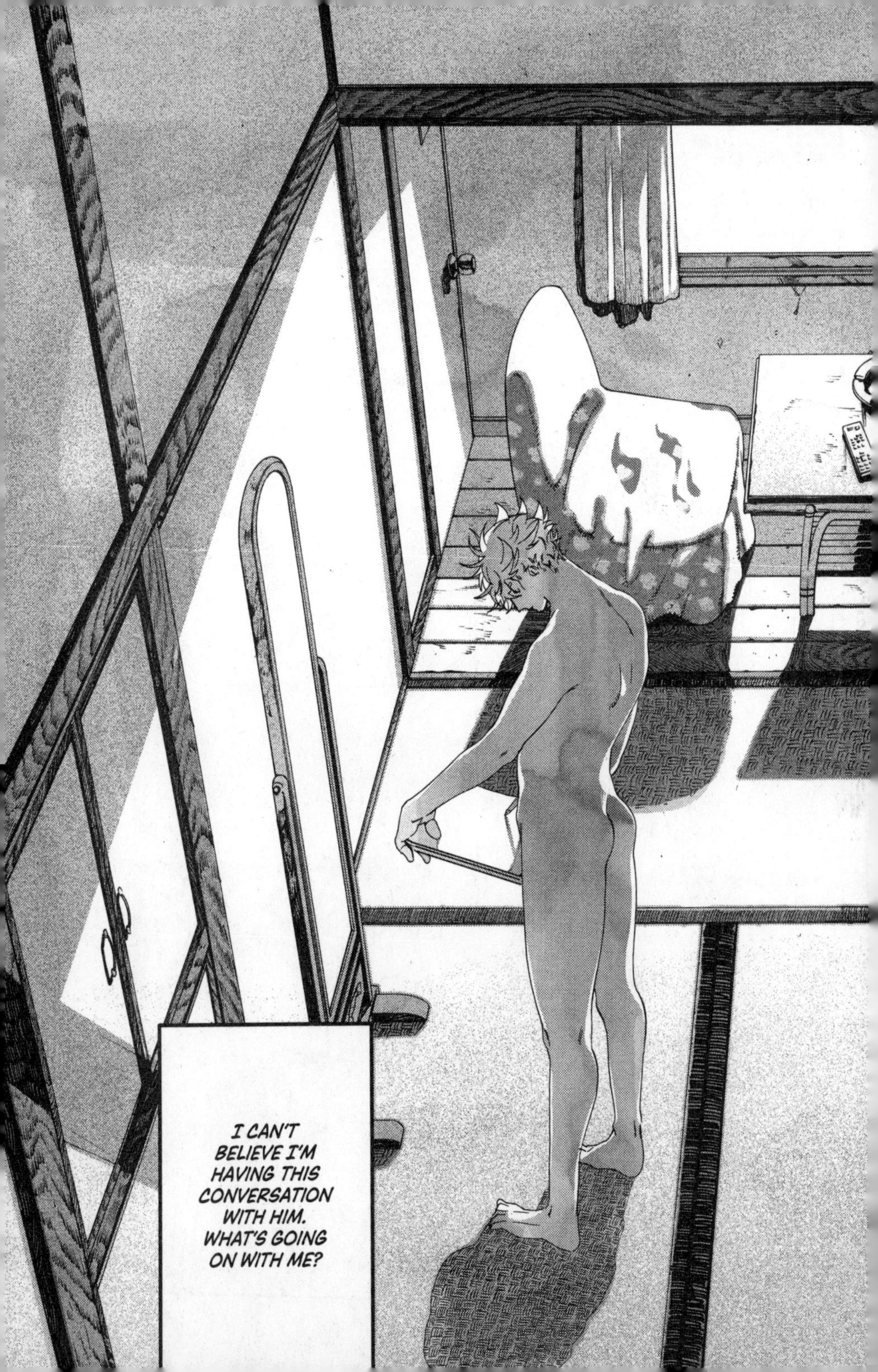
I CAN'T BELIEVE I'M HAVING THIS CONVERSATION WITH HIM. WHAT'S GOING ON WITH ME?

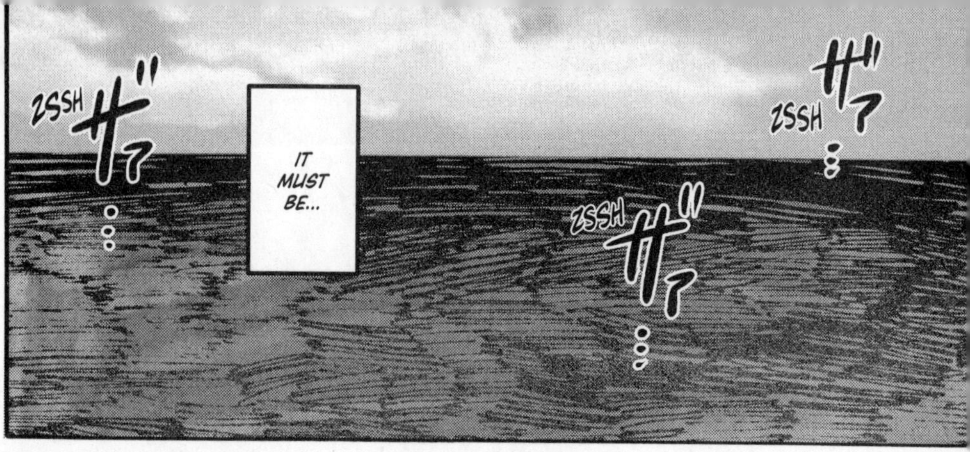
ZSSH ザァ…
ZSSH ザァ…
IT MUST BE...
ZSSH ザァ…

ART: SHOTA YAMAMICHI

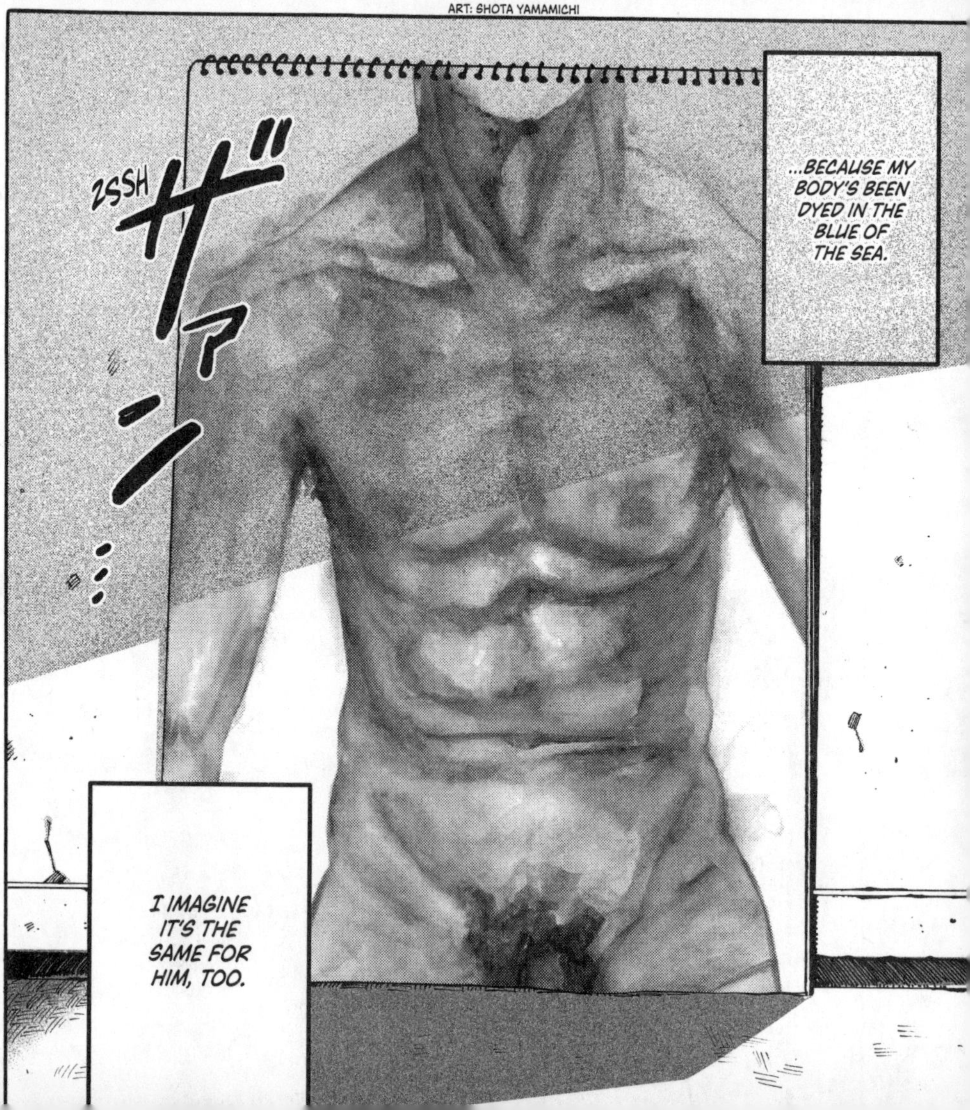
...BECAUSE MY BODY'S BEEN DYED IN THE BLUE OF THE SEA.
ZSSH ザァン…
I IMAGINE IT'S THE SAME FOR HIM, TOO.

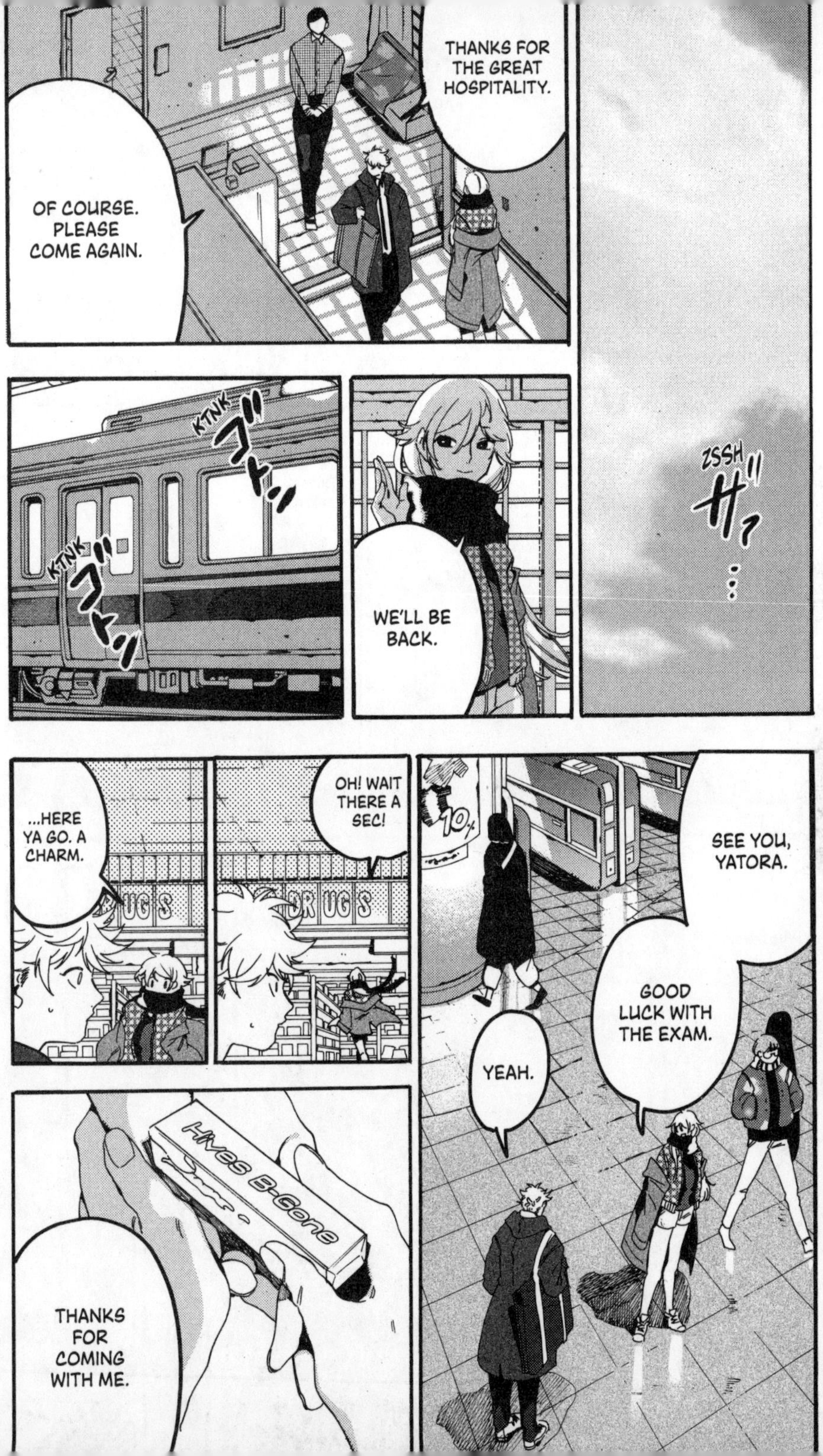
ZSSH
ザッ
THANKS FOR THE GREAT HOSPITALITY.
OF COURSE. PLEASE COME AGAIN.
WE'LL BE BACK.
KTNK
ゴトッ
KTNK
ゴトッ
SEE YOU, YATORA.
GOOD LUCK WITH THE EXAM.
YEAH.
OH! WAIT THERE A SEC!
DRUGS
...HERE YA GO. A CHARM.
Hives B-Gone
THANKS FOR COMING WITH ME.

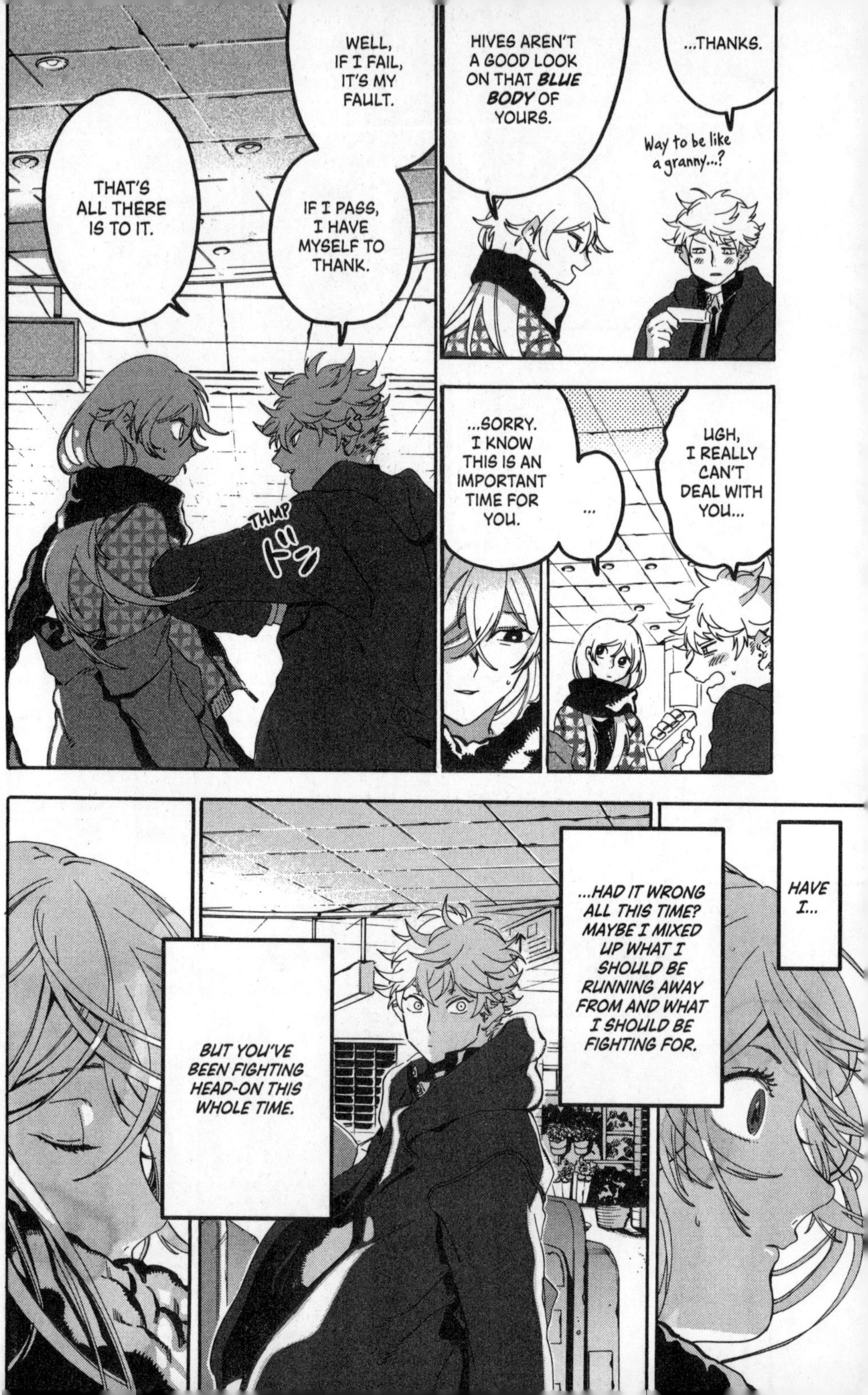

...THANKS.
HIVES AREN'T A GOOD LOOK ON THAT ***BLUE BODY*** OF YOURS.
Way to be like a granny...?
UGH, I REALLY CAN'T DEAL WITH YOU...
...
...SORRY. I KNOW THIS IS AN IMPORTANT TIME FOR YOU.
WELL, IF I FAIL, IT'S MY FAULT.
IF I PASS, I HAVE MYSELF TO THANK.
THAT'S ALL THERE IS TO IT.
THMP
ドッ
HAVE I...
...HAD IT WRONG ALL THIS TIME? MAYBE I MIXED UP WHAT I SHOULD BE RUNNING AWAY FROM AND WHAT I SHOULD BE FIGHTING FOR.
BUT YOU'VE BEEN FIGHTING HEAD-ON THIS WHOLE TIME.

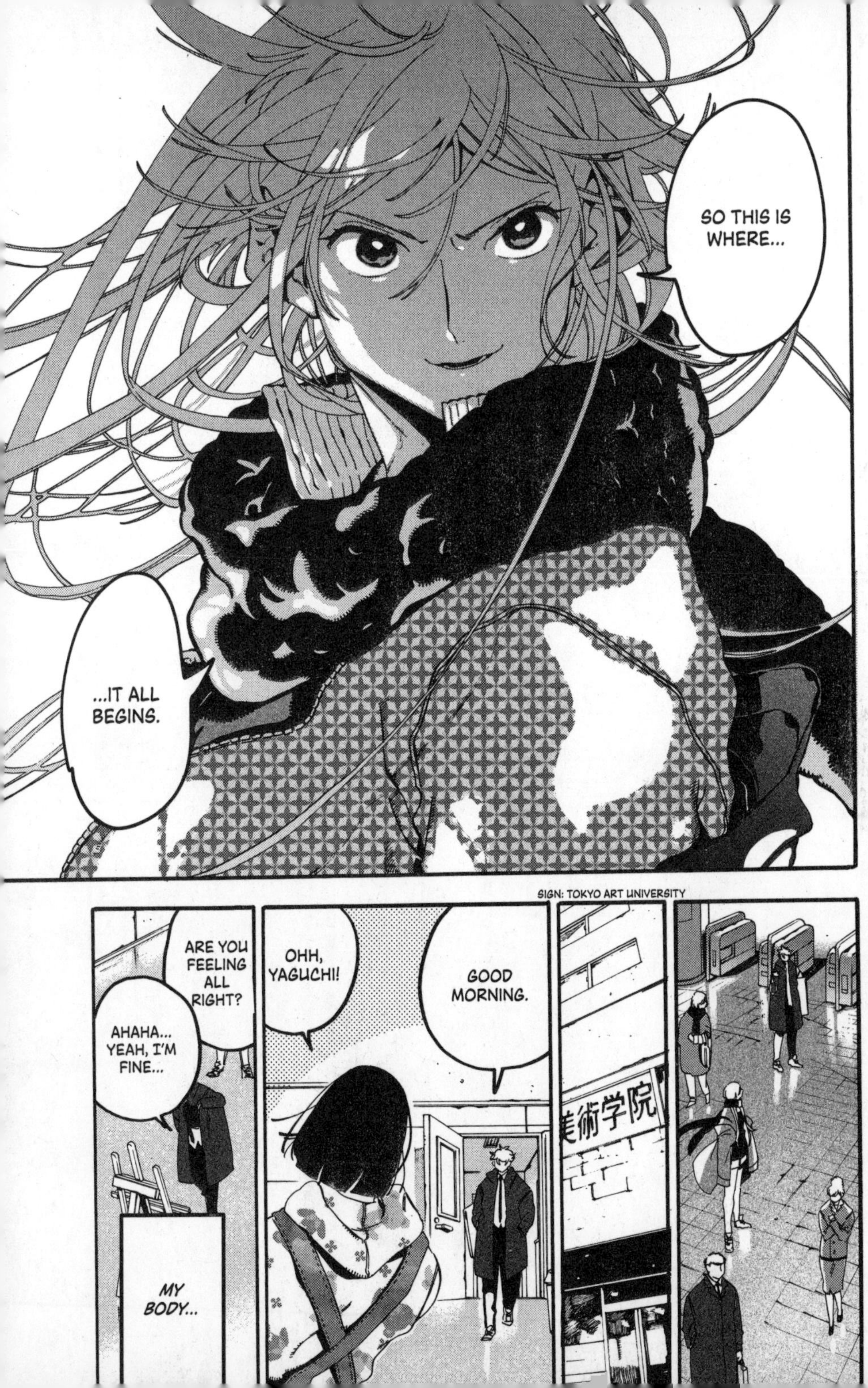
SO THIS IS WHERE...
...IT ALL BEGINS.
SIGN: TOKYO ART UNIVERSITY
美術学院
GOOD MORNING.
OHH, YAGUCHI!
ARE YOU FEELING ALL RIGHT?
AHAHA... YEAH, I'M FINE...
MY BODY...

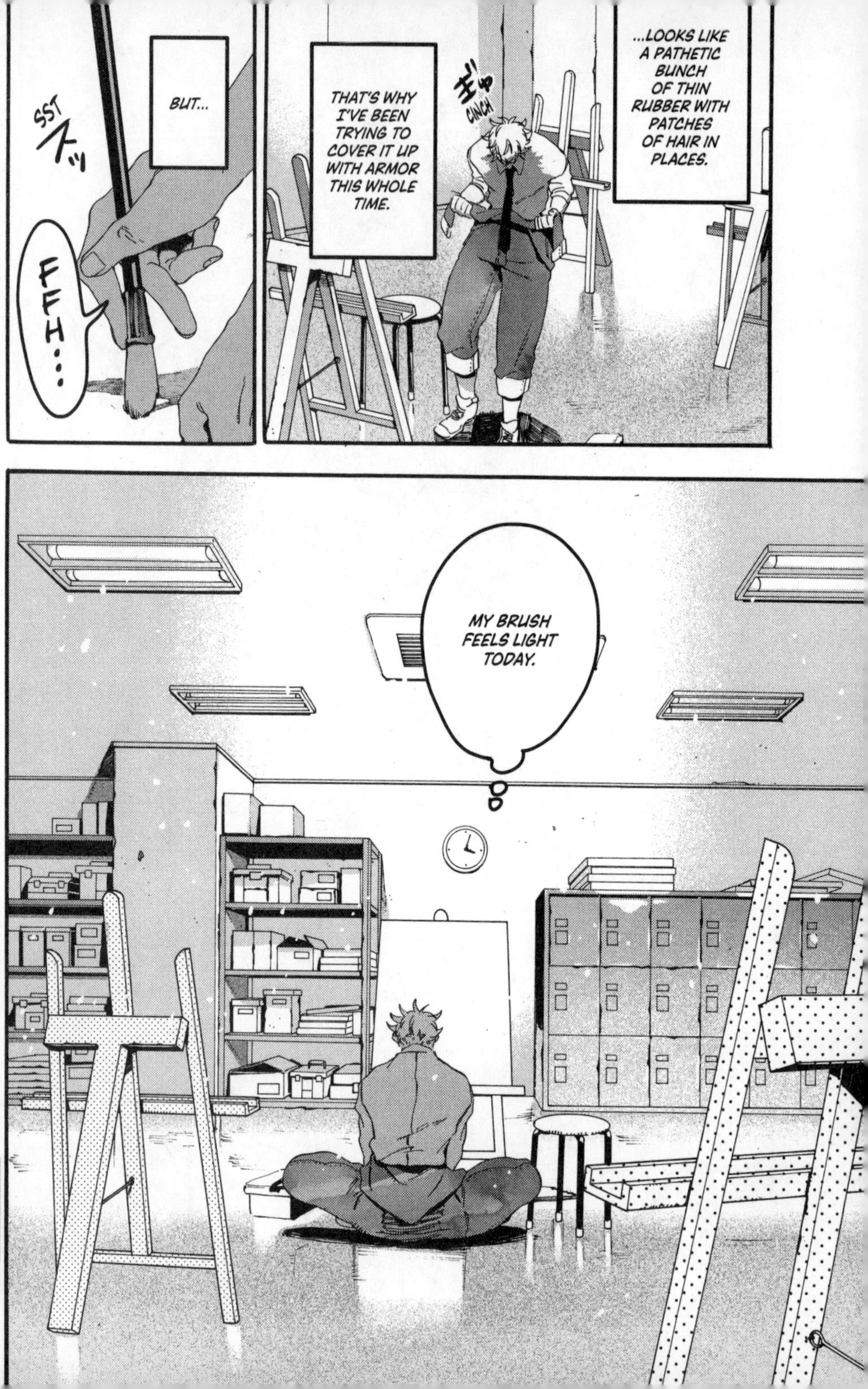
...LOOKS LIKE A PATHETIC BUNCH OF THIN RUBBER WITH PATCHES OF HAIR IN PLACES.
ぎゅ
CINCH
THAT'S WHY I'VE BEEN TRYING TO COVER IT UP WITH ARMOR THIS WHOLE TIME.
BUT...
SST
スッ
FFH...
MY BRUSH FEELS LIGHT TODAY.

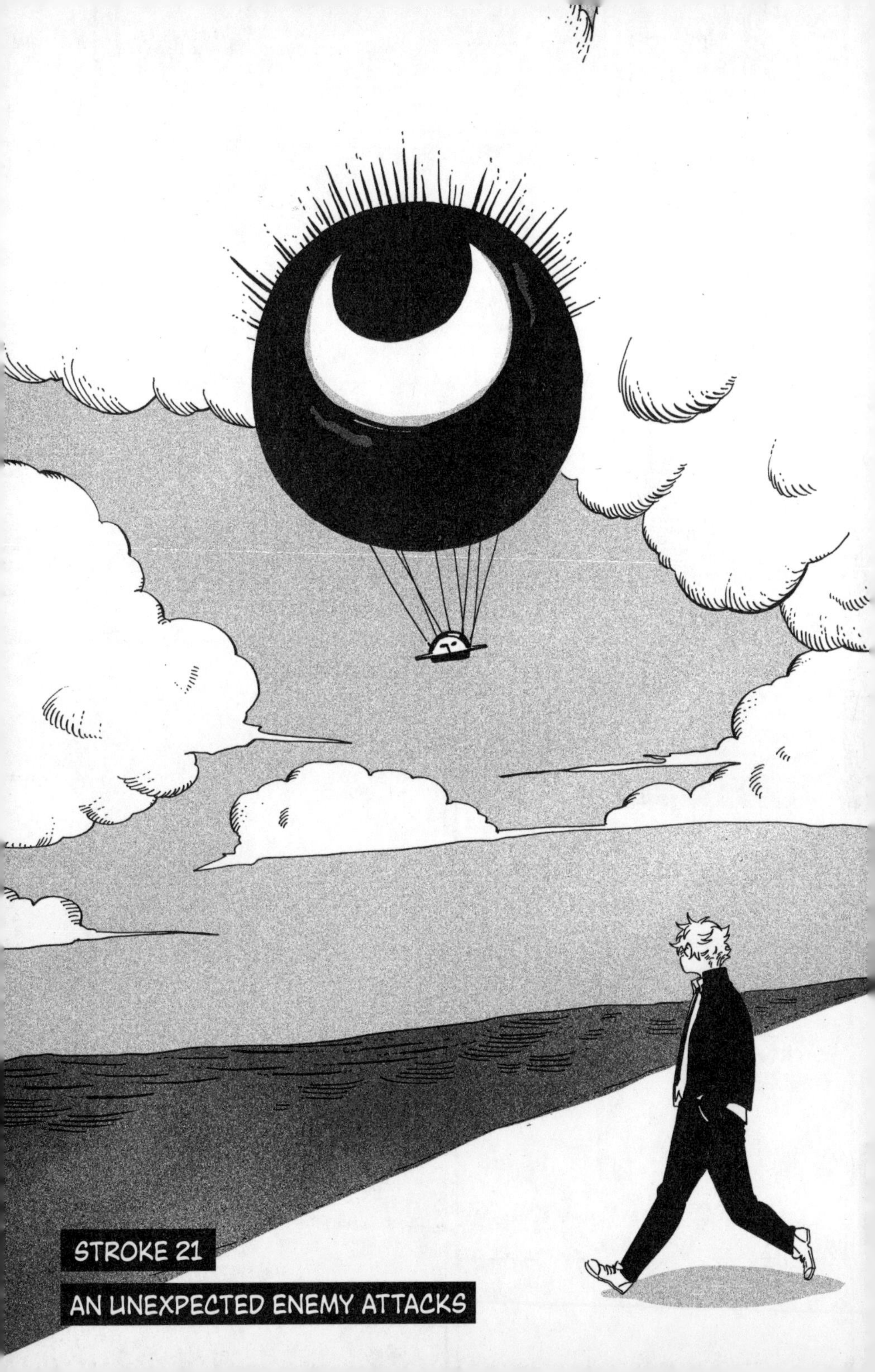
STROKE 21
AN UNEXPECTED ENEMY ATTACKS

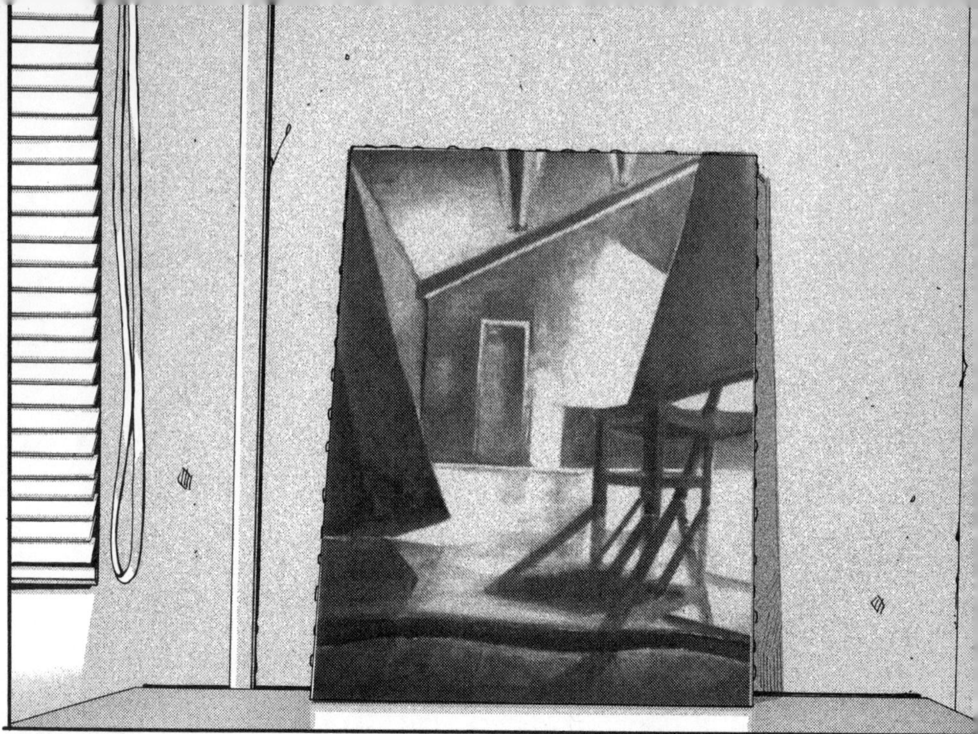

ART: SHOTA YAMAMICHI

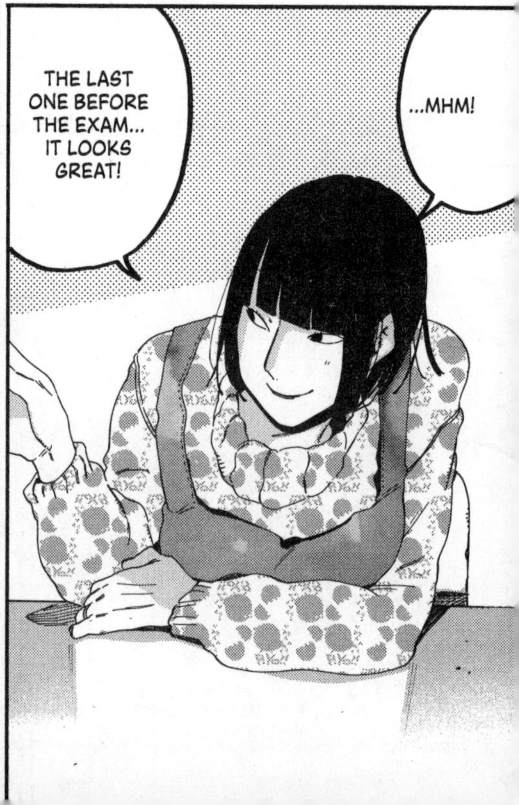
...MHM!
THE LAST ONE BEFORE THE EXAM... IT LOOKS GREAT!

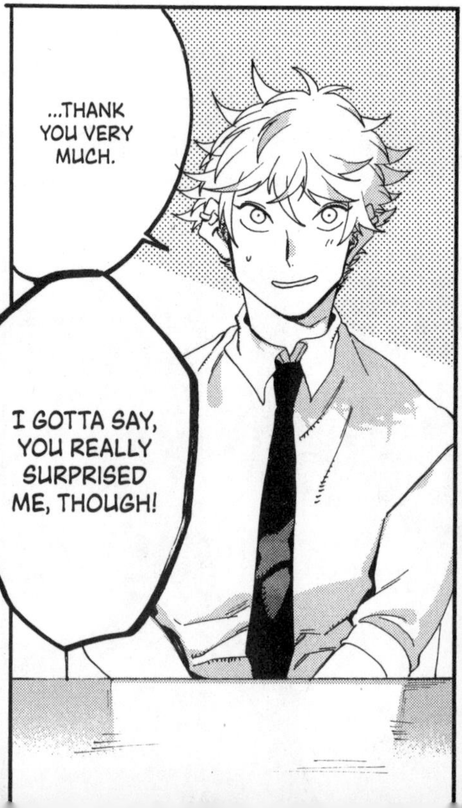
...THANK YOU VERY MUCH.
I GOTTA SAY, YOU REALLY SURPRISED ME, THOUGH!

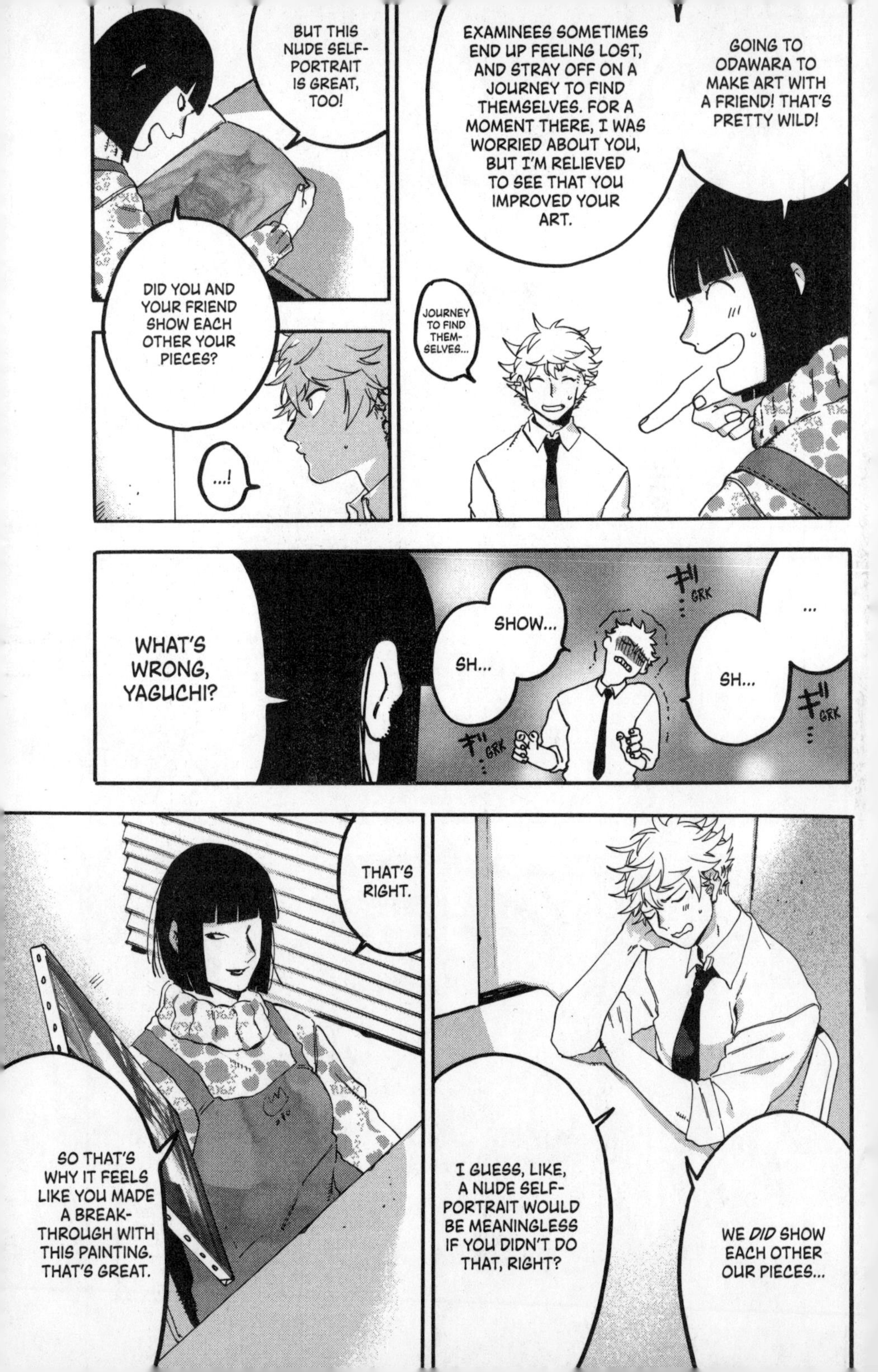
GOING TO ODAWARA TO MAKE ART WITH A FRIEND! THAT'S PRETTY WILD!
EXAMINEES SOMETIMES END UP FEELING LOST, AND STRAY OFF ON A JOURNEY TO FIND THEMSELVES. FOR A MOMENT THERE, I WAS WORRIED ABOUT YOU, BUT I'M RELIEVED TO SEE THAT YOU IMPROVED YOUR ART.
JOURNEY TO FIND THEMSELVES...
BUT THIS NUDE SELF-PORTRAIT IS GREAT, TOO!
DID YOU AND YOUR FRIEND SHOW EACH OTHER YOUR PIECES?
...!
...
SH...
GRK
SHOW...
SH...
GRK
GRK
WHAT'S WRONG, YAGUCHI?
WE *DID* SHOW EACH OTHER OUR PIECES...
I GUESS, LIKE, A NUDE SELF-PORTRAIT WOULD BE MEANINGLESS IF YOU DIDN'T DO THAT, RIGHT?
THAT'S RIGHT.
SO THAT'S WHY IT FEELS LIKE YOU MADE A BREAK-THROUGH WITH THIS PAINTING. THAT'S GREAT.

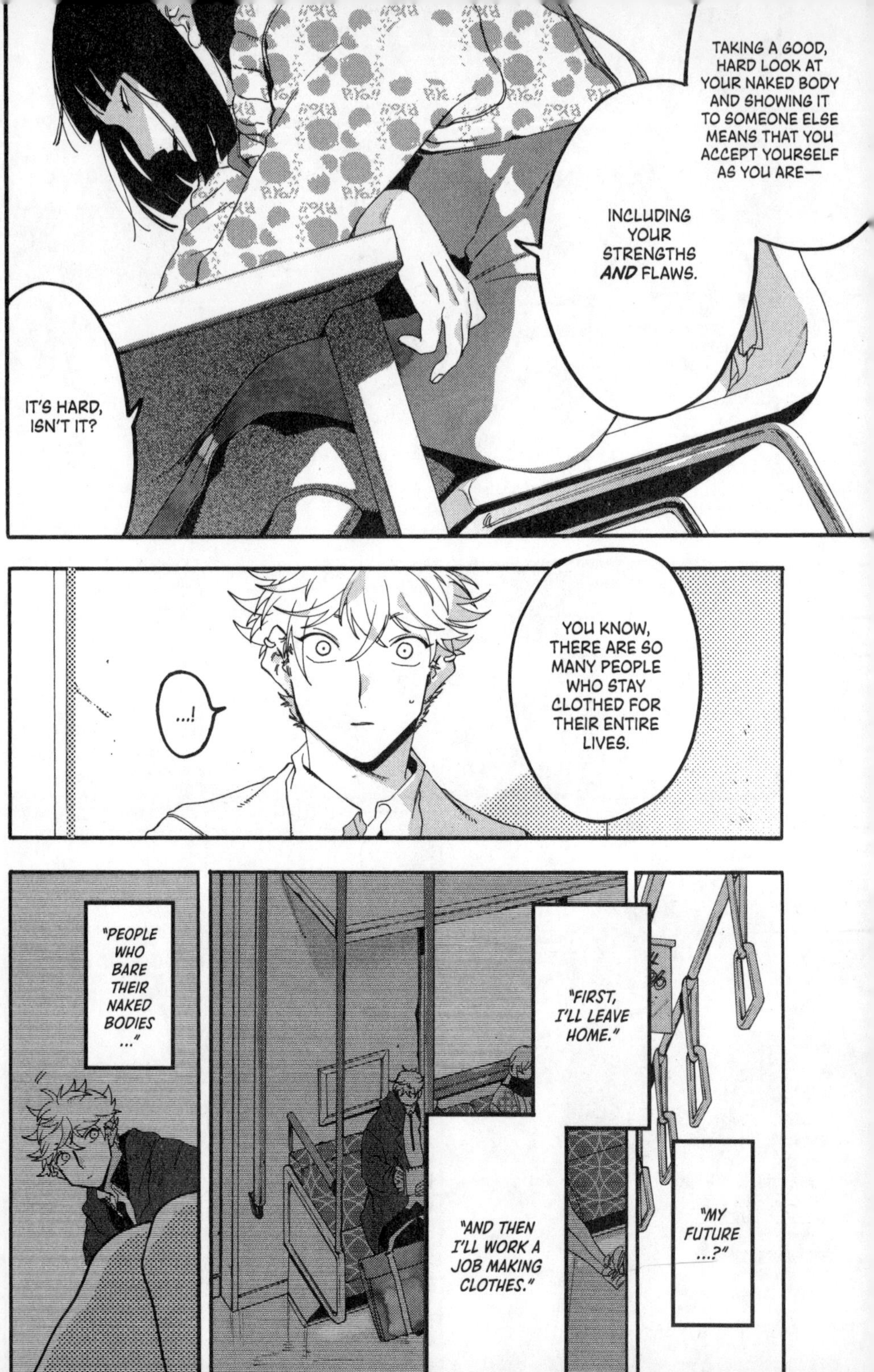
TAKING A GOOD, HARD LOOK AT YOUR NAKED BODY AND SHOWING IT TO SOMEONE ELSE MEANS THAT YOU ACCEPT YOURSELF AS YOU ARE—
INCLUDING YOUR STRENGTHS *AND* FLAWS.
IT'S HARD, ISN'T IT?
YOU KNOW, THERE ARE SO MANY PEOPLE WHO STAY CLOTHED FOR THEIR ENTIRE LIVES.
...!
"MY FUTURE ...?"
"FIRST, I'LL LEAVE HOME."
"AND THEN I'LL WORK A JOB MAKING CLOTHES."
"PEOPLE WHO BARE THEIR NAKED BODIES ..."

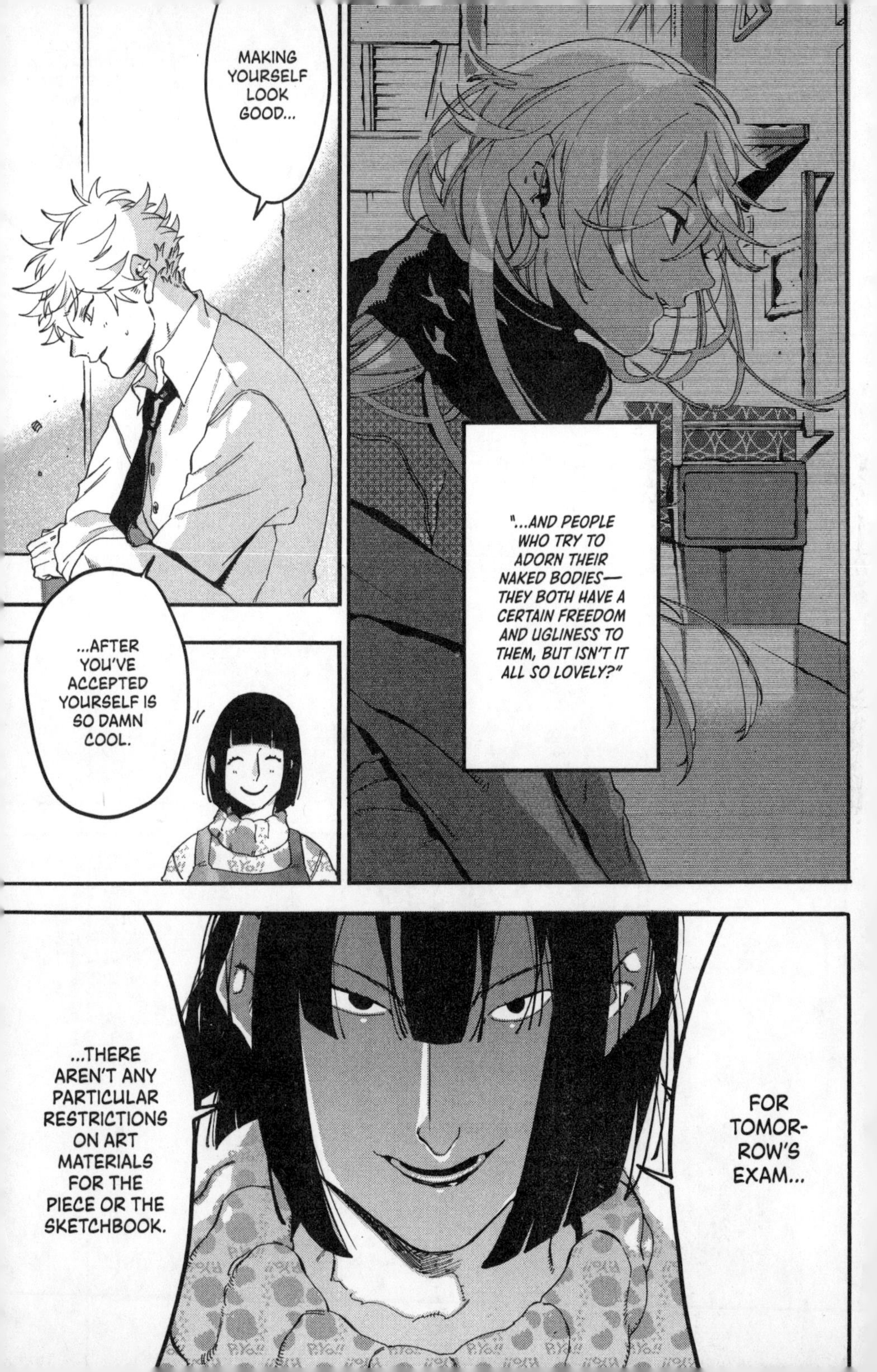
"...AND PEOPLE WHO TRY TO ADORN THEIR NAKED BODIES—THEY BOTH HAVE A CERTAIN FREEDOM AND UGLINESS TO THEM, BUT ISN'T IT ALL SO LOVELY?"
MAKING YOURSELF LOOK GOOD...
...AFTER YOU'VE ACCEPTED YOURSELF IS SO DAMN COOL.
FOR TOMORROW'S EXAM...
...THERE AREN'T ANY PARTICULAR RESTRICTIONS ON ART MATERIALS FOR THE PIECE OR THE SKETCHBOOK.

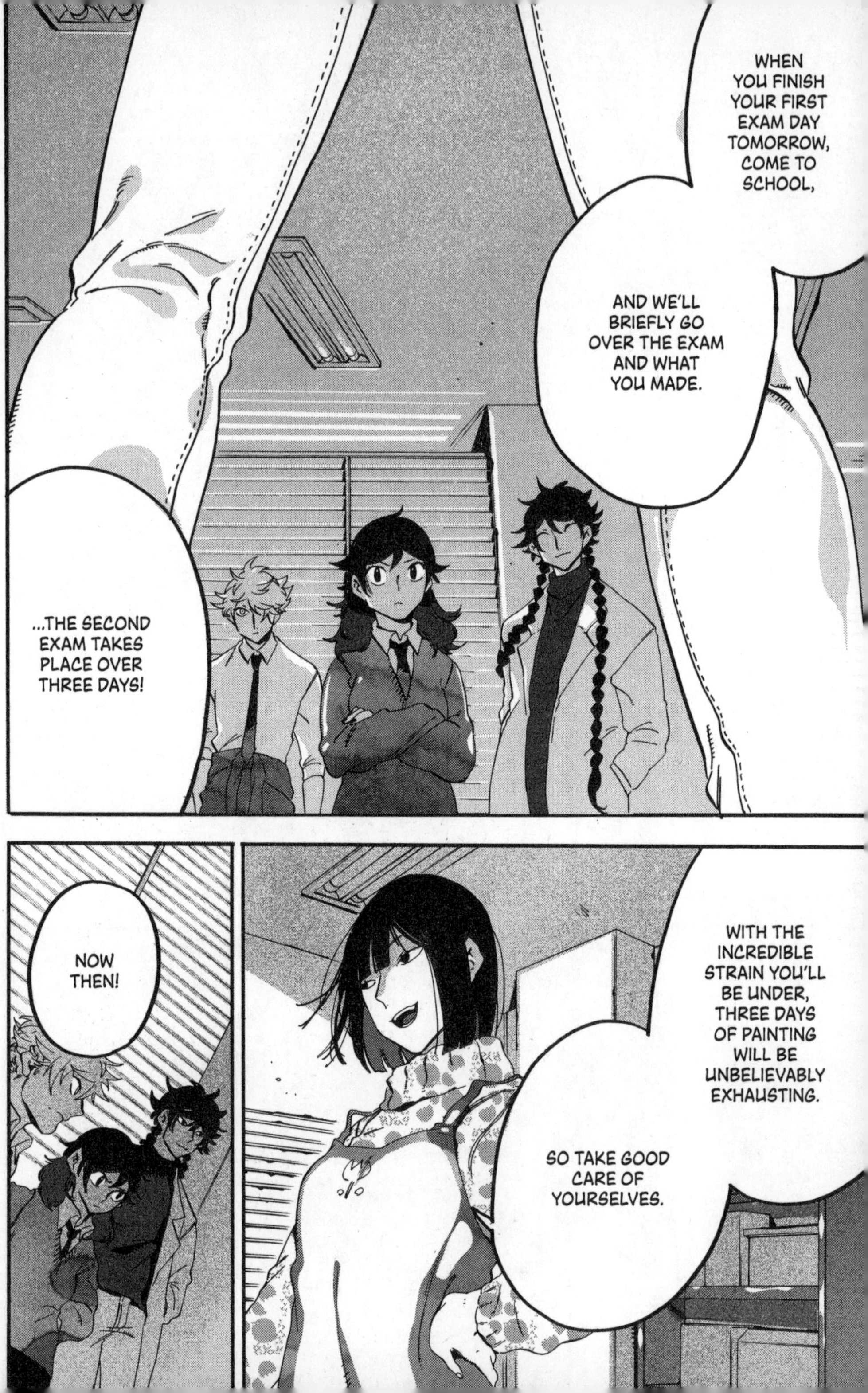
WHEN YOU FINISH YOUR FIRST EXAM DAY TOMORROW, COME TO SCHOOL,
AND WE'LL BRIEFLY GO OVER THE EXAM AND WHAT YOU MADE.
...THE SECOND EXAM TAKES PLACE OVER THREE DAYS!
WITH THE INCREDIBLE STRAIN YOU'LL BE UNDER, THREE DAYS OF PAINTING WILL BE UNBELIEVABLY EXHAUSTING.
SO TAKE GOOD CARE OF YOURSELVES.
NOW THEN!

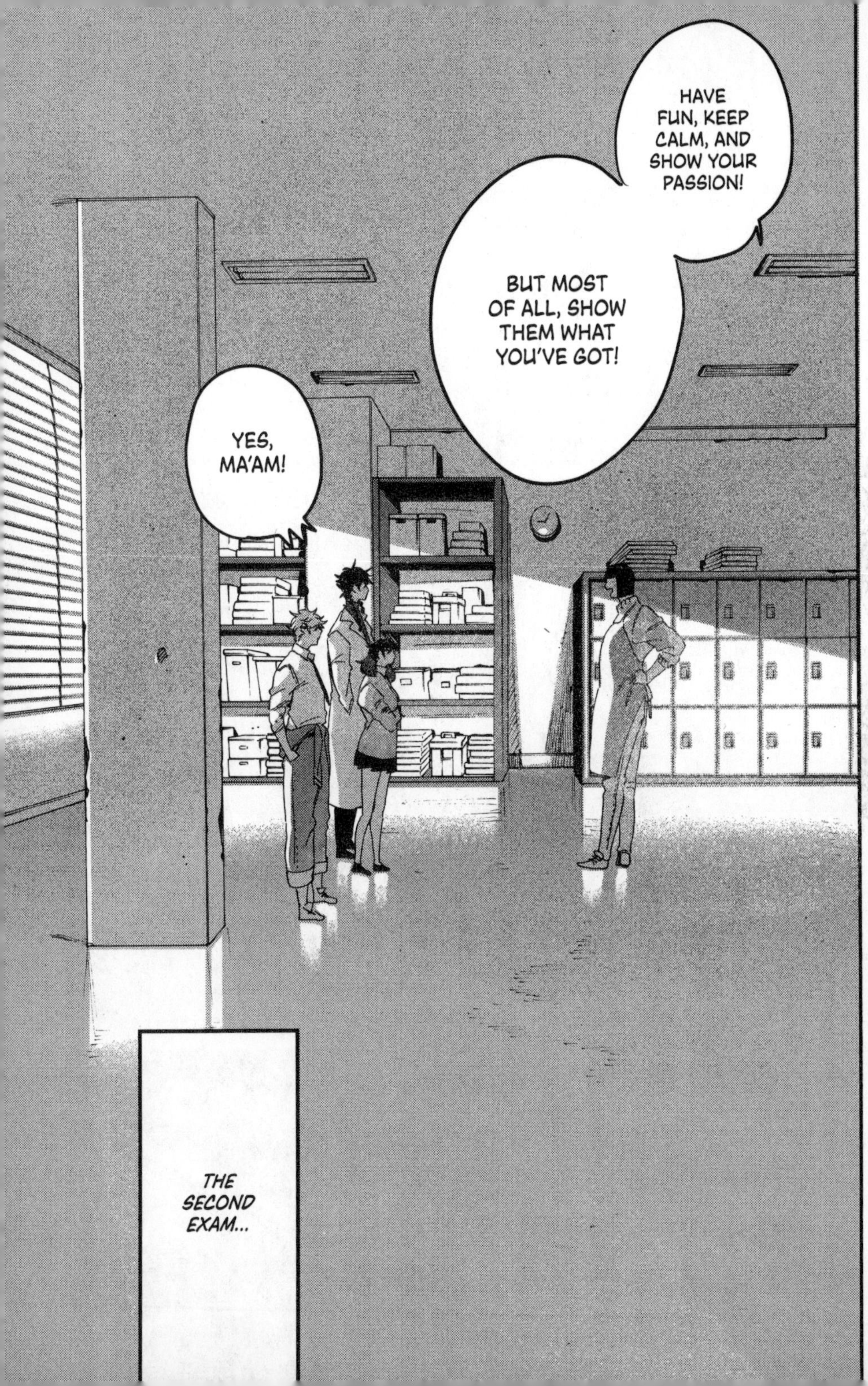
HAVE FUN, KEEP CALM, AND SHOW YOUR PASSION!
BUT MOST OF ALL, SHOW THEM WHAT YOU'VE GOT!
YES, MA'AM!
THE SECOND EXAM...

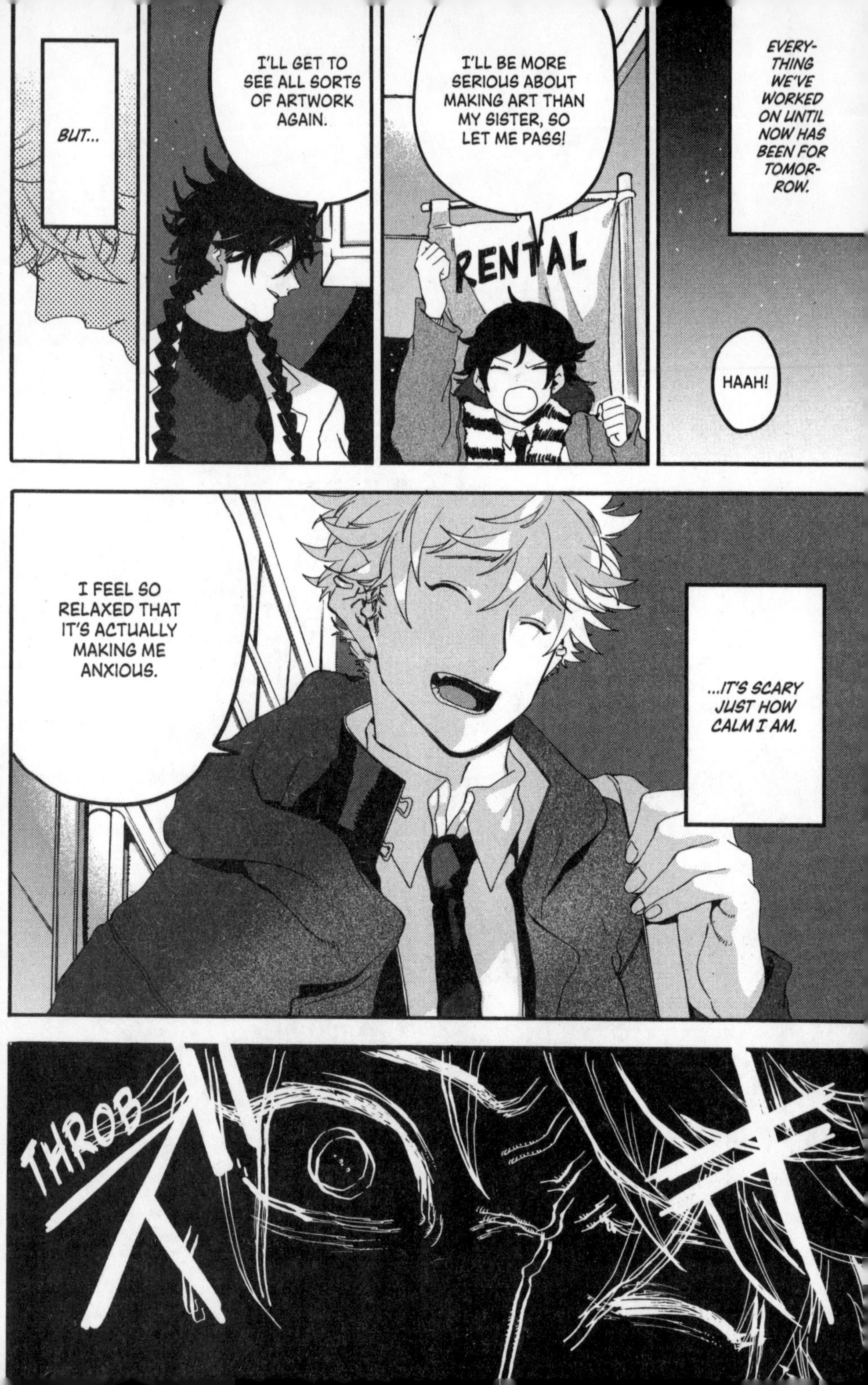
EVERY-THING WE'VE WORKED ON UNTIL NOW HAS BEEN FOR TOMOR-ROW.
HAAH!
I'LL BE MORE SERIOUS ABOUT MAKING ART THAN MY SISTER, SO LET ME PASS!
RENTAL
I'LL GET TO SEE ALL SORTS OF ARTWORK AGAIN.
BUT...
...IT'S SCARY JUST HOW CALM I AM.
I FEEL SO RELAXED THAT IT'S ACTUALLY MAKING ME ANXIOUS.
THROB

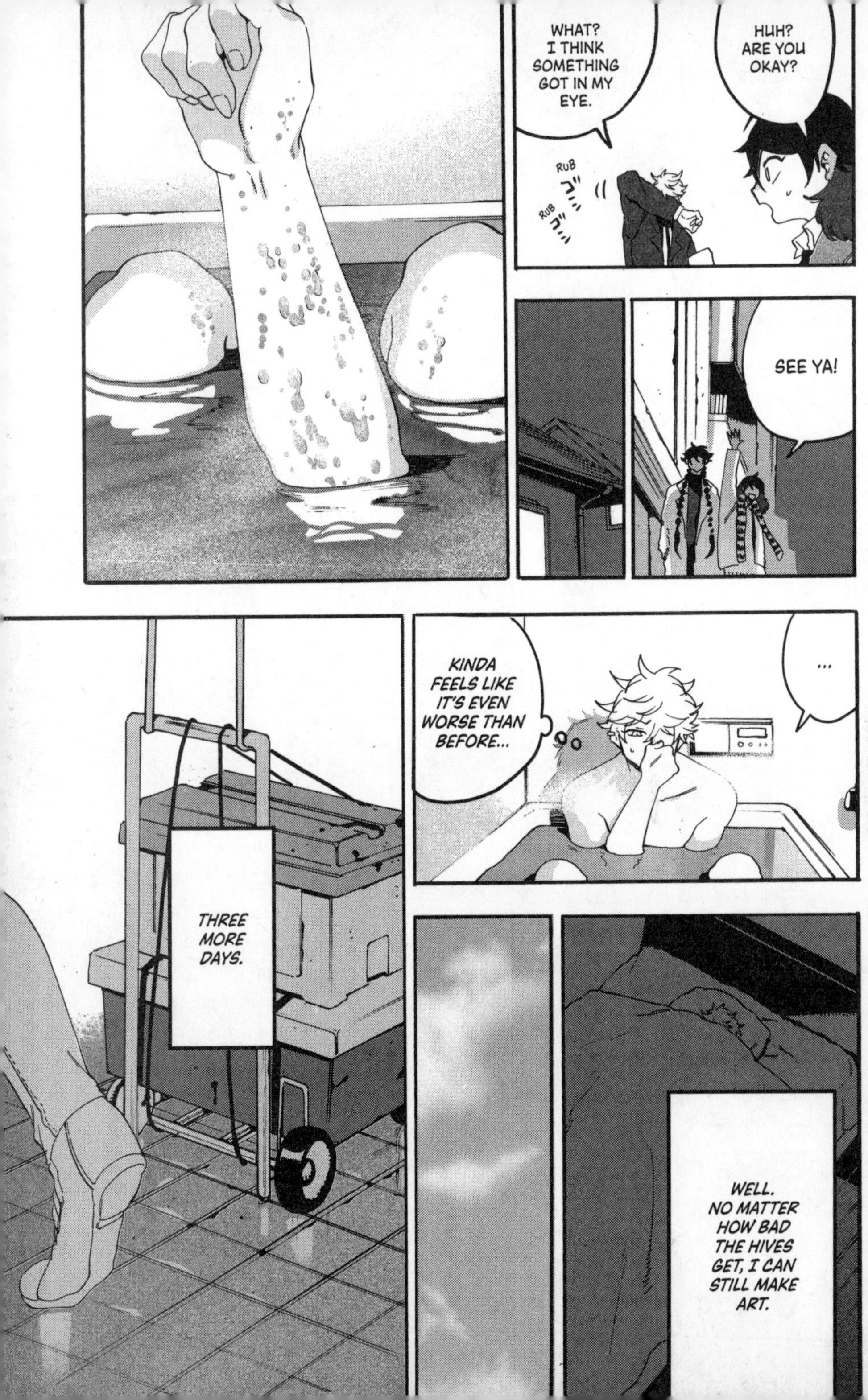
HUH? ARE YOU OKAY?
WHAT? I THINK SOMETHING GOT IN MY EYE.
RUB
RUB
SEE YA!
...
KINDA FEELS LIKE IT'S EVEN WORSE THAN BEFORE...
WELL. NO MATTER HOW BAD THE HIVES GET, I CAN STILL MAKE ART.
THREE MORE DAYS.

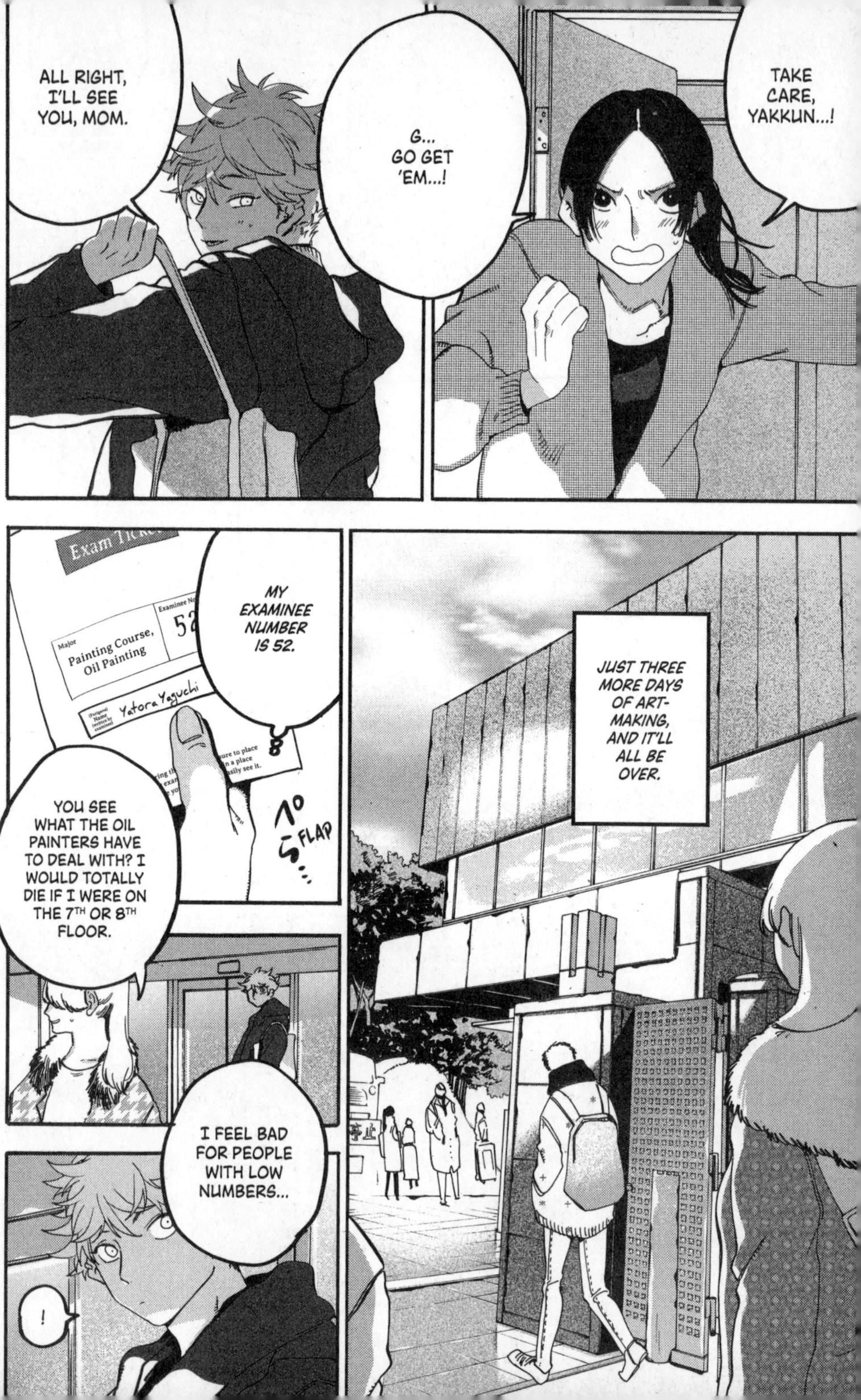
TAKE CARE, YAKKUN...!
G... GO GET 'EM...!
ALL RIGHT, I'LL SEE YOU, MOM.
JUST THREE MORE DAYS OF ART-MAKING, AND IT'LL ALL BE OVER.
Major
Painting Course, Oil Painting
Yatora Yaguchi
MY EXAMINEE NUMBER IS 52.
FLAP
YOU SEE WHAT THE OIL PAINTERS HAVE TO DEAL WITH? I WOULD TOTALLY DIE IF I WERE ON THE 7TH OR 8TH FLOOR.
I FEEL BAD FOR PEOPLE WITH LOW NUMBERS...
!

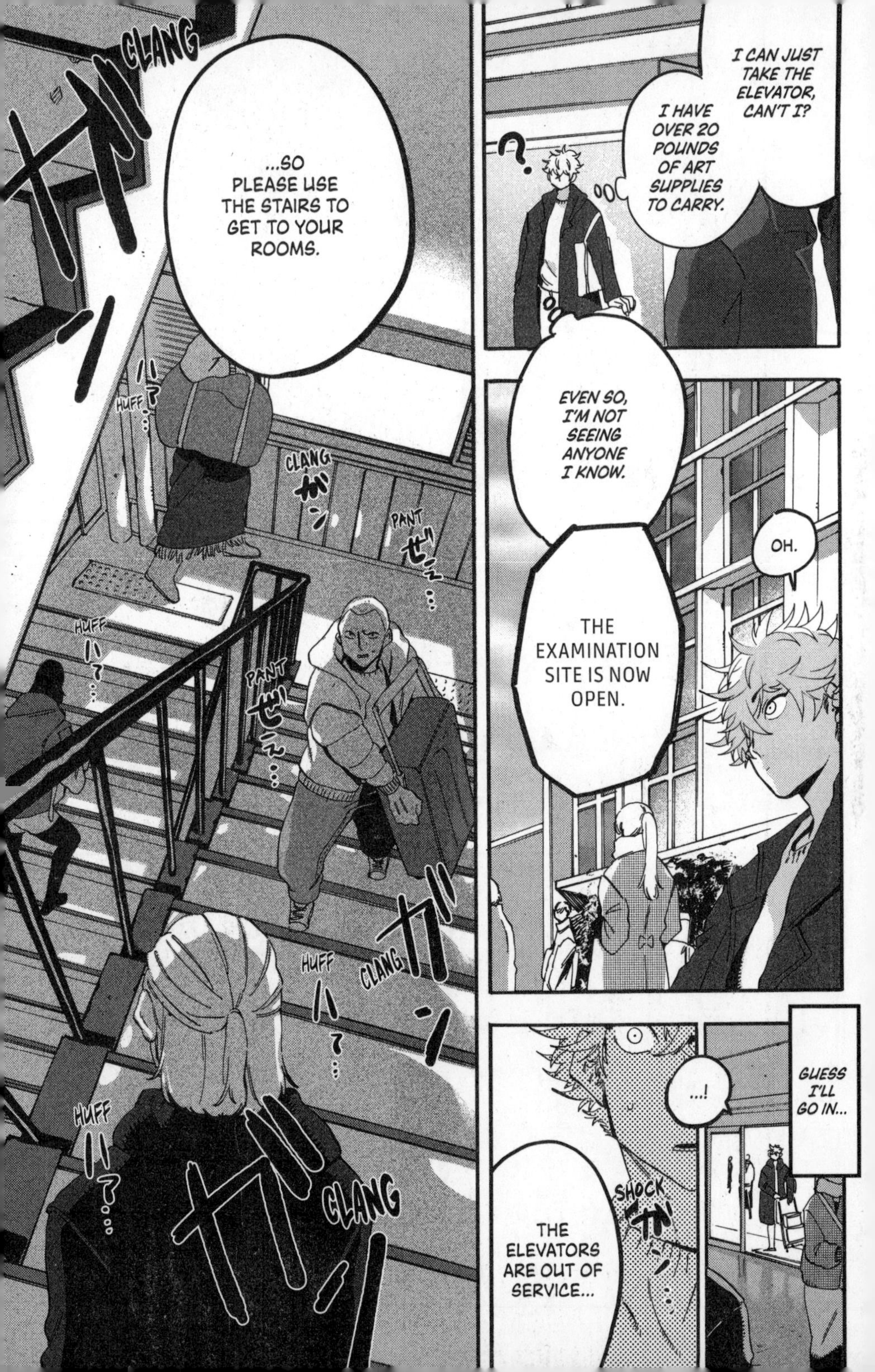
I CAN JUST TAKE THE ELEVATOR, CAN'T I?
I HAVE OVER 20 POUNDS OF ART SUPPLIES TO CARRY.
EVEN SO, I'M NOT SEEING ANYONE I KNOW.
OH.
THE EXAMINATION SITE IS NOW OPEN.
GUESS I'LL GO IN...
...!
SHOCK
THE ELEVATORS ARE OUT OF SERVICE...
CLANG
...SO PLEASE USE THE STAIRS TO GET TO YOUR ROOMS.
HUFF
CLANG
PANT
HUFF
PANT
CLANG
HUFF
HUFF
CLANG

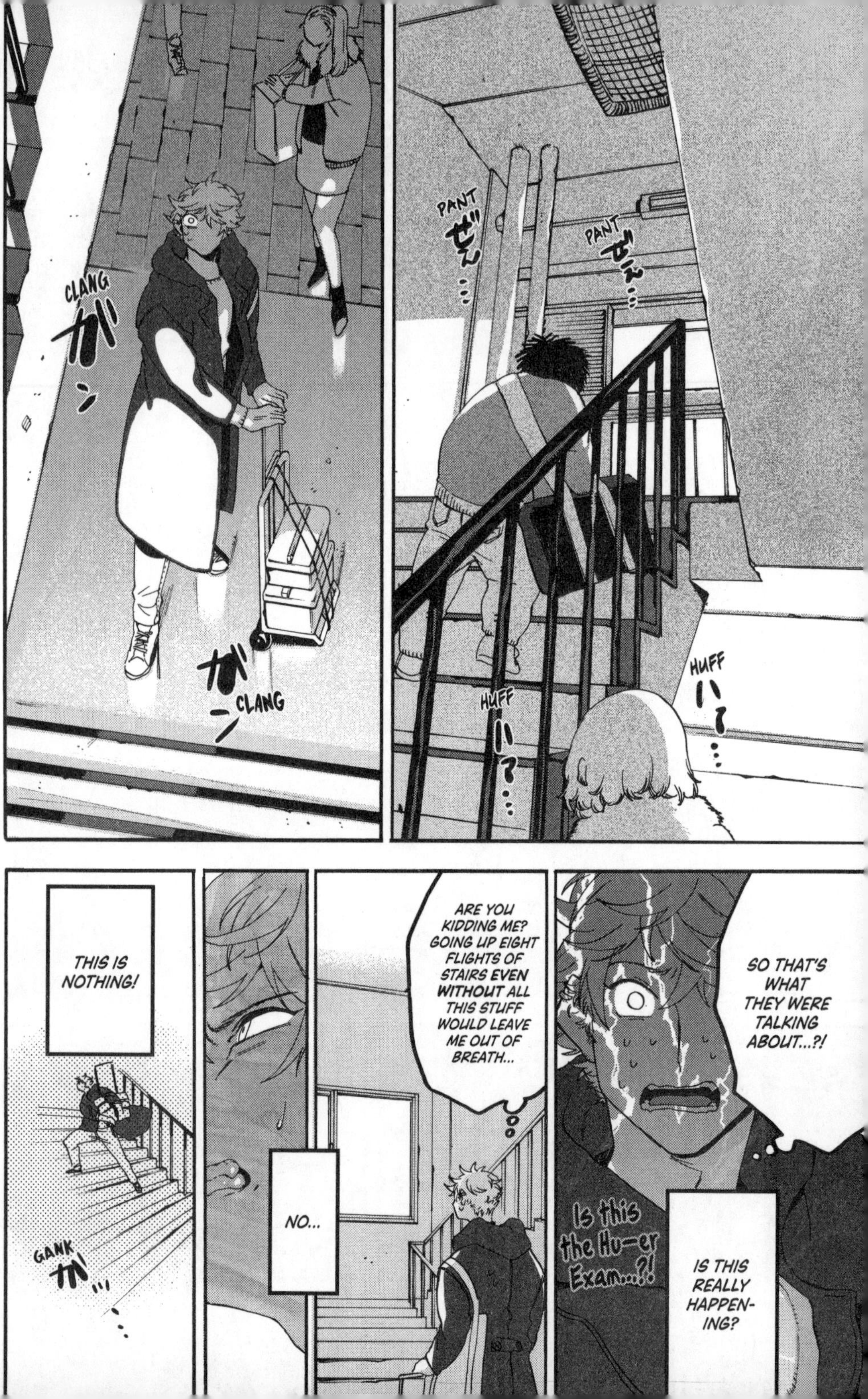
PANT
PANT
HUFF
HUFF
CLANG
CLANG
SO THAT'S WHAT THEY WERE TALKING ABOUT...?!
Is this the Hu—er Exam...?!
IS THIS REALLY HAPPEN-ING?
ARE YOU KIDDING ME? GOING UP EIGHT FLIGHTS OF STAIRS EVEN WITHOUT ALL THIS STUFF WOULD LEAVE ME OUT OF BREATH...
NO...
THIS IS NOTHING!
GANK

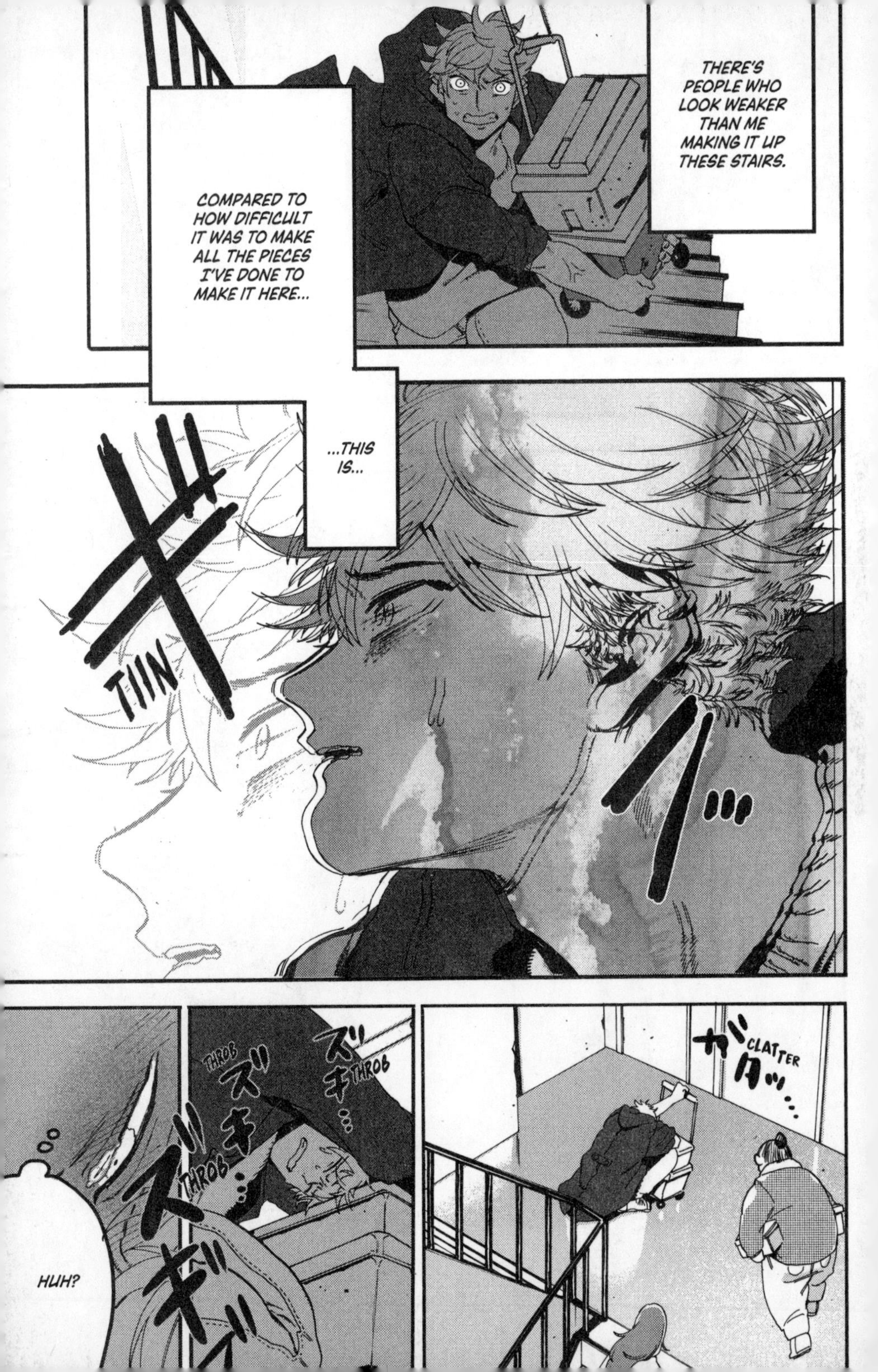
THERE'S PEOPLE WHO LOOK WEAKER THAN ME MAKING IT UP THESE STAIRS.
COMPARED TO HOW DIFFICULT IT WAS TO MAKE ALL THE PIECES I'VE DONE TO MAKE IT HERE...
...THIS IS...
TIIN
CLATTER
THROB
THROB
THROB
HUH?

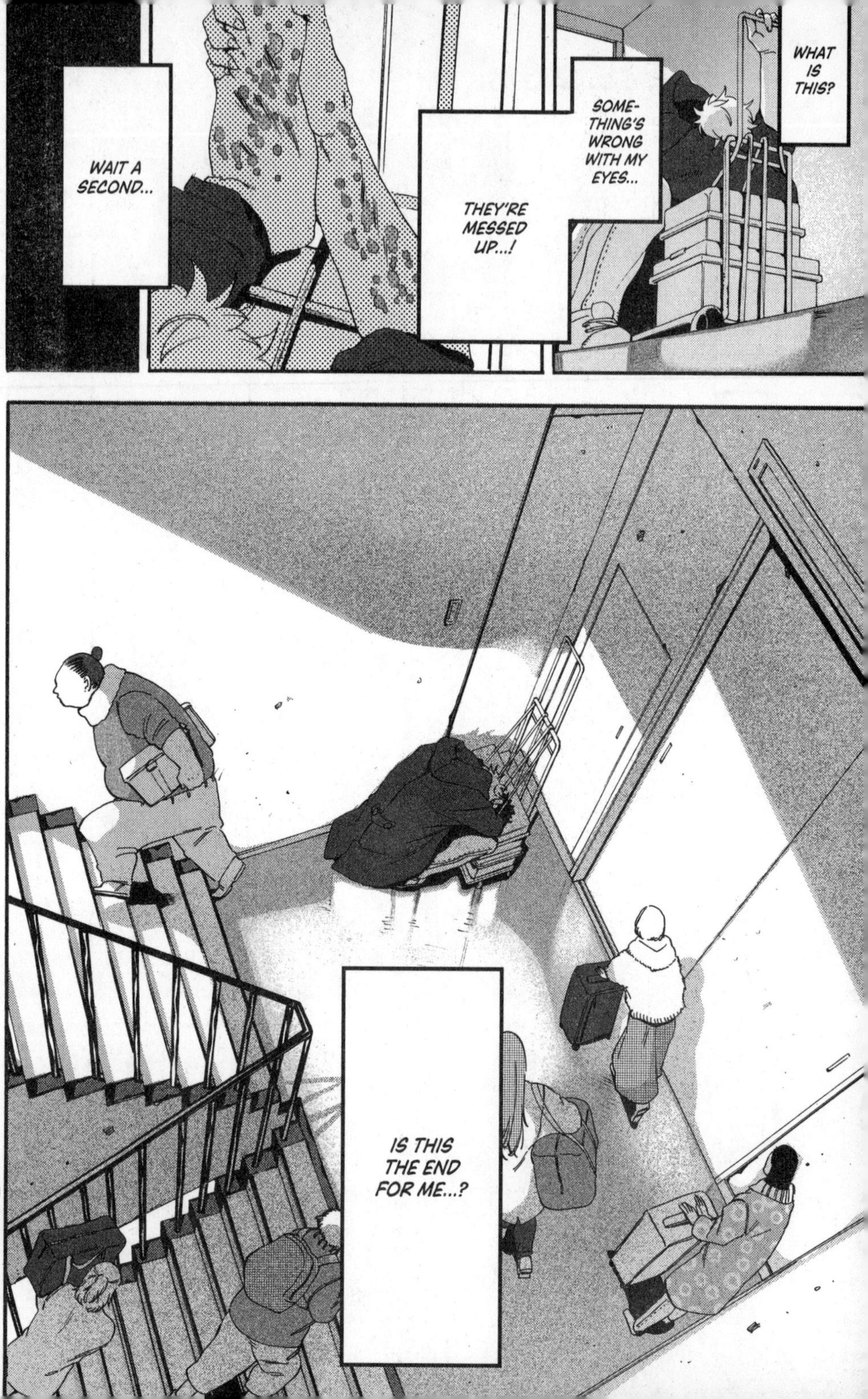
WHAT IS THIS?
SOME-THING'S WRONG WITH MY EYES...
THEY'RE MESSED UP...!
WAIT A SECOND...
IS THIS THE END FOR ME...?

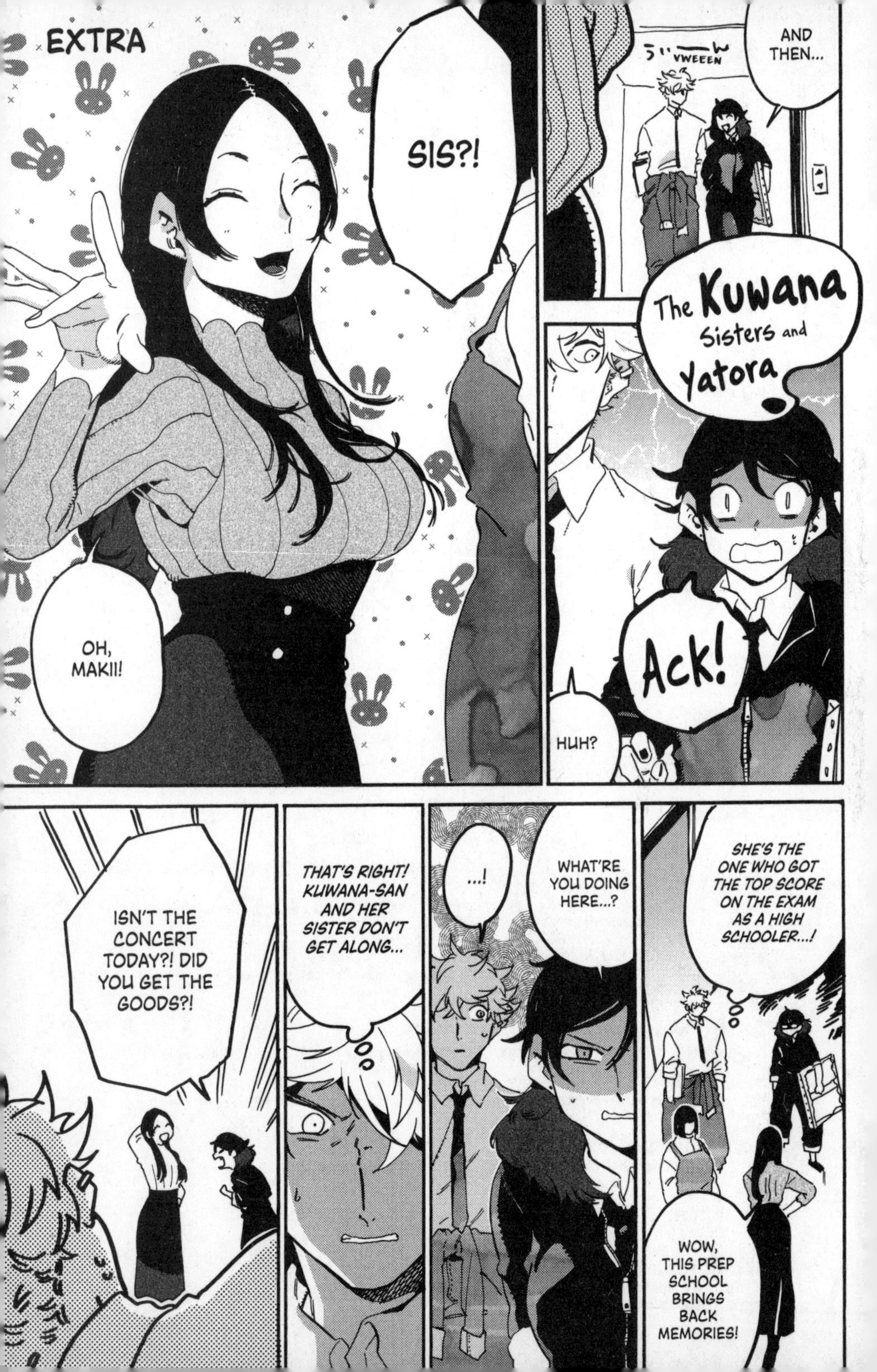

VWEEEN
AND THEN...
The Kuwana Sisters and Yatora
Ack!
HUH?
SIS?!
EXTRA
OH, MAKII!
SHE'S THE ONE WHO GOT THE TOP SCORE ON THE EXAM AS A HIGH SCHOOLER...!
WOW, THIS PREP SCHOOL BRINGS BACK MEMORIES!
WHAT'RE YOU DOING HERE...?
...!
THAT'S RIGHT! KUWANA-SAN AND HER SISTER DON'T GET ALONG...
ISN'T THE CONCERT TODAY?! DID YOU GET THE GOODS?!

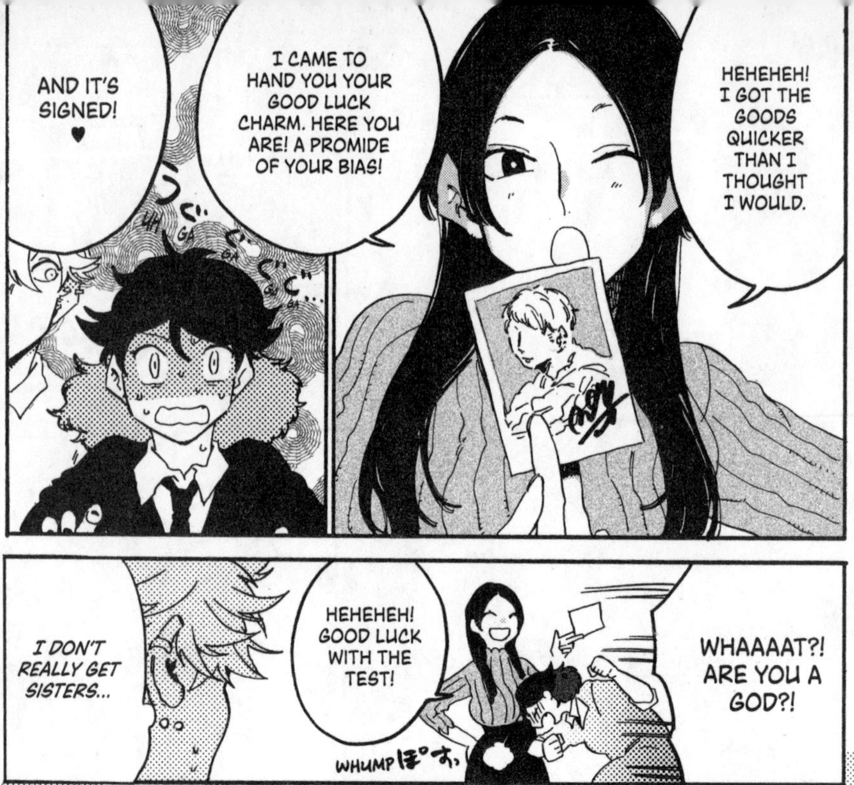
HEHEHEH! I GOT THE GOODS QUICKER THAN I THOUGHT I WOULD.
I CAME TO HAND YOU YOUR GOOD LUCK CHARM. HERE YOU ARE! A PROMIDE OF YOUR BIAS!
AND IT'S SIGNED! ♥
UH GA GA GA
WHAAAAT?! ARE YOU A GOD?!
HEHEHEH! GOOD LUCK WITH THE TEST!
WHUMP
I DON'T REALLY GET SISTERS...

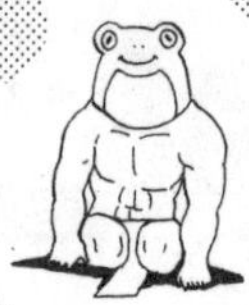

*Blue Period* was created with the support of many people!

## Special Thanks

Thank you so very much!

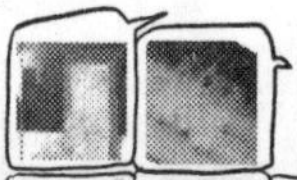

**Moeko Natsui-san**
Thank you so much once again...! And thanks again for the wedding reception...! You'll have to tell me all about that thing we were talking about!

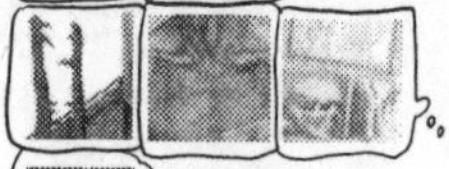

**Shota Yamamichi-san**
Thank you for more of your wonderful pieces! I'm looking forward to seeing your future pursuits...!

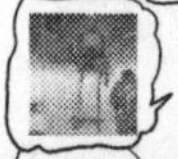

**Takeru Nakajima**
Thank you for painting when you're so busy. I'm so looking forward to your future pursuits.

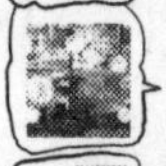

**Saki Uchida**
Thank you for painting when you're so busy. School must be a lot, but I'm looking forward to what you'll produce from now on.

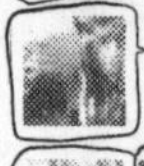

**Haru Ookawa**
I borrowed your painting! Thank you so much...! You must be going through a lot with work and your drafts, but please take care of your health.

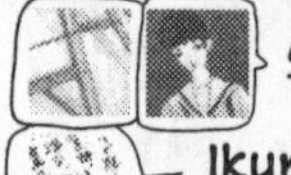

**Akemi Akamine**
Thanks for lending me your valuable pieces! Please give my regards to Hara-san, too!

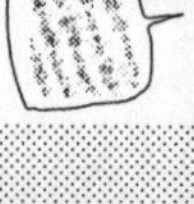

**Ikumi Arai**
It might be a little hard to make out here, but thank you for lending me your work. I'm looking forward to more of your palindromes in the future.

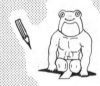

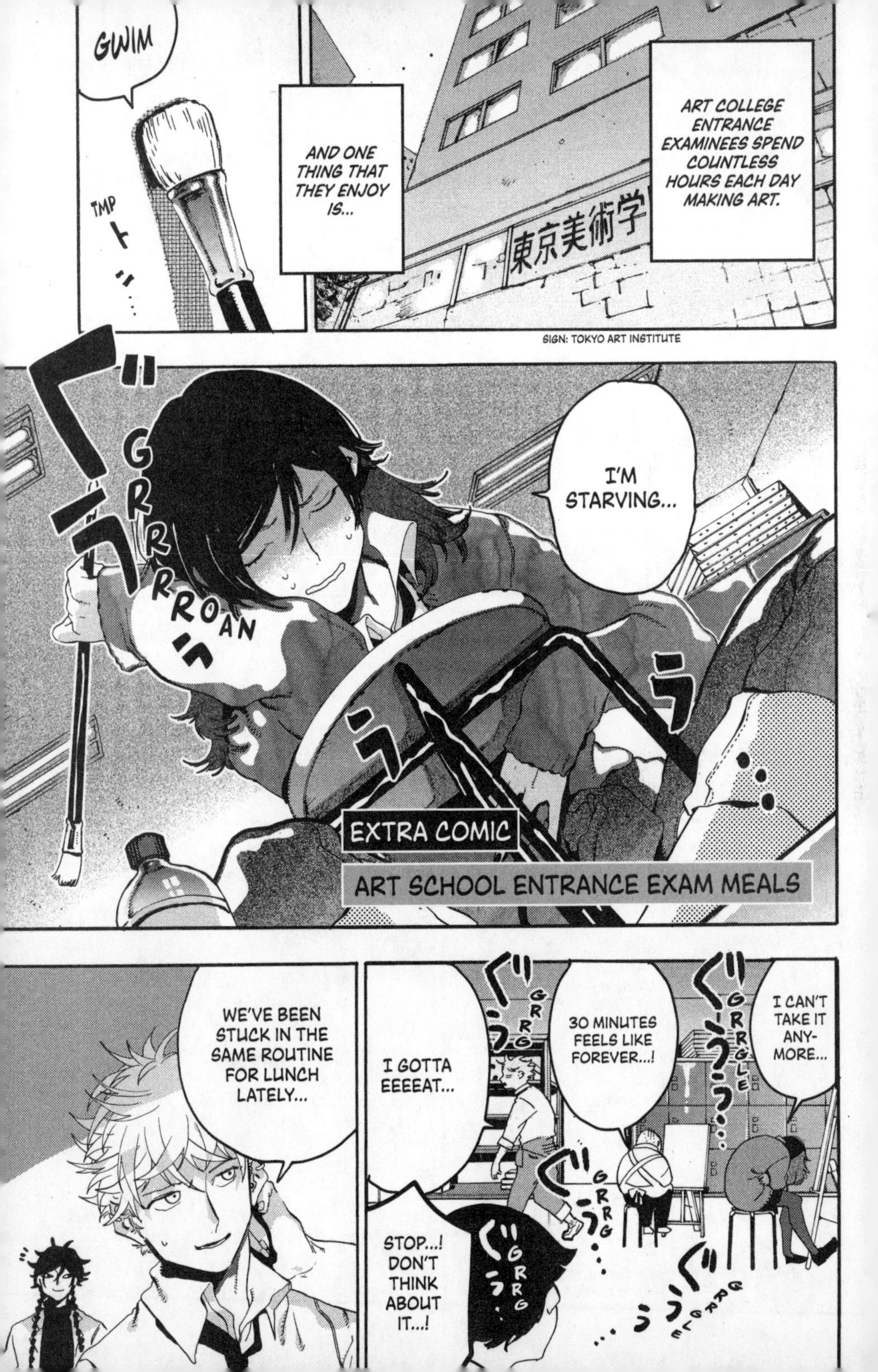
ART COLLEGE ENTRANCE EXAMINEES SPEND COUNTLESS HOURS EACH DAY MAKING ART.
東京美術学
AND ONE THING THAT THEY ENJOY IS...
GWIM
TMP
SIGN: TOKYO ART INSTITUTE
I'M STARVING...
GRRRROAN
EXTRA COMIC
ART SCHOOL ENTRANCE EXAM MEALS
I CAN'T TAKE IT ANY-MORE...
GRRGLE
30 MINUTES FEELS LIKE FOREVER...!
GRRG
I GOTTA EEEEAT...
GRRG
STOP...! DON'T THINK ABOUT IT...!
GRRG
GRRGLE
WE'VE BEEN STUCK IN THE SAME ROUTINE FOR LUNCH LATELY...

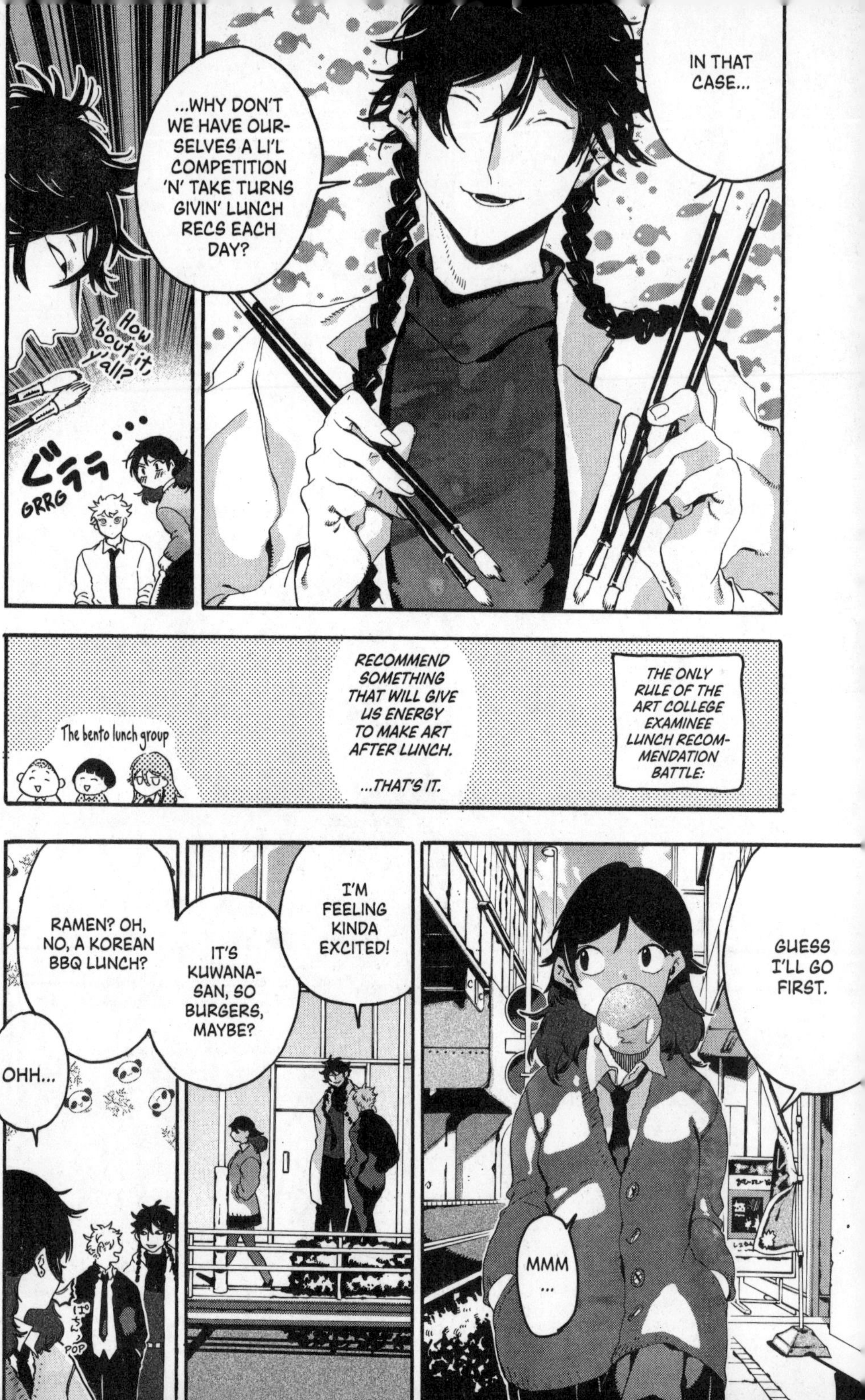
IN THAT CASE...
...WHY DON'T WE HAVE OURSELVES A LI'L COMPETITION 'N' TAKE TURNS GIVIN' LUNCH RECS EACH DAY?
How 'bout it, y'all?
GRRG
THE ONLY RULE OF THE ART COLLEGE EXAMINEE LUNCH RECOMMENDATION BATTLE:
RECOMMEND SOMETHING THAT WILL GIVE US ENERGY TO MAKE ART AFTER LUNCH.
...THAT'S IT.
The bento lunch group
GUESS I'LL GO FIRST.
MMM ...
I'M FEELING KINDA EXCITED!
IT'S KUWANA-SAN, SO BURGERS, MAYBE?
RAMEN? OH, NO, A KOREAN BBQ LUNCH?
OHH...
POP

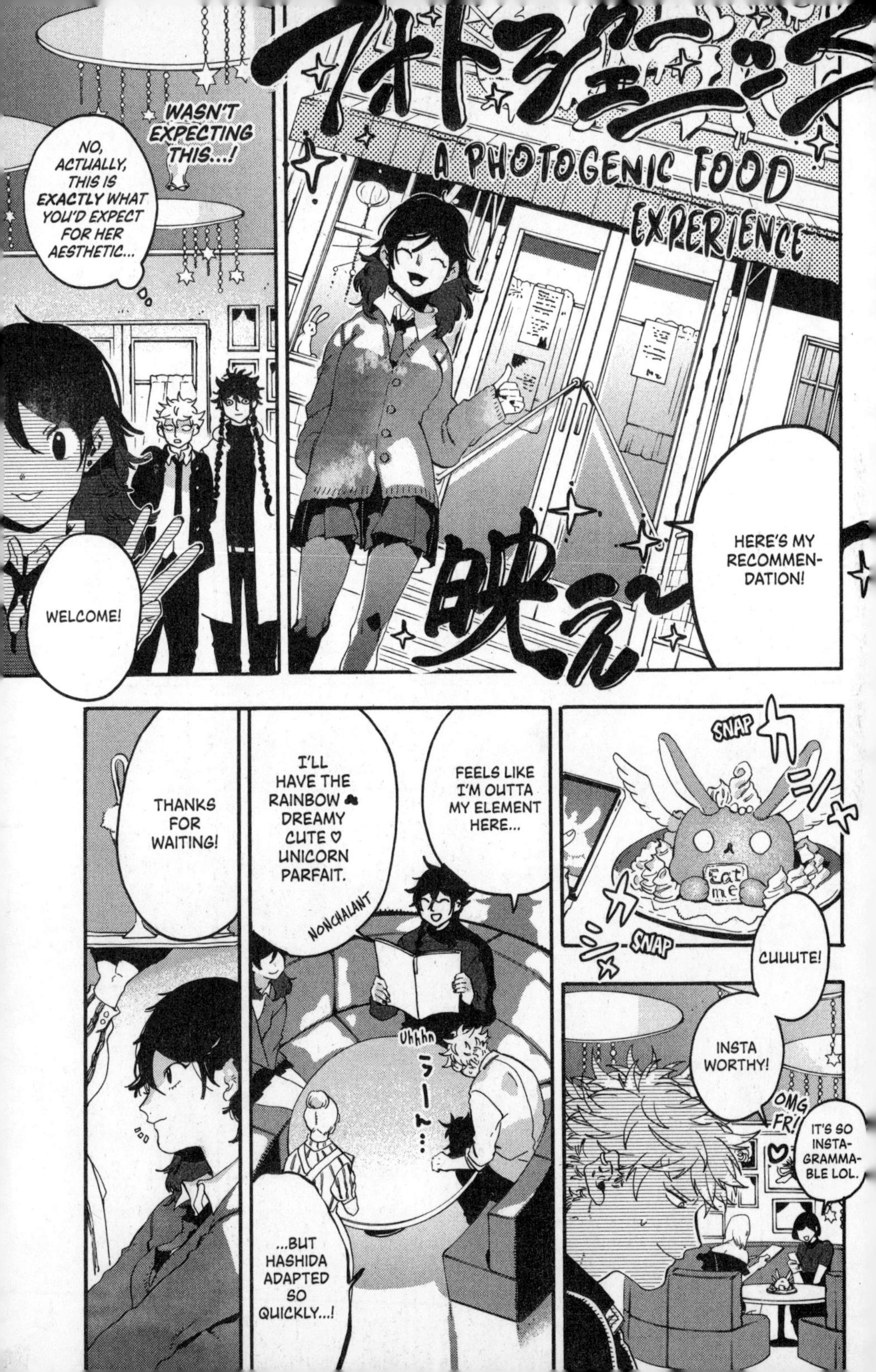
フォトジェニック
A PHOTOGENIC FOOD EXPERIENCE
映え
HERE'S MY RECOMMENDATION!
WASN'T EXPECTING THIS...!
NO, ACTUALLY, THIS IS EXACTLY WHAT YOU'D EXPECT FOR HER AESTHETIC...
WELCOME!
SNAP
SNAP
CUUUTE!
INSTA WORTHY!
OMG FR!
IT'S SO INSTA-GRAMMABLE LOL.
FEELS LIKE I'M OUTTA MY ELEMENT HERE...
I'LL HAVE THE RAINBOW ♣ DREAMY CUTE ♡ UNICORN PARFAIT.
NONCHALANT
Uhhhn
...BUT HASHIDA ADAPTED SO QUICKLY...!
THANKS FOR WAITING!

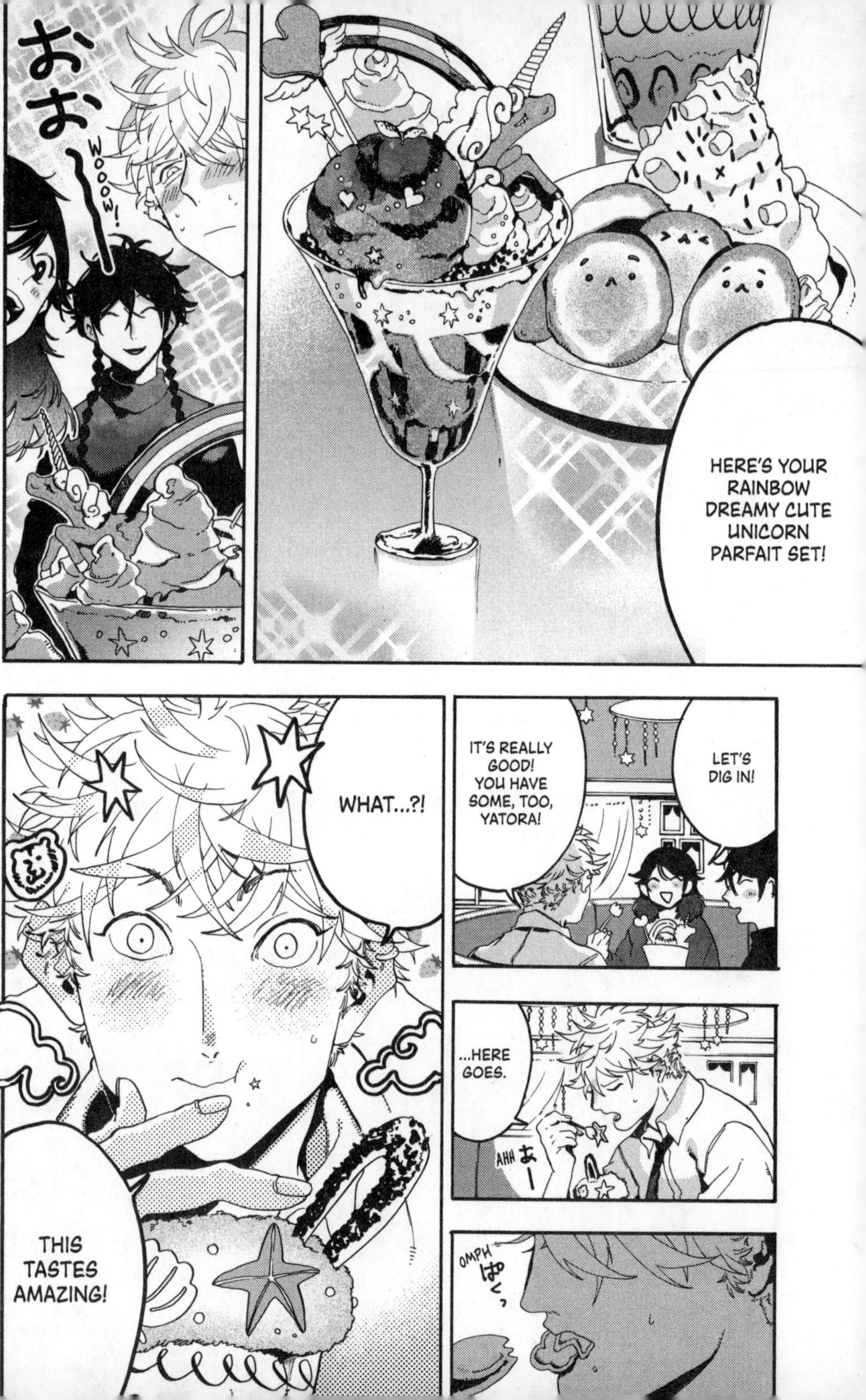
HERE'S YOUR RAINBOW DREAMY CUTE UNICORN PARFAIT SET!
おお〜
WOOOOW!
LET'S DIG IN!
IT'S REALLY GOOD! YOU HAVE SOME, TOO, YATORA!
...HERE GOES.
AHH あー
OMPH はくっ
WHAT...?!
THIS TASTES AMAZING!

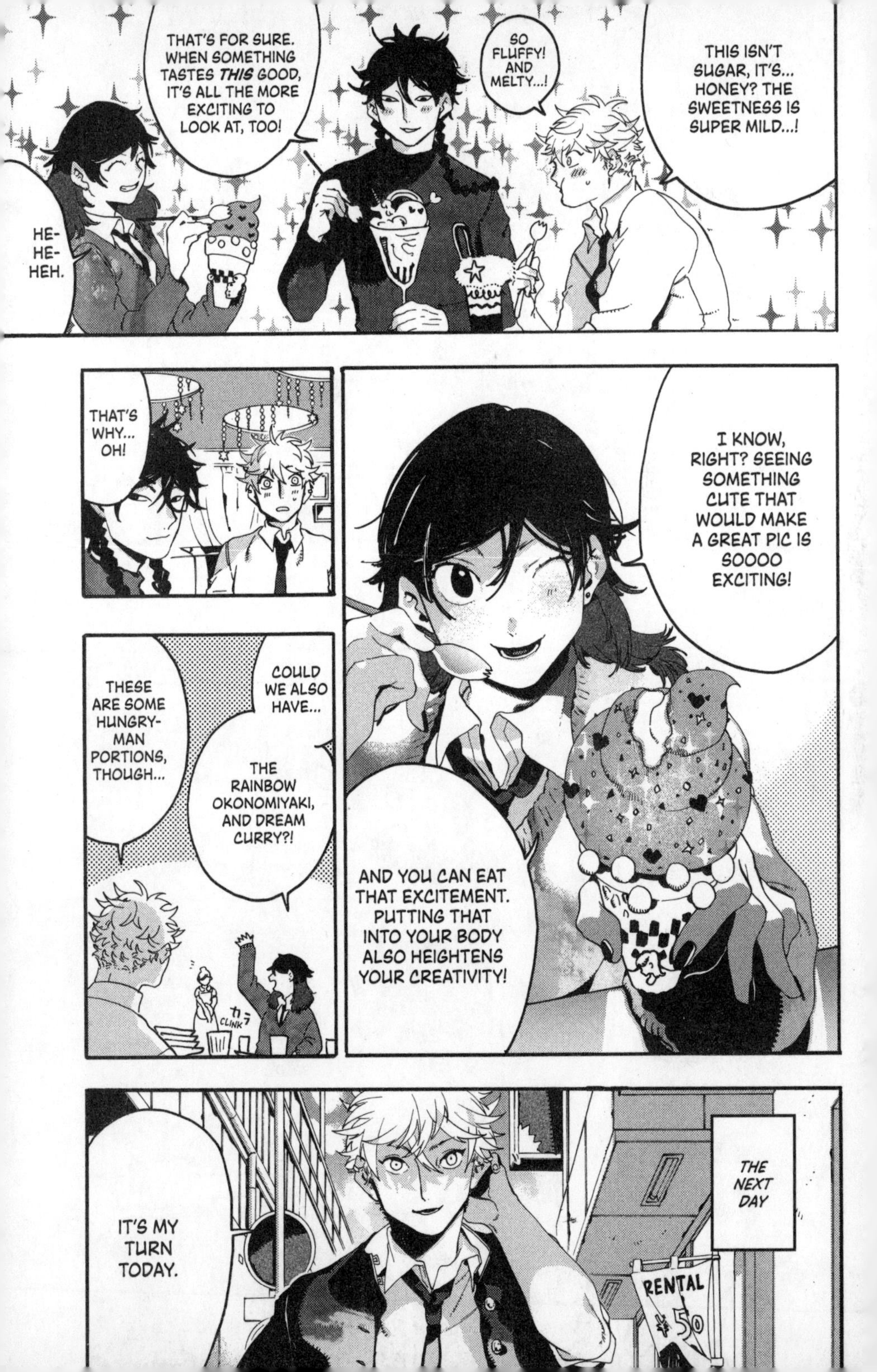
THIS ISN'T SUGAR, IT'S... HONEY? THE SWEETNESS IS SUPER MILD...!
SO FLUFFY! AND MELTY...!
THAT'S FOR SURE. WHEN SOMETHING TASTES *THIS* GOOD, IT'S ALL THE MORE EXCITING TO LOOK AT, TOO!
HE-HE-HEH.
I KNOW, RIGHT? SEEING SOMETHING CUTE THAT WOULD MAKE A GREAT PIC IS SOOOO EXCITING!
AND YOU CAN EAT THAT EXCITEMENT. PUTTING THAT INTO YOUR BODY ALSO HEIGHTENS YOUR CREATIVITY!
THAT'S WHY... OH!
COULD WE ALSO HAVE...
THE RAINBOW OKONOMIYAKI, AND DREAM CURRY?!
THESE ARE SOME HUNGRY-MAN PORTIONS, THOUGH...
CLINK
THE NEXT DAY
IT'S MY TURN TODAY.
RENTAL ¥50

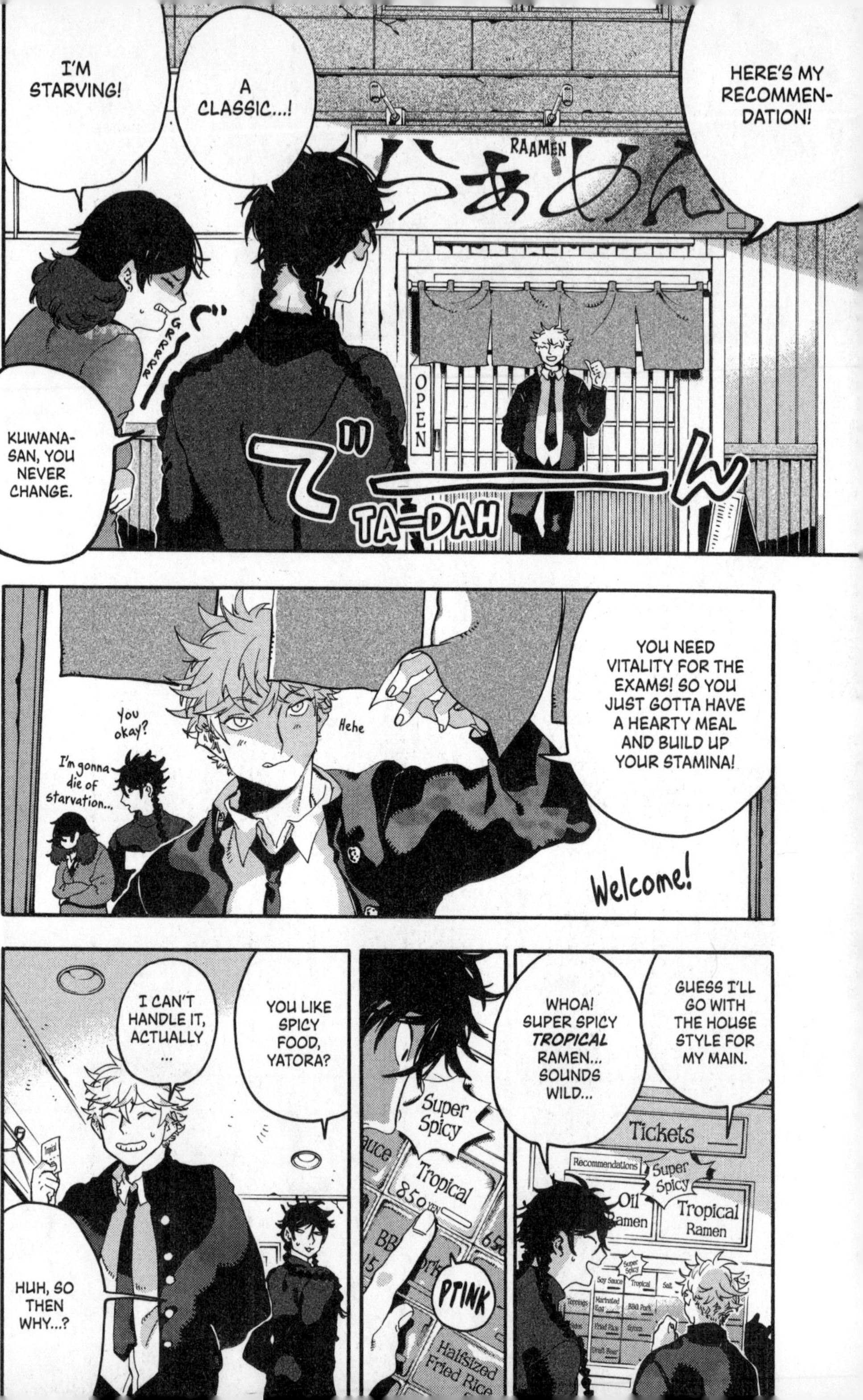
HERE'S MY RECOMMENDATION!
RAAMEN
A CLASSIC...!
I'M STARVING!
OPEN
GRRRR
TA-DAH
KUWANA-SAN, YOU NEVER CHANGE.
YOU NEED VITALITY FOR THE EXAMS! SO YOU JUST GOTTA HAVE A HEARTY MEAL AND BUILD UP YOUR STAMINA!
Hehe
You okay?
I'm gonna die of starvation...
Welcome!
GUESS I'LL GO WITH THE HOUSE STYLE FOR MY MAIN.
WHOA! SUPER SPICY *TROPICAL* RAMEN... SOUNDS WILD...
Tickets
Recommendations
Super Spicy
Oil Ramen
Tropical Ramen
Super Spicy
Tropical
850 YEN
PTINK
Halfsized Fried Rice
YOU LIKE SPICY FOOD, YATORA?
I CAN'T HANDLE IT, ACTUALLY ...
HUH, SO THEN WHY...?

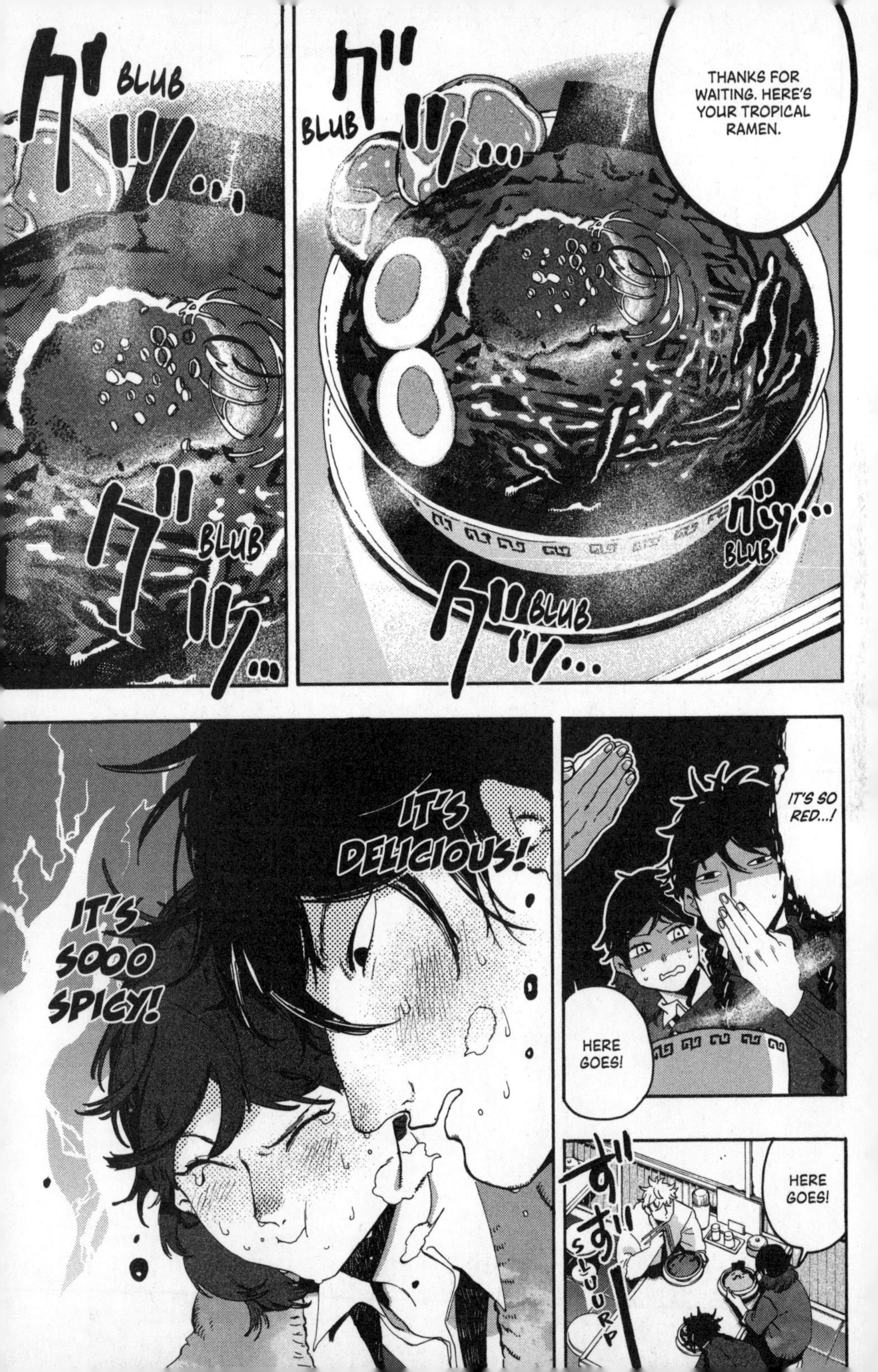
THANKS FOR WAITING. HERE'S YOUR TROPICAL RAMEN.
BLUB
BLUB
BLUB
BLUB
BLUB
BLUB
IT'S SO RED...!
HERE GOES!
HERE GOES!
SLUUURP
IT'S DELICIOUS!
IT'S SOOO SPICY!

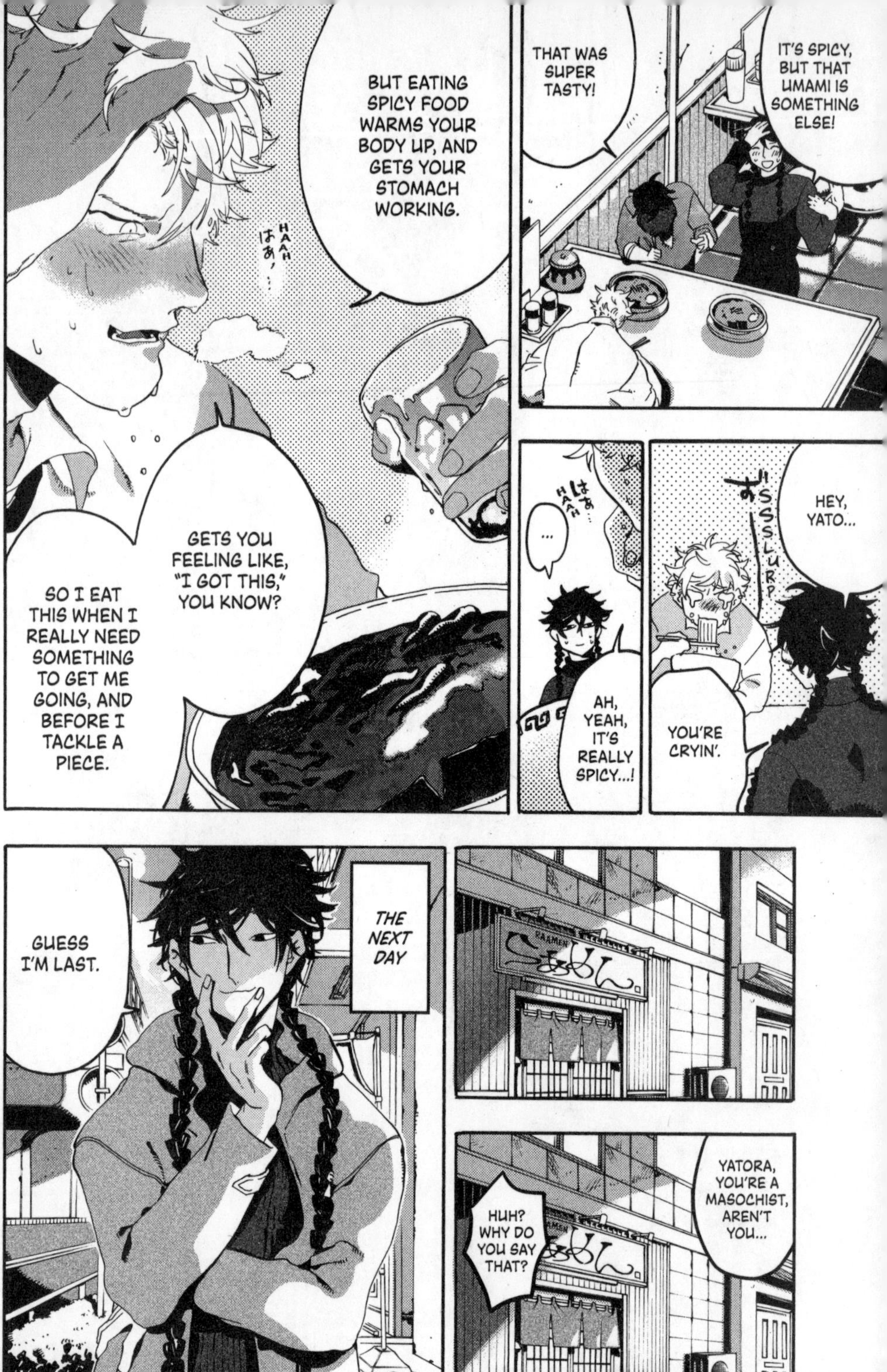
IT'S SPICY, BUT THAT UMAMI IS SOMETHING ELSE!
THAT WAS SUPER TASTY!
HEY, YATO...
SSSLURP
YOU'RE CRYIN'.
はあ HAAH
...
AH, YEAH, IT'S REALLY SPICY...!
BUT EATING SPICY FOOD WARMS YOUR BODY UP, AND GETS YOUR STOMACH WORKING.
はあ、、、 HAAH
GETS YOU FEELING LIKE, "I GOT THIS," YOU KNOW?
SO I EAT THIS WHEN I REALLY NEED SOMETHING TO GET ME GOING, AND BEFORE I TACKLE A PIECE.
RAAMEN
YATORA, YOU'RE A MASOCHIST, AREN'T YOU...
HUH? WHY DO YOU SAY THAT?
THE NEXT DAY
GUESS I'M LAST.

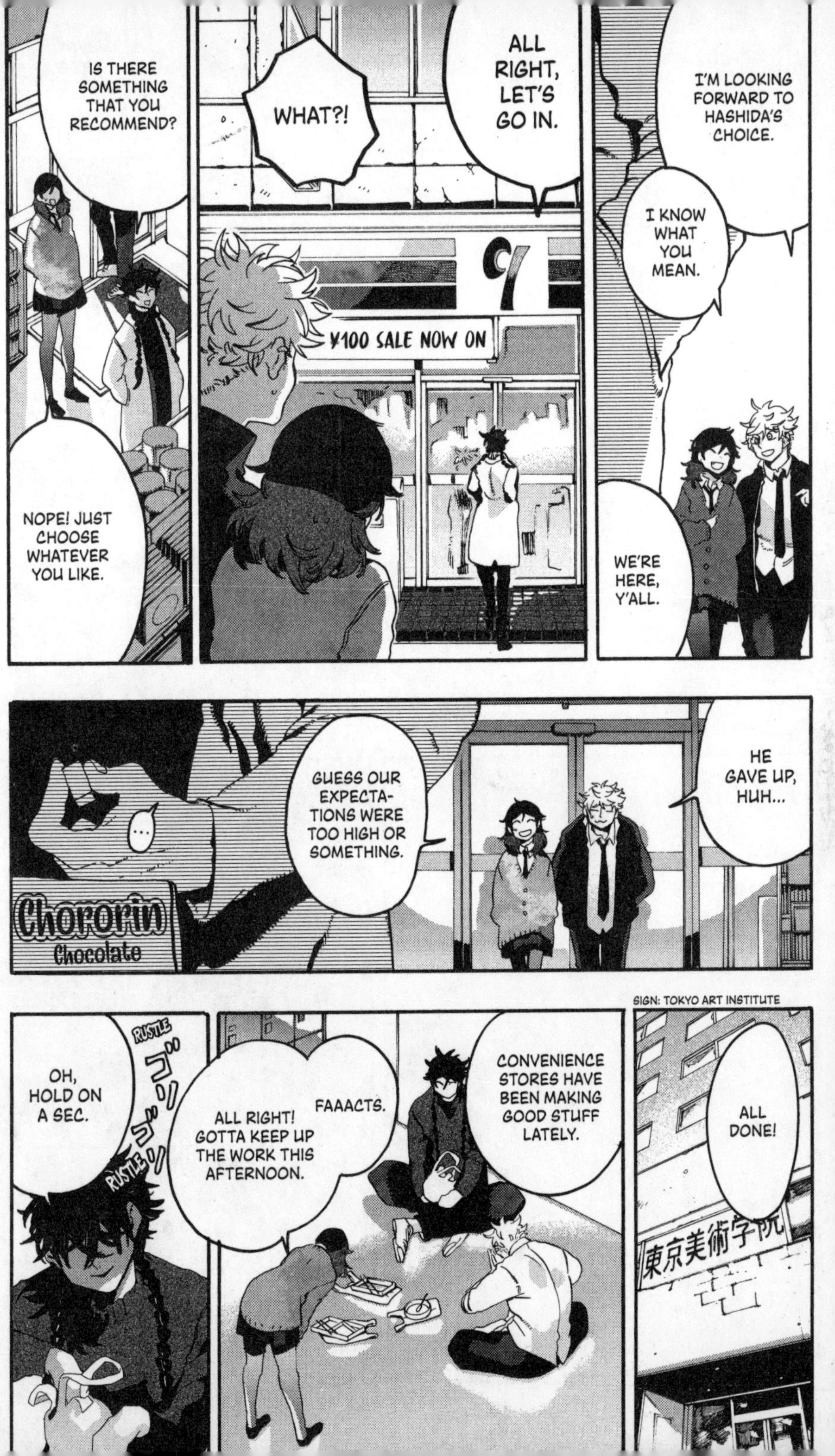
I'M LOOKING FORWARD TO HASHIDA'S CHOICE.
I KNOW WHAT YOU MEAN.
WE'RE HERE, Y'ALL.
ALL RIGHT, LET'S GO IN.
WHAT?!
¥100 SALE NOW ON
IS THERE SOMETHING THAT YOU RECOMMEND?
NOPE! JUST CHOOSE WHATEVER YOU LIKE.
HE GAVE UP, HUH...
GUESS OUR EXPECTATIONS WERE TOO HIGH OR SOMETHING.
...
Chororin
Chocolate
SIGN: TOKYO ART INSTITUTE
ALL DONE!
東京美術学院
CONVENIENCE STORES HAVE BEEN MAKING GOOD STUFF LATELY.
FAAACTS.
ALL RIGHT! GOTTA KEEP UP THE WORK THIS AFTERNOON.
RUSTLE
OH, HOLD ON A SEC.
RUSTLE

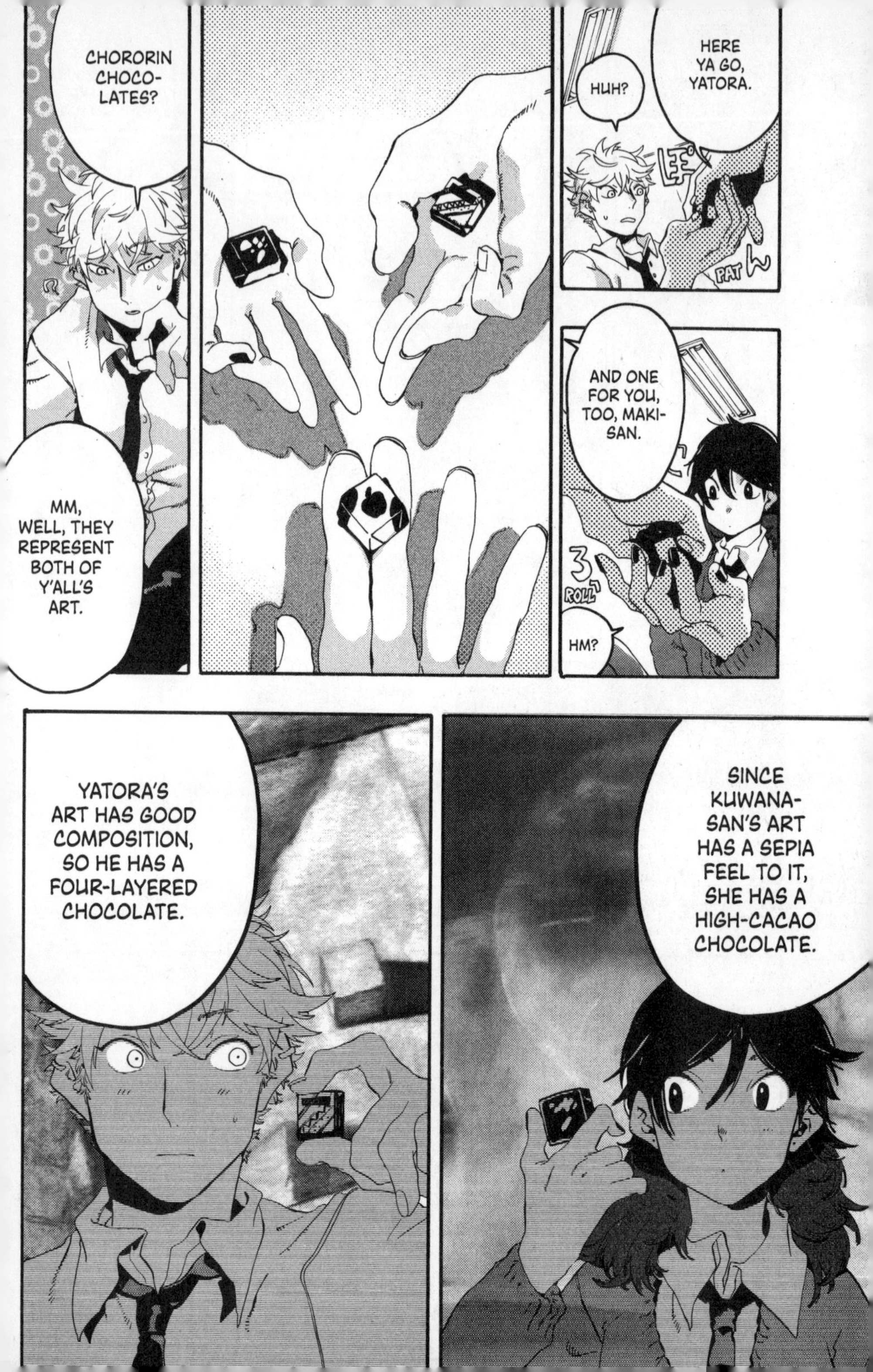
HERE YA GO, YATORA.
HUH?
PAT
AND ONE FOR YOU, TOO, MAKI-SAN.
ROLL
HM?
CHORORIN CHOCOLATES?
MM, WELL, THEY REPRESENT BOTH OF Y'ALL'S ART.
SINCE KUWANA-SAN'S ART HAS A SEPIA FEEL TO IT, SHE HAS A HIGH-CACAO CHOCOLATE.
YATORA'S ART HAS GOOD COMPOSITION, SO HE HAS A FOUR-LAYERED CHOCOLATE.

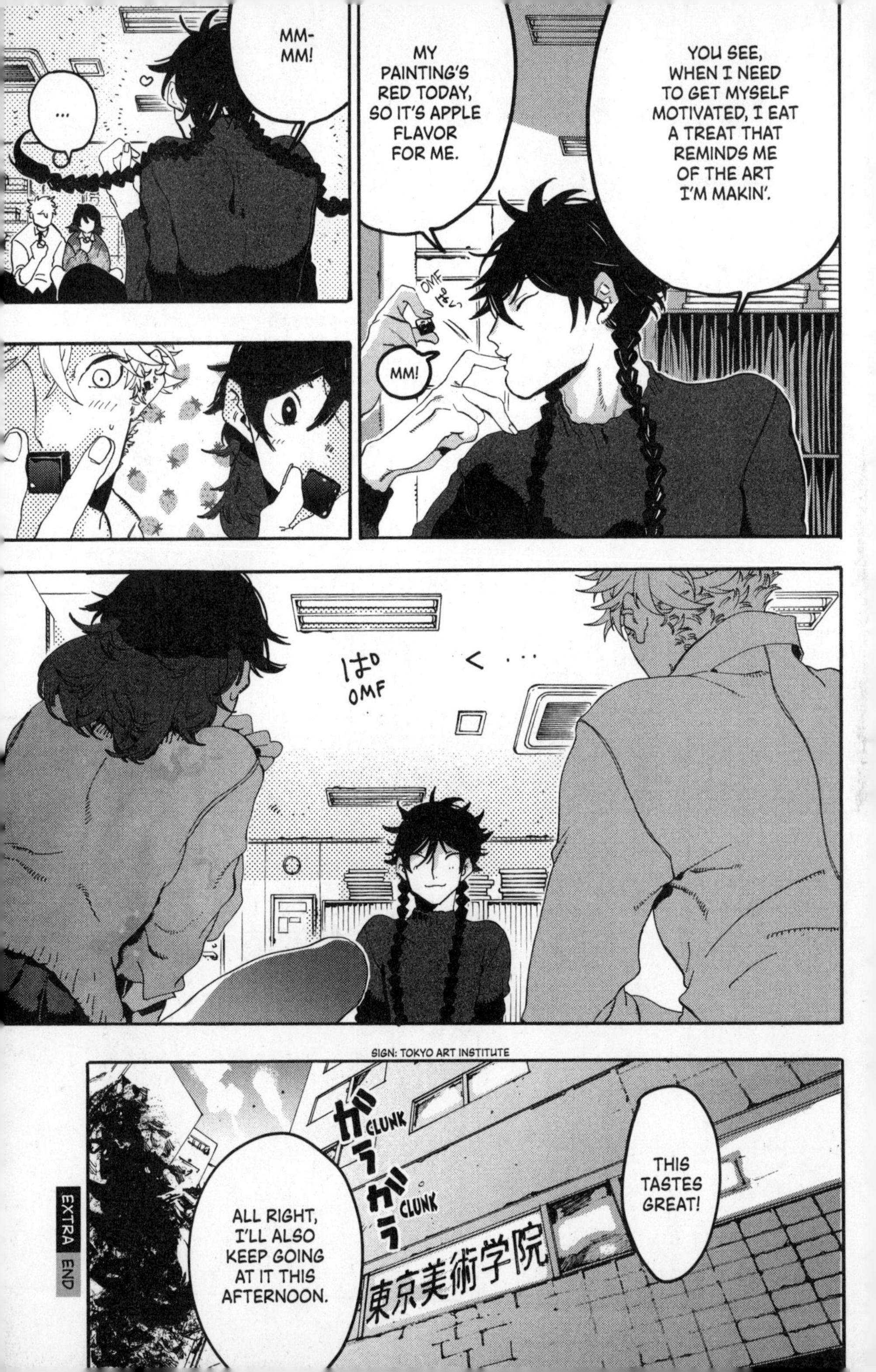
YOU SEE, WHEN I NEED TO GET MYSELF MOTIVATED, I EAT A TREAT THAT REMINDS ME OF THE ART I'M MAKIN'.
MY PAINTING'S RED TODAY, SO IT'S APPLE FLAVOR FOR ME.
OMF
MM!
MM-MM!
...
OMF
<...
SIGN: TOKYO ART INSTITUTE
THIS TASTES GREAT!
がらがら
CLUNK
CLUNK
ALL RIGHT, I'LL ALSO KEEP GOING AT IT THIS AFTERNOON.
東京美術学院
EXTRA END

# TRANSLATION NOTES

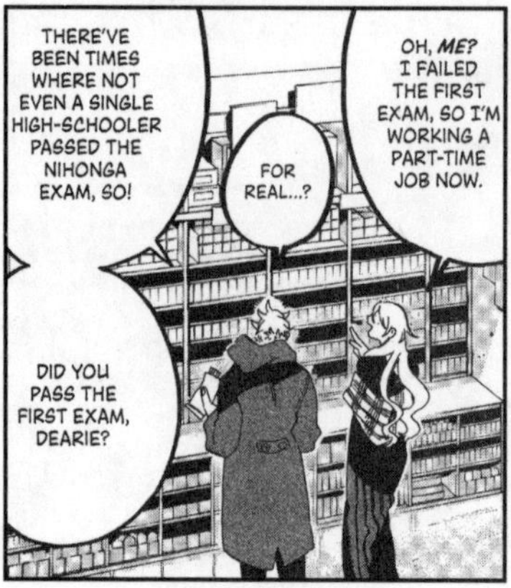
OH, *ME?* I FAILED THE FIRST EXAM, SO I'M WORKING A PART-TIME JOB NOW.
FOR REAL...?
THERE'VE BEEN TIMES WHERE NOT EVEN A SINGLE HIGH-SCHOOLER PASSED THE NIHONGA EXAM, SO!
DID YOU PASS THE FIRST EXAM, DEARIE?

**Oh, Me? ...Dearie?, page 62**
In this passage, Yatora hears Yuka-chan use the Japanese first-person pronoun *atashi* (a shortened version of the first-person pronoun *watashi*) for the first time. *Atashi* is often used by a young woman to refer to herself in friendly, informal conversation. Since *atashi* is socially understood to be a "feminine" pronoun, it is also used by people who may want to be preceived as such, or are in such a community together. For example, at the Bearded Lady, it would be natural to hear staff like Yuka-chan use *atashi* in the bar or in their daily lives. Later on, Yatora asks if the switch in speech is Yuka-chan's way of being "easier to understand" because it is an identifiably gendered method of communication.

**Madam, page 75**
In the original Japanese, "Madam" was "Mama-san," a term used for a woman who is the proprietor of a bar or other night-time entertainment establishment.

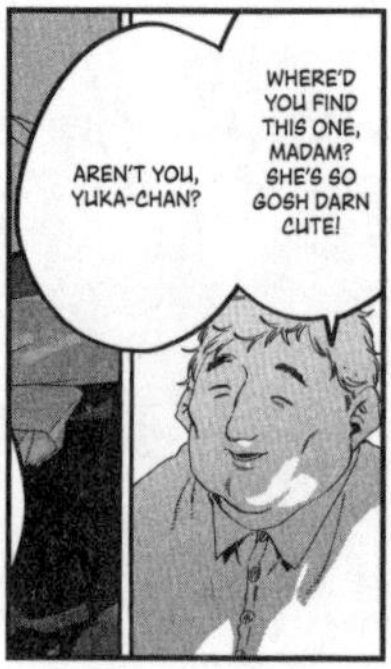
WHERE'D YOU FIND THIS ONE, MADAM? SHE'S SO GOSH DARN CUTE!
AREN'T YOU, YUKA-CHAN?

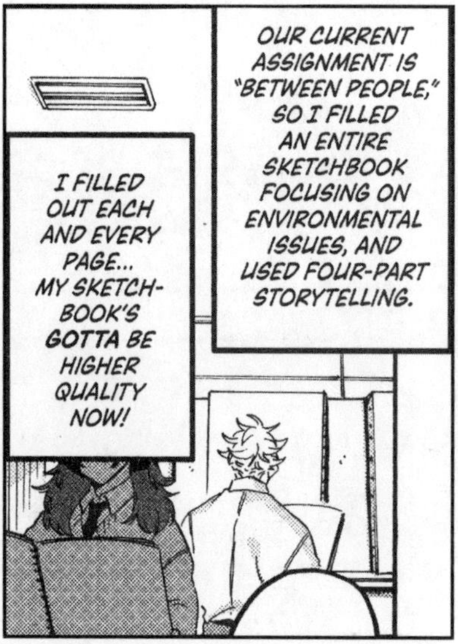
OUR CURRENT ASSIGNMENT IS "BETWEEN PEOPLE," SO I FILLED AN ENTIRE SKETCHBOOK FOCUSING ON ENVIRONMENTAL ISSUES, AND USED FOUR-PART STORYTELLING.
I FILLED OUT EACH AND EVERY PAGE... MY SKETCH-BOOK'S GOTTA BE HIGHER QUALITY NOW!

**Four-part storytelling, page 104**
Known as *kishōtenketsu* in Japanese, this four-part structure is the basis for many stories, arguments, songs, etc. *Kishōtenketsu* can be broken down as follows: *ki* (introduction), *shō* (development), *ten* (twist), *ketsu* (conclusion). The *yonkoma* (four-panel) manga is a great, simplified example of this structure in action—like the Utashima and Okada *yonkoma* on pages 126 and 127.

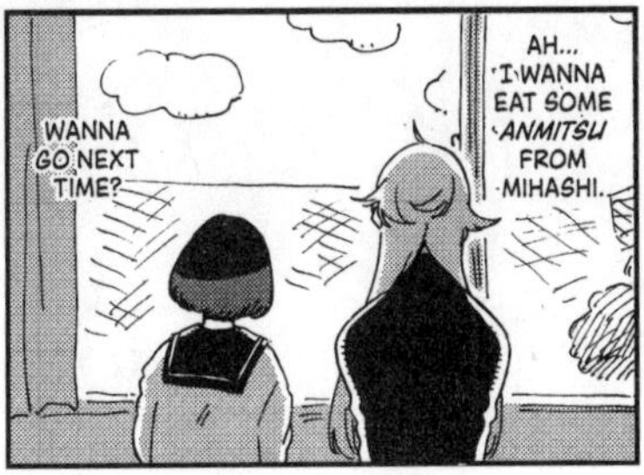

AH... I WANNA EAT SOME *ANMITSU* FROM MIHASHI.
WANNA GO NEXT TIME?


**Anmitsu, page 126**

*Anmitsu* is a Japanese dessert that consists of agar jelly cubes served with azuki bean paste, as well as things like boiled peas, a soft type of mochi known as *gyuhi*, and fruit slices. This dessert is usually served with dark sugar syrup. The name *anmitsu* comes from the names of two of the dessert's ingredients: *an* (from *anko* or azuki bean paste) and *mitsu* (sugar syrup).

**Yaotsu kurikinton, page 126**

Yaotsu is a town in Gifu prefecture, which is located in the center of Japan's main island (*Honshu*). One of the city's delicacies is *kurikinton*, a confection made from chestnuts (*kuri*) that are mashed, boiled with sugar, and then reshaped to resemble chestnuts. Yaotsu *kurikinton* are typically in season from September and until winter.

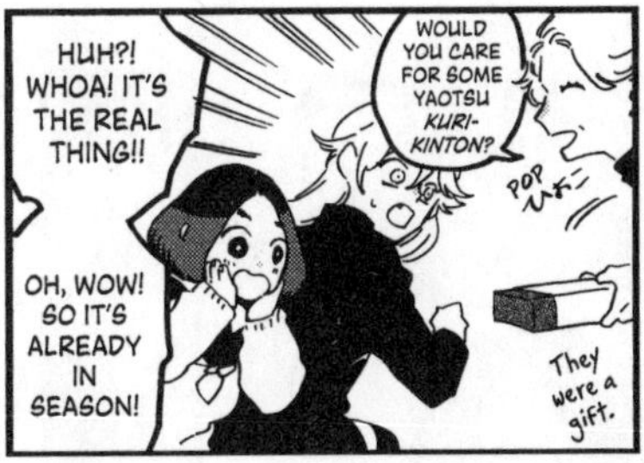

WOULD YOU CARE FOR SOME YAOTSU *KURI-KINTON?*
POP
They were a gift.
HUH?! WHOA! IT'S THE REAL THING!!
OH, WOW! SO IT'S ALREADY IN SEASON!


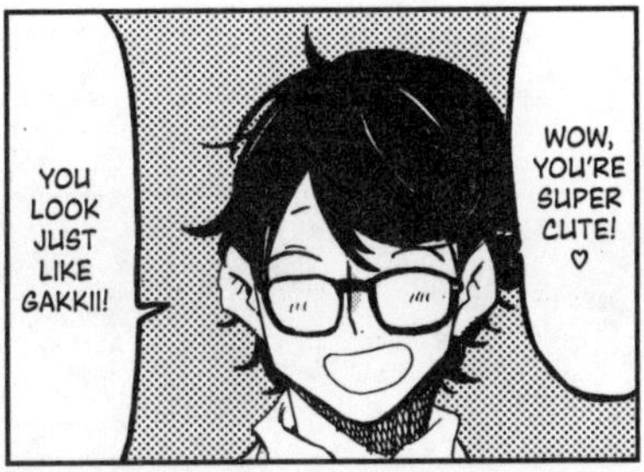

WOW, YOU'RE SUPER CUTE! ♡
YOU LOOK JUST LIKE GAKKII!


**Gakkii, page 127**

Gakkii is the nickname for Yui Aragaki, a Japanese multi-hyphenate entertainer who is admired for her beauty and popularity. She has acted in many films and TV dramas, including the live-action adaptations of *Ranma ½* and *The Full-Time Wife Escapist*.

**Graduation trip, page 147**

In Japan, schools will traditionally have a big excursion for each class of students (i.e. elementary, junior high, and high school). For high school students, this typically happens during their second year because the third-year students are busy with exams, and this type of trip is similar to the big senior trip that some high schools in the US have. There is also a tradition of third-year high school students taking "graduation trips," which the students plan themselves. The owner of the Japanese-style inn that Yatora and Yuka-chan are staying at is assuming that they're in Odawara on such a trip.

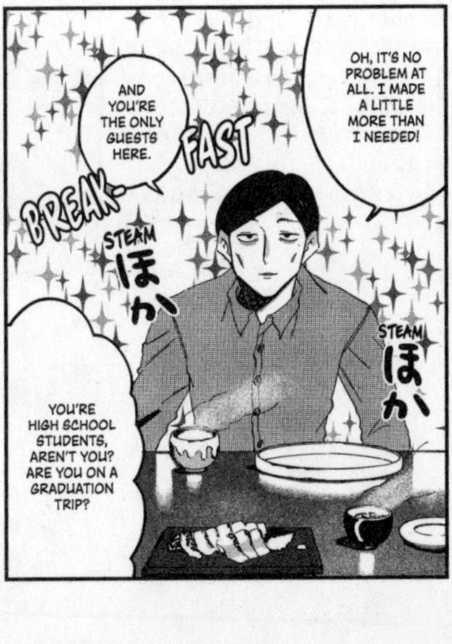

OH, IT'S NO PROBLEM AT ALL. I MADE A LITTLE MORE THAN I NEEDED!
AND YOU'RE THE ONLY GUESTS HERE.
BREAK-FAST
STEAM ほか
STEAM ほか
YOU'RE HIGH SCHOOL STUDENTS, AREN'T YOU? ARE YOU ON A GRADUATION TRIP?

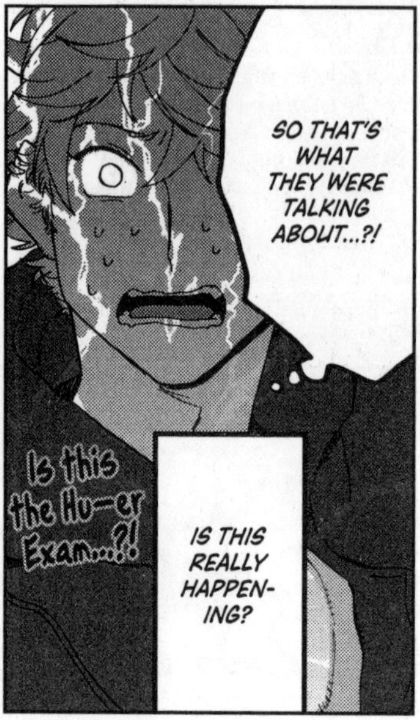
SO THAT'S WHAT THEY WERE TALKING ABOUT...?!
IS THIS REALLY HAPPEN-ING?
Is this the Hu—er Exam...?!

**Hunter Exam, page 182**

This is a reference to the Hunter Exam from the long-running manga and anime series *Hunter x Hunter.* Yatora thinks of this because the physical challenge that he faces is reminiscent of the extreme and often fatal difficulty of the Hunter Exam from *Hunter x Hunter.*

**A promide of your bias, page 186**

Promides (and "bromides") typically refer to professionally produced photos of celebrities and entertainers that are sold to fans. They are printed on bromide paper. These types of photos are also popular with K-pop fans. "Bias" is a term that comes from K-pop fan culture, and it refers to someone's favorite member in a band. This is similar to the term *oshi* in Japanese idol culture.

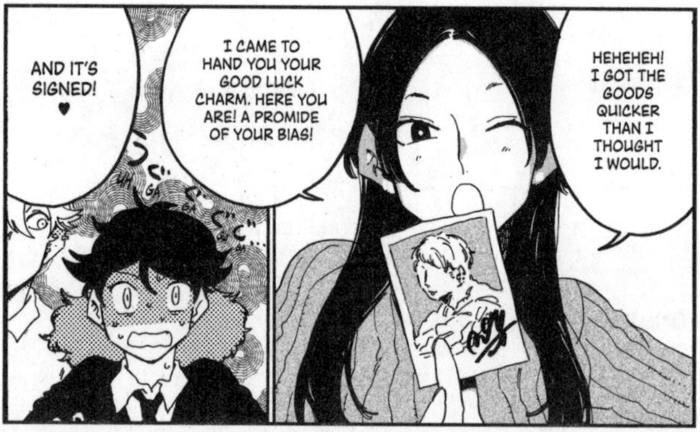
HEHEHEH! I GOT THE GOODS QUICKER THAN I THOUGHT I WOULD.
I CAME TO HAND YOU YOUR GOOD LUCK CHARM. HERE YOU ARE! A PROMIDE OF YOUR BIAS!
AND IT'S SIGNED! ♥

BLUE PERIOD

# The prince in his dark days

### By Hico Yamanaka

A drunkard for a father, a household of poverty... For 17-year-old Atsuko, misfortune is all she knows and believes in. Until one day, a chance encounter with Itaru–the wealthy heir of a huge corporation–changes everything. The two look identical, uncannily so. When Itaru curiously goes missing, Atsuko is roped into being his stand-in. There, in his shoes, Atsuko must parade like a prince in a palace. She encounters many new experiences, but at what cost...?

# Princess Jellyfish

Akiko Higashimura

**ALSO AN ANIME!**

"One of the best manga for beginners!"
—*Kotaku*

Tsukimi Kurashita is fascinated with jellyfish. She's loved them from a young age and has carried that love with her to her new life in the big city of Tokyo. There, she resides in Amamizukan, a safe-haven for geek girls where no boys are allowed. One day, Tsukimi crosses paths with a beautiful and fashionable woman, but there's much more to this woman than her trendy clothes...!

# PERFECT WORLD

### Rie Aruga

> A TOUCHING NEW SERIES ABOUT LOVE AND COPING WITH DISABILITY

An office party reunites Tsugumi with her high school crush Itsuki. He's realized his dream of becoming an architect, but along the way, he experienced a spinal injury that put him in a wheelchair. Now Tsugumi's rekindled feelings will butt up against prejudices she never considered — and Itsuki will have to decide if he's ready to let someone into his heart...

"Depicts with great delicacy and courage the difficulties some with disabilities experience getting involved in romantic relationships... Rie Aruga refuses to romanticize, pushing her heroine to face the reality of disability. She invites her readers to the same tasks of empathy, knowledge and recognition."
—Slate.fr

"An important entry [in manga romance]... The emotional core of both plot and characters indicates thoughtfulness... [Aruga's] research is readily apparent in the text and artwork, making this feel like a real story."
—Anime News Network

Knight of the Ice

*Yayoi Ogawa*

Knight of the Ice ©Yayoi Ogawa/Kodansha Ltd.

# SKATING THRILLS AND ICY CHILLS WITH THIS NEW TINGLY ROMANCE SERIES!

A rom-com on ice, perfect for fans of *Princess Jellyfish* and *Wotakoi*. Kokoro is the talk of the figure-skating world, winning trophies and hearts. But little do they know... he's actually a huge nerd! From the beloved creator of *You're My Pet* (*Tramps Like Us*).

Chitose is a serious young woman, working for the health magazine *SASSO*. Or at least, she would be, if she wasn't constantly getting distracted by her childhood friend, international figure skating star Kokoro Kijinami! In the public eye and on the ice, Kokoro is a gallant, flawless knight, but behind his glittery costumes and breathtaking spins lies a secret: He's actually a hopelessly romantic otaku, who can only land his quad jumps when Chitose is on hand to recite a spell from his favorite magical girl anime!

KC KODANSHA COMICS

# A SMART, NEW ROMANTIC COMEDY FOR FANS OF *SHORTCAKE CAKE* AND *TERRACE HOUSE*!

A romance manga starring high school girl Meeko, who learns to live on her own in a boarding house whose living room is home to the odd (but handsome) Matsunaga-san. She begins to adjust to her new life away from her parents, but Meeko soon learns that no matter how far away from home she is, she's still a young girl at heart — especially when she finds herself falling for Matsunaga-san.

# Yuri Is My Job!

miman

JOIN US FOR
AFTERNOON TEA
WITH EQUAL PARTS
YURI, ROM-COM,
AND DRAMA!

Hime is a picture-perfect high school princess, so when she accidentally injures a café manager named Mai, she's willing to cover some shifts to keep her façade intact. To Hime's surprise, the café is themed after a private school where the all-female staff always puts on their best act for their loyal customers. However, under the guidance of the most graceful girl there, Hime can't help but blush and blunder! Beneath all the frills and laughter, Hime feels tension brewing as she finds out more about her new job and her budding feelings...

**KC/
KODANSHA
COMICS**

"A quirky, fun comedy series... If you're a yuri fan, or perhaps interested in getting into it but not sure where to start, this book is worth picking up."
— Anime UK News

A Kodansha Comics Trade Paperback Original
*Blue Period* 5 copyright © 2019 Tsubasa Yamaguchi
English translation copyright © 2021 Tsubasa Yamaguchi

Published in the United States by Kodansha Comics, an imprint of Kodansha USA Publishing, LLC, New York.

Publication rights for this English edition arranged through Kodansha Ltd., Tokyo.

First published in Japan in 2019 by Kodansha Ltd., Tokyo.

ISBN 978-1-64651-127-3

Original cover design by Yohei Okashita (Inazuma Onsen)

Printed in the United States of America.

www.kodansha.us

1st Printing
Translation: Ajani Oloye
Lettering: Lys Blakeslee
Editing: Haruko Hashimoto
Kodansha Comics edition cover design by Matthew Akuginow

Publisher: Kiichiro Sugawara

Director of publishing services: Ben Applegate
Associate director of publishing operations: Stephen Pakula
Publishing services managing editors: Alanna Ruse, Madison Salters
Production managers: Emi Lotto, Angela Zurlo
Logo and character art ©Kodansha USA Publishing, LLC